THE VAUDEVILLIANS

**A Dictionary
of
Vaudeville Performers**

THE VAUDEVILLIANS

A Dictionary of Vaudeville Performers

ANTHONY SLIDE

ARLINGTON HOUSE
Westport Connecticut

Library of Congress Cataloging in Publication Data
Slide, Anthony.
    The Vaudevillians.

    Bibliography: p.
    1. Vaudeville—United States—Dictionaries. I. Title. II.
Title: Vaudeville performers.
PN1968.U5S38   792.7'028'0922 [B]   81-3565
ISBN 0-87000-492-1   AACR2
Production Service by Cobb & Dunlop, Inc.

This book is dedicated to the memory
of Sime Silverman and to the past
reporters and reviewers of *Variety*,
who recorded the history of show
business, and in so doing made books
such as this possible.

Acknowledgement

The basic research for this volume was undertaken in the Margaret Herrick Library of the Academy of Motion Picture Arts and Sciences in Los Angeles; the Doheny Library of the University of Southern California in Los Angeles; the Library of Congress in Washington, D.C.; the Lincoln Center Library for the Performing Arts in New York City; and the Library of the Museum of the City of New York. This book could not have been written without access to microfilm copies and bound volumes of *Variety, The New York Dramatic Mirror, The New York Clipper,* and *The Billboard.*

I am particularly indebted to the following individuals:
  Herb Baker, for access to materials relating to his mother, Belle Baker.
  Jesse Block and Eve Sully, for a fascinating afternoon of reminiscences of their act.
  Irene D. Caine and Liz Kaufman (Hazel Bammer), for reminiscences of their days as showgirls.
  Patricia Coward, who acted as my very efficient research associate in London.
  Viola Dana, for telling me of her year as a film star in vaudeville.
  Kitty Doner, for her fascinating memories of a long and great vaudeville career.
  Fifi D'Orsay, for recalling her years in vaudeville and her work with Gallagher and Shean.
  Mary Foy, for memories of her father, Eddie Foy, and her time as a member of the Seven Little Foys; also thanks to her daughter, Madeline, and to Ron Foy for access to the family scrapbooks.
  Mrs. Jack Haley (Flo McFadden), for clearing up some misinformation concerning her vaudeville career and her husband's.
  S. T. Linton Hopps, for memories of his years in vaudeville, and in particular of the female impersonators with whom he worked.
  Mrs. Gus Kahn, for memories of her days as a songplugger and of the vaudevillians that she knew.
  Robert Knutson and Ned Comstock of the Doheny Memorial Library of the University of Southern California, for access to *The New York Clipper* and the scrapbooks of Burns and Allen and Charlotte Greenwood.
  Nick Lucas, for talking with me about his years in vaudeville.
  Polly Miller and the Ted Lewis Museum of Circleville, Ohio, for material on Ted Lewis.
  Ken Murray, for answering questions about his vaudeville career, and for comments on his fellow vaudevillians.
  The late Robert North, for memories of his own career and that of Olga Petrova; also thanks to his son, Edmund H. North, for checking the entry on his father.
  The late Madame Olga Petrova, for years of friendship and those wonderful letters concerning her career.
  Eleanor Powell, for comments on John Bubbles, Gus Edwards, and Bill Robinson.
  Al Rinker, for reminiscences of Paul Whiteman and the Rhythm Boys.
  Virginia Sale, for memories of her brother, Chic Sale.
  Penny Singleton, for comments on Jack Haley.
  Joe Smith, for information on Smith and Dale and the Avon Comedy Four.
  Herb Sterne, for sharing memories of his days as a member of the vaudeville audience, and for checking the entries for factual accuracy.
  Arthur Tracy, for talking with me about his career.
  Bennie Urlik, for access to the journals kept by his father, a stagehand at the Orpheum Theatre in Los Angeles.
  Rudy Vallee, for comments on vaudeville as it related to his career.
  Ted and Priscilla Waldman, for memories of their years in vaudeville, and for their immense help in finding photographs and putting me in touch with fellow vaudevillians.
In addition, I would like to thank the following for their help and assistance: Clyde Allen (KFAC Radio, Los Angeles), Rose Arnold, Irene Atkins, Stephen C. Chamberlain, Bill Doyle, Tom Fulbright, Robert Giroux, Robert Gitt, Herb Graff, the Hollywood Comedy Club, Richard Lamparski, Bill Miles, Dominique Paulve, Edward Wagenknecht, and Ian Whitcomb.
The extracts from *American Vaudeville* by Douglas Gilbert are reprinted by permission of Dover Publications, Inc.
The quotes from *Much Ado about Me* by Fred Allen are reprinted by permission of Little, Brown and Company.
The article on Joe Laurie, Jr. by Abel Green is reprinted by permission of Syd Silverman and *Variety.*
The majority of the photographs in this book come from the author's own collection: others come from Eddie Brandt's Saturday Matinee (with special thanks to Mike Hawks), the Harvard Theatre Collection, the Museum of Modern Art, the Museum of the City of New York, and the Wisconsin Center for Theatre Research (with special thanks to Maxine Fleckner and Holly Yasui). The photograph of Polaire is reproduced by permission of Roger-Viollet (Paris), and the photographs of Alice Lloyd, Marie Lloyd, Ella Shields, Vesta Tilley, and Vesta Victoria are reproduced by permission of the Raymond Mander and Joe Mitchenson Theatre Collection (London).

CONTENTS

INTRODUCTION

Happiness *Was* Being a Vaudevillian

Someone once called vaudeville "the fun garden of show biz" and I wholeheartedly agree, for life to me in the 1920s was like one long, exciting roller coaster ride. I was breaking into show business, and I loved the whole world of vaudeville and the fascinating characters who peopled it.

Possibly it's because I spent the first fifteen years of my career, a very impressionable period, traveling and working with these people of vaudeville that I have such a warm spot for them.

O. O. McIntyre, the noted columnist, once wrote, "Off stage, the most human, kindly, and unwordly people I ever knew were vaudevillians. I do not mean the legitimate stars who took an occasional dip into variety, but the lesser lights who made up the major part of vaudeville entertainment."

The vaudevillian realized he was not regarded by the public as seriously as his legitimate brother, so he merely tried to shine in his own backstage orbit where he and his associates lived.

They were the kind of people who would share their flats and their food with a pal waiting for a break. They would even give him what they most prized—part of their routines—to help him get started. They orbited in a solar system of their own. Maybe they couldn't tell you when Columbus discovered America, unless one of the jokes in their act happened to need that date, but they could tell you the exact day and hour twenty years before when they took that Canadian Pacific train at Winnipeg for the long hop to Vancouver.

Vaudeville families were linked by close-knit ties. Their women were domestic and home-loving. Many had their little houses and gardens in suburban New York or New Jersey towns close to the heartbeat of Broadway. Others cheerfully lived in trunks for years, in the hope of finding a cottage some day. Even so, some of them raised families, but under conditions which most parents couldn't imagine.

The training was tough, and it had to be thorough. And most important, you had to have the amazing patience which only actors seem to acquire, along with an unswerving belief in your own ability, plus the most wonderful attribute of all, that eternal air of expectancy, as if Chirstmas Eve were always just a brief one-night stand away.

Countless tales have been told of sentimental vaudevillians, and few are overdrawn. They were supersentimentalists, but I'm sure no greater than the author of this book, Anthony Slide, seems to be.

Congratulations, Tony! You've done a masterful job. This book belongs in a time capsule for future generations.

Ken Murray
Beverly Hills, California

The Palace in 1928

HISTORICAL INTRODUCTION

VAUDEVILLE WAS ONCE A FLOURISH-ing American entertainment, which prospered for a hundred years and lingered on for another twenty. In some respects, it never died. Instead, it gave birth to radio, which became popular in no small part thanks to its use of vaudeville's greatest performers and newcomers, such as Kate Smith and Arthur Tracy, who learned their craft in vaudeville. Those same vaudeville performers made early television great. Can one imagine television history without Ed Wynn, Milton Berle, Jimmy Durante, or Burns and Allen? All of them came from vaudeville. Now most of the vaudevillians are dead and gone, and television entertainment has lost its bite and its humor. It no longer entertains, but merely satisfies its own laugh tracks. Vaudeville's child and grandchild suffered the same fate as their forebear; times and fashions changed—not for the best—and entertainment went out of style.

In his autobiography, Fred Allen noted the inevitable:

> Vaudeville is dead. The acrobats, the animal acts the dancers, the singers and the old-time comedians have taken their final bows and disappeared into the wings of obscurity. For fifty years—from 1875 to 1925—vaudeville was the popular entertainment of the masses. Nomadic tribes of nondescript players roamed the land. The vaudeville actor was part gypsy and part suitcase. With his brash manner, flashy clothes, capes and cane, and accompanied by his gaudy womenfolk, the vaudevillian brought happiness and excitement to the communities he visited.

Fred Allen was writing in 1956, and yet even by then one generation had grown up without the pleasure of real vaudeville. Today, a second generation is here, a generation that has been led to believe that vaudeville was nothing more or nothing better than one of our typical television variety shows. This book cannot, on the printed page, recapture the greatness—the warmth and spontaneity—of the more than one hundred and fifty vaudeville acts whose history it attempts to chronicle, but the writer has attemped, through looking wherever possible at a film record of a vaudeville star, to provide some critical commentary on the particular performer's act. In addition, each entry contains a capsulated biography of the vaudevillian.

The Vaudevillians: A Dictionary of Vaudeville Performers is not a history of vaudeville. The best history of the medium is still, and probably will always remain, Douglas Gilbert's *American Vaude-ville: Its Life and Times* (first published in 1940 by Whittlesey House and currently available in a reprint by Dover Paperpacks). To many, vaudeville died when the Palace Theatre closed as a two-shows-a-day house in 1932. Its origins are more obscure. According to Douglas Gilbert, the first "vaudeville" house in New York is believed to have opened in the 1840s or 1850s; modern vaudeville can be traced from Tony Pastor's opening of his Fourteenth Street Theatre in Tammany Hall, New York, on October 24, 1881. The term "vaudeville" derives from the French "vaudevire," meaning a popular statirical song, after the town of Vire, in northwestern France, where such songs were first composed and sung in the fifteenth century. By the late nineteenth century, it had come to mean a series of unrelated acts, which might include singers, dancers, animal performers, acrobats, and jugglers, which followed one another in rapid succession. Why Americans adopted the term vaudeville rather than the logical descriptive term of variety is unknown, but adopt it they did, and vaudeville became *the* popular entertainment of the American people.

The focal point of vaudeville—its homebase—was the Palace Theater in the heart of New York's theater district, at Broadway and 47th Street. When an act played the Palace, it had reached the pinnacle of success. As male impersonator Kitty Doner recalls:

> It was every actor's ambition to play the Palace in New York. Monday afternoon was the first show, and the house would be filled with performers from the shows around town. They'd come in for the matinee. And all the Broadway talent scouts and agents would come down to catch the first show Monday afternoon at the Palace, because how you went over determined what your future bookings would be. That was the biggest excitement in your life, I guess, playing a Monday afternoon at the Palace Theatre. It was just thrilling.

The Palace Theater opened on March 24, 1913, and at first it seemed a total failure; its opening program, which included comedians McIntyre and Harty, dancer Napierkowska, cartoonist Hy Mayer, and Ed Wynn (the only remembered name on the bill), did not even draw a capacity crowd on opening night. *The New York World* reported, "The opening bill did not lend much enthusiasm to the occasion." *Variety* was downright scathing in its attack on the Palace (with two seats going for the outrageous sum of two dollars each), declaring the fate of two dollar vaudeville was sealed even before the theatre opened its doors. It took many months for the theatre to gain prominence over its rivals, such as Hammerstein's Victoria, Charles Dillingham's Hippodrome, and B. F. Keith's Colonial and

Alhambra. But by December of 1914, *Variety* had changed its tune and described the Palace as "the greatest vaudeville theatre in America, if not the world." Theatrical entrepreneur Martin Beck was responsible for the Palace's existence, but even before it opened he had lost control of the theatre to E. F. Albee, who with B. F. Keith had built up the greatest and most powerful chain of vaudeville theatres in the nation. Behind Keith-Albee came the Pantages and Orpheum circuits, while at the bottom of the vaudeville ladder was the much-maligned Gus Sun circuit.

To both Keith and Albee, despised as they were by many vaudevillians, must go the credit for the success of vaudeville in America. As one commentator wrote of Keith, who died in March of 1914, he was "the Moses of vaudeville. He brought the children of vaudeville where they are today." At its height in the early twenties, vaudeville was seen by 1,600,000 men, women, and children daily, and there were more than 12,000 performers available to the vaudeville circuits.

In 1923 Albee wrote in *Variety:*

To say that vaudeville is our most nationally representative form of theatrical entertainment is not overstating a condition that has been in process of forming and becoming permanent for more than a third of a century. There are many reasons and causes for this attitude of the American public toward vaudeville on one hand, and of vaudeville toward the public on the other. To begin with, the diversified, contrasted, and all-embracing character of a vaudeville program gives it in whole or part an appeal to all classes or people and all kinds of tastes. For its patrons it draws upon all of the artistic resources of every branch of the theatre—grand opera, the drama, pantomime, choreography, concert, symphony, farce, and all of the kindred fields of stage entertainment. In addition to this wide diversity of its attraction, the personnel of its army of artists is as cosmopolitan as the population of the cities and towns of the United States. Not only are all the acts represented in vaudeville, but all of the nations and races of the civilized world are also represented by and through some characteristic form of expression ... In vaudeville, "there is something for everybody," just as in every state and city, in every country and town in our democratic country, there is opportunity for everybody, a chance for all.

The one thing that Albee did not mention, the one thing not to be found on a Keith-Albee bill was a dirty joke, an immoral sketch, or a vulgar act; both Keith and Albee were fanatics for clean shows.

On November 16, 1932, the Palace closed as a strictly vaudeville theatre. From that point on it became what was known as a presentation house, showing feature films accompanied by vaudeville acts. (Of course, in more recent years, after just about everyone had decided vaudeville was dead, the Palace reverted back to being a variety house, but in this respect it was a curiosity.) By the time the Palace became a presentation house, the theater was controlled by Joseph Kennedy and his powerful Radio-Keith-Orpheum organization. E. F. Albee was forced out of power, and he died, at the age of seventy-two, on March 11, 1930 As *The Billboard* (March 22, 1930) commented, his passing left vaudeville without a champion. Albee might have been the vaudevillians' ... greatest enemy, but he was also vaudeville's greatest ally, and the death of vaudeville can be trace just as easily from the death of Albee as from the death of the Palace.

What killed vaudeville? Not Joseph Kennedy, although it would be nice to fix the blame on him. Radio was vaudeville's first major enemy, but it could have survived that menace simply by embracing the new stars that radio created; for radio needed vaudeville to let its new audience both see and hear celebrities such as Arthur Tracy and Kate Smith. What vaudeville could not fight was the sound motion picture. For one thing, too many vaudevillians flocked to the studios of Warner Bros. to film their acts for the Vitaphone—Warner's sound-on-disc process—thus destroying their own careers and negating any possibility that they could continue to play the vaudeville circuits with those same routines for years to come.

Between 1928 and 1930, the following vaudevillians all starred in Vitaphone shorts: Elsie Janis, Willie and Eugene Howard, George Jessel, Blossom Seeley, Webber and Fields, Jack Benny, Kitty Doner, Trixie Friganza, Julia Sanderson, Frank Crumit, Fannie Ward, Raymond Hitchcock, Irene Franklin, El Brendel and Flo Burt, Baby Rose Marie, Burns and Allen, Miller and Lyles, Ruth Etting, Fred Allen, Bert Lahr, Edgar Bergen, Lou Holtz, Helen Morgan, and Jack Haley. Today, of course, we should be thankful for the short-sightedness of these and other vaudeville performers, for in recording their acts for the Vitaphone, they preserved on film the quality and uniqueness of their talent.

When Variety viewed one of the first sound programs from Warner Bros. and the Vitaphone (Sydney Chaplin in the feature film *The Better 'Ole* and a program of shorts with Al Jolson, Elsie Janis, and others), on October 13, 1926, it carried a front page headline hailing the program, which cost a mere $40,000 to produce, as "Better Than Vaudeville." As early as October of 1927, *American Mercury* announced, "The leisurely presented two-a-day all-star vaudeville bill has gone for ever."

The New York Hippodrome

The fate of vaudeville was sealed. An uneasy merger with the motion picture was tried, in the form of film and vaudeville bills at the previously mentioned presentation houses, which had already worked with some success in the twenties in New York at the Capitol Theater and continued to work from the thirties through the seventies at the Radio City Music Hall, but this merger only tended to drag out vaudeville's death for another ten years. As early as February 27, 1909, a critic in *The Moving Picture World* had written, "The writer cannot see that vaudeville sketches add anything to the attractiveness of motion picture shows and it would seem good policy to cut out this expense and invest it in better films and more of them." It took thirty years, but eventually the film industry listened, and second features, newsreels, and selected short subjects more and more replaced the vaudeville acts.

Vaudevillians came, as Albee wrote, in every form and type, although, there is a lot of truth in a 1915 Billy Murray phonograph recording which asked, "What would you do for amusement? There would be no place to go," and answered with, "If it wasn't for the Irish and the Jews." Musical comedy owed much to vaudeville, taking from it the best performers—and later some of the audience—but then vaude (as *Variety* always called it) responded by taking away the musical comedy stars and the musical comedy audience. In particular, there was a great deal of interchange between the vaudeville and the revue stages. Most major vaudevillians were to be seen at one time or another in Florenz Ziegfeld's *Follies, George White's Scandals, The Passing Show,* or *The Greenwich Village Follies.* So interwoven are vaudeville and revue in the minds of most people that Al Jolson, who was a revue star and never played vaudeville per se, is thought of as vaudeville's most famous headliner. By 1912 vaudeville had become so influential that even the great David Belasco announced he would produce playlets for a vaudeville stage. Vaudeville was certainly a training ground, one which the entertainment world no longer has and desperately needs. "Vaudeville is an art, a profession, a craft," wrote Ashton Stevens in *The Billboard* (April 8, 1939). "Ask W. C. Fields, Eddie Cantor, Ed Wynn, G. M. Cohan, Burns and Allen. Tough, devoted, upclimbing years in the patrician two-a-day of yesterday made them what they are today in broader but no better fields."

The acts changed with the years. "Freak" acts were just about dead by 1919. The first World War saw all the "Dutch" comedians with their German accents switching to Hebrew dialects for the duration, while the lack of young men—busy at the Front—saw sister acts come into vague in 1917. The acts varied, but there was always a standard policy as to the order of a vaudeville show. The bill would open with an animal, pantomime or acrobatic act, which would not require any listening or much attention as the audience was generally being seated while it performed. The headliner always appeared immediately prior to the intermission and as the penultimate act on the bill. When there were two headliners, the better position was considered to be the latter one. Like the opening act, the final turn would neither demand nor receive much attention, because the audience would be walking out while it performed. In the thirties the policy changed, and a big band would often close the bill or there would be a grand finale with the entire company, including the headliner.

The Vaudevillians: A Dictionary of Vaudeville Performers features all of the great headliners, from Nora Bayes, Sophie Tucker, and Eva Tanguay from vaudeville's golden age to Jimmy Durante, Olsen and Johnson, and Señor Wences from its dying years. Also included are a sampling of vaudeville's opening and closing acts, forgotten performers such as Alphonse, Marcelle and Sea Lion, and the On Wah Troupe. The passage of time has dealt many former vaudeville greats a terrible blow in that tastes have changed—style in humor is definitely a transitory thing—and phonograph recordings once crisp and clear now sound scratchy and quaint. But in listening to today's disco music, has the world really changed that much when one compares the Village People's "Y.M.C.A." to Irving Berlin's First World War song, "I Can Always Find a Little Sunshine in the Y.M.C.A."?

Raymond Hitchcock. "Hitchy, as he was affectionately known, had his greatest triumph with Hitchy-Koo, which he both produced and starred in. The show opened at the Cohan and Harris Theater, New York City, in June, 1917 (See entry page 72).

THE VAUDEVILLIANS
A Dictionary
of
Vaudeville Performers

ABBOTT AND COSTELLO

Abbott and Costello

After years of semiobscurity in burlesque, as solo acts and in partnership with others, Bud Abbott and Lou Costello burst on the vaudeville, radio, and film scenes in the late thirties and early forties. Their brand of humor was pure corn and routines such as their classic "Who's on First" had origins hidden in the obscurity of burlesque. Most critics agree that the pair's success came about as a result of the Second World War and the prewar jitters which had the public seeking simple, uncomplicated entertainment.

Bud Abbott (October 2, 1895–April 24, 1974) began his career in burlesque, and soon became known as one of the best straight men in the business. Lou Costello (March 6, 1906–March 3, 1959) had hopes of becoming a movie star, but when they came to nothing, he entered vaudeville in the late twenties. From vaudeville, Costello took the

downward path to burlesque. By 1936 both comedians were working at the Eltinge Theatre in New York, Costello with Joe Lyons and Abbott with Harry Evanson. They watched each other perform, and decided they would make a perfect team, or, as Lou Costello once remarked, "Bud and I was right for each other." Abbott and Costello clicked in vaudeville, and in the summer of 1937 had a successful engagement on Atlantic City's Steel Pier. Also in 1937, they played their first nightclub engagement, at Billy Rose's Casa Mañana in New York, which led to a successful vaudeville tour on the Loew's circuit.

Ted Collins, Kate Smith's manager, saw the pair in vaudeville, and booked them to appear on "The Kate Smith Hour," one of the most popular shows on radio, on which the two became regulars for more than a year, and where they introduced "Who's on First" to millions of radio listeners. (Between 1942 and 1949, Abbott and Costello were to have their own radio program, first on NBC and later on ABC.) From Kate Smith's program Abbott and Costello were signed to a Universal Pictures contract and embarked on a film career which was to include thirty-five feature films together, the best known of which are probably *Buck Privates* (1941), *Rio Rita* (1942), and *The Naughty Nineties* (1945).

Of course, as the years rolled by, the Abbott and Costello humor became a little too familiar and a little too broad for most people's tastes, and in the era of Mort Sahl and Lenny Bruce it was quite definitely out of style. Today, with burlesque again in vogue, there is little doubt that Abbott and Costello are regarded as one of the greatest teams in the history of that peculiarly American institution. And, thanks to their films, that familiar cry of "Heyyyyyyy Abbott-t-t-t-t-t" will be heard for many years to come.

References: "Laborers in the Cornfield: Abbott and Costello," in *There's Laughter in the Air!* by Jack Gaver and Dave Stanley (Greenberg, 1945), pages 125–137. *The Abbott and Costello Book* by Jim Mulholland (Popular Library, 1975). *Bud and Lou* by Bob Thomas (J. B. Lippincott Company, 1977).

FRED ALLEN

Fred Allen in his early vaudeville days

"In vaudeville, "wrote Douglas Gilbert, "Allen was a carefree, irresponsible performer, a clean nut comic who presented any ridiculous thing that occurred to him. He'd quit off in the middle of a routine, sit flat on the stage almost in the footlights, and read his press notices to the orchestra leader. At one time he used a shapeless and dilapidated ventriloquist's dummy for a purposely atrocious ventriloquial specialty; another time he used a frightful banjo to accompany an equally wretched song. His dead pan was superb, making the foolish things he did get over for riotous laughter." From vaudeville, Fred Allen went into radio—"this drudgery, this sham, this gold mine," as he once called it—and became one of the medium's biggest stars. S. J. Perelman called Allen "the great sourpuss," and his cynical, dour, baggy-eyed style came over to radio listeners through Allen's scripts, for which he was almost entirely responsible.

Born John Florence Sullivan in Cambridge, Massachusetts, on May 31, 1894, Fred Allen began his working life in the Boston Public Library before breaking into vaudeville in the early 1910s. He was initially known as Freddy James and billed—with some justification—as "The World's Worst Juggler." In 1914 he toured Australia, juggling and telling jokes like "She was so old when they lit the candles on her birthday cake six people were overcome by the heat," and "I don't have to look up my family tree, because I know that I'm the sap." Returning to the States, Allen played small-time vaudeville for a while and then, in an attempt to break into the big time, changed his name to Fred Allen, borrowing his last name from the Fox circuit booker Edgar Allen.

As Fred Allen, he played the Fifth Avenue Theatre in January of 1918. Sime Silverman saw him and was devastating in his review published in the January 4, 1918, issue of *Variety:* "If Fred Allen is his right name he should change it, and if Fred Allen isn't his right name, someone should tell what it was, for this Fred Allen has copped and copped until he may think he has an act. . . . His is a nutty talking juggling turn and if he gets away with it on the big time, then he is not near as nutty as the big time is." Silverman had no problem in recognizing gags and routines "stolen" from a number of other vaudevillians, in particular Felix Adler, Edwin George, and Joe Cook. Back Allen went to the small time, and it was not until 1922 that he became an established vaudeville headliner. When the comedian played the Colonial in June of 1921, *Variety* (June 10, 1921) had changed its opinion of Allen, perhaps because he had disposed of all his paraphernalia such as the ventriloquist's dummy and the juggling and was now relying on his monolog. "Allen's present act is big time and it looks all his own," reported the paper.

From vaudeville, Fred Allen went into revue with *The Passing Show* of 1922, which played an important part in his life in that he first met his future wife, Portland Hoffa, who was a member of the chorus. They were married in 1927. Allen was also a member of the cast of the 1924 edition of *The Greenwich Village Follies,* and later starred with Libby Holman and Clifton Webb in *First Little Show* (1929) and *Three's a Crowd* (1930). During this period, Allen was also to be seen on the vaudeville stage, most notably in a twenty-two-minute sketch titled "Disappointments of 1927," in which he was joined by Portland Hoffa. The premise of the sketch was that Allen was the prolog singer about to introduce the rest of his cast, from Paul Whiteman and His Band to a line of voluptuous chorus girls. Unfortunately, a phone call tells him that none of them is able to appear. Allen then proceeded to do the entire show, aided by Portland Hoffa who wanted to disgrace herself and was thus willing to work with Fred Allen. In addition to working with Portland Hoffa, Allen developed a double act with Bert Yorke as his straightman in which the two opened at the Palace on October 4, 1926.

Fred Allen's years in vaudeville are recorded in detail in the second volume of his autobiography, *Much Ado about Me,* a volume which is, without question, the finest autobiography of a vaudevillian ever written. Its style and its use of comedy validate Herman Wouk's definition of Fred Allen as "a classic humorist."

Radio listeners first heard Fred Allen on CBS on October 23, 1932, on "The Linit Bath Club Revue." Other radio programs followed, but it was not until 1934 and "Town Hall Tonight" that Allen's radio style became established. In 1939 "Town Hall Tonight" became "The Fred Allen Show," which continued in popularity for a decade and introduced the famous characters of Allen's Alley, Mrs. Nussbaum (Minerva Pious), Ajax Cassidy (Peter Donald), Titus Moody (Parker Fennelly), and Senator Beauregard Claghorn (Kenny Delmar). On radio,

Fred Allen was noted for his running gag feud with Jack Benny and his outspoken attacks on the radio executives, which resulted in frequent censorship of his program. Allen was the great pessimist—or perhaps one should say realist—of the entertainment world, and his radio scripts emphasized this attitude. At the close of his book on the radio years, *Treadmill to Oblivion,* he noted, "All that the comedian has to show for his years of work and aggravation is the echo of forgotten laughter."

"The Fred Allen Show" was last aired on June 26, 1949, and Allen was not heard from again on a regular basis until he joined the panel of "What's My Line?" on CBS television. Fred Allen had made the occasional film appearance from 1929 onward, most notably in *Thanks a Million* (1935), *Sally, Irene and Mary* (1938), *Love Thy Neighbor* (1940), and *It's in the Bag* (1945).

Fred Allen died alone while walking his dog in New York City on March 17, 1956. His death did not end an era in radio entertainment, because that era had already passed seven years earlier and television had put an end to the type of class humor for which Fred Allen stood. Allen was an intellectual and his comedy appealed as much to the highbrow as to the lowbrow. He was a genius at barbed wit and the fast, devastating comeback gag. In the early thirties he came back with a riposte to an aggressor against his character, "Tell me, did your parents ever consider birth control?" Fifty years later that joke is being heard again, but now it is considered sophisticated and daring. Fred Allen was not just a man for his time. He was also a man of our time.

As a stage attraction at New York's Bedford Theatre, appearing before the movie, she proved so popular in February of 1920 that fifteen minutes into the film (*The Clouds Roll By* with Douglas Fairbanks) the lights had to be brought up so she could reappear to take another bow and ask the audience to watch the feature because she had no further songs in her repertoire. Aunt Jemima made her Palace debut in 1922, when *Variety* announced she had "a place in big-time vaudeville" (October 30, 1922). By 1924 "the cheery purveyor of pop songs" (as *Variety* dubbed her) was singing "It Had to Be You" and "The Charleston," and was proclaimed the season's biggest hit at the Hippodrome. Her natural conviviality overwhelmed audiences, and as *The Billboard* noted in 1931, she personified "the colored mammy." In fact, the secret of her success probably lay in her being the black mammy of the Ethel Waters type in *A Member of the Wedding,* in whose arms everyone wished to be held and loved. Aunt Jemima represented warmth and joy, and the fact that she was really white doubtless helped to win over those with racial antagonisms.

Tess Gardella had appeared in the 1921 edition of *George White's Scandals,* but her best-known nonvaudeville appearance was as Queenie in the original Broadway production of *Showboat,* which opened at the Ziegfeld.

References: *Treadmill to Oblivion* by Fred Allen (Little, Brown and Company, 1954). *Much Ado about Me* by Fred Allen (Little, Brown and Company, 1956). *Fred Allen's Letters,* edited by Joe McCarthy (Doubleday and Company, 1965).

ALPHONSE

Alphonse was a popular opening act on vaudeville bills during the late twenties and early thirties. Three girls would stand in their skin suits while Alphonse draped clothes around them from bolts of material; he would carry on a continuous narration as he worked, and within five minutes would have the girls clothed in the most beautiful of dresses. Irene D. Caine was one of Alphonse's girls from 1926 through 1928 and she recalls earning a salary of seventy-five dollars a week, a considerable sum of money at that time and a sure indication of how popular and well-paid Alphonse was. In the early forties, Alphonse Berge was featured in Ken Murray's *Blackouts.*

Late in his career, as part of a night club act, Ed Wynn performed a routine similar to that of Alphonse. Audiences liked it, but it is probable few remembered that it had originated with Alphonse.

AUNT JEMIMA

Today Aunt Jemima is a familiar name on pancake syrup, but fifty years ago Aunt Jemima meant a plump, jovial Italian woman in blackface, whose real name was Tess Gardella. Born in Wilkes-Barre, Pennsylvania, Tess Gardella came to New York after the death of her father, a miner, and entered show business by way of singing at political rallies, dances, and night clubs in Chinatown. It was Lew Leslie—of *Blackbirds* fame—who changed her name to Aunt Jemima and brought her to vaudeville. Theatre on December 27, 1927, singing "Hey, Feller!," "C'mon, Folks," and "Can't Help Lovin' dat Man." After leaving *Showboat* in March of 1930, she returned to vaudeville and to the Palace. *The Billboard* (April 12, 1930) wrote, "She has pipes that are golden, a knack of selling them, and a marvelous sense of humor. A great act anywhere."

In 1949 Tess Gardella played the Palace again as Aunt Jemima. It was her last public performance; she died a few months later in Brooklyn, on January 3, 1950, at the reported age of fifty-two. As a blackface act, Aunt Jemima was unique, and one of the longest-running acts of its type in the history of vaudeville.

AVON COMEDY FOUR see Smith and Dale

BELLE BAKER

Belle Baker was one of vaudeville's great singing stars, remembered for the way she put over a song with a sob in her voice, but to describe Miss Baker merely as a great torch singer is tantamount to labeling Fanny Brice a singer of comedy numbers. For Belle Baker could handle comedy as well as melancholy. As proof of this, one need look no further than to three songs which she introduced, all written by Irving Berlin, the composer with whom she was most associated. In 1913 at her debut at the Palace, Belle Baker sang Berlin's comic number "Cohen Owes Me

Belle Baker

Ninety-seven Dollars," the death bed lament of "Old Man Rosenthal" to his son. Two very different Irving Berlin numbers with which she will always be associated are the poignant "What'll I Do?" and the carefree "Blue Skies," which she introduced in the 1926 Ziegfeld show *Betsy*.

"She doesn't croon, nor does she coon shout," wrote *Variety* (November 10, 1931). "She sobs her lyrics with a cry in her voice that's catching." And never was this more evident than in Belle Baker's rendering of the Hebrew chant, *"Eli, Eli,"* in which she sang in Yiddish, of the troubles and sorrows of the Jewish people. Her recordings ran the gamut from "Poor Little Butterfly Is a Fly Gal Now" (1919) and "I've Got the Yes! We Have No Bananas Blues" (1923), to "My *Yiddishe* Momma" (1925) and "I Cried for You" (1923). On May 15, 1920, The *New York Dramatic Mirror* noted, "Everybody knows Belle Baker and the sort of songs she sings. She has been one of the most popular of all the singers in the realm of vaudeville for several years, and has been responsible for more songs than you can shake a stick at."

Belle Baker was not particularly beautiful. She was short and plump, with dark hair and dark features. It was her voice and her mannerisms which made her great, an artful blend of intimacy and clowning, with the hint of her Jewish background never far below the surface. After her death, Eddie Cantor wrote of Belle Baker:

Her talent was enormous. She was Dinah Shore, Patti Page, Peggy Lee, Judy Garland, all rolled into one. Her voice filled the theatre and her words—

every one of them—reached you in the very last row of the gallery. All this, mind you, without the aid of a microphone. She could make you laugh, she could make you cry. She could make you a fan for life.

A product of New York's lower East Side Jewish ghetto, Belle Baker was born Bella Becker on December 25, 1895, the daughter of penniless Russian immigrants. After a little schooling and working in sweatshops, the child began to sing—at the age of eleven—at the Cannon Street Music Hall, where she was heard by Jacob Adler, one of the great names in the New York Jewish theatre, and offered a position with his company at the Grand Theatre. Producer and promoter Lew Leslie was the next person in Belle Baker's life. He taught her how to put over a song and began booking Belle into small theatres in the New York area; eventually Belle Baker made her first vaudeville appearance in Scranton, Pennsylvania, at the age of fifteen. A year later, Belle Baker and Lew Leslie were married—they were divorced in 1918.

Belle Baker made her major vaudeville debut at Hammerstein's Victoria Theatre in 1911, and was soundly criticized for the quality of her songs, her dress and her material. One theatrical critic, C. F. Zittell, was particularly scathing, but a few weeks later he telephoned Belle and offered to help her improve the act. Recalling that time in the March 2, 1923, issue of *Zitt's,* the publisher-critic wrote, "I selected songs for the young lady, personally staged her songs, and then obtained an opening for her at the Manhattan Opera House." Within two years, Belle Baker was a vaudeville headliner.

During the 1910s Belle Baker developed a close friendship with Irving Berlin, and the composer wrote many songs for her, including "My Wife's Gone to the Country," "Wake Up, America," "Always," and "Prohibish." In the December 26, 1919, issue of *Variety* Belle Baker contributed a short piece on "Singing Popular Songs":

If I think a number has possibilities, I try it. It would be out of reason to believe I could sing all the songs I hear. But I try to send them all away with a smile for the writer of a bad song today may write a good song tomorrow. The life of any of my songs depends upon the audience. I sing a song as long as I believe the audience wishes to hear it. Often I have discarded a number upon this impression, to later find I am singing it again, by request. Song writers are among the greatest benefactors in the world. They lyrically tell the public in seriousness or laughter those things the public likes to hear, when accompanied by a pretty melody that sends the blues out of your system. Or a ballad hits you just right. The writers give their all for the public, to make them laugh or forget.

By November of 1917, it was reported that Belle Baker had outdrawn all "name" headliners in gross receipts in the New York area B. F. Keith theatres. In 1919 the singer married for a second time—Maurice Abrahams, a composer responsible for such hits as "He'd Have to Get

Under," "Hitchy Koo," "Ragtime Cowboy Joe," and "America, I Love You." A year later, Miss Baker gave birth to a son, Herbert, who was to become a prominent Hollywood scriptwriter, and to whom Belle dedicated a number of her songs, in particular "Ten Little Fingers, Ten Little Toes." In 1924 Belle Baker wrote her first song (with Gracie Deagon), the mildly popular "Pretending." Belle Baker left vaudeville briefly to star in Florenz Ziegfeld's production of *Betsy,* which opened at the New Amsterdam Theatre on December 27, 1926, but ran for a mere thirty-nine performances. In 1929 Miss Baker made her feature film debut in the Columbia Pictures production of *The Song of Love;* she appeared in one other American feature, *Atlantic City* (1944).

Maurice Abrahams died in New York on April 13, 1931. (On September 21, 1937, Belle Baker married Elias H. Sugarman, editor of *The Billboard,* but they were divorced on November 28, 1941.) Abrahams's death affected his wife greatly, and for over a year she restricted her performing to radio, before returning to vaudeville in the summer of 1932 when she introduced one of her biggest hits, "All of Me." In 1934 Belle Baker coheadlined with Beatrice Lillie at the London Palladium, and also costarred in an English feature film, *Charing Cross Road,* released the following year. On May 22, 1936, Belle made her American night club debut at New York's Versailles Club (she had first starred in London at the Kit Kat and the Café de Paris).

Belle Baker's stage appearances dwindled in the forties, and the performer made her last important public appearance at the Palace in May of 1950. In 1955 Belle Baker was honored on Ralph Edwards's "This Is Your Life." She died in Los Angeles on April 25, 1957.

References: "Singing Popular Songs" by Belle Baker in *Variety,* Vol. 57, No. 5 (December 26, 1919), page 20. *Belle Baker—The Incomparable* by Nicole Baker (unpublished manuscript by the singer's granddaughter).

BARBETTE

In the world of female impersonation, Barbette was unique in that he appeared as a, from all accounts, superb female trapeze artist, thrilling American vaudeville audiences in the 1910s and delighting Parisian society in the twenties. Barbette performed aerial acrobatics on the trapeze, often coupled with a slack wire walking routine, and audiences never ceased to be amazed when he removed his wig after taking three or four bows. "It is a real shock as no one would for a moment think he is a man while the act is in progress," reported the *New York Dramatic Mirror* (September 4, 1919).

Barbette was born Vander Clyde in Round Rock, Texas, on December 19, 1904, and learned his craft in his mother's back yard. After his first visit to a circus in nearby Austin, Barbette was determined to be a performer. Upon graduating from high school at the age of fourteen, he answered an advertisement in *The Billboard* inserted by one of the Alfaretta Sisters, who were billed as "World Famous Aerial Queens." One of the sisters had died, and the other was looking for a partner. She ex-

plained to the boy that audiences were far more impressed by female trapeze artists and suggested he dress as a girl. After a stint with Alfaretta, and later with Erford's Whirling Sensation, Barbette developed a single act, which appears to have made its New York debut at the Harlem Opera House in 1919. Barbette was then just the opening act on the bill, but he quickly became a headliner.

In 1923 Barbette came to Paris, to appear at the Casino de Paris. He was not the star attraction on the bill—that was actor Sessue Hayakawa—but he was the hit of the evening, appearing in a white gown covered with ostrich feathers, and ending his act with a *"chute d'ange"* from the trapeze to the white-carpeted floor of the stage. When he pulled off his wig to show his nearly-bald head, and took the stance of a professional wrestler, the audience went wild with surprise and delight. In the years to come, Barbette was to be one of France's most popular cabaret stars. His friend Jean Cocteau wrote of Barbette, "He walked the tightrope high above the audience without falling, above incongruity, death, bad taste, indecency, indignation. . . . Ten unforgettable minutes. A theatrical masterpiece. An angel, a flower, a bird." In 1930 Cocteau had Barbette appear, in drag, in the writer's best-known film *Blood of a Poet.* Alfred Hitchcock's 1930 film *Murder* features a homosexual female impersonator trapeze artist as the murderer, and there can be little question that the character is based on Barbette, even to his stage costume, a parody of that worn by the artist.

While Barbette was being feted by European audiences, he still found time to appear on the American vaudeville stage. He headlined at the Palace in February of 1927, first seen at the head of a grand staircase wearing a long ostrich feather train, which he discarded before beginning his act. *Variety* (February 9, 1927) wrote, "As an impersonator Barbette will fool anybody; as an aerial artist, he is superb. A tendency to overaccentuate the feminine gestures in spots should be watched." Barbette was one of the featured players in *Billy Rose's Jumbo* (1935). As Jimmy Durante sang of beautiful women, he performed his aerial acrobatics. Upon returning to the ground, Barbette removed his wig at the close of Durante's song, leading the comedian to cry, "Betrayed!"

While appearing at Loew's State in 1938, Barbette caught pneumonia, and the long illness which followed put an end to his performing. He continued to train new performers, served as an "aerial consultant" for the stage show *Disney on Parade,* and was "aerial choreographer" for the film *The Big Circus* (1959). He also worked with a number of circuses, and was the subject of a *New Yorker* profile, surely the only female impersonator to be so honored, although he was recognized more as Jean Cocteau's inspiration than as a personality in his own right. Barbette died on August 5, 1973, incongruously, in Austin, Texas —a state not noted for its liberal attitude toward female impersonators and a city which Barbette found offensive, noting, "since those years in Paris, I've never been able to readjust to crudity."

Reference: "Onward and Upward with the Arts: An Angel, a Flower, a Bird" by Francis Steegmuller in the *New Yorker,* Vol. 45, No. 32 (September 27, 1969), pages 130–143.

NORA BAYES

Nora Bayes in 1911

"Nora Bayes was the American Guilbert, mistress of effortless talent in gesture, poise, delivery, and facial work," wrote Douglas Gilbert. "No-one could outrival her in dramatizing a song. She was entrancing, exasperating, generous, inconsiderate—a split personality; a fascinating figure." She was also one of the biggest names in vaudeville, on a par with Elsie Janis and Eva Tanguay. With a voice that on phonograph recordings sounds far from memorable, Nora Bayes introduced such standards as "Shine on Harvest Moon," "Down Where the Wurzburger Flows," and "Has Anybody Here Seen Kelly?"

She was born Eleanor or Leonora Goldberg in 1880 in Milwaukee, according to *Who's Who in the Theatre;* according to *Variety,* she was born in Chicago, while others say that Nora Bayes's home town was Los Angeles. The performer's first stage appearance seems to have been at the Chicago Opera House in 1899, and by 1907 she was appearing successfully at New York's Fifth Avenue Theatre. The following year, Nora Bayes married Jack Norworth, a former blackface comedian, and the couple worked together until their divorce in February of 1913. They were known as "The Happiest Married Couple of the Stage," but their billing as "Nora Bayes, Assisted and Admired by Jack Norworth" indicates not only Bayes's difficult, egocentric personality but also that the marriage was a far from equal partnership.

Jack Norworth, who was born in Philadelphia on January 5, 1879, and died in Laguna Beach, California, on

September 1, 1959, had formerly been married to actress Louise Dresser. (Bayes had been married once before and was to enter into three later marriages following her divorce from Norworth.) He was a prolific composer, usually working in association with lyricist Albert Von Tilzer; among his many compositions are "Shine on Harvest Moon," "Take Me Out to the Ball Game," "Meet Me in Apple Blossom Time," and "Since My Mother Was a Girl." The couple's life was filmed in 1944 by Warner Bros. under the title of *Shine on Harvest Moon,* with Ann Sheridan playing Bayes and Dennis Morgan portraying Norworth.

Nora Bayes was brought in as the headliner to play Topsy, a soubrette girl, with the 1907, and first, edition of Flo Ziegfeld's *Follies,* after the show transferred from the Jardin de Paris on the roof of the New York Theatre to the Liberty Theatre. She and Norworth starred in the 1908 *Follies* and introduced "Shine on Harvest Moon," which was to be revived by Ruth Etting in the 1931 *Ziegfeld Follies;* the couple made their last *Follies* appearance the following year.

Besides her vaudeville appearances, Nora Bayes appeared in many successful Broadway shows, including *The Jolly Bachelors* (1910), with Jack Norworth, and *Little Miss Fix-It* (1911), in which she and Norworth sang the delightful courting couple's lament, "Mister Moon-Man, Turn Off Your Light." In 1915 she starred in the revue *Maid in America,* with "All kinds of music rewritten by Sigmund Romberg" and "Words by the actors and their friends." In *The Cohan Revue of 1918,* described as "a hit and run play batted out by George M. Cohan,"

Jack Norworth

Nora Bayes performed a satire on the knitting craze, in which she was seen ceaselessly working on a sweater for a soldier, heedless of burglary and fire in her household. The musical play *Ladies First* opened at the Broadhurst Theatre in October of 1918, and was subsequently moved over to the newly opened Nora Bayes Theatre—to have a theatre named after one must surely be the supreme wish of every egotistical performer—on December 30, 1918. (The Nora Bayes Theatre was later the Forty-Fourth Street Theatre and is now part of the *New York Times* plant.) In 1922 Nora Bayes, along with Harry Richman and Norma Terriss, starred in *Queen o' Hearts,* a musical comedy by Lewis Gensler, in which Bayes played the proprietress of a matrimonial agency. Gensler had written "Black Eyed Susan" for Nora Bayes to sing in vaudeville some years earlier.

In vaudeville, following her divorce from Norworth, Nora Bayes was billed modestly as "The Greatest Single Woman Singing Comedienne in the World." Typical of her vaudeville repertoire was the 1915 song "I Work Eight Hours a Day, I Sleep Eight Hours a Day, That Leaves Eight Hours for Lovin'." As *Variety* noted, "Miss Bayes had an extensive repertoire of songs which ranged from semi-classics to the comedy types. She had the exceptional knack of putting over a song which continually brought her countless copyists." During the First World War, Nora Bayes tirelessly entertained the troops, and also introduced, in 1917, the most famous of all wartime songs, George M. Cohan's "Over There."

Her salary was at least $2,500 a week; in September of 1921 she played the Winter Garden at $3,500 a week, and shortly before her death, Nora Bayes was touring at $5,000 a week. Her health began to deteriorate in the early twenties, and, as it did, her temperamental behavior increased. She was more interested in telling audiences about her adopted children than in providing them with comedy and song, and at one point E. F. Albee refused to have her play in his houses any longer.

As early as November of 1905, Nora Bayes had appeared in London, at the Palace Theatre. In 1924 she was back in London, aiming for a comeback by playing the Palladium at $300 a week. Cissie Loftus was on stage doing an impersonation of Nora Bayes when the real thing appeared and helped her out. So popular was the routine that the two repeated it at the Palace. But it was at the Palace, a year later, that Nora Bayes's temperament got the better of her again, with disastrous results for her career. She was to appear in a National Vaudeville Artists benefit on a bill which also included Sophie Tucker, who had been promised number five spot on the program. Bayes was to follow Tucker, but she refused claiming her reputation would be damaged by allowing Sophie Tucker to go on before her. The Palace's booker, E. V. Darling, refused to reconsider his decision, and, remembering Bayes's past rudeness and temperament, suggested she leave the theatre. Darling then told the show's master of ceremonies, Emmett Keane, to tell the audience what had happened, leaving out nothing but Miss Bayes's bad language.

In March of 1928, Nora Bayes came to Eddie Darling and begged him to put the large photographs of her out in the lobby of the Palace Theatre so that when she drove past she would know they were there—he could take them down when the matinee performance was to begin. Darling did as she requested. On March 19, 1928, days later, Nora Bayes was dead of cancer. Her last stage appearance had been at the Fox circuit's Audubon Theatre (at 168th Street and Broadway) for the week of February 20th. She had told Edgar Allen of the Fox vaudeville staff, "I'd love to play one more week and retire." Critic Burns Mantle's description of her seems to be most appropriate and to the point: "A singer of popular songs."

JACK BENNY

When Jack Benny died in Los Angeles on December 26, 1974, his age was listed as eighty. But to millions of his radio and television fans, Jack Benny passed away at the age of thirty-nine, a beloved American entertainer whose beginnings were in vaudeville, but who never really established his familiar style until he started his radio career in the thirties. In radio Benny learned how to use silence to his advantage. A lengthy pause would follow a burglar's demand, "Your money or your life," and eventually Benny's voice would be heard: "I'm thinking it over." Benny used the pause in the opening line on his first radio broadcast, on an Ed Sullivan talk show over CBS on March 29, 1932. "Ladies and gentlemen," he said, "this is Jack Benny talking. There will be a slight pause while you say, 'Who cares?'" On television, he used that famous, long, hard stare to add to the impact of the joke; it was a meaningful pause. The Jack Benny trademarks, in particular his meanness and his theme song, "Love in Bloom," all came along after his vaudeville days were over, although he had used the pregnant pause to limited effect in his vaudeville act.

Jack Benny was born Benjamin Kubelsky, the son of Polish Jewish immigrants, on February 14, 1894, in Chicago, Illinois. He grew up in Waukegan, Illinois, and there, at the age of six, he was forced to take violin lessons by parents who were hopeful their son might grow up to be a classical violinist. At the age of fifteen, Benny was earning eight dollars a week, playing in the pit orchestra of Waukegan's Barrison Theatre. Two years later, he entered vaudeville with Cora Salisbury, also from the Barrison Theatre orchestra, as one half of Salisbury and Benny; Miss Salisbury played the piano and Benny the violin, and their straight music act was billed as "From Grand Opera to Ragtime." When America entered the First World War, Jack Benny enlisted in the Navy; here he discovered his talent for comedy, entertaining troops at the Great Lakes Naval Training Station with violin solos interspersed with wisecracks.

Benny returned to vaudeville after the First World War as a solo performer, initially calling himself Ben K. Benny. He changed his name in 1921 because it created confusion with that of another violinist-vaudevillian, Ben Bernie, to whom, in terms of their style of delivery, he bore a certain resemblance. *Variety*'s Sime Silverman saw Benny at the Fifth Avenue Theatre and reported in the January 21,

Jack Benny, Mary
Livingstone, George
Burns, and Gracie Allen

1921, issue of his paper that the comedian had "gags, presence, and assurance." Among the gags in the era of prohibition, was the following: "An optimist is a bartender still paying dues to his union." The only suggestion that Silverman made for improvement was that Benny discard his violin—the comedian did not.

Aside from vaudeville, Jack Benny worked in night clubs and in *Earl Carroll's Vanities.* In 1927 he teamed with a musical group called The New Yorkers, with whom he had been appearing at New York's Little Club, and returned to vaudeville with a twenty-one-minute act. The running gag was to have Joe Venuti direct the band, which played well until Benny took over when the result was disastrous. *Variety* (November 30, 1927) reported, "Benny and New Yorkers are a fine layout for vaude or picture houses. Benny scores with his gags, sells his band and the band adds to the sale by its excellent playing."

There was a certain effeminate quality to Jack Benny's later work; this originated in the late twenties, when it seemed all masters of ceremonies should appear somewhat limp-wristed and effete. Frank Fay worked this way when he was a master of ceremonies, and the most effeminate performance this writer has seen from this period was by comedian-singer Harry Rose. It is fascinating to watch Benny perform as master of ceremonies for a 1930 M-G-M short titled *The Song Writers Revue,* in which he introduces ten composers and exchanges jokes with the very amusing Fred Fisher. The exasperated expression is there, but the timing seems a little unsure and the jokes are best forgotten.

Benny's film career began in 1929 with *Hollywood Revue of 1929,* in which he also served as a poor—from today's viewpoint—master of ceremonies. Although his

most famous feature was *The Horn Blows at Midnight* (1944), which was so poorly received that it became a perennial gag with the comedian, Benny was featured in more than twenty films, including *Chasing Rainbows* (1930), *Love Thy Neighbour* (1940, which was based on the famous Jack Benny-Fred Allen radio feud), *Charley's Aunt* (1941), *To Be or Not to Be* (1942), and *The Meanest Man in the World* (1942).

The first of Jack Benny's own radio shows was "The Canada Dry Ginger Ale Program," which received its first airing on NBC on May 2, 1932. It was followed by "The Chevrolet Program" (1933), "The General Tire Program" (1934), "The Jello Program" (1934), "The Grape Nuts Program" (1942), and eventually, "The Jack Benny Program," sponsored by Lucky Strike, which began on October 1, 1944. Within a few years of Benny's having his own show, all the familiar names had become regulars on the program: announcer Don Wilson, Eddie Anderson as Rochester, singer Dennis Day, and, of course, Benny's wife, Mary Livingstone, whom he had met when she was Sadie Marks, a salesgirl at the May Company in Los Angeles—yes, she really did work for the May Company —and married in 1927. Also featured on "The Jack Benny Program" was bandleader Phil Harris and Mel Blanc with his famous cry, "Train now loading on track three—all aboard for Anaheim, Azusa and Cuc—amonga." In 1949 Benny moved to CBS and continued with his radio show until May 22, 1955. If nothing else, Jack Benny's radio show established him in the self-created role of one of the world's meanest men, the exact opposite of his real life character. The radio image certainly paid off financially, for by January of 1935 Benny was receiving $15,000 a week for personal appearances, a far cry from the few hundreds a week that had been his vaudeville salary ten years earlier. Benny's radio and later television success was due in no small part to his writers, for Benny was never great at ad-libbing and stopped providing his own material when his vaudeville career ended. During one of his verbal bickerings with Fred Allen, he said, "You wouldn't dare say that if my writers were here."

Jack Benny made his first television appearance on March 9, 1949, on a variety program with Bing Crosby and others. "The Jack Benny Program" was first televised on October 28, 1950, and continued through April 16, 1965. Benny, of course, continued to appear on television after that date on "Shower of Stars," "The Jack Benny Hour," and other programs.

Almost to the end, Jack Benny never stopped working. Just prior to his death, it was announced that Benny would star opposite Walter Matthau in the film of *The Sunshine Boys,* a role which was subsequently played by Benny's close friend George Burns. Benny's funeral, attended by so many of his colleagues and friends, demonstrated the affection in which he was held by his profession. In his eulogy Bob Hope said, "The world lost a national treasure. . . . He had the geniousness of a Picasso and a Gershwin. . . . He didn't stand on the stage, he owned it. He was stingy to the end—he only gave us eighty years and that wasn't enough. . . . He never used his sharp wit to injure or belittle anyone." *Newsweek* admirably summed up Jack Benny when it described him as "the ageless fussbudget who played straight man to the world."

References: *Jack Benny Checklist: Radio, Television, Motion Pictures, Books and Articles* by David R. Smith (University of California Library, 1970). *An Intimate Biography* by Irving Fein (G. P. Putnam's, 1976). *Jack Benny* by Mary Livingstone Benny and Hilliard Marks with Marcia Borie (Doubleday, 1978).

EDGAR BERGEN

There can be little doubt that Edgar Bergen was America's most famous ventriloquist. Not that he was a great ventriloquist, for after all those years on radio he seemed incapable of preventing his lips from moving when they should not, but somehow one believed in Charlie McCarthy and Bergen's other dummies. They were his alter egos, and when he conversed with them one forgot to notice that Bergen's lips were moving. There was a gentleness to his humor; it might not create belly laughs, but it made one feel good inside. One felt that Edgar Bergen really believed in Charlie McCarthy and Mortimer Snerd, and that the conversation between them continued long after the audience had departed.

Through the years Bergen's act changed drastically, and the ventriloquist who appeared at the Palace in 1926 bore little resemblance to the star of radio, television, and night clubs of more recent years. Edgar Berggren was born in Chicago on February 16, 1903. He decided to be a ventriloquist after watching the Great Lester in vaudeville and reading a twenty-five-cent book of magic titled *Herrman's Wizard's Manual.* The prototype for Charlie

Edgar Bergen with Charlie McCarthy and Mortimer Snerd

McCarthy was fashioned by an Irish woodcarver named Charlie Mack around 1920, and his features were borrowed from an Irish newsboy who used to deliver newspapers to the Berggren family. The name Charlie McCarthy came from the woodcarver as well. The original doll was four feet tall and weighed twenty-four pounds; he was made of Michigan pine and the head was attached to the body by a shaft about nine inches long.

Bergen claimed that he was shy and nervous as a young man, and that through Charlie McCarthy's uninhibited personality he was able to express himself. Edgar Bergen and Charlie McCarthy appeared together in small Chicago theatres and on the Redpath Chautauqua circuit during the summer months. Years later, the ventriloquist remembered his first theatrical engagement: "It was on a Saturday in a suburban theater and the contract price was three dollars for five shows. When the manager paid me off about midnight, he said I'd been a tremendous hit and that he was going to give me something extra. He did—a quarter out of his own pocket. And that's the only time anyone in show business has ever paid me more than I contracted for."

Gradually, Edgar Bergen advanced his career until in June of 1926, he was appearing in a fifteen-minute act at the Palace. It was a sketch which had Bergen and a nurse, played by Christine Caldwell, finding Charlie McCarthy, as a newsboy and orphan, crying on a park bench. The couple took McCarthy to a doctor who discussed various operations he wished to perform on the dummy. The sketch closed with Bergen and the nurse becoming engaged and keeping Charlie as an office boy. "Neatly set and well manipulated it clicked heavy here," reported *Variety* (June 30, 1926). From this sketch developed another, with Bergen as the doctor about to operate on Charlie McCarthy, which ended with the dummy coming out of the ether and shouting, "Was it a girl?"

In 1930 Edgar Bergen and Charlie McCarthy made their first film appearances in a series of Vitaphone shorts, but the pair's biggest break came on December 17, 1936, when they guest starred on Rudy Vallee's radio show. The two worked regularly with Vallee until April of 1937. Then Edgar Bergen and Charlie McCarthy began their own radio show—on May 9, 1937—under the sponsorship of Chase and Sanborn Coffee; they were to be on the radio for the next twenty years. As Bergen once remarked, "It was absolutely the last place in the world a ventriloquist should go, and sometimes doing the absolutely wrong thing works." The most famous aspect of Bergen and McCarthy's radio work was the long-running feud between Charlie and W. C. Fields, from 1938 through 1944, which led to a feature film together, *You Can't Cheat an Honest Man* (1939). Among Charlie McCarthy's best-known quips to W. C. Fields are "Mr. Fields, is that your nose or a new kind of flame thrower?", "Do you mind if I stand in the shade of your nose?", and "Why don't you fill your nose with helium and rent it out for a barrage balloon?"

Other dummies which Bergen introduced on radio were, of course, Mortimer Snerd, as well as Effie Klinker (who looked like Sneezy in Disney's *Snow White and the Seven Dwarfs*); Ophelia (a querulous old lady); Maisie and Matilda (two barnyard hens); Podine Puffington (a tall, glamorous blonde); Lars Lindquist (A Swedish fisherman); and Gloria Graham (who "wouldn't sit still and stop talking . . . she gushed herself right out of show business"). For the record, Charlie McCarthy weighed 40 pounds, wore size 4 clothes, 2-AAA shoes and a 3-⅜ hat. The head has always remained the same, but the body has been replaced from time to time. Charlie's remarks have often been quoted: to Admiral Halsey, "Hiya Sailor;" to Paulette Goddard, "Take away your face and figure and what have you got?;" and to Marilyn Monroe (who told him she was wearing her wedding dress with "something borrowed"), "You didn't borrow enough!"

In 1947 Edgar Bergen deserted Charlie McCarthy to play Mr. Thorkelson in the film version of *I Remember Mama,* which he described as his favorite role because it was one in which he did not have to be Edgar Bergen. The ventriloquist has appeared in many films through the years, including *The Goldwyn Follies* (1938), *Song of the Open Road* (1944), and *Don't Make Waves* (1967); his last screen appearance was a cameo in *The Muppet Movie,* released in 1979, which is dedicated to his memory. On September 21, 1978, Bergen announced he was retiring from show business and that Charlie McCarthy was to be bequeathed to the Smithsonian Institution—to which Charlie responded, "Well, at least I won't be the only dummy in Washington." A month later, while playing a farewell engagement at Caesar's Palace in Las Vegas, Edgar Bergen died, on September 30, 1978. He had ended his show with the words, "All acts have a beginning and an end . . . and I think that time has come for me. So I think I'll just pack up my jokes and my friends." Edgar Bergen's audience was long lasting and affectionate, perhaps because, as Sam Goldwyn remarked in his unique style, "the popularity of Charlie McCarthy and the Seven Dwarfs proves that people are getting tired of people."

References: "Cultivated Groaner" in *Time* (November 20, 1944), pages 54–57. "Alter Ego! Bergen and McCarthy" in *There's Laughter in the Air!* by Jack Gaver and Dave Stanley (Greenberg, 1945), pages 65–82. "Edgar Bergen" in *The Vaudevillians* by Bill Smith (Macmillan Publishing Company, 1976), pages 38–49.

MILTON BERLE

Milton Berle

Milton Berle, as his nickname "Mr. Television" indicates, belongs more in a volume on the history of television than a study of vaudevillians, but Berle's early success on television was thanks entirely to the years of training he spent in vaudeville. The comedian himself has acknowledged that "The Texaco Star Theater," which was first seen on NBC on June 8, 1948, began as little more than a glorified vaudeville show. The first show was introduced with the words, "Welcome to the Texaco Vaudeville Theater," at which point Berle appeared as master of ceremonies, a role he had played on the vaudeville stage in the late twenties and thirties. "The Texaco Star Theater" was full of the sort of wisecracking quips that had assured Milton Berle's success in vaudeville; he would come out at the start of the program and announce, "We had a wonderful show prepared for you—but it won't be ready till next week." He was never at a loss for words or for a joke, although many of the gags had probably been "borrowed" from other comedians. In the early days of his vaudeville career, one prominent vaudevillian told me, "Nobody had any respect for him. He stole everyone's material." In time, Berle became known as "The Thief of Bad Gags."

Berle himself has explained this by saying: "Material won't do; it's personality. If you don't have a directional point of view or a style, you better toss out what you've got and find yourself. Personality is what people tune in to watch or turn out to see. And funny is funny. Nothing's old if you haven't heard it before and nothing's new if you have."

"The Texaco Star Theater" also featured Berle's trick of intruding himself into others' acts, another vaudeville device about which there is some controversy. Berle insists that he never butted into another performer's act without his permission and without their rehearsing the situation. Some vaudevillians disagree. Ted Waldman recalls that Berle interrupted Beatrice Lillie's act at the Palace, completely destroying her rapport with the audience. At one point he asked her, "Are you Lady Peel?" To which Lady Peel, alias Beatrice Lillie, responded—in total disregard of the ban on swearing on-stage at the Palace—"Goddam right, I am." Whatever the truth of the matter, Berle had been doing this interrupting from 1924 on, and it had become one of his trademarks.

Milton Berlinger was born in the Harlem district of New York City on July 12, 1908. The biggest influence in his life was his mother Sarah, of whom he once said, "She was my mother, but she was also my father, my best friend, my sweetheart." It would be easy to call her aggressive, but that would be unfair, because there is no doubt that Berle was happy to follow where his mother led. Legend has it that Milton Berle made his stage debut at the age of five in a Charlie Chaplin look-alike contest at a theatre in Mount Vernon, New York. As Chaplin did not make his film debut until Berle was six, this cannot be, but whatever the truth of the matter, Milton Berle did enter vaudeville as a young child, chaperoned by his mother, who was to see every performance her son gave until she died in 1954. In the 1910s Berle worked in the Philadelphia area for a Gus Edwards type of entrepreneur named E. W. Wolf, who put on "kid" shows with names like "Playmates," "The Melody of Youth," "Ting-a-Ling," and "Tid-Bits." In 1920 he appeared in a revival of *Florodora* as part of the Baby Sextette, six little boys and girls who sang a reprise of the hit song from the show "Tell Me Pretty Maiden." On his mother's advice, he turned the number into a comedy by starting off on the wrong foot, which made him stand out and perhaps taught the young Berle how to steal the show, or to be more precise, how to steal a gag out of others' acts.

In 1921 Berle teamed with Elizabeth Kennedy for a vaudeville act called Kennedy and Berle, and the two appeared in a sketch, "Broadway Bound," written and produced by Milton Hocky and Howard Green. It featured the two young players in scenes from Shakespeare's *Romeo and Juliet,* classic melodramas such as *Orphans of the Storm,* and popular stage plays such as *Lightnin'* and *The Gold Diggers.* The two played the Palace for the first time on May 2, 1921, opening the second half of the bill. However, Milton Berle soon grew too big to play opposite Miss Kennedy, and the act broke up in 1924. He became a single, offering an opening song, a comedy routine and, more often than not, an impersonation of Eddie Cantor (which he had first performed while with E. W. Wolf).

Berle made his single debut in New York at Loew's State on December 29, 1924. As the years passed, Berle's act changed, and he grew in popularity. In 1927 he had a sketch titled "Memoirs of Milton," in which he sang "I Get the Girls That Get What I Have." The high spot of the sketch was a routine in which one girl would come on the stage, set as a dockside, and announce she was planning suicide. She would flirt with Berle, then take his money and depart; when a second girl appeared and announced her suicide plans, Berle tipped her into the water. Reviewing the act at the American Theatre, *Variety* (April 27, 1927) was not wildly enthusiastic, noting that "Berle is worthy of something better than he does here."

From vaudeville Milton Berle graduated to night clubs, where his gags were deliberately geared to insult the customers. He would turn to one of the gentlemen in the audience and comment, "Oh, I see it's novelty night; you're out with your wife." He informed the guests that there were two waiters per person, one to hand them the check and one to revive them. Between 1932 and 1934, Berle's weekly salary rose from $450 to $2,500. He made his radio debut in 1934, and became a regular on that medium in 1936 on CBS's "Community Sing." Although he was not entirely successful on radio, Milton Berle was heard on the air almost continuously through 1948, his best-known program being the 1944 series "Let Yourself Go," which encouraged the audience to do precisely that and to act out its secret desires. Berle had been in silent films as a child "bit" player, appearing in a Pearl White serial and other films shot at the Fort Lee, New Jersey, studios. He made his major film debut in 1937, in *New Faces of 1937,* followed by *Sun Valley Serenade* (1941), *Always Leave 'em Laughing* (1949), *Let's Make Love* (1960), *It's a Mad, Mad, Mad, Mad World* (1963), and *The Oscar* (1965), among many others.

Milton Berle achieved his greatest success with his 1948 television debut on "The Texaco Star Theater", which, incidentally, allowed him his first major opportunity to appear in drag, a talent which Berle had learned, as he acknowledges in his autobiography, from some of the great female impersonators of the 1910s. Berle appeared under Texaco sponsorship until 1953, when his program became "The Buick-Berle Show." A year later it became "The Milton Berle Show," and as such it lasted until 1956, when it was cancelled; Berle returned in 1958 with a new program which continued, on and off, through 1967. With his theme song "Near You," Milton Berle was, without question, the most popular star on television in its early years, and it is said that he was responsible for the sale of more television sets than any other personality or advertising campaign. In fact, *Limelight* (March 16, 1961) claimed that Berle's "Texaco Star Theater" could be credited with selling almost all of the 353,000 television sets in use in the New York area in 1950.

The zenith of Milton Berle's career came in the late forties, when he became the only show business personality to be featured on the covers of both *Time* and *Newsweek* on the same date, May 16, 1949; on the latter cover he appeared in typically grotesque drag as Carmen Miranda. In 1951 Berle signed an unprecedented thirty-six-year, six-million-dollar contract with NBC, which still remains in force, with some revisions, today. Certainly, show business (particularly television) has been kind to Milton Berle, but at the same time Berle has given back much in the delight he has afforded millions of members of his audience through the years. Berle himself shrugs off his unique position in entertainment, noting merely that "the milestones weren't milestones at the time, just chances to work."

References: *Milton Berle: An Autobiography with Haskel Frankel* (Delacorte Press, 1974). "Conversation with Milton Berle" in *Oui* (December, 1975), pages 71, 72, and 110–115. "Milton Berle" in *The Vaudevillians* by Bill Smith (Macmillan, 1976), pages 68–73.

SARAH BERNHARDT

Sarah Bernhardt

There were many great actresses who played vaudeville, but only one legend ever graced the vaudeville stage, and that was Sarah Bernhardt (October 23, 1844–March 26, 1923), who made a triumphant American vaudeville tour in the winter of 1912 and the spring of 1913. In February

of 1912, Martin Beck (who built the Palace Theatre and controlled the Orpheum circuit) arranged for the actress to make what was billed as one of her many American farewell tours, at a reported salary of $7,000 a week. She performed single acts from her repertoire, and her leading man was Lou Tellegen, who went on to become a minor matinée idol in films and to marry opera singer Geraldine Farrar. At this time, according to Bernhardt critic and scholar Gerda Taranow, the actress was appearing in roles that she liked and which were repetitions or imitations of those she had played from her break with the Comédie-Francaise in 1880 through her direction of the Renaissance in 1898. The vaudeville program might include Bernhardt as the Empress in *Theodora,* as Marion la Vivandiere in *Une Nuit de Noel sous le Terreur* (translated for vaudeville audiences as *A Christmas Night Under the Terror*), or as Marguerite Gautier in *La Dame aux Camélias.*

Sarah Bernhardt had the right to select her supporting acts; for example, she would allow no animal performers on the same bill. But she appears to have been extremely relaxed as to whom she would accept. W. C. Fields presented no problems for her and indeed she even wrote letters of recommendation for some of her fellow performers. One act which did not fare well was that of the Heras family of acrobats, which was booked to close the Bernhardt program in Chicago. When the actress learned of it she cabled Beck that she would not have acrobats following her. She did not! The story is told that Beck was worried about her response to the requirement for Sunday performances in certain cities; but the star replied, "Monsieur Beck, the theatre is my life. Of course I shall play on any Sunday!"

The Sarah Bernhardt twenty-week vaudeville tour, managed by Eddy Sullivan of the Charles Dillingham forces, opened at the Majestic Theatre, Chicago, on December 2, 1912. It almost got no farther, because Bernhardt became ill during Christmas week, but she recovered sufficiently to continue. She traveled by private Pullman car with nineteen members of her company, a chef, a porter, and a maid. Playing the Opheum circuit, Sarah Bernhardt appeared at theatres in St. Louis, Milwaukee, Winnipeg, Edmonton, Kansas City, Los Angeles, San Francisco, Seattle, Denver, and Omaha, among others.

At the close of her triumphant American vaudeville tour, Bernhardt, appeared for three-and-a-half weeks at the Palace in May of 1913. For her first week at the Palace, the supporting acts included McMahon, Diamond and Clemence, performing a scarecrow dance; Harris, Boland and Holtz, a trio presented by Elsie Janis; the Edison talking films, which used sound on disc, and which were screened out of sync and greeted with derision by the opening night audience; Mlle. Fregoleska, and Seldom's Poems in Marble, which closed the program. On her opening night at the Palace, Bernhardt took eighteen bows after appearing in the piece *A Christmas Night Under the Terror. Variety* (May 9, 1913) reported, "Her vaudeville tour has not improved Mme. Bernhardt's physical self for it was noticed she did not display the same confidence in her movements as at her opening in Chicago some few months ago. She moved round more carefully, always making sure to find a prop and did part of her work on a chair. But it was Bernhardt which is enough." The Palace show cost $10,000 to produce, which with Bernhardt's salary meant very little for the other performers, and brought in an average of $22,000 a week.

In 1915 one of Bernhardt's legs was amputated. According to Robert Grau, $250,000 was vaudeville's estimate of her worth for twenty-five weeks after the amputation, but the actress turned down the offer. She also rejected an offer from a San Francisco showman to display the amputated leg, with a cable stating, "If you wish my left leg, see the doctors; but if it is my right leg you want, you must see my American impressario, Mr. Connor."

After a legitimate stage tour of America closed in Montreal in December of 1917, Sarah Bernhardt let it be known that, for financial reasons, she would be willing to appear once again in vaudeville. Because of wartime restrictions of "foreign acts," as Sarah Bernhardt was classified, negotiations for a vaudeville tour broke down, but the divine Sarah did play three weeks at the Palace, beginning on Monday, December 17. She introduced a new playlet, *Du Theatre au Champ d'Honneur (From the Theatre to the Field of Honor)*, and also offered such favorites as *Camille* and *Jeanne d'Arc*. Belle Baker was one of the supporting acts during Bernhardt's stay at the theatre. "Remarkable what this grand old lady can do in the varieties as against her drawing power on the road at the head of her own company," noted *Variety* (January 4, 1918). "It must be deduced that in vaudeville at lower prices and with an entertaining bill surrounding her, it's just the people who want to see Bernhardt rather than to see her play who are drawn in. And Bernhardt does draw a different crowd from the customary vaudeville attendance."

After her three weeks at the Palace, Bernhardt played a week at the Riverside Theatre. *Variety* (January 11, 1918) reported:

That the divine one is still wonderfully possessed with the power of inspiring her audience is the marvel of the stage. Perhaps most mystifying is her retention of voice power. She thrilled the house which after her half-hour playlet applauded for fully two minutes. Mme. Bernhardt again played the role of the wounded color bearer in *From the Theatre to the Field of Honor*. The playlet has been slightly changed over the initial Palace presentation. Then the surgeon and stretcher bearers were in French uniforms, but now they wear the khaki of America, which brings the story into fuller tune since Americans were long in the hospital corps even before our entrance into the fray.

Sarah Bernhardt was an amazing woman, not only in that she could draw vaudeville audiences to hear her speak in a language that they could not understand, but could arouse those audiences with the emotion of her portrayals. Here was a woman in her seventies, playing two shows a

day and one-night stands in towns she had probably never even heard of. "Bernhardt is seventy-three now," commented *Variety* (January 4, 1918), "but she doesn't look it upon the stage, and played the eighteen-year-old Joan without spoiling the illusion of the young girl."

References: *Madame Sarah* by Cornelia Otis Skinner (Houghton Mifflin Company, 1967). *Sarah Bernhardt: The Art Within the Legend* by Gerda Taranow (Princeton University Press, 1972).

BLOCK AND SULLY

Block and Sully

Jesse Block and Eve Sully had a husband and wife act, he the straight man and she the dumb dame (in this case a brunette rather than a blonde), which became popular in vaudeville at around the same time as Burns and Allen came to the fore. As the following routine indicates, there was a great similarity between the two acts, even down to their having the same writer, Al Boasberg. However, there was never any animosity between Block and Sully and Burns and Allen, and they always remained firm friends.

BLOCK:	Why are you late?
SULLY:	I was watching the show and I had to change my seat six different times.
BLOCK:	Why, were you molested?
SULLY:	Yes, finally.
BLOCK:	Where were you born?
SULLY:	In a hospital.
BLOCK:	Why, were you sick?

SULLY:	No, I wanted to be near my mother.
BLOCK:	I saw your sister on the street today, but she didn't see me.
SULLY:	I know, she told me.
BLOCK:	Say, where can I get a hold of your sister?
SULLY:	I don't know, she's awfully ticklish.
BLOCK:	I never met anyone as dumb as you.
SULLY:	My sister's dumber than me.
BLOCK:	You mean dumber than I.
SULLY:	She's dumber than both of us.
BLOCK:	Did you ever hear the story of the Scotsman who found a corn plaster on the street and went out and bought tight shoes?
SULLY:	No, you didn't tell me about it. Did I ever tell you about the Scotsman who found a corn plaster on the street and went out and bought tight shoes?
BLOCK:	I just told you that story.
SULLY:	That's where I heard it!

As *Variety* (May 14, 1930) wrote, it was "smooth, easy dialog that can't miss." Sully would end the routine with a silly giggle, go into the wings, and return with a soft shoe dance, saying, "Look Ma, I'm dancing." As readers will note, whereas Gracie Allen was forever discussing her brother, Eve Sully's major topic of conversation was her sister. Unlike George Burns with his cigar, Block and Sully had no particular props. They would appear on stage in street clothes, with Jesse Block often wearing a straw hat. When they first developed their routine, they would carry a suitcase on stage and sit on it while engaging in crosstalk.

In addition to the crosstalk, for some of which they paid Al Boasberg twenty-five dollars a week, other material was written by "a pimply-faced kid of twenty-one" (as Jesse Block recalls) named Herman Wouk. Eve Sully would also read short poems such as the following:

There once was a butcher named Hutton,
Whose wife was a glutton for mutton.
He sneaked up behind her,
Threw her in the grinder.
No Hutton, no mutton, no glutton—no nuttin!

Although they may not have been aware of it, the Block and Sully and the Burns and Allen routines were interchangeable. Jesse Block recalled for me a routine he and Eve Sully did with Jack Benny, when Benny was the master of ceremonies at the Palace Theatre in Chicago. At the close of Block and Sully's act, he said:

BENNY:	Jesse, come here. I always knew you were clever, but that girl you work with, she was wonderful.
BLOCK:	Did you ever meet her?
BENNY:	No, I never met her. I'd love to meet her. (Eve came on stage and said hello)
BENNY:	You're awfully cute. Do you smoke?
SULLY:	No.
BENNY:	Do you drink?

SULLY:	No.
BENNY:	Do you go out?
SULLY:	No.
BENNY:	What do you do?
SULLY:	I tell lies.
BENNY:	I'd like to take you out.
SULLY:	I can't, I'm married.
BENNY:	To whom?
SULLY:	To Jesse. (And Eve went giggling off while Benny stood there with his typically exasperated look)
BLOCK:	Sorry Jack, I did the best I could.

This routine, with Bing Crosby substituting for Jack Benny, is performed almost word for word by Burns and Allen in a Paramount short titled *Hollywood on Parade* from the early thirties.

New York-born Jesse Block had performed wherever he could as a child. At the age of fifteen he auditioned for Gus Edwards, and when an opening came, Edwards sent two of his kids—Jack Weiner and Walter Winchell—down to the East Side of New York where Block lived. He made his debut in Edwards's *Song Revue of 1915* in Madison, Wisconsin; also in the *Revue* were Georgie Price, Lila Lee, and Arthur Freed. Eventually, Block developed a song and dance act with a girl titled Block and Dunlap. When that act broke up four years later, he met Eve Sully through Bert Gordon. Except for a sister in the Yiddish theatre, Eve Sully had no theatrical background. She had been touring in a song and dance act with Jeanette MacDonald's sister Blossom (who was later professionally known as Blossom Rock).

Block and Sully got together in 1926 and were married in 1930. "We rehearsed for four years," jokes Jesse Block. He continued:

Our act always remained the same. A dumb dame and a soft shoe dance. We immediately clicked. We played all the important theatres in this country, two a day. And then, when we went to the presentation houses, we were responsible for talking acts coming into the Chicago Theatre. Up to that time it had been singing acts and acrobats, but we were the first talking act ever to play there—5,000 seats. In 1930 we went to England and played the Palladium with Burns and Allen—not on the same bill, of course. They played the Holborn Empire and we played the Palladium. Then we played the Holborn Empire and they played the Palladium.

In 1929 Block and Sully played the Palace for the first time, worried about trying to put over their act at the height of the Depression. They need not have been concerned. Block came on stage from one side and Sully from the other. She walked up to him and asked, "Did you vote for Hoover for President?" He replied, "Certainly I did." Eve Sully commenced to hit him over the head, and the more she hit him the more the audience laughed. "From then on we were set," notes Jesse Block. Reviewing their act a couple of months later, *Variety* (March 12, 1930) commented, "Jesse Block and Eve Sully have a talk routine with lapses into song and action. Okay on the smart retorts, the girl playing dumb." After jumping from vaudeville to the presentation houses, Block and Sully became major headliners.

In the early thirties Block and Sully had their own radio program on Monday nights, with Paul Douglas as the announcer, Arlene Francis as Eve's sister, and Gertrude Niesen providing a few songs. The couple also appeared in a number of film shorts and were featured, in the roles of Ben Ali and Fanya, in the 1934 Samuel Goldwyn production of *Kid Millions,* starring their friend Eddie Cantor. In 1940 Block and Sully were to be seen on the New York stage in George Abbott's production of *See My Lawyer,* which also starred Madge Bellamy; many years earlier they had taken over from Fred and Adele Astaire in the Chicago production of *For Goodness Sake.*

In 1938, with Lou Holtz and Belle Baker, Block and Sully were the last vaudevillians to appear on the stage of the Capitol Theatre. During the Second World War, they toured with the USO, and then, in 1948, Block and Sully played their last vaudeville engagement—at Loew's State —and Jesse Block embarked on a new career as a stockbroker. Today, fifty-four years after the debut of Block and Sully, Jesse Block and Eve Sully are as entertaining as ever, although audiences are usually limited to those privileged enough to be invited to their luxurious Central Park South apartment in New York City.

Reference: "Block and Sully" in *The Vaudevillians* by Bill Smith (Macmillan, 1976), pages 74–82.

EL BRENDEL AND FLO BURT

El Brendel, the Swedish-dialect comedian who made the phrase "yumping yimminy" famous, was born not in Scandinavia but in Philadelphia—on March 25, 1898. With his wife Flo Burt, he entered show business there under the guidance of Bart McHugh, telling jokes and performing sleight-of-hand tricks. But before coming to fame as a vaudeville act in 1917, the couple was forced to play apart, Flo Burt in *The Suffragette Revue* (1916) and El Brendel in burlesque shows.

The couple's 1917 vaudeville routine consisted of songs by Miss Burt and eccentric dancing by Brendel, with comedy patter in which Brendel flirted with his wife, telling her he earned eight dollars a week, paid seven dollars for board, and spent the other dollar on women. *Variety* was impressed by both performers, commenting that "Brendel has a unique style of characterizing a funny Swede," and "Miss Burt as a singer of songs is going to attract a lot of attention." For the next ten years, Brendel and Burt were vaudeville headliners, until El Brendel embarked on a screen career as a comic Swede. Between films, El Brendel and Flo Burt found time for the occasional vaudeville tour. In the late thirties, they traveled with their own *Hollywood Surprises* show which included a supposed love scene between Garbo and Stokowski.

From 1926 through 1956, El Brendel was featured in more than fifty films, including *Wings* (1927), *Sunnyside*

El Brendel in 1922

Up (1929), *Just Imagine* (1930), and *Mr. Lemon of Orange* (1931). In all of these Brendel leaves an impression of comic mediocrity, an impression which those who saw Brendel on the stage assure us is a false one. Most vaudeville audiences agreed with *Variety* (October 12, 1917) that "he is genuinely funny" or with the *New York Dramatic Mirror* (December 18, 1919), "an unqualified uproariously funny act." El Brendel died in Hollywood, California, on April 9, 1964.

FANNY BRICE

At the time of her death, *Variety* described Fanny Brice as "one of the greatest singing comediennes in the history of the American theatre." There were no other singers in her class, for she was equally at home with both comedy songs and tragic lyrics. She was a great torch singer, as evidenced by the rendition of her most famous song "My Man," a French hit from 1920 for which Channing Pollock supplied English lyrics. Her comedy songs—"Becky Is Back in the Ballet," "I Should Worry," and "Second-Hand Rose"—are as entertaining today as they were fifty years ago. If you want to understand how Fanny Brice could handle a lyric, just listen to her perform "Cooking Breakfast for the One I Love," which she introduced in a 1930 film, *Be Yourself!* At first she sings the lyrics straight, with warmth and affection; then, as the lyrics start to get silly, with talk of oatmeal sprinkled with lox, a Yiddish accent begins to creep into her voice, until the number has become a comic song. No other singer had such control of a song, such ability to drastically change

Fanny Brice

its impact.

As a comedienne, Fanny Brice had the advantage of a funny face with expressive eyes and mouth, a mouth which when she grinned broadly seemed to be an ugly gash in her features. (And yet that same face could be poignantly and hauntingly expressive when necessary, although the necessity for Fanny Brice's brand of pathos seemed to disappear in the thirties, when she was at the height of her radio fame.) Her comedy dialogue was distinctly Jewish, and it is interesting that before it became a classic Sam Goldwyn remark, Fanny Brice had said, "A verbal agreement is not worth the paper it's written on."

When Fanny Brice was once asked about her career, she responded:

Listen, kid! I've done everything in the theatre except marry a property man. I've been a soubrette in burlesque and I've accompanied stereopticon slides. I've acted for Belasco and I've laid 'em out in the rows at the Palace. I've doubled as an alligator; I've worked for the Shuberts; and I've been joined to Billy Rose in the holy bonds. I've painted the house boards and I've sold tickets and I've been fired by George M. Cohan. I've played in London before the King and in Oil City before miners with lanterns in their caps.

Not bad for a girl named Fannie Borach, born on New York's Lower East Side, on October 29, 1891.

Like most vaudevillians, Fanny Brice always wanted to entertain. Her brother Lew (who also played vaudeville as a comedian, and who died on June 16, 1966) recalled that, as a child, Fanny appeared one amateur night at Keeney's Theatre in Brooklyn singing—with tears of emotion— "You Know You're Not Forgotten by the Girl You Can't Forget." She auditioned for George M. Cohan, but was rejected because she could not dance. She toured in burlesque, first in *The Transatlantic Burlesque* and then in *College Girl,* and while appearing in the latter at the Colombia Theatre in New York she was seen by Florenz Ziegfeld, who was casting the 1910 edition of his *Follies.*

When the *Follies* opened at the New York Theatre on June 20, 1910, a new star was unquestionably born. Despite the presence of Lillian Lorraine and Bert Williams, not to mention three-and-a-quarter hours of glamor, there was little doubt that the real star of the *Follies* was Fanny Brice. She was "the individual hit of the show," reported *Variety* (June 18, 1910), viewing the *Follies* during its tryout at the Apollo Theatre in Atlantic City. "Her first song, 'Lonely Joe,' was a riot, while the second, 'Grizzly Bear,' was nearly so." Fanny Brice was to be starred by Ziegfeld in his *Follies* of 1911, 1916, 1917, 1920, 1921, and 1923, although the showman never really gave her an opportunity to do anything but comedy; he once told her about a *Follies* audience, "They'll never take you home because of your tears, but because of your laughter."

When not in the *Follies,* Fanny Brice was busy in vaudeville and on the musical comedy stage; she starred in *The Honeymoon Express* (1913), *Nobody Home* (1915), *Why Worry?* (1918), *Fanny* (1926, written especially for her by David Belasco), *Fioretta* (1929), and *Sweet and Low* (1930). The spelling of her name changed through the years, and until the twenties she was always Fannie, becoming Fanny permanently only in the late twenties, and then only on the stage; when she wrote an article for *Cosmopolitan* in 1936, she called herself Fannie.

Fanny Brice became a vaudeville favorite as quickly as she became a *Follies* favorite. On April 27, 1912, *Variety* reported that she was "unquestionably 'the goods' for vaudeville. Miss Brice is chock full of unction and has a keen sense of travesty." She made her first appearance at the Palace in February of 1914, and was to be a regular there for the next twenty years. At the Palace, in September of 1915, she introduced "Becky Is Back in the Ballet," wearing a short ballet skirt and flesh pink stockings to sing about the girl who graduated from a ballet school in the Hester Street neighborhood of New York. She gave impersonations of a salesgirl in a millinery shop and a Yiddish mother boasting of her daughter's cleverness, and concluded her act with a song in male attire. "When Miss Brice learns to refrain from starting to disrobe before she is out of sight of the audience her new act will be a step —several of them in fact—in the right direction," commented *Variety* tartly. (September 10, 1915).

A few years later, Fanny Brice was back at the Palace with her torch number "The Song of the Sewing Machine," a lament for the women of the sweatshops. On the same program—between 1915 and 1925 the length of her vaudeville act had grown from twelve to forty minutes, and the audience still wanted more—she gave the marvelous monolog of "Mrs. Cohen at the Beach" with its punch line to the kids, "Why didn't you do it when you were in the water?" In March of 1930 she gave her classic "Dying Swan Ballet" at the Palace, and in order not to stop the show completely she had to appear at the end of the program as well as in the headliner spot.

Fanny Brice's private life was involved but exciting. She once joked, "I've been poor and I've been rich. Rich is better!" A first, teenage marriage to Frank White was soon dissolved, as was her second marriage, in 1918, to gambler Nicky Arnstein who inspired the song "My Man," which Fanny introduced in 1921. In 1930 she married Billy Rose but divorced him eight years later. Her language was extremely colorful and she made no allowances for it off stage. "Anyone who can't say f— is deceitful," she told her biographer.

Her memory would sometimes fail her, but never where money was concerned. Jesse Block recalls an incident from the thirties:

> We played the Oriental Theatre in Chicago with Fanny Brice. She had just closed with the *Follies*. She was a tremendous headliner. This was the first time we met and we became great friends after that. We were together for a number of years until she moved to California. She had a heart condition. She never went any place, except to Eddie Cantor's house. Now we come to California, and we haven't seen her for a couple of years. And, in the meantime, because of her illness, she became very absentminded. Now out there, Eddie has a dinner party for us, George and Gracie Burns, Jack and Mary Benny, and Fanny Brice. So that night, we're reminiscing. I say, "Remember Fanny when we played on the same bill at the Oriental Theatre?" She says, "Kid, I don't remember playing the Oriental Theatre." I say, "Sure, remember we went down to the College Inn and we saw Ben Bernie and His Band?" "I don't remember Ben Bernie." "This I'm sure you'll remember. Al Capone gave you a party." "No." I say, "Fanny, I remember everything. I remember you got $7,500 for the week." She says, "I got $8,000." That she remembered!

In 1928 Fanny Brice made her film debut in *My Man*. She appeared in four other features, *Be Yourself!* (1930), *The Great Ziegfeld* (1936), *Everybody Sing* (1938), and *Ziegfeld Follies* (1946), but aside from *Be Yourself!*, in which she was given a chance to act, the films were chiefly an excuse for recreations (sometimes unsatisfactory) of her vaudeville and *Follies* sketches. Fanny Brice's most famous characterization, thanks to radio, was Baby Snooks, which had its antecedents in her vaudeville "Babykins" skits, and which, according to legend, she had first tried out at a party after the opening of the 1910 *Follies*. Baby Snooks was first heard on radio on February 29, 1936, and continued intermittently until Fanny Brice's death. Snooks's lisping voice and inquisitive "Why, Daddy?" were popular with radio audiences.

Fanny Brice planned to end Baby Snooks's career on June 12, 1951, when her NBC contract ended, and to devote herself to her hobby of interior decoration. She announced she wanted to retire because, "It's too much work." Unfortunately, fate had another idea; Fanny Brice suffered a massive cerebral hemorrhage and died in Los Angeles on May 29, 1951. Since her death she has been the subject of stage and screen biographies starring Barbra Streisand—nothing new, for in 1939 Twentieth Century-Fox filmed a fictionalized account of her romance with Nicky Arnstein in *Rose of Washington Square*. Fanny Brice is one of the handful of vaudevillians whose appeal has not diminished with the passing of the years. At screenings of *Everybody Sing,* audiences still laugh at her Baby Snooks routine with Judy Garland, just as they laughed at her in the *Follies* sixty years ago and more.

References: "Fannie of the Follies" by Fannie Brice in *Cosmopolitan* (April, 1936), pages 64, 65, 101, and 102. *The Fabulous Fanny* by Norman Kratkov (Alfred A. Knopf, 1953).

BOTHWELL BROWNE

Bothwell Browne

Bothwell Browne was one of the best-known female impersonators of the vaudeville stage, hailed by *Variety* as early as 1910 as second only to Julian Eltinge. Like most female impersonators, Browne relied on beautiful gowns to put his act across, but would also generally appear in a sketch or playlet supported by a number of beautiful women—none of whom was allowed to be quite as beautiful as he. Browne was certainly a handsome man, slimmer and far better looking than Julian Eltinge.

San Francisco-born, Bothwell Browne appears to have started his career with the Cohan and Harris Minstrels. As early as 1908 he was popular in New York vaudeville theatres, and when his sketch "Winning a Gibson Girl" was featured at the Fifth Avenue Theatre, Sime Silverman in *Variety* (September 12, 1908) found him "a decidedly clever female impersonator." Browne was back at the Fifth Avenue Theatre in September of 1910, playing a variety of females, including a showgirl, a suffragette, and "The Pantaloon Girl," and closing with a dance as Cleopatra. *Variety* noted that his one weakness was the lack of a strong singing voice. Browne starred in at least one musical comedy, *Miss Jack,* which opened at the Herald Square Theatre on September 4, 1911, and ran for a mere sixteen performances.

Despite these early New York appearances, Bothwell Browne proved more popular on the West Coast, and throughout the 1910s tended to play San Francisco, Los Angeles, Spokane, and Seattle almost exclusively. In 1913 he produced a sketch titled "The Serpent of the Nile," which featured his cousin, Frances Young, as Cleopatra. Young was also featured in Bothwell Browne's "Exotic Art Dances," which first played at the Hippodrome in San Francisco on September 4, 1916. The act opened with Browne, dressed in a gold cloth, introducing Young who performed a dance as an ancient Persian swordsman. *Variety* (September 15, 1916) reported, "This lad is about as handsome a built boy as one wants to see and he danced so easily and gracefully his efforts met with good results." Browne then reappeared to perform "The Dance of Vanity" as a Japanese Maid. The act closed with Young, as a scantily clad Egyptian slave, tending to the needs of Browne as Cleopatra. From today's point of view, the whole thing sounds somewhat effete, but *Variety* called it "the best staged, produced, costumed and elaborate dancing turn that ever left the Pacific Coast."

In 1919, Mack Sennett, the comedy film producer, starred Browne in a vulgar, antiGerman comedy titled *Yankee Doodle in Berlin,* which had Browne playing an American aviator who dons female attire to obtain German secrets. *Photoplay's* critic, Julian Johnson, found Browne's impersonation "very creditable and inoffensive," As a result of the film, Browne put together a vaudeville act with a group of Mack Sennett Bathing Beauties and headlined with them at the Palace in December of 1919. Bothwell Browne's fame may be judged by his making the front cover of the December 12, 1919, issue of *Variety* and the front covers of the *New York Dramatic Mirror* on October 30, 1919, and January 21, 1920. The last announced that he was topping the Keith bills with his Bathing Beauties in a *20th Century Revue,* assisted by the Browne Sisters.

Browne's popularity declined in the twenties. In October of 1923 he appeared in an Egyptian sketch at Los Angeles's Hill Street Theatre playing the Queen (!). Like most female impersonators, no breath of scandal was ever attached to his name, and his private life remains a mystery. Bothwell Browne ended his career producing night club shows in New York. He died in Los Angeles on December 12, 1947.

BUCK AND BUBBLES

Buck and Bubbles

Ford Lee Washington (Buck) and John W. Sublett (Bubbles) were two of the best loved and most talented black entertainers in vaudeville. "They were a tremendous act," recalled Jesse Block. "John Bubbles is one of the most talented boys. He can singer better than anyone. He can dance better than anyone." With Buck vamping at the piano, Bubbles would dance up a storm in a routine for which he noted, "I took the white boys' steps and the colored boys' steps and mixed 'em up all together so you couldn't tell 'em, white or colored." He became the greatest exponent of syncopated tap.

Eleanor Powell told me, "I think Bubbles is fantastic. He did things with his feet. . . . I don't know how many times Buck and Bubbles and I played the Paramount together. When Bubbles was on, I'd be in the wings, on my stomach, watching the feet, and it got so he was playing to me, not to the audience. And I'm doing the same thing when he's on. And after the show, we'd go down to the basement and knock our brains out jamming around."

Buck and Bubbles got together in Louisville, Kentucky, when Buck was nine and Bubbles thirteen. After four years, the two made it to the stage of B. F. Keith's Mary Anderson Theatre in Louisville—the first blacks to play there—dancing and singing "Curse of an Aching Heart" and "Somebody Loves Me." Next they came to New York, playing the Columbia Theatre at 47th Street and Seventh Avenue. Within months they were playing the Palace. That was in 1920, and the act never had to worry from that point on. As headliners, Buck and Bubbles toured the Keith circuit. In 1923 they had their own revue, with five girls and two boys, which opened in New York in July of that year at the City Theatre. There was comedy, singing and dancing, plus a first-rate impression by Buck and Bubbles of Williams and Walker. "The revue has plenty of entertainment," reported *Variety* (July 26, 1923).

Aside from vaudeville, Buck and Bubbles were featured in Lew Leslie's *Blackbirds of 1930* and the 1931 edition of the *Ziegfeld Follies.* Their films included *Varsity Show* (1931), *Atlantic City* (1944), and *A Song Is Born* (1948). They sang "Breakfast in Harlem" in the 1936 London revue *Transatlantic Rhythm,* which also featured Ruth Etting, Lupe Velez, and Lou Holtz. Most important, Buck played Mingo and Bubbles played Sportin' Life in George Gershwin's *Porgy and Bess,* which opened at Boston's Colonial Theatre on September 30, 1935. Those who were privileged to view that original production state that no one could sing "It Ain't Necessarily So" and "There's a Boat dat's Leavin' for New York" like John Bubbles.

Buck died on January 31, 1955, and Bubbles returned to the Palace as a single act in August of 1967 with the Judy Garland Show. Despite a stroke, he returned to the New York stage in May of 1980 in the revue *Black Broadway,* leading the audience in singing "It Ain't Necessarily So." At the show's close John Bubbles and the entire company sang Eubie Blake's "Memories of You." Certainly Bubbles must have had some wonderful memories of sixty years on the New York stage, breaking down racial barriers not with violence and anger but with talent.

References: "Bubbles" in the *New Yorker* (August 26, 1967), pages 21–23. "John Bubbles" in *The Vaudevillians* by Bill Smith (Macmillan, 1976). "John Bubbles: A Hoofer's Homage" by Jane Goldberg in *The Village Voice* (December 4, 1978), page 112.

GEORGE BURNS AND GRACIE ALLEN

If the man in the street was asked to name one act which symbolized all that was great about vaudeville, an act that has endured in popularity for more than fifty years, there is no question that the answer would be Burns and Allen. As a comedy team, they were unrivaled in the annals of show business, and now that Gracie Allen is gone, George Burns finds new success as a new style—senior citizen—leading man in films. The reason for the lasting fame and success of Burns and Allen is not hard to ascertain. It was not simply talent, although they certainly had that, but rather the ability to grasp and prosper in each new medium of entertainment as it came along. First they rose to the top in vaudeville, then radio, followed by the movies and eventually television.

George Burns and Gracie Allen's routines do not need repeating here, for there can be no one who is not familiar with George's straight-man questions and Gracie's "dizzy" responses, dialogue that more often than not was concerned with Gracie's family, and in particular her brother:

George Burns and Gracie Allen

GRACIE: Did you know my brother was held up by two men last night?
GEORGE: For how much?
GRACIE: Oh, all the way home!

Whatever George Burns had to say, Gracie had a response. When, as her boss, George commented angrily, "You should have been here two hours ago," secretary Gracie innocently responded, "Why, what happened?" Gracie would always misunderstand with hilarious results. On a bus tour of New York City, which included Grant's Tomb and the George Washington Bridge, she was outraged that the nation could find a tomb for Grant while the father of her country was consigned to his final rest under a bridge.

In an interview with the *New York Times,* George Burns once noted what he considered the reason for the pair's success: "We were kicking around for eight years telling the same jokes before anything happened. Suddenly people got the idea that Gracie's crazy and needs protection. We had nothing to do with the things that happened to us. The public makes and breaks people like us too fast." The public may make or break a vaudevillian, but it can also come to adore and cherish an act, and such was the case with Burns and Allen.

George Burns was born Nathan Birnbaum in New York City on January 20, 1896. He first tried his hand at show business at the age of seven, when his father died and he formed the Pee Wee Quartette. Later, he joined forces with Abie Kaplan, and because the two of them followed the truck of the Burns Brothers coal yard, in the hopes of picking up any coal that might drop on the street, they became known as the Burns Brothers. The first name of George the comedian took from an elder brother, Isadore, whom he admired and who was called George by his friends. At the age of thirteen, George Burns linked up with an entertainer named Mac Fry to become the Company in Mac Fry and Company. Next was a partnership with Sam Brown as Brown and Williams (after a former member of the act). And so it went. Burns was Glide in Goldie, Fields and Glide, followed by participation in an act titled The Fourth of July Kids. In his autobiography, *I Love Her, That's Why!*, George Burns wrote that he often changed his name because the booker of a specific theatre threatened not to give Burns another job if he knew who he was. To add to the confusion, at one time George Burns was playing in an act titled Burns and Links —and he was Links!

Eventually, at the age of twenty-four, George Burns's vaudeville fortunes began to improve. He found a new partner in Sid Gary, who was later to become a popular entertainer on radio noted for his high soprano voice. Two years later Burns and Gary split up, and Burns joined forces with a man named Billy Lorraine in an act titled Burns and Lorraine—Two Broadway Thieves, so called because part of their act consisted of imitations of Broadway stars like Al Jolson and Eddie Cantor. In his autobiography, Fred Allen recalled some of the dialogue from the Burns and Lorraine act:

BURNS: I had a fight with my wife last night.
LORRAINE: What happened?
BURNS: She chased me around the house with a red-hot poker. I finally ran into a closet and shut the door.
LORRAINE: And then?
BURNS: My wife started knocking on the closet door and yelling, "Come out of that closet, you coward! Come out of that closet, you coward!"
LORRAINE: Did you come out of the closet?
BURNS: Not me. In my house, I'm boss!

While working with Billy Lorraine, George Burns was also developing an act of his own. The last place that Burns and Lorraine played was the Union Hill Theatre in New Jersey, and while there Burns told the headliner, Rena Arnold, of his plans; at the same time he told her a risqué story. Miss Arnold was offended by the story but told her friend Gracie Allen that she should approach Lorraine, who was looking for a new partner. Gracie Allen saw the act, confused Burns with Lorraine, and asked him for a job. It was three days before she discovered her mistake.

Gracie Allen was born in San Francisco on July 26, 1905, the daughter of a song-and-dance man named Edward Allen whom she once described as "the first and best clog and minstrel man in San Francisco." Of her birth Gracie Allen said, "I was so surprised I couldn't talk for a year and a half." Gracie first worked on stage as a child with her father. Later she appeared with her sisters, Bes-

sie, Pearl, and Hazel, in an act titled Larry Reilly and Company, in which she danced an Irish jig and sang. Burns and Allen made their first appearance together in 1922 at the Hill Street Theatre in Newark, New Jersey; they were married four years later, on January 7, 1926, in Cleveland, Ohio. At first Gracie played the straight role and Burns was the comedian, but in a matter of months the roles had been reversed, and George Burns was established as the cigar chomping straight man with Gracie Allen as his dizzy partner.

GRACIE: All great singers have their trials; look at Caruso. Thirty years on a desert island with all those cannibals.
GEORGE: You've got the wrong man.
GRACIE: No, you're the man for me.
GEORGE: But they say I'm through as a singer. I'm extinct.
GRACIE: You do not!

Variety (April 12, 1923) saw Burns and Allen at the Fifth Avenue Theatre and reported, "He has a good delivery for this style of talk and the girl is an excellent foil. They have more than average personalities. The act lets down in spots, due to the dialog, and can be strengthened in this respect." *Variety* also noted the act was similiar in style to that of an earlier team called Matthews and Ayres. Of course, *Variety* was not always impressed by Burns and Allen; a few months later, on June 28, 1923, it commented, "A brighter and smarter vehicle will have to be secured if they expect to advance."

Burns and Allen's first great success was with a sketch titled "Lamb Chops," written for them by Al Boasberg, who was later to be much in demand as a comedy writer for films. Abel Green saw the pair perform at the Palace and wrote in *Variety* (August 25, 1926): "George N. Burns and Gracie Allen have a new skit in *Lamb Chops*, by Al Boasberg; funny stuff, almost actor proof, but further enhanced by the team's individual contributions. Miss Allen is an adorable 'dizzy' with an ingratiating prattle. Burns foils and wisecracks in turn and the laugh returns are fast and many. They dance off before the routine encore, which brings him back for a bit wherein he reclines on a prop mat on the stage, 'feeding' his partner. A tip-top comedy interlude for the best vaudeville."

The dialogue for "Lamb Chops," which became so well known that the audience would often join in, went something like this:

GEORGE: Do you care about love?
GRACIE: No.
GEORGE: Do you care about kisses?
GRACIE: No.
GEORGE: What do you care about?
GRACIE: Lamb chops.

In the summer of 1929 Burns and Allen went to England for a total of twenty-one weeks, several of which were spent in London, alternating between the Holborn

Empire and the London Palladium. They were billed as "The Famous American Comedy Couple," and the English people took Gracie, in particular, to their hearts. One critic wrote, "Excepting Beatrice Lillie, she is perhaps the most adroit female laugh-getter in vaudeville.... Sweet simplicity gushes from her eyes and her lips though it is obvious from the first that she is full of guile." While in England—in June of 1929—the couple made a series of radio broadcasts for the BBC, happy precursors of what lay ahead.

When Burns and Allen returned to the United States, there was no question about their popularity. Their film career began with a series of shorts for Paramount, including *Lamb Chops,* and the couple blossomed into features with *The Big Broadcast* in 1932, followed by *International House* (1933), *Six of a Kind* (1934), *We're Not Dressing* (1934), *The Big Broadcast of 1936, The Big Broadcast of 1937, Damsel in Distress* (1937), and *Honolulu* (1939), among others. Gracie was even featured in a few films on her own, most notably *The Gracie Allen Murder Case* (1939).

The two became radio regulars on CBS in 1932, when they were signed to appear on the Guy Lombardo program, sponsored by Robert Burns Cigars; soon after, "The Burns and Allen Show" made its appearance. It began as a vaudeville-style entertainment and did not develop into a situation comedy until the early forties. Of course, the running gag on the show in the early thirties was Gracie's search for her lost brother (in reality, an employee of Standard Oil in San Francisco); CBS would have Burns and Allen wander in and out of other radio programs asking about Gracie's daft brother, who had hurt his leg falling off an ironing board while pressing his pants. Not everyone was entranced by the program; *Time* magazine (January 30, 1933) commented, "Burns and Allen have shot into first place as the most annoying broadcast on the air—the climax of sub-moronic radiodrivel." In 1940 Gracie Allen declared her candidacy for president of the United States on the Surprise Party Ticket, campaigning for the repeal of prohibition. When told this had already been accomplished, Miss Allen replied, "Oh really? I can hardly wait for my brother to sober up so I can tell him about it."

On October 12, 1950, "The George Burns and Gracie Allen Show" made a successful transition to television— on CBS—after eighteen years on the radio. The show's thirty-minute format was that of a situation comedy, with the pair playing themselves, aided by Harry Von Zell (the announcer as himself), Ronnie Burns (the couple's adopted son as himself), Bea Benaderet (as Blanche Morton, Gracie's friend and neighbour), and Larry Keating (as the best-known actor to play Blanche's husband, Harry Morton). One of the show's sponsors was Carnation Milk, and Gracie would say innocently, "I never will understand how they get milk from carnations." Each episode ended with George and Gracie performing one of their vaudeville routines and the close, George's "Say goodnight, Gracie," was one of the best known in the history of television. The show ended in September of 1958, when Gracie Allen announced her retirement.

George Burns carried on for another year with his own show, featuring the same characters as the original.

Gracie Allen died on August 28, 1964. At her funeral Jack Benny said, "Her love was so great it never waned in a span of forty years.... Gracie Allen was an institution. Her timing and delivery were the most natural I have ever known." George Burns continued to work, and in recent years his career has blossomed; in 1975 he won the Academy Award for Best Supporting Actor for his work in *The Sunshine Boys.*

References: *I Love Her, That's Why* by George Burns, with Cynthia Hobart Lindsay (Simon and Schuster, 1955). "Gracie Allen—Just the Name Evoked a Smile" by Albin Krebs in *New York Herald Tribune* (August 29, 1964), page 8. *Living It Up* by George Burns (G. P. Putnam's Sons, 1976). *The Third Time Around* by George Burns (G. P. Putnam's Sons, 1980).

MARIE CAHILL

Marie Cahill in 1904

Marie Cahill was a popular comedienne and singer on the legitimate stage who made infrequent forays into vaudeville from 1919 on. She was born in Brooklyn, circa 1870, into a strict Roman Catholic family (who insisted that she wear extremely full costumes when appearing on stage). Miss Cahill's first appearance was in Brooklyn in the late 1880s, as a soubrette in the romantic Irish melodrama *Kathleen Mavourneen.* Her New York debut came on July 1, 1889, at Poole's Eighth Street Theatre in *C.O.D.,* and later that same year she appeared in her first musical, *A Tin Soldier.* For three years she appeared in Augustin

Daly's productions, but her first major success was in *The Wild Rose* (1902) produced by George Lederer, in which she sang "Nancy Brown." That song became the title for a musical comedy, written by George Broadhurst and Frederick Rankin, with music by Silvio Hein and George Hadley, which made Marie Cahill a star in 1903. By this time Miss Cahill was under the management of Daniel V. Arthur, whom she later married. Perhaps the greatest success of Marie Cahill's early career was *Marrying Mary,* which opened at Daly's Theatre in August of 1906.

The comedienne did not make her vaudeville debut until March of 1919, when she headlined at the Palace. Her songs included "As Long as the Congo Flows" and "If You Like Me and I Like You." She also performed a telephone sketch, carrying on a monolog with her friend Ethel. Her debut was, in the words of the *New York Dramatic Mirror* (March 25, 1919), "a theatrical function of importance," and the magazine continued:

> Miss Cahill's dates in vaudeville are as assured as was from the first the United States' and the Allies' victory against the Hun. Hereafter she will be a distinctive vaudeville institution of a status which will have the admiration of the whole family. Each member of the family, too, will attend her performances which fact will make her one of the best drawing cards on the Big Time.

Despite her religious background, some of her numbers were slightly risqué, like her 1920 hit "It's Right Here for You (If You Don't Get It 'Taint No Fault o' Mine)." Marie Cahill continued to appear on the legitimate stage and vaudeville through the twenties; she was one of the headliners on the April, 1925, old-timers bill at the Palace. Her last stage role was as Gloria Wentworth in *The New Yorkers,* which opened at the Broadway Theatre in December of 1930. She died at her New York home on August 23, 1933, still revered as one of the great musical comedy stars of her day.

MRS. PATRICK CAMPBELL

"No, I'm not dreaming of appearing at any music hall," Ellen Terry, the great English dramatic actress, told *Variety* in October of 1910, after receiving several offers to appear in vaudeville on her arrival in the United States. "No actors in their senses should, in my opinion, at least not while the regulations and privileges are so different for the different places." She went on to say:

> I don't think actors show to advantage in a music hall. They cannot entertain the visitors as some to the manner born (of music halls can do). To be sandwiched in between past masters of the art of vaudeville entertainment, such as Paul Cinquevalli and Alice Lloyd, really shows off an actor to ill advantage. Music hall artists are out of place in a theatre—actors are out of place in a music hall—at least, that is my opinion.

Mrs. Patrick Campbell

Ethel Barrymore was one actress who did not agree. She earned large salaries playing vaudeville, and was, in fact, the first star to play the Palace—in April of 1913—and be a hit. Another actress who took a point of view opposite to that of Ellen Terry was Mrs. Patrick Campbell (1865–1940). In need of money, Mrs. Campbell arrived in New York in 1910 and telephoned a friend to announce, "Here I am. I have a good one-act play and a lovely frock, and I would be glad of a vaudeville engagement. What shall I do?" She was told to telephone E. F. Albee, who gave her ten weeks work at a salary which Mrs. Pat claims in her autobiography was $500 a week and which Douglas Gilbert states was $2,500 a week. Legend has it that in the middle of her conversation with Albee (when she was setting down her rules of two performances a day, no work on Sundays, and no obligation to speak to any other performers on the same bill), she asked for a telephone, rang her hotel suite, and apologized to Pinkie, her Pekinese, for being late. "I am," she explained, "with those horrible men in the vaudeville business."

The one-act play in which Mrs. Pat starred on the vaudeville stage was titled *Expiation!*; she had originally planned to appear in it in England. In her autobiography the actress recalled, "Oh, those two performances of *Expiation!* I had to kill a man twice a day and shriek—and it had to be done from the heart—the Americans see through 'bluff'—and I was advertised as a 'Great tragic actress'!" *Variety* (February 19, 1910) reviewed *Expiation!* and commented, "Any legitimate of rank who enters vaudeville, and gives a little for the money received has done something. In comparison, Mrs. Pat has done a lot."

Variety was not so kind about Mrs. Campbell's second vaudeville offering, *The Ambassador's Wife,* a twenty-four-minute playlet by her son Alan Patrick Campbell, which opened at the Majestic Theatre, Chicago, in May of 1910. The paper thought it unfair that the actress' son was allowed to practice as a storywriter while the audience was forced to suffer. As to Mrs. Pat herself, according to Douglas Gilbert's *American Vaudeville,* she complained about everything and "a hundred and forty-six Tanguays couldn't tie her for temperament."

While appearing in Hollywood productions in the early thirties, Mrs. Patrick Campbell apparently found time to appear at vaudeville houses, concert halls, in fact anywhere, to lecture on "Diction in Dramatic Art," a subject on which she had first spoken at the Lyric Theatre in Hammersmith, London, in July of 1927. To listen to Mrs. Pat talk about "beautiful speech," and to hear her impersonate a man of the cloth preaching a sermon with and without the correct vocal intonations, was devastating. Her voice could have the power of a volcano, the crispness of water from a mountain spring, or the warmth of a log fire, and, of course, she was much too good for American audiences, whether in movie houses or vaudeville palaces.

Reference: *My Life and Some Letters* by Mrs. Patrick Campbell (Dodd, Mead and Company, 1922).

EDDIE CANTOR

Eddie Cantor

In his 1929 book *Caught Short! A Saga of Wailing Wall Street,* there is a cartoon that typifies Eddie Cantor's humor. He is in blackface, knocking on J. P. Morgan's door

and announcing, "I am the Kuhn, of Kuhn, Loeb and Company." When not in blackface, Cantor was best with Jewish humor (certainly less offensive, in view of his own religion, to today's audiences). As a Jewish aviator from Newark, who named his plane *Mosquito—the Spirit of New Jersey,* he could not emulate Lindbergh's crossing of the Atlantic because he couldn't eat ham sandwiches. He changed his name to Ginsberg from Levey, explaining, "I was in the South, around the Mississippi during the floods, and I read headlines in the papers that they were going to blow up all the levees." He announced that, "I'd go to war for my mother country, Russia—darkest Russia—for all my relatives there, General Walkowitch, Itzkowitch, Eczema." When queried on eczema, he replied, "Yes, that's another itch."

Eddie Cantor's stage characterizations were always effeminate, or at least effete. In *Whoopee!* he is weak and a chronic hypochondriac; when not running away from his strong and domineering female nurse, he is commenting to the hero about how cute he looks without his shirt. (When the hero, supposedly a half-breed Indian, confides that "I went to your schools," Cantor asks in surprise, "You went to a Hebrew School?") In one highly suggestive scene in *Whoopee!,* he discusses operations with another man, and both begin pulling up shirts and pulling down pants to reveal their scars. The sequence ends with them rolling around together on the floor. In his famous 1919 *Ziegfeld Follies* sketch, Cantor played the effeminate, college-educated son of railway porter Bert Williams, complete with horn-rimmed glasses and a mincing walk. The tough old porter is horrified that his son has not turned into a football hero, at least, and is about to hit him when Cantor exclaims in a girlish voice, "Remember, Daddy, I have a temper." Williams replies, "I'll show you where you got it from!" The sketch ended with Williams putting his porter's cap on Cantor's head and saying, "Pick up them bags! This is my graduation and your commencement."

In an introduction to his *World's Book of Best Jokes,* Eddie Cantor explained that he preferred humorous insults to all other types of jokes, because ordinary jokes are forgotten ten minutes after delivery but insults are repeated until they become classics. Cantor also confessed to having used more than twenty thousand jokes over an eleven-year period on the radio. Cantor had first embraced blackface in 1910, figuring it would help him get his material over. With the addition of horn-rimmed glasses he became more than an average blackface minstrel; the glasses added a hint of intelligence and brought the characterization away from the Southern cotton fields and into the twentieth century and the liberated life of a northern Negro. The comedian was a great defender of blackface and ethnic humor. "When this kind of harmless humor was barred," he told the *Los Angeles Times,* "it took half of the fun out of show business."

Dancing, clapping his hands, eyes popping, the energetic comedian sang the songs with which he will always be associated—"Making Whoopee," "My Baby Just Cares for Me," "If You Knew Susie," "Hungry Women," and "You'd Be Surprised." His recordings were always immensely popular. In 1920 Cantor signed a new contract with Brunswick Records for $220,000 over five years, the biggest contract of its kind, easily beating out those offered to Caruso and John McCormack.

Eddie Cantor was born Isidore Itzkowitz on New York's East Side on January 31, 1892, and raised by his grandmother, Esther Kantrowitz. When he enrolled in school at the age of six, he started to give his grandmother's name and never finished it. The school registrar told him Isidore Kantor was sufficient. Soon after, the *K* became a *C*, and his wife-to-be persuaded him to adopt Eddie as his first name because it was "cute." Cantor's entry into vaudeville was typical of his generation: amateur shows and burlesque, abortive partnerships with Al Lee and Sam Kessler in 1914, and even an unsuccessful 1914 engagement in an Andre Charlot show, *Not Likely,* in London. The first break in Cantor's early career came in 1912, when he was signed by Gus Edwards to appear in his *Kid Kabaret* with George Jessel, Eddie Buzzel, George Price, and Lila Lee. "It was not first class vaudeville," wrote Cantor, "but the best and only acting school of its kind, where poor young boys and girls could learn the art of entertainment in all its forms and get paid for learning." A close friendship developed between Cantor and Jessel, which endured through the remainder of Cantor's life. In 1931 the two had a highly successful engagement together at the Palace.

Cantor's second break came in 1916, when he left an engagement with the Oliver Morosco production of *Canary Cottage* in Los Angeles to return to New York and a tryout with Florenz Ziegfeld. The comedian made a big hit in Ziegfield's *Midnight Frolics* and, as a result, was put into the 1917 edition of *The Ziegfeld Follies.* The 1918 and 1919 editions followed, and Cantor might have continued in the *Follies* through the twenties had he not walked out of the 1919 *Follies* to join the Actors' Equity strike. Ziegfeld announced he would have nothing more to do with Cantor, and the performer formed a new alliance with the Shuberts, for whom he appeared in *Broadway Brevities of 1920* and *Make It Snappy* (1922). Happily, Cantor and Ziegfeld patched up their differences, and Cantor returned to star in the two most important musical comedies of his career, *Kid Boots* (1923) and *Whoopee!* (1928), plus the 1927 edition of *The Ziegfeld Follies.* In 1954 Eddie Cantor reminisced,

Those never-to-be forgotten Ziegfeld nights when the entrances were crowded with the stars and the showgirls listening to the devastating, cheer-provoking lines of Will Rogers!—lines that would be just as big today. "We never lost a war or won a conference," he drawled. "America is an open book—a checkbook," he'd say, and nothing could follow his act—nothing but the finale. The pantomine of Bert Williams, the robust humor of W. C. Fields, the songs of Fannie Brice, they're all gone now, but I have my memories. Today, with television, a fellow can have a big time, a big salary, a big rating and security—but the satisfaction, the joy of being part of the Ziegfeld tradition is no more. I could cry.

Eddie Cantor returned to vaudeville in 1923, and proved he was still as popular with vaudeville audiences as he was with those for musical comedy. He opened his vaudeville tour at the Orpheum, Brooklyn, delivering popular songs such as "How Ya Gonna Keep Your Mind on Dancing," "Oh, Gee! Oh, Gosh!," and "Yes, We Have No Bananas." *Variety* (June 7, 1923) reported, "Eddie Cantor is an entertainer with a capital 'E.' He is value received for vaudeville."

In 1926 Cantor made his screen debut in the film version of *Kid Boots,* but it was not until 1930 and the film version of *Whoopee!* that he made his mark on the screen. Among his best known features are *Palmy Days* (1931), *The Kid from Spain* (1932), *Roman Scandals* (1933), and *Kid Millions* (1934). In 1953 his life story was filmed as *The Eddie Cantor Story,* with Keefe Brasselle in the title role.

Cantor was an early performer on radio, but came into his own on "The Chase and Sanborn Hour" on NBC in 1931. As "The Eddie Cantor Show," the program was heard on CBS from 1935, and Cantor became known for his radio discoveries, which included Deanna Durbin, Bobby Breen, and Dinah Shore. In 1939 he was blacklisted for his outspoken criticism of certain government officials as fascists, but he came back on NBC in 1940. In 1944 he raised forty million dollars for war bonds on a twenty-four-hour marathon radio show. Cantor moved over to television in 1950 with "The Colgate Comedy Hour."

Aside from his work on radio, stage, and screen, Eddie Cantor was a distinguished and prolific author, writing two autobiographical works and a number of amusing short volumes, *Caught Short!, Yoo Hoo Prosperity, Your Next President, Between the Acts,* and *Who's Hooey?* Cantor also took a great interest in political and social activities. He was a founder of Actors' Equity, the American Federation of Radio Artists (AFTRA), and the Screen Actors Guild. To Eddie Cantor goes the credit for the creation of the March of Dimes. He was an outspoken leader in Jewish affairs, so much so that the neofascist Catholic priest Father Coughlin said in 1935, "Jews have only three enemies to fear—Bernard Baruch, Eddie Cantor, and the Motion Picture Industry." The State of Israel awarded Cantor the Medallion of Valor in 1962 for his "extraordinary achievements" on behalf of that nation. In 1956 the Academy of Motion Picture Arts and Sciences presented him with a special Oscar "for the distinguished service to the film industry," and in 1964 President Johnson gave Cantor the U.S. Service Medal in recognition of his humanitarian work.

Eddie Cantor never really recovered from the death of his wife, Ida, on August 8, 1962—they were married on June 9, 1914 and had five daughters—and he died at his Beverly Hills home on October 11, 1964. He was indeed a great entertainer and a great humanitarian, whose vigor and zest for life was as apparent off stage as on.

References: *My Life Is in Your Hands* by Eddie Cantor, as told to David Freedman (Blue Ribbon Books, 1928). *Take My Life* by Eddie Cantor, with Jane Kesner Ardmore (Doubleday and Company, 1957).

EMMA CARUS

Emma Carus was a combination singer and comedienne; she was the former because she had a good voice, and the latter, in part, because she was not attractive. Her famous opening line was, "I'm not pretty, but I'm good to my family." Mrs. Gus Kahn recalls, "She had a beautiful baby face, but she was quite stout. And Gus and I wrote a song for her called 'Henry, Oh Henry, Your Mother Is Looking for You'—a little kid's song. And it was kind of strange seeing this big, fat woman standing up there, singing a song like a child."

The daughter of a noted prima donna, Henrietta Rolland, Emma Carus was born in Berlin on March 18, 1879, and first sang publicly at the age of six. She made her first New York appearance in 1894 and became a popular favorite in musical comedy, starring in such shows as *The Giddy Throng* (1900), *The Wild Rose* (1902), *Forty-Five Minutes from Broadway* (1907, succeeding Fay Templeton), *Up and Down Broadway* (1910), and *The Wife Hunters* (1911). She was featured in the original 1907 edition of *The Ziegfeld Follies,* and went into vaudeville for the first time that same year. After 1915 Emma Carus appeared exclusively on the vaudeville stage. She died on November 18, 1927.

THE CHERRY SISTERS

The best contemporary description of the Cherry Sisters is given by Robert Grau in his 1910 book *The Business Man in the Amusement World:*

> They were just a quartette of incompetents, and they were so indifferent to their reception by the public, that they were in demand for many years, at a salary far higher than would have been accorded them if they had possessed real ability. There was, though, something approaching cruelty in the spectacle which these poor females presented, night after night, in exhibiting their crudities to howling, insulting audiences.

There were originally five Cherry Sisters—Jessie, Ella, Lizzie, Addie, and Effie—and they came from a small community named Marion, just outside of Cedar Rapids, Iowa. To raise money to visit the 1893 Chicago World's Fair, the sisters put on shows for their friends; because these friends were so uncritical the sisters were persuaded, when they did get to Chicago, to approach a vaudeville agent and become professional entertainers. The agent was quick to realize the potential he had in an act which was so bad it was good; he signed them to appear in one-act melodramas, such as *The Gypsy's Warning,* interspersed with songs, and the sisters toured through Iowa, Kansas, and Illinois.

In 1896 Oscar Hammerstein brought four of the girls to New York to appear at his Olympia Theatre, at Forty-fourth Street and Broadway, the forerunner to Hammerstein's Victoria Theatre. They were billed as "The Cherry Sisters—Something Good, Something Sad," but the emphasis was definitely on the latter, for they were indeed a sad act, being pelted with rotten vegetables before Effie Cherry could finish her first song, "Three Cheers for the Railroad Boys." Legend has it that Hammerstein explained to the sisters that other stars, jealous of their talents, had hired people to throw vegetables at them. There is little doubt that Hammerstein himself hired those first vegetable throwers. Perhaps the sisters really didn't care, earning as they were $1,000 a week until they retired in 1903, when Jessie died.

None of the sisters ever married. Effie was the most active, twice running unsuccessfully for Mayor of Cedar Rapids; she even considered running for Congress on an antiliquor, antitobacco platform. The sisters tried a comeback in May of 1924, playing the Orpheum in Des Moines, and *Variety's* local reviewer wrote, "If it were not for a reputation for being a bad act gained 30 years ago, the Cherry Sisters could not get a hearing. . . . As terribleness, their skit is perfection." In 1935 Addie and Effie Cherry were invited to appear at a New York night club, The Gay Nineties, but audiences by this time were frankly embarrassed by the pitiful sight of two old ladies unaware of their shortcomings. Addie died on October 26, 1942, and Effie, the last of the Cherry Sisters, on August 5, 1944, at the estimated age of eighty-five.

Reference: "So Bad They Were Good" by Avery Hale in *Coronet* (December, 1944), pages 92–96.

ALBERT CHEVALIER

The coster comedian—the performer with a cockney accent born within the sound of London's Bow Bells—has been an integral part of British music hall from Gus Elen through Flanagan and Allen to Max Bygraves, but only one gained international fame and was as popular in American vaudeville as in the music halls of England, and that was Albert Chevalier. In this country his salary in vaudeville in the early years of this century was $1,750 a week.

Albert Chevalier's songs, which he usually wrote himself, were, and are, gems of working class English life. Once heard, no one can forget "Mrs. 'Enry 'Awkins, "Knocked 'Em in the Old Kent Road" (a song also associated with Marie Lloyd), or "My Old Dutch," in which an elderly cockney recalls the forty years spent with his wife, his old Dutch: "She's stuck to me through thick and thin, when luck was out, when luck was in; Oh what a wife to me she's been, and what a pal." "My Old Dutch" could not fail to move an audience to tears—particularly when Chevalier asked that death might take him first in order that he might prepare the way in Heaven for his Old Dutch. Similarly, in "The Fallen Star" he enumerated in perfect theatrical English the woes of a stage actor down on his luck, who remembers yet again forty years ago— a cherished period of time with Chevalier—when he was a "favorite at the Vic. But now I pass unrecognized in crowded streets and bars. The firmament of fame holds no record of my name; the name of a fallen star." These songs

Albert Chevalier

were never really sung by Chevalier, but rather carefully recited in the same style as that of the Professor Higgins character in *My Fair Lady.*

Albert Chevalier was born on March 21, 1861, the son of a French father and an English mother. He was on the legitimate stage for many years before moving over to music hall and vaudeville. No doubt those years spent with such prominent British actors as Arthur Roberts, Squire Bancroft, and John Hare helped him tremendously when it came to the conception of his vaudeville characterizations. Most references agree that Chevalier first sang a cockney song, "Our 'Armonic Club," in London's Strand Theatre production of the pantomime *Aladdin* in 1889. Chevalier's first music hall appearance was at London's Tivoli Theatre in 1891.

Chevalier toured the world singing his coster songs, with the French chanteuse Yvette Guilbert, and the pair made their American vaudeville debut at Koster and Bial's Music Hall in 1896; they continued to appear together until 1906. In 1907 Albert Chevalier returned to the legitimate stage in the Theatre Royal, Drury Lane, production of *The Sins of Society.* From this point on, the actor alternated between the legitimate stage and vaudeville. He even starred, opposite the American actress Florence Turner, in a 1915 film production called *My Old Dutch,* based on the song. That same song was also the basis for a stage play by Chevalier, which was presented at New York's Lyceum Theatre in July of 1920.

Death came to Albert Chevalier on July 11, 1923, after he had announced his final retirement from the stage. *Variety* (July 26, 1923) hailed him as "the greatest of all

coster comedians," but that is a title which does not do justice to a vaudevillian whose characterizations were always uniquely English and yet which, through his artistry, transcended the barriers of nationality.

PAUL CINQUEVALLI

One of the greatest classic jugglers of all time, Paul Cinquevalli was described by *Variety* (July 19, 1918) as "a model for gracefulness in juggling." The *New York Clipper* (May 19, 1904) wrote of him, "Cinquevalli is of medium size, but is the personification of muscular development and graceful action." He was born in Lissa, Poland, on June 30, 1859, and at an early age ran away to join a circus. Cinquevalli made his first appearance as a wire walker in Odessa, Russia, and soon became a leading exponent of the art of wire walking and trapeze artistry, until a fall from the trapeze put him in the hospital for eight months. There he began to practice juggling and balancing and, on his release, embarked on a new career. Cinquevalli made his London debut in 1885 at a circus in Covent Garden; he first visited the United States with Rich and Harris's Howard Athenaeum Company in 1888 and made a triumphant reappearance here in 1901, playing the Keith circuit and appearing for ten consecutive weeks at the Union Square Theatre. According to the *New York Clipper* (November 16, 1901), "Australia, South Africa, India, Mexico, and the South American countries alike bowed down in amazement at his marvellous work, so much better was he than those who had preceded him that they were forgotten." Paul Cinquevalli died at his home in the Brixton section of London—a residential area popular with music hall artists—in July of 1918.

CLARK AND McCULLOUGH

It is curious that youngsters today thrive on the Marx Brothers, imitating Groucho Marx's walk, leer, and voice at the drop of a hat, yet they have never heard of Bobby Clark and Paul McCullough, who were equally funny (especially Bobby Clark, who was more outrageous and perhaps worthier of imitation than Groucho Marx). Clark was the funny man, with black glasses painted on his face, a cigar in one hand, and a leer and walk that were unique. On his head was a pork pie hat; he wore a short topcoat and carried a cane which, sooner or later, would be used to smack a retreating chorus girl. Like Groucho, Bobby Clark was both witty and intelligent, announcing, for example, that the team's motto was "Omnia Cafeteria Rex" (We Eat All We Can Carry). McCullough was the straight man, although he could crack a joke when required. As a team, they delighted vaudeville, burlesque, and revue audiences from 1912 through the thirties, when they made occasional excursions into films, transferring some of their better sketches from the transience of the stage to the permanence of motion picture film.

No matter what production he appeared in, Bobby Clark would completely take over the show. While playing the comedy lead in a 1947 revival of Victor Herbert's *Sweethearts,* Clark provided his own gags and at one point

Clark and McCullough

confided to the audience, "Never was a thin plot so complicated." When appearing in the 1946 production of Moliere's *The Would-Be Gentleman,* he was told that the alphabet was divided into vowels and consonants, to which he responded, "That's only fair." In a 1942 production of *The Rivals,* directed by Eva Le Gallienne, he refused to stand still on stage for a moment; while the other actors were delivering their lines, Bobby Clark was climbing over the furniture, deploring the pictures, leering and winking at the rest of the company, and carrying on imaginary conversations. Eventually Miss Le Gallienne said to him, "I've never worked with anybody like you, Mr. Clark. I think you'd do a better job by yourself. I'll just try to keep the other actors out of your way." Bobby Clark's favorite dramatist was William Shakespeare, "because the clowns never get killed."

Both Clark and McCullough were born in Springfield, Ohio, Clark in 1888 and McCullough in 1883. Bobby Clark made his stage debut in May of 1902 at the Grand Opera House in Springfield, as an attendant in *Mrs. Jarley's Waxworks.* The two met in grammar school in Springfield; they attended tumbling classes at the Springfield YMCA and practiced in each other's back yards. One day in 1900 Paul McCullough said, "I'll tell you what. Let's become partners. Maybe we can go into show business or something." They did. After placing an advertisement for their act in *The Billboard* and the *New York Clipper,* the two were invited to join first the Culhane, Chace and Weston Minstrel Show, and later, Kalbfield's Greater California Minstrels. Eventually the pair joined Ringling Brothers' Circus. The story is told that Al Rin-

gling complained about the amount of luggage that Clark carried with him and constantly added to, to which the comedian responded that he was only traveling with so much luggage because he had noticed the circus was advertised as "Bigger and Better." For six years, between 1906 and 1912, Clark and McCullough worked in various circuses as clowns and musical performers, billed as the Jazzbo Brothers, the Prosit Trio, or Sunshine and Roses.

Clark and McCullough (unlike most comedy duos, the funny man's name was first in their billing) entered vaudeville on December 2, 1912, at the Opera House in New Brunswick, New Jersey, with an act which consisted chiefly of trying to set a chair on top of a table. In those early years the act was chiefly pantomime with little or no dialogue. Later the pair developed a sketch in which Clark volunteered to act as a lion tamer in a circus if McCullough would wear a lion skin and substitute for an escaped lion. In the meantime, unknown to Clark, the lion returned, and he played out the sketch with such comments as "Great boy, great! You're doing a grand job;" "Put some life into it! We're getting fifty cents for this job" and "This is one of the classic performances of history. You even smell like a lion!"

Clark and McCullough toured in vaudeville for five years, until the 1917 White Rats strike against the vaudeville management, which the two supported. This ended with management's barring any vaudeville act which participated in the strike from their theatres. To continue working, Clark and McCullough entered burlesque, and there, rather than in vaudeville, achieved their greatest success. Clark once reminisced about burlesque comedy and noted, "We had a lot of good people then. It would be hard to pick out the best. Maybe Joe Welch with his Jewish comedy, or his brother Ben Welch, or Dave Marion, or maybe Frank Tinney. I used to catch them all whenever I could. They were good—better than anybody today, I think. Real funny fellows. Make you laugh like you meant it." A classic Clark and McCullough burlesque sketch was titled "The Courtroom," which had Clark as the judge at the trial of a strip-tease performer. Every time an attorney spoke, Clark would hit him with a bladder and shout, "You're trying to inject hokum into this case!" Eventually a fight broke out involving everyone in the courtroom, which was stopped only by the suggestion that the stripper demonstrate her act for the judge in his chambers. Clark returned soon after to announce, "Case settled out of court!"

Critic Howard Lindsay recalled,

The core of their vaudeville act was pantomime, but they learned the use of dialogue, the value of the feed line and the timing of the comedy line. They learned another lesson vaudeville could teach better than any branch of the entertainment field—economy. In the eighteen or twenty minutes a vaudeville act was allowed, there could not be a wasted word or an insignificant movement.

As burlesque stars, Clark and McCullough were featured in *Puss Puss,* which opened at the Columbia Theatre in New York on December 9, 1918. Clark played Count Rolling No Moss, while McCoullough was Baron Few Clothes, and the two sang "They Go Wild over Us" and "Spanish Onions," described as "a strong specialty." In addition, the pair made their London debut in *Chuckles of 1922,* which opened at the New Oxford Theatre on June 19. From *Chuckles of 1922,* the team went into the 1922 edition of *The Music Box Revue,* which made them Broadway stars. In 1930 Clark and McCullough were starred in *The Ramblers,* set in a motion picture studio on the Mexican border.

Despite their fame on Broadway, Clark and McCullough were still not major headliners in vaudeville. They played the Capitol—which featured both vaudeville and films—in January of 1928, and *Variety* (January 11, 1928) commented that few in the audience knew who they were. However, it was not long before the audience was roaring with laughter, because, as *Variety* noted, "They cash in heavily on ability rather than on laurels gained through past successes." Audiences everywhere soon knew who Clark and McCullough were after their many film appearances between 1929 and 1935.

In the spring of 1936, the partners were resting; Clark in New York and McCullough in a sanitarium in Massachusetts. They had just finished touring in a version of the revue *Thumbs Up,* in which they had starred on Broadway the previous year. On March 23, 1936, Paul McCullough walked into a barber's shop in Medford, Massachusetts, and ordered a shave. After the shave was finished, he picked up the razor and slashed his throat and wrists. He died two days later in a Boston hospital. "I think it was just something Paul couldn't help. Something that had been with him all the time and he didn't even know it," said Bobby Clark. *Variety* (April 1, 1936) noted that McCullough might have been only a straight man, but "the fact that he was a vital part of the noted team was never doubted, least of all by Bobby Clark."

Clark remained in seclusion for several months, but he reappeared to play solo for the first time in the 1936 version of *The Ziegfeld Follies.* He sang "I Can't Get Started" with Gypsy Rose Lee, and proved that even without McCullough he was as funny as ever. Bobby Clark worked continuously through the years, appearing in *Streets of Paris* (1939), *Star and Garter* (1942), *Mexican Hayride* (1944), *As the Girls Go* (1948), and *Jollyana* (1952), among others. In 1956 he toured as Mephisto in *Damn Yankees,* playing it straight except for the cigar— "It seems to me that the devil would smoke cigars," he explained.

For the last few years of his life, Bobby Clark lived in retirement in New York with his wife, Angele Gaignat, whom he had married in 1923. He died at his home on February 12, 1960. The leer that "lit up the whole theatre" was no more.

References: "Enter, Crouching Low and Smoking a Cigar" by Robert Lewis Taylor in the *New Yorker,* Vol. 23, No. 30 (September 13, 1947), pages 37–42 and 45. "Minstrel and Circus Days" by Robert Lewis Taylor in the *New Yorker,* Vol. 23, No. 31 (September 20, 1947), pages 32–6 and 38–40. "Up from Jaw Moose" by Robert Lewis Taylor in the *New Yorker,* Vol. 23, No. 32 (September 27, 1947), pages 36–46.

GEORGE M. COHAN

George M. Cohan

"The first president—he can be a king and emperor if he chooses—of the republic of Broadway" was the fitting description coined by the *New York Dramatic Mirror* on February 8, 1919, for George M. Cohan, the man who symbolizes popular American theatre in the first decades of this century. Cohan may not have participated in vaudeville during its heyday in the years from 1900 through 1925. But there can be little question about his importance in the vaudeville field in view of the eight-foot-tall bronze statue, of George M. Cohan, unveiled on September 11, 1959, which stands as the dominant feature in New York's theatre district, directly opposite the home of American vaudeville, the Palace Theatre.

George M. Cohan was born, as befitted the author of "Yankee Doodle Dandy," "Over There," and "You're a Grand Old Flag," on July 4, 1878, in Providence, Rhode Island, the son of Jerry and Nellie Cohan, two minor variety artists. At the age of eight, George M. Cohan had learned to play the violin and at the age of twelve he was performing the title role in *Peck's Bad Boy.* But even before that, in the spring of 1889, a vaudeville act was born. It was originally titled The Cohan Mirth Makers, and consisted of Mr. and Mrs. Cohan and their children George and Josie, collectively described as "The Celebrated Family of Singers, Dancers, and Comedians with

Their Silver Plated Band and Symphony Orchestra." (The last, depending upon the family's finances, was usually augmented to eight members.) Under the management of B. F. Keith—"We were always welcome at Keith's," George M. Cohan noted in his autobiography—the family toured America, singing, dancing, and joking until, as the Four Cohans, they became the highest paid act of their size in vaudeville. George M. Cohan began to provide the material for his family's act, in particular a playlet titled "Running for Office," just as he was providing sketches for other vaudeville acts. The youngster also contributed enthusiasm to the act, explaining, "I am not a comedian, and I can't get laughs. So I try for enthusiasm."

At the turn of the century, George M. Cohan and his family left vaudeville, not of their own accord, but through a dispute with B. F. Keith about billing. When Cohan complained to Keith, the latter accused him of manufacturing the complaint in order to force him to pay the act more money. In anger, Cohan told Keith, "I'll make you a promise right now—that no member of the Cohan family will ever play for you again as long as you are in the theatrical business." Perhaps the break with vaudeville was for the best, for on February 25, 1901, Cohan saw his first play, *The Governor's Wife,* open on Broadway, starring—who else?—but The Four Cohans. It was followed by *Running for Office* (a play-length adaptation of Cohan's earlier vaudeville sketch, produced in 1903), *Little Johnny Jones* (1904), *Forty-Five Minutes from Broadway* (1906), and *George Washington, Jr.* (1906).

In 1906 the producing partnership of Sam Harris and George M. Cohan came into being, and together the two men presented forty-five plays by Cohan and others, including *The Honeymooners* (1907), *The Man Who Owns Broadway* (1909), *The Cohan and Harris Minstrels* (1909), *Get-Rich-Quick-Wallingford* (1910), *The Little Millionaire* (1911), *Broadway Jones* (1912), *Seven Keys to Baldpate* (1913), *The Miracle Man* (1914), *Hello, Broadway!* (1914), *Hit-the-Trail Holliday* (1915), *The Cohan Revue of 1916* (1916), *The Cohan Revue of 1918* (1917), and *A Prince There Was* (1918), all written by Cohan. Cohan's lack of support for the 1919 Actors' Equity strike (in fact, he opposed it) damaged his reputation in the theatre, and even to this day he has his detractors within Equity. This did not prevent his continuing a distinguished theatrical career as an author, as a producer, and as an actor. In 1922 he produced and wrote *Little Nellie Kelly.* In 1923 he produced, wrote, and starred in *The Song and Dance Man,* an appropriate title for the little man with the big talent, and one of the more than thirty plays he produced between 1920 and 1937, when he and Sam Harris were reunited for the production of *Fulton of Oak Falls,* written by and starring Cohan. In 1933 he surprised everyone by successfully starring in the Theatre Guild production of Eugene O'Neill's *Ah, Wilderness!* George M. Cohan's last great stage success was as F.D.R. in the Rodgers and Hart musical *I'd Rather Be Right,* which opened at the Alvin Theatre on November 2, 1937, and ran for 266 performances. Whatever his critics may have said, there is no question that George M. Cohan was

extraordinarily gifted, a man of boundless energy and talent.

Thanks to his plays and his songs—which included, aside from those already mentioned, "Give My Regards to Broadway," "Harrigan," "Forty-Five Minutes from Broadway," and "Mary's a Grand Old Name"—George M. Cohan became a national institution, the male Betsy Ross of America, as Joe Laurie, Jr. called him. It was little wonder that in 1936 Congress awarded him the Medal of Honor. It was little wonder, also, that Hollywood should film his life (with James Cagney portraying Cohan) in *Yankee Doodle Dandy* (1942). (Cohan appeared, not too successfully, in a number of films, including *Seven Keys to Baldpate* [1917], *Broadway Jones* [1918], *Hit-the-Trail Holliday* [1918], *The Phantom President* [1932], and *Gambling* [1934]. In addition, many of his plays were filmed, starting in 1917.)

George M. Cohan died at his New York apartment on November 5, 1942. As to what Cohan himself considered the most interesting part of his life, one can only accept what Gilbert Seldes wrote in 1934. "He seriously says today that the only theatre he really loved was the theatre which was essentially his father's, the theatre of one-night stands, of six performances a day, of small houses in small towns, of Brooklyn and Coney Island, the theatre in which he had grown up and his father had grown up."

References: *Twenty Years on Broadway* by George M. Cohan (Harper and Brothers, 1924). "Song and Dance Man" by Gilbert Seldes in *Profiles from the New Yorker* (Alfred A. Knopf, 1938), pages 342–361. *George M. Cohan: Prince of the American Theatre* by Ward Morehouse (J. B. Lippincott Company, 1943). *George M. Cohan: The Man Who Owned Broadway* by John McCabe (Doubleday and Company, 1973).

COMPOSERS

There was a time when composers were a fairly popular commodity on vaudeville bills. Some spent most of their careers playing vaudeville, while others went on to more lucrative employment. In the latter division was Erno Rapee, who made his vaudeville debut in 1914 playing classical numbers and patriotic medleys on the piano. "The pianist hasn't yet found out how to get his hair cut in the American style" was the chief criticism from Sime Silverman in *Variety* (January 9, 1914). Rapee was later to embark on a highly successful career as a composer for silent films; he was responsible for the theme song from *What Price Glory,* "Charmaine." Harry Von Tilzer made his vaudeville debut at Hammerstein's in October of 1907, singing his own compositions including "Just Help Yourself," "Lulu and La La La," "Top of the Mornin'," and "Dearie."

ERNEST BALL

Ernest Ball was a professional composer of Irish songs, despite the fact that he was born in Cleveland; he wrote many ballads for the popular Irish tenor Chauncey Olcott. Among Ball's best-known songs are "Will You Love Me in December as You Do in May?," "Mother Machree," "A Little Bit of Heaven," "Let the Rest of the World Go By," and "When Irish Eyes Are Smiling." One of Ball's earliest vaudeville appearances was at Hammerstein's in May of 1911; he accompanied himself on the piano, and *Variety's* Dash wrote, on May 6, 1911, "As a regular vaudeville act Ernest Ball will do nicely if not placed in too heavy running." Ball did continue in vaudeville, working first with Maude Lambert as a partner and later, in 1922, with George MacFarlane. He died in his dressing room at the Yost Theatre in Santa Ana, California, on May 3, 1927, while touring with his act, "Ernie Ball and His Gang," the Gang being a male octet. He was forty-nine years old.

IRVING BERLIN

Irving Berlin, one of the greatest popular composers of all time, also had an extensive vaudeville career. He first came to prominence in vaudeville playing Hammerstein's in September of 1911, singing "Don't Wait Until Your Father Comes Home" and "The Mysterious Rag," among others. Despite complaining, as apparently did much of the audience, that the composer of "Alexander's Rag Time Band" did not use a piano on the stage, Jess in *Variety* (September 16, 1911) thought that Berlin had "a dandy style in delivering a song." During the First World War, of course, Berlin was busy in the army with his *Yip Yip Yaphank* revue, which introduced "Oh How I Hate to Get Up in the Morning," and which Sime Silverman described in *Variety* (August 23, 1918) as "a great show by a great bunch." After the war Irving Berlin returned to the vaudeville stage, and the *New York Dramatic Mirror* reviewed his act on October 23, 1919:

Irving Berlin has undertaken a vaudeville route that will serve to increase the popularity of his many songs. He is one of the most facile of present day song writers, and every one is glad to see this stalwart young composer in civies once more, after so nobly springing to arms for the defense of his country. With Harry Akst at the piano, his repertoire includes "Mandy," "Oh How I Hate To Get Up in the Morning," and his latest, "You'd Be Surprised."

JOE COOK

Joe Cook's unique place in vaudeville is explained by two of his advertisements, one from 1909 and the other from 1920. The first reads, "Master of All Trades. Introducing in a fifteen-minute act, juggling, unicycling, magic, hand-balancing, ragtime piano and violin playing, dancing, globe rolling, wirewalking, talking, and cartooning. Something original in each line—Some Entertainment." In 1920 Cook was billing himself as a humorist with a one-man vaudeville show, for as *Variety* (December 18, 1909) noted, "A doer of many things is Joe Cook," and as a funny man he had few peers in the history of American vaudeville.

Born in Evansville, Indiana, in 1890, Joe Cook's real

Joe Cook

name was Joseph Lopez. He took the name of Cook from a family that raised him after the death of his parents. *Variety* once suggested there should be a marker at the Cook house on the corner of Fourth and Oak Streets in Evansville, where Joe Cook learned the tricks that were to bring good clean fun to millions. Cook first worked with his brother in an act titled "The Juggling Kids," but appeared as a single turn at Proctor's 125th Street Theatre in July of 1907. Within two years Joe Cook was a vaudeville headliner, whose classic routine featured an imitation of four Hawaiians. Before he began, Cook would explain that he was actually imitating only two Hawaiians; he could imitate four, but he did not wish to do it as it would put all the performers who could only imitate two Hawaiians out of work. Cook would appear on stage with a ukelele in his hand and begin:

I will give an imitation of four Hawaiians. This is one (whistles); this is another (plays ukelele); and this is the third (marks time with his foot). I could imitate four Hawaiians just as easily, but I will tell you the reason why I don't do it. You see, I bought a horse for $50 and it turned out to be a running horse. I was offered $15,000 for him and I took it. I built a house with the $15,000 and when it was finished a neighbour offered me $100,000 for it. He said my house stood right where he wanted to dig a well. So I took the $100,000 to accommodate him. I invested the $100,000 in peanuts and that year there was a peanut famine, so I sold the peanuts for $350,000. Now why should a man with $350,000 bother to imitate four Hawaiians?

Another vaudeville gag had Cook as a landlord attempting to collect rent on a miniature cottage. After arguing with the imaginary tenant, Cook would walk off with the cottage under his arm. An Indian lecture had a stooge holding up a beer mug as a sample of early Indian pottery, while the chief's collection of bows and arrows consisted of bow ties and Arrow collars. A stooge from the audience would be invited to drink a bottle of beer while blindfolded, with the blindfold misplaced over his mouth instead of his eyes. Joe Cook would enter with three papier-mâché figures of gymnasts on his shoulders, and stagger around pretending to be under a terrible strain in supporting them. The act always included numerous contraptions, such as one that dropped a weight on an assistant's head to remind him when to ring a bell during the performance. Few would disagree with a 1925 *Variety* review, "The act is as it always was, one of the greatest comedy novelties in vaudeville. Cook is as versatile as he is clever and is blessed with a gift for travesty and a whimsical personality that would bring him laughs at an undertakers' convention."

Aside from vaudeville, Joe Cook appeared on stage in *Hitchy-Koo* (1919) and starred in the first *Earl Carroll's Vanities* in 1923. He was immensely successful as "Smiley" Johnson in *Rain or Shine* (1928), and in *Fine and Dandy* (1930) and *Hold Your Horses* (1933) he appeared with his long-time stooge Dave Chasen (later of restaurant fame). Without the visuals that the stage offered, Joe Cook proved equally popular on radio in the thirties. His last stage appearance was in *It Happens on Ice*—the first of the ice shows—at New York's Center Theatre, beginning in October of 1940.

In 1942 Joe Cook was stricken with Parkinson's disease, which became progressively worse through the years. He died at his home in Staatsburg, New York, on May 16, 1959. Reviewing *Rain or Shine,* critic Brooks Atkinson described Joe Cook as "the greatest man in the world." Many who had the privilege of viewing his act would agree.

References: "Greatest Man in the World" by Glendon Allvine in *Variety,* Vol. 214, No. 12 (May 20, 1959), pages 1 and 68. "Death of an Amazing Performer" by Robert J. Landry in *Variety,* Vol. 214, No. 12 (May 20, 1959), page 64.

FRANK CRUMIT AND JULIA SANDERSON

It is doubtful that any other singing couple endeared themselves so much to vaudeville and radio audiences as did Frank Crumit and Julia Sanderson. Their relaxed style of delivery and their charm of manner added much to any vaudeville bill, for, as *Variety* noted in 1925, "An abundance of 'class' surrounds the couple to the extent they unquestionably tone up any vaudeville bill besides which their mild and unassuming manner of delivery is restful."

Julia Sanderson's career predated her husband's by many years. She was born in Springfield, Massachusetts, on August 20, 1887, the daughter of a well-known actor, Albert Sackett. As a child, she appeared in Philadelphia with Forepaugh's Stock Company, and in 1903 was ap-

Frank Crumit

pearing as a member of the chorus and as an understudy to Paula Edwardes in *Winsome Winnie*. In April of 1904 Miss Sanderson opened in *A Chinese Honeymoon* at New York's Lyric Theatre, in the role of Mrs. Pineapple, and later that same year she supported De Wolf Hopper in *Wang*. Later stage successes included *The Tourists* (1906), *The Dairymaids* (1907), *The Arcadians* (1910), *The Sunshine Girl* (1913), *The Girl from Utah* (1914), *Sybil* (1916), *The Canary* (1918), and *Hitchy-Koo* (1920). She made her London stage debut, as Suzanne in *The Hon'ble Phil,* in October of 1908.

The star's vaudeville debut came in January of 1907 at Keeney's Theatre in New York. *Variety* (January 12, 1907) noted that "Miss Sanderson has a delightful full, rich voice and an altogether charming stage presence." Both the voice and the presence were to delight vaudeville audiences for many years to come.

Frank Crumit was born in Jackson, Ohio, on September 26, 1889; he was educated at the University of Ohio, for which he wrote the school football song, "The Buckeye Battle Cry." After graduation, Crumit toured in vaudeville as a singer and a ukelele player. He also began to write songs, many of which have stood the test of time as mild-mannered comic numbers of considerable humor. "Song of the Prune," "A Parlor Is a Pleasant Place To Sit In," "There Is No One with Endurance Like the Man Who Sells Insurance," and especially "Abdul Abulbul Emir" can still be sung and enjoyed to this day.

On August 9, 1921, *Tangerine,* a musical comedy about a South Sea Island where women do all the work and a man's place is in the home, opened at the Casino Theatre.

Julia Sanderson

It starred Julia Sanderson as Shirley Dalton and, in a lesser role, Frank Crumit as Dick Owens. From this first meeting a romance developed, and the couple teamed up, at first professionally and later in private life. Crumit was Julia Sanderson's third husband; her first marriage had been to the well-known jockey James Todhunter Sloan. The couple were regular headliners on the vaudeville stage, (1925–26), and took over the leads from Gertrude Lawrence and Oscar Shaw in the original Broadway production of George and Ira Gershwin's *Oh, Kay!* in January of 1928.

Frank Crumit had already built up a reputation for himself before he teamed with Julia Sanderson. On November 15, 1923, *Variety* commented, "For vaudeville Crumit is as sure as rent day." Thanks largely to his many phonograph recordings, he was fast becoming a radio favorite as well. In 1928 he and Julia Sanderson made their radio debut as a team, and the following year they were signed to star in "Blackstone Plantation," sponsored by Blackstone Cigars and initially broadcast over the CBS network. When that show expired in 1933, the couple returned briefly to vaudeville, but they were soon back on the air, guesting on a number of variety shows until 1938, when they were signed to star in the NBC quiz program "The Battle of the Sexes." In 1942 they hosted "The Crumit and Sanderson Quiz" on Saturday nights on CBS.

When Frank Crumit died in New York City, on September 7, 1943, he and his wife had two radio shows on the air, a daily entertainment program, sponsored by the Southern Cotton Oil Company, and the weekly quiz for the Lewis Howe Company. After her husband's death,

Julia Sanderson appeared for a while on the Mutual network with the program "Let's Be Charming," and then announced her retirement. She died at her home in Springfield, Massachusetts, on January 27, 1975.

DANCE TEAMS

The idea of dance teams in vaudeville seems rather ludicrous. Fred Astaire and Ginger Rogers dancing on film is perfectly acceptable, but somehow one cannot imagine watching them dance on stage, from the rear of the gallery. And yet dance teams were popular with vaudeville audiences and did flourish from the early 1910s through the mid-twenties, although it is obvious from a reading of contemporary reviews that the stage settings for such dance teams were as important as the dancing itself.

Many dance partnerships have long been forgotten. In the late 1910s Bryan and Broderick presented an act titled "Let's Dance." "Their technique is well grounded," reported the *New York Dramatic Mirror* (March 1, 1919), "and when they become better molded in the design of their numbers, the inspiration and poetry strongly evident at present will add continuity and charm to their act." From England came Ted Trevor and Diane Harris, with an eleven-minute act of ballroom dancing. Reviewing their performance at the Riverside Theatre, *Variety* (October 29, 1924) reported, "The first impression is that the dancers are lightning fast, but subsequent numbers, of which there are three, detract from that through a certain tenor of similarity which prevails throughout the dances. Each is executed with no mean sense of showmanship, and to this, which must be added, the likable appearance of the pair, may be attributed the foundation upon which the team rests." From France, in 1922, came Mitty and Tillo, billed as "France's greatest dancers" (Mitty being announced as a former member of the Folies Bergère company).

Mae Murray and Clifton Webb, before their respective film careers, toured in vaudeville as a dance team presenting "Society Dances." Five black musicians accompanied the couple on stage as they performed "D'Arlequin Waltz" *(sic)*, "Brazilian Maxine," a tango titled "Cinquante Cinquante," and "Barcarole Waltz," which was claimed as a creation of Miss Murray. *Variety* (March 20, 1914) reported, "In a becoming pink charmeuse outfit over chiffon Miss Murray's pretty arms, hands, and feet seemed set to music. That Palace audience Monday night went plumb daffy over her dancing. In praising her splendid dancing Webb should not be overlooked." After her film career ended, Mae Murray returned to vaudeville in 1930, but she succeeded more because of her good-looking clothes than her dancing.

Actually, Clifton Webb was a prominent dancer on the New York stage for many years. In the twenties he and Mary Hay (a former *Ziegfeld Follies* show girl featured in D. W. Griffith's film of *Way Down East,* and one-time wife of matinee idol Richard Barthelmess) were a popular dancing team on the vaudeville stage and in *Sunny* (1925). In January of 1929 they headlined at the Palace, with an act that featured two pianos, played by Victor Arden and

Irene and Vernon Castle

Phil Ohman; the latter, of course, went on to become a popular band leader in the thirties. *Variety* (January 23, 1929) commented, "As mixed comedy dancers, and dancers who do not exert themselves, Webb-Hay could dance twice as long as they do at present and still please. As class dancers and names, they seem to condescend in doing comedy, but if attempted by others the same comedy would appear amateurish."

In the 1910s Ivy and Douglas Crane were dancing headliners on the Orpheum circuit, known as the Vernon and Irene Castle of the West. In later years, Ivy Wilson became a fan magazine writer and Hollywood columnist for a British newspaper; she died in Woodland Hills, California, on December 7, 1977, at the age of ninety. Another early husband and wife dancing partnership was that of Dorothy Dickson and Carl Hyson. They were two of America's leading exponents of ballroom dancing, featured in vaudeville and, in 1919, at New York's Palais Royal Dance Club. Dorothy Dickson appeared in *Oh Boy!* (1917) and the 1918 edition of *The Ziegfeld Follies;* she came to London in 1921 to star, with Carl Hyson (whom she was later to divorce), in *London, Paris and New York* at the London Pavilion. From that point on, she appeared almost continuously on the London stage through the fifties.

Emma Haig was popular in vaudeville both as a solo dancer and in partnership with various male dancers. Before George White created his famous *Scandals* he was one of Emma Haig's partners; he was replaced in 1919 by Jack Waldon. Reviewing Emma Haig's solo act at the Palace in the summer of 1919, *Variety* (June 27, 1919)

described Miss Haig as "a whirlwind of speed, a gifted kicker, and a tireless worker," but noted that without a partner "that touch of gracefulness and team rhythm is absent." Emma Haig was back at the Palace in March of 1923, working with a young tenor named George Griffin; she tried a little singing herself, but it was marred by a noticeable lisp. For fifteen minutes, Miss Haig performed a variety of dances, including a Spanish number and a Jackie Coogan impersonation. "The finale, with her most difficult steps, gets the tiny lady off heartily liked. There is no straining for recognition and the several bows are healthy and called for. This is a first rate number for any bill and a headliner for the average big-time house, especially West, where Miss Haig is a favorite," reported *Variety* (March 29, 1923).

From today's viewpoint, the two most famous dancing teams in vaudeville were Fred and Adele Astaire and Vernon and Irene Castle. The Castles took over the mantle of Maurice and Florence Walton, whom Mrs. Castle described as "the best known dancers of our day." In her autobiography, *Castles in the Air,* Irene Castle wrote, "Maurice waltzed beautifully and had undoubtedly taught Florence everything she knew. She was a little wooden from the waist up, but she had lovely legs and feet and handled them beautifully." Vernon and Irene Castle achieved fame with their appearance in *Watch Your Step* (1914), and with their famous dance, "The Castle Walk," continued to be the biggest dancers of their day until Vernon Castle's death on February 15, 1918. They were more at home in musical comedies and revues, or at private soirées, and Irene Castle noted, "We only went into vaudeville when we were hard up."

Fred and Adele Astaire claim to have made their professional debut in vaudeville in Paterson, New Jersey, in 1910, but as early as October 17, 1908, *Variety* saw them perform at New York's Hudson Theatre, and commented,

> The Astaire Children are a nice looking pair of youngsters, prettily dressed, and they work in an easy style, without the predominating "freshness" which usually stands out above everything else with "prodigies." Dancing is the feature. It ranges from toe to the more popular (in vaudeville) hard-shoe. The singing falls almost entirely to the boy, who has a surprisingly powerful voice for a lad of his years. . . . The toe-dance following the song could be replaced to advantage. It has a tendency to make the boy appear girlish, something to be guarded against. His actions throughout are a trifle too polite, which is probably no fault of his own, as he appears to be a manly little chap with the making of a good performer.

In 1918 Fred and Adele Astaire were featured in *The Passing Show,* and Heywood Broun wrote in the *New York Tribune,* "In an evening in which there was an abundance of good dancing, Fred Astaire stood out. He and his partner, Adele Astaire, made the show pause early in the evening with a beautiful, careless, loose-limbed dance in which the right foot never seemed to know just what the left foot was going to do, or cared either. It almost seemed as though the two young persons had been poured into the dance." After *The Passing Show of 1918,* Fred and Adele Astaire were marked as major revue and musical comedy stars; they never returned to vaudeville.

VAUGHN DeLEATH

Vaughn DeLeath

Born in Mount Pulaski, Illinois, on September 26, 1896, Vaughn DeLeath was one of the great names in early radio; in fact, she was the first lady of radio, the medium's first crooner, whose voice was selected by Dr. Lee De Forest as that best suited to the radio microphone. She was also a radio executive and a song writer, best remembered for "I Wasn't Lying When I Said I Love You." She made literally hundreds of popular recordings in the twenties.

Vaughn DeLeath's large size—Kate Smith had nothing on her—and her warm, engaging personality made her a natural for occasional vaudeville appearances in the twenties and thirties. She was also seen on stage, as Signora Calvaro, in *Laugh, Clown, Laugh,* which opened at the Belasco Theatre on November 28, 1923. Vaughn DeLeath died in Buffalo, New York, on May 28, 1943.

LEW DOCKSTADER

One of the last and one of the greatest of the old-time blackface minstrels, Lew Dockstader was born George Alfred Clapp in Hartford, Connecticut, in 1856. In 1873 he came to New York, where he joined the Earl, Emmet,

and Wilde Minstrels; the following year he toured the country with the Whitmore and Clark Minstrels, gaining great popularity with his song "Peter, You're in Luck This Morning." Dockstader's first vaudeville appearances were in the 1890s, but in 1898 he teamed with George Primrose to form the Primrose and Dockstader Minstrel Men, which became America's best known blackface troupe. When the couple split up in 1904, Lew Dockstader's Minstrels, with a company of forty artists, was formed. Lew Dockstader was also one of the headliners, along with Weber and Fields, at the opening of Proctor's Pleasure Palace on Fifty-eighth Street, between Lexington and Third Avenues, on Labor Day of 1895.

Lew Dockstader's vaudeville act consisted of blackface characterizations of prominent figures of the day, and was apparently based on an earlier blackface act of Frank Bell's. As he grew older and more portly, Dockstader abandoned blackface and became a monologist, but he continued to poke mild fun at the personalities of the day. Reviewing his act in 1920, the *New York Dramatic Mirror* (September 18, 1920) reported, "He is the only monologist

Lew Dockstader

today who can skilfully touch upon the (political) campaign candidates and do it in just the humorous, satirical manner that an audience will take kindly to." Lew Dockstader died in New York City on October 26, 1924; he had remained active until the year of his death.

THE DOLLY SISTERS

Reviewing the Dolly Sisters at the Palace, Sime Silverman wrote in *Variety* (February 24, 1922), "As two dandy looking twins who can not be told apart, with class and

The Dolly Sisters

who can dance if they want to, the Dolly Sisters are always worth the price of admission just to look." The Dolly Sisters were as much a part of the twenties as art deco, which somehow they resembled, and yet their career goes back well before 1920, to 1909, when they first played vaudeville as a dance team at Keith's Union Square Theatre.

The Dolly Sisters were, as one commentator wrote, the Gabors of their era. They married well and often, and were at home in all the world's glamor spots, from Westhampton, Long Island, to Monte Carlo (where Roszika Dolly claimed to have won $400,000 at roulette in one night). They were elegant and they were beautiful, and in their company one might find the world's most eligible bachelors from the Prince of Wales to Diamond Jim Brady (who Roszika said gave her a Rolls-Royce, "not merely a Rolls-Royce, but one wrapped up in ribbons").

Roszika and Yansci (more commonly known as Rosie and Jenny) Dutsch were identical twins born on October 25, 1892, in Hungary. From vaudeville they went into the 1911 edition of *The Ziegfeld Follies,* in which they performed a dance routine as Siamese twins. They were also starred in *His Bridal Night,* a farce by Lawrence Rising, revised and elaborated by Margaret Mayo, which opened at the Republic Theatre on August 19, 1916. They starred in one feature film, *The Million Dollar Dollies,* released by Metro in 1917. From 1916 on, the Dolly Sisters were regulars at the Palace, although critics often complained that their singing abilities were almost nonexistent and they seldom bothered to change their dance routines. However, dancing and singing were always minor considerations compared to how the Dollys would dress for their

vaudeville appearances and how many costume changes they would make. As *Variety* (July 20, 1917) noted, "The Dollys are the Dollys, and people accept them in that way."

In the twenties the Dolly Sisters were to be seen more in Paris and London music halls than on the New York stage; one of their last major French revues was *Broadway à Paris,* the most popular show of 1928. However, the Dolly Sisters were starred, along with Vincent Lopez and Moran and Mack, in *The Greenwich Village Follies,* which opened at the Shubert Theatre on September 16, 1924, with lyrics and music by Cole Porter. The high spot, apparently, was a routine featuring the Dolly Sisters with Jud Brady's Dogs imitating them.

After retirement in the late twenties, the Dolly Sisters concentrated on the social scene. On June 1, 1941, Yansci Dolly was found dead in her Beverly Hills apartment. She had formed a noose from the drapes and hanged herself. Eight years before, she had been seriously injured in a motoring accident in France that necessitated major plastic surgery. Yansci Dolly had never fully recovered from the trauma of losing her beauty. In 1945 George Jessel produced a feature film at 20th Century-Fox based on the girls' lives, *The Dolly Sisters,* featuring Betty Grable and June Haver. Roszika Dolly died in New York on February 1, 1970; according to *Variety,* her one philosophy of life had been, "If you drink scotch, make it Black and White. It will never hang you over."

KITTY DONER

Kitty Donner as "The Devil of the Jazz" in the early Twenties

Male impersonation was very much a British prerogative as far as vaudeville was concerned, with Vesta Tilley and

Kitty Doner in drag

Ella Shields being Britain's best known exponents of the art. In America, Emma Don (active in 1911), Grace Leonard (active in 1919), and Evelyn Wilson (active in 1929) tried their hands at male impersonation, but the best-known American male impersonator and the only one on a par with Tilley and Shields was Kitty Doner. Reviewing her act on November 26, 1924, *Variety* commented, "If our cousins across the pond think they have a patent on the raising of male impersonators, they ought to get a load of this baby. In male clothes, she is as masculine as a Notre Dame guard, and in female togs as feminine as bare legs. As a dancer, she is in a class by herself."

Kitty Doner was born in Chicago in 1895 and, in view of her vaudeville speciality, it is not surprising that both of her parents were British. Her father, Joe Doner, was born in Manchester on September 25, 1864, while her mother, Nellie, was born in London on December 15, 1874. Nellie was a popular principal boy in English pantomime before joining up with Joe Doner in an act titled The Escaped Lunatics. One of Joe Doner's routines was to play Dr. Jekyll and Mr. Hyde. Kitty recalls, "My dad was a very fine actor and a beautiful dancer. He wanted to be a prize fighter and he trained, but his brother, who was a very fine actor and a top star who changed his name from Doner to John D. Gilbert, didn't want Dad to be a prize fighter. He said, 'He's a good mimic and a good actor, and he's got to go on the stage.' "

The reasons why Kitty Doner first dressed as a boy are quite fascinating from a purely psychological point of view. "I was the first-born," she recalls, "and my dad was very, very disappointed that I wasn't a boy, and as I grew I turned out sort of gawky. I wasn't considered a pretty

girl. I was very boyish, and because my dad taught me dancing, my dancing was mannish. The story goes that my father and mother were in the shows, and when the time came for me to go into a show, they put me in an act with them, and Dad dressed me as a boy. He said, 'She might as well get started dressed as a boy because she's not pretty enough to compete with the beautiful girls in show business.' " Kitty Doner was to appear in other guises as well; in 1905 she appeared as a canary in the children's bird ballet at the New York Hippodrome. In 1909 she made her vaudeville debut with Brady's Dancing Dogs, as one of the four girls featured with the four collies in the act.

In 1912 Kitty Doner appeared in her first show, *The Candy Shop,* which opened Broncho Billy Anderson's Gaiety Theatre in San Francisco. In *The Candy Shop,* she appeared in both male and female attire and made a reputation for herself, at least as far as the West Coast was concerned. As a result, she was invited to join *The Passing Show of 1913.* Her father took over her management and brought her to see Florenz Ziegfeld, who she begged to allow her to play a female role (until she discovered she would have to do pratfalls and would not wear the beautiful clothes of the Ziegfeld show girls). Kitty Doner was with the *Follies* for one night—then her father took her out of the show, and she decided that from then on, she would play a boy.

Kitty Doner's biggest break came in 1914, when she was signed to play opposite Al Jolson in *Dancing Around,* a revue which also featured Clifton Webb; it was based on a popular song of the period, with music by Sigmund Romberg. The show opened at the Winter Garden Theatre on October 10, 1914. Kitty was to play with Jolson, with whom she was romantically involved, in two further revues: *Robinson Crusoe, Jr.,* which opened at the Winter Garden on February 17, 1916, with music again by Romberg, and *Sinbad,* which opened at the Winter Garden on February 14, 1918, with music by Romberg and Jolson.

During the run of *Dancing Around,* Kitty Doner began perfecting her male impersonation routine. She would study the men in the cast. "I followed them around until the men in the show were just nuts," she remembers. "I was under their tail; I was under their feet. I was mimicking everything they would do, the way they would twirl their moustaches or the way they would brush their hair back." This stood her in good stead when she returned to vaudeville in the late 1910s. Reviewing her act, the *New York Dramatic Mirror* (October 30, 1919) wrote,

It's a real delight to watch a clever little artiste like Kitty Doner in action. And when it comes to dancing steps with the soft shoes in the masculine attire, Kitty is head and shoulders above the majority of men and women cracked up as dancing stars. Kitty Doner is a graceful dancing dynamo and isn't a bit afraid of hard work. Other feminine vaudevillians should watch her and profit accordingly.

Kitty's vaudeville act, "A League of Song Steps," gained for her the title of "The Best Dressed Man on the American Stage." It also landed her an engagement in the home of male impersonation, England, where she topped the bill at London's Victoria Palace in 1922.

Kitty Doner's brother, Ted, and sister, Rose, were also in show business, and the three appeared together often on the vaudeville stage. Ted and Kitty took over the Fred and Adele Astaire roles in the touring company production of *Lady, Be Good* in the mid-twenties. At that time she was offered a film contract by Joe Schenck, but turned it down; she was to make only one film appearance, in a 1928 Warner Bros. short, *A Bit of Scotch,* for which she was paid $1,575. Throughout the twenties, Kitty Doner's weekly vaudeville salary averaged $1,000; when she toured on the William Fox circuit in 1927 she was paid $1,500 a week, and when she performed at the Hill Street Theatre, Los Angeles, she received $1,200.

In May of 1926, Kitty Doner returned to the Palace with an act which typified her vaudeville performances. With Jack Carroll at the piano, she appeared first in evening dress, followed by a song as a French dandy. Next came an appearance in skirts to perform some high kicking. Then, on-stage, she stripped down to a pair of briefs and a bra for a fast change to a Scotsman. Kitty Doner recalls that a pink floodlight was used for her strip change, which gave the audience the distinct impression that she was naked and caused great concern to E. F. Albee. Reviewing that act, Sisk wrote in *Variety* (May 5, 1926),

Monday night she appeared to fine advantage, combining the enthusiasm and infectious pleasure of working with the already good material which helps her attractive and unique talents. She rivals Ella Shields in the male impersonations and that is no scant praise. What makes her an even more important figure is that marvellous dancing stuff. Kitty Doner, then, is not just a headliner—she's a headliner who offers not only a well known name but some honest-to-John entertainment.

Kitty Doner never gave impersonations of well-known men; rather her male impersonations were unique unto themselves. Equally unique were her female impersonations, such as the tough gal, Tillie from Tenth Avenue, with her opening line, "Yeh, this is the joint. My gang hangs out here."

She was a performer who moved with the times, and when her type of old-time vaudeville died she was the first to admit it, telling the *San Francisco Chronicle* in a headline story on November 25, 1934, "There ain't any vaudeville, but some people won't believe it." She developed a night club act, singing with Harold Stern and His Orchestra. In the forties, she became show director with *Holiday on Ice,* and during 1950 and '51, Kitty Doner was responsible for auditioning talent on "Ted Mack's Amateur Hour." It was not Kitty's first involvement with television; on August 1, 1931, she had performed her act in front of a television camera at the CBS studios on the top floor of New York's Vanderbilt Hotel, the first complete stage act to be televised to a radius of over one hundred miles.

Kitty Doner was the pet of Broadway in the twenties and remains one of vaudeville's great names, living up to the title given her by the *New York Dramatic Mirror* (August 7, 1920): "Just another name for pep."

FIFI D'ORSAY

Fifi D'Orsay

Fifi D'Orsay, the saucy French bombshell from Montreal, is better known today for her screen appearances, but she served her apprenticeship in vaudeville, and there she learned her craft. Fifi is quick to point out that there is a big difference between being a moving picture actress and being an entertainer. "As I sit here talking to you now," she comments, "I can say I'm both. And I'm a comedienne and I can be a dramatic actress. I have a lot of tricks under my belt. I work to everybody—that's the secret of my success. Maurice Chevalier taught me that— not to work just to the people in front of you; turn to everybody, work the circumference of the room."

Born Yvonne Lussier in Montreal, Canada, in 1904, Fifi D'Orsay worked as a secretary in order to raise enough money to come to the United States and make her ambition to become an actress a reality. She came to New York in 1924 and was met by Helen Morgan, whom Fifi had known in Canada. Helen Morgan let Fifi stay in her apartment and advised her to check the adverts for jobs in show business. This Fifi did, and she spotted a notice that director John Murray Anderson was auditioning for the touring company of *The Greenwich Village Follies.* "I was singing 'My Man' in French and in English too," recalls Fifi, "and I was singing 'Yes, We Have No Bananas' in French, and then I sang 'Chicago.' Well, John Murray

Palace Theatre marquee for Fifi D'Orsay's 1950 appearance

Anderson liked me, and right away he chose me to be in the show. He said, 'Where do you come from?' and straight away I told him the Folies Bergère in Paris. I wanted to make myself important! Do you know that he chose me to be a chorus girl, but then, when we started rehearsing, he gave me a specialty to do." The specialty turned out to be an apache dance, which later had to be dropped because, as Fifi D'Orsay is quick to point out, she is not a dancer.

Karyl Norman, the Creole Fashion Plate, was the original star of this version of *The Greenwich Village Follies,* but because he proved to be a poor draw on the road, he was replaced after a month. Jane and Katherine Lee were brought in next, but they also failed to draw. Finally, Gallagher and Shean joined the show and were its stars for a year. With charming frankness, Fifi D'Orsay comments,

I became Mr. Gallagher's little sweetheart. He was thirty-seven years older than me, but it was good for me because he knew all the little tricks of the business and I was a beginner. I wanted to learn everything about show business and he taught me—believe me! He was the greatest straight man in the business. Mr. Shean was the comic, but without Mr. Gallagher he couldn't have done very well. He was always talking to me with a highball in his hand. He was drinking all the time!

John Murray Anderson had named Yvonne Lussier Fifi, and her billing in *The Greenwich Village Follies* was "Mademoiselle Fifi," a name which she took with her when she left the *Follies* and worked as a vaudeville act with Ed Gallagher. "I was his guardian, I was his nurse, I was his lover, I was like a wife, but I wasn't his wife. I would be the one to dress him before he went on the stage. I would stand him on the stage. He was always drunk, but, boy, when he got on the stage, he could say his lines. But I was proud to do it, because he was my teacher. I helped him because he was helping me, although it was no fun," remembers Fifi.

After two years with Ed Gallagher, Fifi D'Orsay was living with her aunt, who rented out rooms in her New York City apartment, and among the tenants was Charlie Butterworth. It was Butterworth who sent Fifi over to see Herman Timberg, a noted creator of vaudeville sketches. At eight o'clock in the morning, Fifi arrived, full of pep, sat down at the piano, and began to sing "Chicago." Timberg was suitably impressed and teamed her with Herman Berrens in a vaudeville sketch titled "Ten Dollars a Lesson," in which Berrens was a professor giving piano lessons to the saucy Mademoiselle Fifi, who sang "Everything Is Hotsy Totsy Now." Fifi wore a striking red outfit, had her hair cut in a boyish style, and dyed it black. She made her first entrance with a ukelele under her arm, and when she told Berrens that her ukelele teacher had given it to her, Berrens would cast anxious glances at his piano. The sketch ended with the two singing "We're So in Love." Berrens and Fifi became a popular vaudeville act, booked onto the Orpheum circuit forty-five weeks of the year.

Eventually Fifi D'Orsay decided she would like to work as a single act, which she did, first as a mistress of ceremonies on the Publix circuit. While playing at the Harris Theatre in Pittsburgh, on a bill headlined by Rubinoff the violinist, Fifi received a telegram asking her to come to New York and make a screen test for Fox. She was engaged to marry Herman Berren's brother, Freddie, who had a musical vaudeville act, but decided that a moving picture contract was more important at that time than a marriage contract. For her test, she sang exactly the same songs she had performed for John Murray Anderson five years earlier; the result was a seven-year contract. Her first film was *They Had to See Paris,* which starred Will Rogers in his first sound feature. (It was Rogers who had recommended Fifi, having remembered meeting her with Ed Gallagher in 1925.) To Rogers, she was "Froggie," but by now Fifi had added the name of D'Orsay, because she liked the perfume of the same name. "Now they think my name is spelt Dorsey," she comments, "and they asked me if I'm Jimmy Dorsey's mother!"

Fifi D'Orsay played opposite Will Rogers again in *Young as You Feel* (1931) and since then has been featured in a number of films, including *Hot for Paris* (1930), *Those Three French Girls* (1930), *Mr. Lemon of Orange* (1931), *Going Hollywood* (1933), *Wonder Bar* (1934), *The Gangster* (1947), and *What a Way to Go!* (1964). While starring in films in the early thirties, she was also appearing at presentation houses with her vaudeville act, earning as much as $5,000 a week. "After I became a film star, I was busy all the time," she remembers. Fifi played the Palace, the Paramount, the Capitol, and the Roxy. At one point, she had a vaudeville act with Edmund Lowe and Victor McLaglen. In 1933 she obtained a release from her Fox contract in order to concentrate on her stage appearances.

When the Palace returned to a policy of presenting vaudeville acts and feature films in 1950, Fifi D'Orsay returned to the site of many of her early triumphs. Her act still had "oomph," and audiences had not forgotten her. Along with the marvelous musical comedy star Ethel Shutta, Fifi D'Orsay brought the sparkle that once lit up the vaudeville and revue stages to the Stephen Sondheim musical *Follies,* during 1971 and 1972. Fifi was sixty-seven years old, but the energy and vitality were still there. Today, Fifi D'Orsay is still performing, with an act titled "I'm Glad I'm Not Young Any More;" she tells jokes like "Years ago, they used to call me a sexpot, now I'm a sexagenarian" and "I'm old enough for Medicare but not too old for men to care." In her act today, Fifi D'Orsay plays on her age, but she is ageless, a vital reminder of the exhilaration that was vaudeville.

MARIE DRESSLER

Marie Dressler

"A great scout with the mob, loves a good story and knows how to tell one, and a tireless worker. A good woman, that's all," summed up *Variety* (August 22, 1919) on Marie Dressler. Today, of course, Marie Dressler is remembered for her screen roles in *Anna Christie* (1930), *Min and Bill* (1930), *Dinner at Eight* (1933), and *Tugboat Annie* (1933); but she was already a major stage and vaudeville performer even before films became a popular form of entertainment, and the beginning of her career predates the cinema by many years.

Marie Dressler was born Leila Koerber, in Cobourg, Canada, on November 9, 1869, the daughter of an itinerant musician who moved his family from one town to the next with sickening regularity. Because of her weight and lack of beauty—"I was born homely," she wrote in her autobiography—Marie Dressler took to clowning. At the age of fourteen, she joined the Nevada Stock Company; parental opposition led her to take the name of Marie Dressler from an aunt. Engagements in other stock companies followed, until Marie Dressler arrived in New York and began singing at the Atlantic Garden on the Bowery and Koster and Bial's Twenty-third Street Theatre. Marie Dressler's first major success came in an operatic comedy titled *The Lady Slavey,* which opened in Washington, D.C., in September of 1896, and in which she played Flo Honeydew of the Music Halls.

At the turn of the century, Marie Dressler became a favorite in burlesque and vaudeville as a coon singer. Coon songs, as one might expect, poked gentle fun at the black race, and were sung by black as well as white entertainers.

Popular songs included "Every Race Has a Flag But the Coon!" (1900), which Marie Dressler and Williams and Walker made famous; "I Never Liked a Nigger with a Beard" (1900), described as "the funniest descriptive coon song ever written"; "All Coons Look Alike to Me" (1900); "My Chilly Baby" (1900); "The Emblem of an Independent Coon" (1900); and "Coon! Coon! Coon!" (1901).

Marie Dressler quickly became a vaudeville favorite, not only for her coon songs but for her imitations. On April 4, 1903, *The Billboard* wrote of her, "She is a very shapely woman, large and heavy, and her ways immediately captivate an audience." After Weber and Fields split in 1904, Joe Weber asked Marie Dressler to join his company, which included Anna Held, in *Higgledy-Piggledy.* Because of her lengthy stay with Joe Weber, Marie Dressler gained the somewhat unglamorous title of "Joe Weber's Amazon." At the Colonial in January of 1907, she gave imitations of Mrs. Leslie Carter and Blanche Bates (from the legitimate stage), and delighted audiences with her song, "A Great Big Girl Like Me." Back at the Colonial in April of 1908, Marie Dressler portrayed a chesty elocutionist and a classy prima donna, and as *Variety* (April 25, 1908) noted, "there is just enough accuracy and truth in her burlesques to make the picture ridiculously plain."

On May 5, 1910, at the Herald Square Theatre, Marie Dressler appeared for the first time in her best-known farce, *Tillie's Nightmare,* "a melange of mirth and melody" in which she played Tillie Blobbs, a Broadway House Drudge. In it, she sang "Heaven Will Protect the Working Girl," a classic of lower class mentality and middle class morality, whose last chorus went something like this:

Stand back there, villain, go your way.
Here I will no longer stay;
Although you were a Marquis or an Earl
You may tempt the upper classes

With your villainous demi-tasses,
But Heaven will protect the working girl!

Tillie's Nightmare led, of course, to the film of *Tillie's Punctured Romance,* a 1914 Mack Sennett feature-length comedy, in which Charlie Chaplin and Mabel Normand supported Marie Dressler. It might have helped Chaplin's film career, but it did little for Marie Dressler except make her appear crude and vulgar. She did, however, star in two more Tillie films without Chaplin: *Tillie Wakes Up* and *Tillie's Tomato Surprise.*

Marie Dressler continued to work in musical comedy and vaudeville throughout the 1910s, taking time out to participate in Liberty Loan drives during 1917 and '18, and the Actors' Equity Strike of 1919, in which she headed the chorus girls' division. In April of 1919, Marie Dressler headlined at the Palace, but was paid the very small sum of $1,500 a week. "She was in all her cut-up glory, exactly like the old days of Weber and Fields," commented the *New York Dramatic Mirror* (April 8, 1919). "She satisfied everyone. In doing so she made herself a matter of importance to the Associated Press. Few actresses, even considering those who play Ibsen and other queer fellows' scribbling, are quoted by the transcontinental press as much as she for the reason that she has always something to say that even college professors can understand as well as servant girls."

The performer's career took a downward turn in the twenties, with engagements becoming fewer and fewer, although she did appear on an October, 1925 old-timers bill at the Palace. By 1927 she was thinking of leaving America for good and opening a small hotel in Paris. (Interestingly, as early as 1901, Marie Dressler had told the press of her interest in retiring from the stage and running a hotel.) However, she was offered a small part in a film, *The Joy Girl,* which led to an invitation from screenwriter Frances Marion to come to Hollywood. This led to other screen roles, and especially *Anna Christie,* Garbo's first talkie, which established Marie Dressler as the screen's foremost character comedienne. Dressler was also teamed with Polly Moran in a series of comedies which, in her autobiography, she states did justice neither to her nor to Polly Moran. (The latter had also been in vaudeville, and in 1918 *Variety* applauded "her semi-nut impromptu way" of performing.)

Marie Dressler died at the height of her new career, in Los Angeles, on July 28, 1934. She was, as Will Rogers said in a radio tribute, "a marvelous personality and a great heart."

References: *The Life Story of an Ugly Duckling* by Marie Dressler (Robert M. McBride and Company, 1924). *My Own Story* by Marie Dressler, as told to Mildred Harrington (Little, Brown and Company, 1934).

THE DUNCAN SISTERS

The Duncan Sisters were one of the greatest sister acts on the vaudeville stage; their humor and their harmonizing has never dated and today, on film, they are as entertaining as they were on the live stage fifty and more years ago. Singing straight songs such as "Remembering," "Baby's Feet Go Pitter Patter' Cross My Heart," "I'm Following You," and "Side by Side" or comic songs like "I Gotta Code in By Dose," "It Must Be an Old Spanish Custom," "In Sweet Onion Time," "The Prune Song," or "The Cupsidor My Father Left to Me," Vivian and Rosetta Duncan represent vaudeville at its most entertaining. They had a presence and a sense of timing and, as *Variety* once commented, they were performers in the full sense of the word.

Born in Los Angeles, the daughters of a real estate agent, Hymie and Jake (as Rosetta and Vivian were affectionately known) took to the stage around 1916 with a yodeling act. They worked briefly for Gus Edwards, who is generally credited with having discovered them, and by May of 1917 the sisters had their own act, twelve minutes long, which was first seen in New York at the Fifth Avenue Theatre. *Variety* (May 11, 1917) reported,

> The Duncan Sisters are two blonde girls presenting what should be termed a stereotyped sister-act. The girls possess a restricted song routine, with the possible exception of a patriotic number used as an encore. One is a pianiste, accompanying her sister, who leads all the numbers, with the exception of two duets, in which the girls lack harmony. The number leader has not been sufficiently groomed to handle character songs and it would be advisable to drop the one number of this order. The Duncan Sisters are not ripe as yet for the big time.

The Duncans gradually perfected their vaudeville act, with Vivian, very much the leader of the team, providing most of the comedy. After a couple of stints in musical comedy, the sisters developed the idea for a show of their own. They took Uncle Tom's Cabin, jazzed it up a little and added a lot of comedy; the result was *Topsy and Eva,* which opened at San Francisco's Alcazar Theatre on July 9, 1923. The book was by Catherine Chisholm Cushing, while the music and lyrics, including the hit song "Remembering," were by the Duncan Sisters. Vivian appeared as the sweet, innocent, peaches-and-cream heroine, Little Eva, while Rosetta donned blackface to clown, quite brilliantly, as Topsy.

Outrageous is perhaps the only description one can give to Rosetta Duncan's impudent Topsy, with her philosophy, "I'se mean an' ornery, I is, mean an' ornery. I hate everybody in the world, and I only wish there were more people in the world so I could hate them too." Even Vivian, despite the sweetness of the character that she was playing, would kid around during the show. Others in the production included Basil Ruysdael (as Uncle Tom), Frank W. Wallace (as Simon Legree), and Myrtle Ferguson (as Ophelia St. Clair). Ferguson's Aunt Ophelia was a perfect foil to Rosetta Duncan's Topsy. It would be easy to brand her portrayal as insulting to blacks but, as *Variety* (December 9, 1959) noted, "memory does not suggest that there was anything invidious racially in Rosetta Duncan's Topsy, though in that more innocent long-ago before

The Duncan Sisters as themselves

Adolph Hitler brought racial 'stereotypes' in worldwide bad odor, there was not the same quickness to take notice which prevails today.''

Topsy and Eva opened in Chicago in December of 1923. During its twenty-week run at the Selwyn Theatre, it grossed $462,387, despite distinguished critic Burns Mantle's description of it as "a freak of the season ... purports to be a musical comedy version of *Uncle Tom's Cabin;* and it is a terrible thing." The show opened in New York at the Sam Harris Theatre on December 23, 1924, and after it closed there the Duncan Sisters were constantly taking it on the road, particularly on the West Coast where they were especially popular. They even took *Topsy and Eva* to England, France, Germany, and South America, playing the roles in the language of the particular country in which they were appearing.

The Duncan Sisters filmed *Topsy and Eva* as a silent feature in 1927, but the film was not particularly successful, for one needed to hear the girls as well as see them to totally appreciate their talents. The sisters appeared in two other features, *Two Flaming Youths* (1927), in which they had a cameo, and *It's a Great Life* (1929), which introduced "I'm Following You" plus a somewhat risqué version of "Tell Me Pretty Maiden." In the late twenties, Rosetta and Vivian were back on the vaudeville stage, singing some of the songs from *Topsy and Eva* plus numbers such as "Sittin' on the Curbstone Blues" (wearing children's clothes). *Variety* (January 23, 1929) reported, "The Duncans are a vaudeville act, in or out of picture houses. . . . There are many who insist the Duncan Sisters could entertain with bows only."

In 1942 the Duncan Sisters announced their retirement, but they returned ten years later, chiefly playing night

The Duncan Sisters as Topsy and Eva

clubs. On December 1, 1959, while driving home from a night club engagement at Mangam's Chateau in Lyons, on the outskirts of Chicago, Rosetta Duncan's car struck a bridge. Rosetta died three days later, on December 4; she was fifty-eight years old. Charlotte Greenwood called her "the greatest clown on the American stage." For a while, Vivian worked as a solo act. She made her Los Angeles debut at Billy Gray's Bandbox in December of 1960, joining comedienne Alice Tyrrell to sing one of the more outrageous numbers from *Topsy and Eva,* Topsy's lament of "I Never Had a Mammy." Today, Vivian Duncan resides in the San Francisco area.

Literary scholar Edward Wagenknecht, who always had a particular fondness for *Topsy and Eva,* wrote,

> The Duncan Sisters suggested a fresh wholesomeness which was not the quality most frequently encountered in the musical comedy stars of their time, but they also had a good deal of tart commentary on hypocrisy and pretension, much of which was no less effective for being implicit rather than explicit.... Their career was a record of splendid generosity; they always gave freely of their means and of themselves, and I am sure many theatregoers must remember them, as I do, with great affection.

References: *"Topsy and Eva"* in *As Far as Yesterday* by Edward Wagenknecht (University of Oklahoma Press, 1968), pages 119–125. "The Fabulous Duncan Sisters" by Robert Kendall in *Hollywood Studio Magazine* (May, 1976), pages 28–29.

JIMMY DURANTE

Jimmy Durante in the early Twenties

Jimmy Durante had a comic style which is hard to analyze. He was not particularly funny, yet because of the warmth of his personality he could win you over. As the

New York Times (March 26, 1944) commented, "He is essentially a clown. He doesn't dazzle you with jokes; he overwhelms you with the sheer power of his exuberant good nature and a tumultuous sense of the ridiculous." If the appeal of his comedy is hard to understand, the appeal of his singing is even more puzzling, for as Fred Allen said, Durante's singing "can only be described as a dull rasp calling its mate." And yet, who else could possibly sing those Durante songs: "I Can Do without Broadway, But Can Broadway Do without Me?," "Toscanini, Stokowski and Me," "Who Will You Be with When I'm Far Away?" and, of course, "Inka Dinka Doo."

It does not seem possible that Jimmy Durante, "Schnozzola," as he was affectionately known to millions of fans, is no longer with us, for that craggy face, huge nose, and wide grin, plus that exuberant personality were an essential part of show business for more than sixty years. Those famous sayings of Durante's have become part of the English language (a language that he mangled in his act): "That's my boy," "Stop the music," "I got a million of 'em," and, of course, "Goodnight Mrs. Calabash, wherever you are." A typical Durante joke might be, "An operetta? That ain't music. It's a dame that woiks for the phone company." It was not particularly funny, but the way Durante delivered the line, one just had to laugh. The biggest Durante joke of all was the nose, about which he first started making cracks in 1923 at the Club Durant: "Here it is, folks! Yes, it's real! It ain't gonna bite you, and it ain't gonna fall off!"

"I got my nose from my mother, a piano from my father and a taste for indoor plumbing from the jernt where we lived. The bathroom was out inna backyard," Durante would often recount, recalling his childhood and birth on New York's Lower East Side, as James Francis Durante, on February 10, 1893. By the age of fifteen, Durante was playing piano at neighborhood parties, working his way up slowly—very slowly—in show business. In 1916 he organized a five-piece novelty band for the Club Alamo in Harlem, and joined forces with a singing waiter named Eddie Jackson and a young girl named Jeanne Olsen. Durante formed a partnership on stage with Jackson and married the girl.

According to Durante himself, shortly after he and Jeanne Olsen were married they stayed in a rooming house in Chicago, owned by a Mrs. Calabash. She was "a truly wonderful woman and we loved her," and years later Durante began calling his wife, as an affectionate nickname, Mrs. Calabash. After Jeanne's death in 1943, Durante was on a television show with Gary Moore; at the end of the show he ad-libbed, "Goodnight Mrs. Calabash." The next time he said it, he added "wherever you are." Who Mrs. Calabash was remained a secret until Durante revealed her identity at a National Press luncheon in Washington, D.C., on March 7, 1966.

In 1923 Durante and Jackson opened a speakeasy called the Club Durant, at 232 West Fifty-eighth Street in New York. There they were joined by a tap dancer and comic named Lou Clayton, and thus was born the team of Clayton, Jackson, and Durante. Clayton nicknamed Durante "Schnozzola," and also coined the phrase, "If that's the

Jimmy Durante with
Eddie Jackson and Lou
Clayton

way you want it, that's the way it's gonna be." So popular
did the Club Durant become, thanks in no small part to
Variety's Sime Silverman, who promoted it and the trio,
that prohibition officers moved in and closed the place
down. Undaunted, the trio moved on to a new club, the
Parody, and from there they moved into big-time vaudeville.

With Harry Donnelly's Parody Club Orchestra, Lou
Clayton, Eddie Jackson, and Jimmy Durante made their
vaudeville debut as a trio at Loew's State in March of
1927. The act was titled "Jest for a Laugh" and included
songs such as "Yucatan," "I'm Going to Tell a Story,"
"The Noose," "She's Just a Cow," and "Jimmy, the Well
Dressed Man." It was, of course, Durante who carried
most of the comedy, panicking the balcony with a comic
turn directing the orchestra. The boys' good friend, Sime
Silverman, reported in *Variety* (March 16, 1927),

Here's a tough break, because it is necessary to say
that those boys went over to a hit Monday night at
the State. . . . It's tough because this was the chance
awaited to send over a receipt in full for the many
checks at their various sawdust joints. . . . Lou Clayton, Eddie Jackson, and Jimmy Durante are cafe
entertainers, by training, instinct, nature, good nature, ability, disposition, love (of coin), and anything
else you may want to add. New to vaude . . . the boys
did exceptionally well in routining by the Monday
night performance. They clipped down to thirty-
four minutes from forty-four minutes at the matinee.

In April of 1928 the trio was headlining at the Palace
at $3,000 a week and breaking the theatre's box office

record. *Variety* (April 18, 1928) described them as "those
three cafe spirits who talk like *Variety* writes." Durante
loved vaudeville. "I like to see 'em on a Sunday night
changin' da billin' on da Loew's State, changin' dat billin',
takin' dose letters down and puttin' dose new letters up,"
he once said. "You can't get nuttin' more excitin' den
dat."

Clayton, Jackson, and Durante made their Broadway
debut a year later, in Florenz Ziegfeld's production *Show
Girl,* with music and lyrics by George and Ira Gershwin
and Gus Kahn, which opened at the Ziegfeld Theatre on
July 2, 1929. Also in the cast of the show, which ran for
111 performances, were Eddie Foy, Jr., Ruby Keeler, and
Harriet Hoctor. The trio's next Broadway appearance was
also their last together, in *The New Yorkers,* with music
by Cole Porter, which opened at the Broadway Theatre on
December 8, 1930; Ann Pennington and Marie Cahill
were also in the cast. *The New Yorkers* was a revue-type
musical comedy centered on Hope Williams, a tired and
disgusted society girl from Park Avenue ("where bad
women walk with good dogs"), who dreamed up acts of
foolishness.

In 1931 the group split, when Durante decided to go
solo in response to an offer from Hollywood. There was
no animosity in the break-up. Clayton remarked of Durante, "You can warm your hand on this man," and for
many years he was Durante's manager. Lou Clayton died
in Santa Monica, California, on September 12, 1950. Eddie Jackson continued to appear on and off with Durante
for many, many years, usually singing "Won't You Come
Home, Bill Bailey?" The two had a tiff in October of 1958
while appearing in Las Vegas, with Jackson claiming that
Durante had slighted him, but they made up in April of

the following year and Jackson was present at Durante's funeral. Eddie Jackson died in Los Angeles on July 16, 1980, at the age of eighty-four.

In the thirties, Durante alternated film work with Broadway appearances. On the stage, he was seen in *Strike Me Pink* (1933), *Policy* (1936), *Red Hot and Blue* (1937), and *Stars in Your Eyes* (1939). In 1935 he appeared as Claudius B. Bowers in *Billy Rose's Jumbo,* a role he repeated for the 1962 film version. In addition, Durante made his first English appearance, at the London Palladium, on June 1, 1936, and British audiences found him as appealing as their American cousins. He found the English very polite, recalling, "One joinalist—from da London Times—tries to kill me wit' politeness. He asks if I minds if he mentions my nose. I'm surrounded by assassins! 'If ya don't mention it,' I says to him, 'you puts me outa business.' " Jimmy Durante was featured in more than thirty motion pictures between 1930 and 1963, but few of them did justice to his talents; a film script seemed too restrictive for Durante's humor. Among the comedian's better-known films are *The Cuban Love Song* (1931), *Blondie of the Follies* (1932), *The Phantom President* (1932), *George White's Scandals* (1934), *Hollywood Party* (1934), *Sally, Irene and Mary* (1938), *Little Miss Broadway* (1938), *You're in the Army Now* (1941), *The Man Who Came to Dinner* (1942), *It Happened in Brooklyn* (1947), *Pepe* (1960), and *It's a Mad, Mad, Mad, Mad World* (1963).

Durante had been starred on radio as early as 1934, but he came to prominence in that medium with "The Camel Comedy Caravan" in 1943, in which he was costarred with Gary Moore. Because of his crewcut Moore was called "The Haircut," while Durante for a very obvious reason, was called "The Nose." The two worked together through 1947, when they both went solo. In 1950 Durante made his television debut in "Four Star Revue," and continued for many seasons with "All Star Revue," "The Colgate Comedy Hour," and "Texaco Star Theatre," in which he is best remembered for his duets with Margaret Truman. He might have continued indefinitely, for as Durante pointed out, "As long as they laugh, as long as they want me to sing, I'll stay," but a stroke put an end to his career in 1972. He died on January 29, 1980, in a Santa Monica, California, hospital. However, as Gene Fowler wrote in his biography of Jimmy Durante, "The great clown stays on with us, as great clowns always stay on in the hearts of men and women and children who seek in the refuge of merriment an hour of escape from the scowls of the long day."

References: "The Great Schnozzola" by Maurice Zolotow in the *Saturday Evening Post* (July 15, 1950), pages 22–3, 122, 124, 126, and 128. *Schnozzola: The Story of Jimmy Durante* by Gene Fowler (The Viking Press, 1951). *Good Night, Mrs. Calabash* by William Cahn (Duell, Sloan, and Pearce, 1963).

GUS EDWARDS

To describe Gus Edwards as a vaudevillian is a misnomer, for his career on the vaudeville stage is unimportant com-

Gus Edwards

pared to his career as a composer, a producer of vaudeville and night club acts, and a discoverer of new talent. He was called "The Star Maker"—the title of a 1939 Paramount feature about his life, with Bing Crosby playing Edwards —in that he was responsible for the careers of Eddie Cantor, the Duncan Sisters, George Jessel, Eleanor Powell, Walter Winchell, Ray Bolger, Larry Adler, Hildegarde, Ona Munson, Lila Lee, and many others.

While Gus Edwards started these people on a show business career, it should not be assumed that he was always the one major force in their lives on stage. For example, Eleanor Powell recalls that in 1925 she was in Atlantic City with her parents:

I was on the beach and I was eleven years old. And the person who ended up being a baby sitter for me on the beach was Johnny Weissmuller. One day I was doing these cartwheels and splits—just a kid, you know—and this man walks over. Now remember, I don't know the name Gus Edwards; I don't know the name Al Jolson; I'd never been to a show. He says, "You're pretty good," and he says he's Gus Edwards. Now Johnny knew who he was. He said, "I'd like to speak to your mother. I'd like you to come up and work at the Ritz Grill." So I tease my mother that night, "Please. . . ." And I did an acrobatic dance to "The Japanese Sandman." The big stars of the show were Lola and Leota Lane. Well, I made seven dollars a night, three nights a week. I came back the next summer when I was twelve. Then, in the winter, I went back to Springfield, Massachusetts, and dancing school. When we finally saved a little money, my mother and I went back to New York, and Ben Bernie put me to work in his club.

In New York, Miss Powell took it upon herself to seek representation by the William Morris Agency and to get into a show at the Capitol Theatre. As she notes, Gus Edwards was not her mentor. He saw her and put her into her first show, but that was basically it.

Gus Edwards was born in Hohensaliza, Germany, on August 18, 1879, and he came to this country as a child. With his fine soprano voice, he attracted the interest of Tony Pastor, who had the notion of having the fourteen-year-old Edwards sing from one of the balcony boxes of his Fourteenth Street Theatre. Before he was twenty, Gus Edwards had become a songwriter and set up his own publishing business. He wrote one of the hit songs from the Spanish-American War, "Goodbye Little Girl, Good-bye"; among his many other songs were "Meet Me Under the Wisteria," "By the Light of the Silvery Moon," "I Can't Tell Why I Love You but I Do," "I Just Can't Make My Eyes Behave," "In My Merry Oldsmobile," "Jimmy Valentine," "If a Girl Like You Loved a Boy Like Me," "I'll Be with You When the Roses Bloom Again," "Sun-bonnet Sue," "If I Was a Millionaire," and "He's My Pal." Edwards's most famous song was "Schooldays," which became his theme song and which he used in the various kiddie acts that he produced for vaudeville.

These kiddie acts, the earliest of which appears to be "The Newsboy Quintet" (which dated back to the 1890s and included Edwards himself), really became popular in 1905. They had titles such as "Kid Kabaret," "The Nine Country Kids," "School Boys and Girls," and "Juvenile Frolic," and featured children such as Herman Timberg, the violinist, Walter Winchell, Georgie Price, Eddie Cantor, and Lila Lee, who was then known as Cuddles. George Price recalled in *Variety* (November 14, 1945) that the kids called Edwards "Woof," because his favorite trick was to stick his head through the door and growl like a dog to frighten the children. "We lived like the royal family," reminisced Price. "Cuddles and I had a governess. We had our schooling on the road. One of the chorus boys would get extra money for teaching us. One of our teachers was Arthur Freed, now the Metro producer."

Typical of Edwards's productions was his "Song Revue," a fifty-minute vaudeville act which played the Palace in October of 1914. There were four principals, Gus Edwards, George Jessel, Lilyan Tashman, and Sallie Seeley, plus a chorus of boys and girls, who provided nonstop songs such as "You Gotta Stop Pickin' on My Little Pick-aninny," "The Bohemian Rag," "Shadowland," "Just Around the Corner from Broadway," and "I Love You, California." In addition, George Jessel gave impersonations of Eddie Foy, Bert Williams, and Raymond Hitchcock. *Variety* (October 3, 1914) noted, "Jessel has apparently a fund of undeveloped talent. . . . He should be instructed to cover up his self-consciousness." *Variety* also singled out a member of the chorus, Lila Lee, who it noted was billed merely as "Cutey Cuddles," and ended

its review by stating, "Edwards has given every detail especial attention and may be credited with one of vaudeville's biggest productions."

After a trip to Hollywood to work for M-G-M, Edwards returned to vaudeville in 1930 with an act titled "Gus Edwards and His Hollywood Protégés"; it was forty-five minutes long, and it also played the Palace in April of 1930. The leading protégé was one Armida, a Mexican singer and dancer who had appeared in a number of early talkies. The remainder of the program sounded like a Major Bowes Amateur Hour, with tap dancers, a violinist, and a boy who gave an impersonation of Ted Lewis. Sime Silverman reported in *Variety* (April 16, 1930) that Edwards was paid $4,250, and that his return to vaudeville was not worth the effort he had put into its preparation.

Sometimes Edwards would work as a solo act in vaudeville. In May of 1909 he was at Hammerstein's singing some of his own songs, including "My Old Lady," "My Cousin Caruso," and "Up in My Aeroplane." "Quite aside from the fact that his own compositions have made him a widely familiar name, he is a decidedly skillfull entertainer," reported *Variety* (May 22, 1909). Just prior to the First World War, Edwards produced what was remembered as one of New York's best cabaret entertainments at Reisenweber's. In addition, he wrote the scores for many Broadway stage successes, including *When We Were Forty-One* (1905, which featured Elsie Janis, whom he had managed), *Hip! Hip! Hooray!* (1907), *School Days* (1908), *The Merry-Go-Round* (1908), and *The Ziegfeld Follies* of 1910.

In the mid-thirties, Edwards produced an amateur talent show on radio from the Los Angeles radio station of KFWB. For the last eight years of his life, Edwards was an invalid cared for by his wife, Lillian, whom he had married on November 28, 1905. He died in Los Angeles on November 7, 1945. "I sat on his knee, and he taught me how to sing," remembered Eddie Cantor.

References: "Gus Edwards's Academy" by S. J. Woolf in the *New York Times* magazine (March 23, 1941), pages 12 and 19. "Geo. Price Recalls His School Days of Show Biz with Gus Edwards" by Georgie Price in *Variety,* Vol. 160, No. 10 (November 14, 1945), page 48. "My Husband, Gus Edwards" by Lillian "Mrs. Gus" Edwards in the *American Weekly* (December 5, 1948), page 16. "Gus Edwards" in *As I Remember Them* by Eddie Cantor (Duell, Sloan and Pearce, 1963).

KATE ELINORE

A singer and comedienne—one of America's foremost according to *Variety* (January 7, 1925)—Kate Elinore was active in vaudeville for more than thirty years, from the mid-1890s through December of 1924. She died on December 30, 1924, from an illness she contracted while playing the Orpheum Theatre in Los Angeles. Her career in vaudeville began in an act with her sister, May, which continued until 1906 when she met and married Sam Williams, who was to write song material for her and also appear with her on stage. When not in vaudeville, Kate

Elinore was active in musical comedy, her most prominent role being that of Lizette in the original 1910 Broadway production of *Naughty Marietta.*

JULIAN ELTINGE

Julian Eltinge in 1926

Julian Eltinge was, without question, the most famous female impersonator of all time. His beauty caused him to be dubbed the Mr. Lillian Russell of his day, while W. C. Fields said of Eltinge, "Women went into ecstacies over him. Men went into the smoking room."

He was born in Newtonville, Massachusetts, on May 14, 1883, and first donned female attire at the age of ten, when he appeared in the annual revue of the Boston Cadets; apparently, he was so successful in the female role that the following year the revue was written around him. Word of his success reached the ears of a number of theatrical managers, and he was soon appearing in minor productions around the country. Eltinge's first major success came in 1904 when he appeared in *Mr. Wix of Wickham,* a musical comedy with music by Jerome Kern and others.

Eltinge began to make vaudeville appearances, and as early as May 14, 1906, made his London debut at the Palace Theatre. The impersonator's New York vaudeville debut came in September of 1907, when he appeared at the Alhambra Theatre in an act which included "The Sampson Girl," a skit on Gibson Girls, and "Willie Green," in which he appeared in kid clothes. He was billed simply as "Eltinge," and *Variety* (September 21, 1907) reported, "The audience was completely deceived as to Eltinge's sex until he removed his wig after the second song. Eltinge

will be liked. He is artistic in everything he does, and his act is far and away above what is described as female impersonation." Eltinge's vaudeville success can be attributed chiefly to the beautiful gowns that he wore, which apparently won over the female members of the audience completely, and to a creditable singing voice, far superior to that of most other female impersonators.

In a 1909 interview, Eltinge explained that he spent two hours transforming himself into a woman, with the help of his male Japanese dresser, Shima. Almost an hour would be devoted to his make-up, and Eltinge noted, "It depends on where you put the paint, not how much you splash on."

Aside from solo vaudeville appearances, between 1908 and 1909 Eltinge toured with the Cohan and Harris Minstrels. On September 11, 1911, *The Fascinating Widow* opened at the Liberty Theatre. As in later plays and films, Julian Eltinge was featured in a dual role, that of Mrs. Monte and Hal Blake, and although the play had only a short New York run, Eltinge was able to tour with it for the next couple of years. (Interestingly, also in the cast was June Mathis who was to become a well-known silent screenwriter and who is generally credited with having discovered Rudolph Valentino for *The Four Horsemen of the Apocalypse.* Before he became a star, Valentino worked with Eltinge in a 1920 film titled *An Adventuress,* which was reedited and reissued in 1922 as *The Isle of Love.*) Two other farces which had short runs in New York, but in which Eltinge toured successfully, were *The Crinoline Girl,* which opened at the Knickerbocker Theatre on March 16, 1914, and *Cousin Lucy* (with music by Jerome Kern), which opened at the Cohan Theatre on August 27, 1915.

After a small cameo role in a 1915 film, Julian Eltinge embarked on a short but profitable screen career in 1917 with *The Countess Charming,* in which he again played a dual role and in a stage version of which he subsequently toured. Reviewing the film in the December, 1917 issue of *Photoplay,* Randolph Bartlett noticed that Eltinge was beginning to show his age and to have weight problems:

> Enter Julian Eltinge, female impersonator, as they miscall him in vodeveel. . . . There is nothing female about Eltinge, and in these days he is now barely able to appear the grande dame, whereas not many years ago he could do you an ingenue that you would find yourself making eyes at. But his picture, *The Countess Charming,* is great fun. The story is not especially important, the entertainment consisting in the swift transitions from masculine to feminine and back again. Here Eltinge has an opportunity that the stage denied him, and it is too bad that he failed to realize it until he had lost his beauty. The film gives an instantaneous change of costume in a flash-back; a similar change in a stage performance would occupy so much time that the value of the juxtaposition would be lost.

While appearing in films, Julian Eltinge also found time to write, cast, and produce vaudeville sketches for his

Julian Eltinge Players. He returned to vaudeville after an absence of several years in January of 1918 with an eighteen-minute act at the Palace which involved four songs and four costume changes, from widow's weeds to a bathing suit. A year later he starred in a new vaudeville show, produced by William Morris, which opened at the Mason Theatre in Los Angeles. Eltinge had lost twenty pounds through a strenuous course of exercise and dieting and appeared in many different costumes, designed by Cora McGeachy, while the scenery was designed by Erté. Frederick James Smith in the *New York Dramatic Mirror* (January 11, 1919) reported,

> Cleverly removing the stigma of "female impersonations," Eltinge's impersonations are always a subtle and good-humored satire on feminine mannerisms and foibles. In his new show, he has several numbers which are really brilliant and penetrating satire, especially the vampire number, in which he satires the screen vampires. . . . There is a one-act play, a little farce, written by Eltinge and June Mathis, which is a gem of fun, in which Eltinge plays the star part. Motion pictures and spoken lines are artistically combined in this. He presents also a bride number and a bathing girl who wears six different costumes.

Supporting Eltinge were Dainty Marie in her aerial act, the Dancing Lavars, and the Arnaut Brothers, who were billed as musical clowns.

Eltinge continued to tour in vaudeville through the mid-twenties. In February of 1921, while appearing at the Majestic Theatre in Chicago, he confided to the audience that his corsets were hurting him, a problem with which many women in the theatre sympathized. When he returned to the Palace in April of 1923, *Variety* (April 19, 1923) found him "as welcome as the flowers in May."

The performer had the ultimate honor of having a New York theatre named after him. Al H. Woods, who had produced *The Fascinating Widow,* told Eltinge, "Sweetheart, you're a big money maker for me, and I'm going to name my theatre for you." A year to the day from the opening of *The Fascinating Widow,* September 11, 1912, the Eltinge Theatre opened on Forty-second Street with *Within the Law.* It is still standing today, virtually unchanged, but it is now called the Empire and used as a movie theatre.

Julian Eltinge went to extraordinary lengths to stress his masculinity; there were endless stories of his beating up stagehands, members of the audience, and fellow vaudevillians who made suggestive remarks about his sexual preferences. Certainly, there was never a hint of scandal attached to Julian Eltinge's name. If he had a lover, male or female, there is no record of it. Eltinge himself never married and for the last years of his life lived with his mother on his ranch in Southern California. The fixation with proving his masculinity does, of course, suggest a lack of that quality or a need to cover up something. At least one vaudeville performer interviewed for this book was quite positive that Eltinge was a homosexual, while others, including Ruth Gordon in a *New York Times*

article, have described him as "as virile as anybody virile."

In the early thirties Eltinge toured with his own company and in July of 1931 opened in *The Nine O'Clock Revue* at the Music Box Theatre in Hollywood. That same year the performer starred in a grade "B" talkie, *Maid to Order.* Also in Los Angeles, Eltinge appeared at a sleazy night club, The White Horse, on Cahuenga Boulevard, but a Los Angeles ordinance created to crack down on homosexual hangouts prohibited men wearing female apparel in night clubs and bars. Thus Eltinge had to content himself with having his costumes on display on a clothes rack and standing by each to give the appropriate impersonation. Herb Sterne, the theatre and film critic for *Script* magazine, was at the opening night and remembers it as pathetic, with not more than a dozen people in the audience. Eltinge closed after a few nights.

Julian Eltinge was not seen on the New York stage from October of 1927, when he headlined at the Palace, until 1940, when he appeared, along with Blanche Ring, Eddie Leonard, and Pat Rooney, in Billy Rose's *Diamond Horseshoe Jubilee.* He died at his New York apartment on March 7, 1941. Certainly there was no other female impersonator who could look back on a career which included a theatre named in his honor and continual critical acclaim for the good taste with which he handled his craft.

Reference: "Julian Eltinge—A Dressing Room Marvel," in *Variety,* Vol. 42, No. 1 (December 11, 1909), pages 28 and 153.

LEON ERROL

Leon Errol in 1927

With his acrobatic clowning, his "rubber legs," and his depiction of a comic drunk, Leon Errol was well known in revue and in films, but he also contributed much to the vaudeville scene. Errol did not rely too strongly on spoken gags; his approach was purely physical. If he was in bed and needed covers, Errol would not simply add them to the bed. He would spread the covers on the floor with the pillow at the head, roll himself in the material, and then make a dive for the bed. His "rubber legs" were so called because of the way he walked. As *Esquire* commented in September of 1947, "It was a walk that was half punch drunk, half plain drunk; it was a stagger, a wobble, it was both legs seeming to give way at the same time but never quite buckling completely." In his day, Leon Errol's walk was as famous as the shuffling step of Charlie Chaplin's Tramp.

Leon Errol was born in Sydney, Australia, on July 3, 1881, and originally planned to be a surgeon until college dramatics lured him away from that field. For many years he toured Australia, New Zealand, and England, appearing in vaudeville, stock companies, and musical comedy. Errol came to New York in 1911, at which time he met Florenz Ziegfeld and was signed to appear in that year's edition of the *Follies,* which opened on June 26, 1911. (Many sources claim that Errol was in the 1910 edition of the *Follies,* but this is simply not true, although certainly he had already appeared on the American stage prior to his *Follies* debut.) The comedian was featured in a sketch with Bert Williams and also performed a dancing skit on Hazel Dawn's *The Pink Lady* with his wife, Stella Chatelaine. (Errol and Miss Chatelaine were married on August 10, 1907, and appeared together frequently on the stage. She died on November 7, 1946.) Of the comedian's *Follies* debut *Variety* (July 1, 1911) wrote, "Errol had plenty to attend to during the evening. Allowing for . . . nervousness, he did it all with credit." Leon Errol was to be a regular feature with Ziegfeld's *Follies* through 1915.

The comedian's vaudeville debut came at the Brighton Theatre in July of 1916 with an eighteen-minute act in which he played a drunk at a subway station, taken from a sketch which he and Bert Williams had performed in the 1915 *Follies.* Assisting Errol were May Hennessy as a newsgirl, Frank McDermott as a ticket collector, Alf P. James as a detective, Harry McBride as the porter (played in the *Follies* by Williams), and Walter Felton as the ticket seller. Sime Silverman, writing in *Variety* (July 21, 1916), was somewhat critical: "If an audience can believe Mr. Errol's 'souse' is funny for sixteen minutes, then they will like him in this skit. . . . While the Errol turn has nothing sensationally funny, this comedian carries it over as a summer attraction, but does so mostly through his reputation gained as a member of the *Follies.* In actualities there is too much of the same thing; Errol does not do enough dancing, and the turn has a very poor finish at present."

After his years with the *Follies,* Leon Errol was featured in *The Century Girl* (1916), *Hitchy-Koo* (1917), and its sequel *Hitchy-Koo, 1918*. On March 25, 1919, *Joy Bells* opened at the London Hippodrome, starring Errol and George Robey, a popular British comedian-singer. A rivalry broke out between the two which, of course, did nothing to hurt the show at the box office. Having recently been named a Commander of the British Empire by King George V, George Robey would sign for his salary each week, adding to his name the initials C. B. E. Not to be outdone, Leon Errol added C. E. W. to his name, meaning "Collect Every Week." As an example of Errol's American popularity, prior to leaving for England and *Joy Bells,* he headlined at both the Palace and the Riverside Theatre in January of 1919. He would close the first half of the bill at the Palace, then take a taxi to the Riverside Theatre for the second-to-closing position there.

From 1924 on, Leon Errol was to be seen chiefly in motion pictures; he appeared in literally dozens of productions, including *Yolanda* (1924), *Paramount on Parade* (1930), *Her Majesty Love* (1931), *Alice in Wonderland* (1933), *We're Not Dressing* (1934), *Make a Wish* (1937), *Six Lessons from Madame La Zonga* (1941), *Higher and Higher* (1943), *Joe Palooka* (1946), and *Footlight Varieties* (1941). In films, Leon Errol was best known for the *Mexican Spitfire* series of features that he made with Lupe Velez in the late thirties and early forties.

Never a great comedian, Leon Errol was not without his admirers, and it says much for his appeal that audiences would come to see him chiefly for the comical way he walked from 1911 through 1951. Leon Errol died in Los Angeles on October 12, 1951.

Reference: "The Man with the Rubber Legs!" in *Esquire* (September, 1947), page 54.

RUTH ETTING

Ruth Etting

In the early thirties Ruth Etting was one of America's most popular singers, the torch singer par excellence, a happy singer of sad songs. She became known as the

Sweetheart of Song and her popularity as a Columbia recording star and as a radio singer was unsurpassed. She was also a prominent vaudeville performer, first in Chicago and later in New York.

Ruth Etting was born in David City, Nebraska, on November 23, 1896. She had originally intended to be a costume designer and even took courses in that subject at the Chicago Art Institute in 1918. The date of Ruth Etting's Chicago stage debut is unclear, but it was certainly many years earlier than the 1925 appearance in a revue at the Marigold Garden Theatre which she claims as her first. Three years earlier, in 1922, Etting had married Martin Snyder, a gangster commonly referred to as Moe the Gimp, who was to manage her career. She divorced Snyder in 1937 and married her pianist Myrl Alderman, who was the victim of a shooting incident involving Snyder. The tempestuous Etting-Snyder-Alderman relationship was the chief subject of a very poor 1954 film biography, *Love Me or Leave Me*, featuring Doris Day as Ruth Etting and James Cagney as Snyder.

Ruth Etting was a popular singer in night clubs and vaudeville houses in Chicago in the mid-twenties. *Variety* (March 10, 1926) reviewed her act at the Chicago Palace and noted, "Here is a single, schooled and developed in the cabarets of Chicago, that big-time vaudeville should not miss." In little over a year, Ruth Etting was making her New York vaudeville debut at the Paramount Theatre, backed by Paul Whiteman and His Orchestra. Sime Silverman reviewed her act in *Variety* (June 15, 1927) and commented, "Miss Etting's quiet delivery leaves a likeable impression right away. She more croons than throws her songs over, and her ballad, 'I See You Sally' cinched her. She did 'Moonbeams' as nicely, and for 'Sam, the Accordion Man' for the encore was furnished an effect of an accordion player, also under the spot to the side."

On August 16, 1927, the twenty-first edition of *The Ziegfeld Follies* opened at the New Amsterdam Theatre, and one of its stars was Ruth Etting, now billed as "The Sweetheart of Columbia Records." Etting was to star in the next, and last, *Ziegfeld Follies* in 1931, singing "Shine on Harvest Moon" and "Cigars, Cigarettes." "I'd go out in front of the curtain dressed in one of those luscious creations that Ziegfeld always had for his girls," she recalled. "I was no actress, and I knew it. But I could sell a song." She also appeared with Eddie Cantor and Ethel Shutta in *Whoopee,* which opened at the New Amsterdam Theatre on December 4, 1928, and with Ed Wynn in *Simple Simon,* which opened at the Ziegfeld Theatre in February of 1930. In the last, she introduced perhaps her most famous song, "Ten Cents a Dance," while from *Whoopee* came "Love Me or Leave Me." Other famous songs associated with Ruth Etting include "It All Depends on You," "Mean to Me," "Shaking the Blues Away," and "Everybody Loves My Baby."

In the early thirties Ruth Etting was featured on a number of radio programs. She also appeared in three feature films, *Roman Scandals* (1933), *Hips, Hips Hooray* (1934), and *Gift of Gab* (1934), plus more than thirty shorts for Paramount and Warner Bros. between 1928 and 1936. That year she announced her retirement, claiming

"there wasn't much satisfaction in singing into a microphone, that the stage lost its glamor when Ziegfeld died, and she didn't think much of the pictures." Ruth Etting did, however, make a reasonably successful comeback on radio and in nightclubs in the forties. She died in Colorado Springs, Colorado, on September 24, 1978.

References: "Ruth Etting Today" by W. Franklyn Moshier in *Film Fan Monthly* (September, 1974), pages 19–25. "Ruth Etting" by George Eells in *Films in Review,* Vol. 27, No. 9 (November, 1976), pages 539–546.

FRANK FAY

Frank Fay

"Showbiz has a name for the likes of Frank Fay—a trouper's trouper," wrote *Variety* at the performer's death. There were, of course, others with less complimentary names for Frank Fay, whose arrogance, drinking, and sharp tongue made him as many enemies in the vaudeville profession as he had friends. In vaudeville, he was the supreme monologist, who could deliver a deadly ad lib with an insouciant Irish charm. When Milton Berle challenged him to a duel of wits, Fay responded, "I never fight with an unarmed man"; he once introduced Rudy Vallee as "certainly the oldest adolescent in existence." With his acid tongue he could destroy a popular song, as he did with "Tea for Two," telling his audience, "a dame getting out of bed before the sun comes up—and what for? To bake a sugar cake." His style of humor reached its zenith in the mid-twenties, when he became one of vaudeville's first regular masters of ceremonies, although an argument could also be made on behalf of Lou Holtz and Ken

Murray. In this role, he could dominate an entire vaudeville bill. He'd exchange patter with other acts, fill in time when necessary, interrupt other performers, and trade barbs with any hecklers in the audience.

Frank Fay was born Francis Anthony Fay in San Francisco on November 17, 1897, the son of stock company troupers, which ensured his making his first stage appearance, at the age of three, in a Chicago production of *Quo Vadis?* In 1903 he played the role of the Teddy Bear in *Babes in Toyland*, and later that year made his first New York appearance as an extra in Sir Henry Irving's company in *The Merchant of Venice*. No wonder that Fay responded to an interviewer's question as to when he entered show business with, "Good Lord—I've never been out of it." After years on the legitimate stage, always in minor roles and usually in minor productions, Fay teamed with Johnny Dyer and started the comedy act of Dyer and Fay, which was rough and crude and which Fay apparently loathed.

By 1918 he was established as a solo monologist, and on March 15 of that year *Variety* noted, "There is something about Fay's work that gets over easily and makes him a favorite." Even at this early stage of his vaudeville career, Frank Fay was beginning to display signs of arrogance. While appearing at the Orpheum, Brooklyn, in May of 1918, he claimed to be having trouble tying his necktie, and four minutes into his scheduled appearance he was still in his dressing room wrestling with the tie and assuring onlookers that he was certain the tie would behave itself sooner or later. Eventually the stage manager came to tell Fay of the audience's impatience, to which the performer responded, "Let 'em wait." When word of this got back to the United Booking Offices, the remainder of Fay's engagements on the Orpheum circuit were cancelled. In February of 1919 he was at the Palace, with a skit on prohibition titled "The Face on the Drug Store Floor," and even then he was not above burlesquing the headliner, Madame Petrova. The *New York Dramatic Mirror* (March 9, 1915) was quick to note, "Fay is headed straight toward a headline position. And when he gets there he'll be a drawing card too."

It did not take long for Frank Fay to reach the top. He was at the Palace in October of 1924, performing card tricks with the aid of two stooges, Lou Mann and George Haggerty, who were invited up from the audience, insulted, and hit over the head. At this time he was billed as "Broadway's Favorite Son," although *Variety* (October 15, 1924) did inquire as to who made the appointment. He was always neatly groomed, elegantly attired, with very much of the air of the dashing Irish-American playboy on stage, yet behind the refinement there was, as *Variety* (February 11, 1925) noted, "a whole power house."

After two marriages—to Lee Buchanan and Frances White—ended in divorce, Frank Fay asked Barbara Stanwyck, who in 1927 was making a name for herself opposite Hall Skelly in *Burlesque,* to become his wife. It was a marriage which was to last until 1935, when Stanwyck was riding high with a major career in motion pictures and her husband was on the way down. As Fay and Stanwyck, the couple appeared in a dramatic sketch, *The Conflict* by

Vincent Lawrence, at the Palace in February of 1929. It was a tale of a young couple, bored with life and each other, who pretend to be happy and discover that they are. It was not a success. "Here's your chance, and probably your last chance, for a view of Frank Fay as a dramatic actor. Don't miss it. You'll die," commented *Variety* (February 13, 1929). "Miss Stanwyck looks very cute in three-piece black and white pajamas with flared coat, and looks better than she acts, dramatically."

Fay entered films in 1929, but was relatively unsuccessful. It is interesting to view him as the master of ceremonies in Warner Bros. 1929 production of *Show of Shows* (a role in which he excelled on stage) and see how dismally he handles the chore. Perhaps the only good thing that came out of Fay's Hollywood years was his talking Columbia Pictures into hiring his wife.

While in vaudeville, Fay had continued to appear in revues such as *The Passing Show of 1918* and *Jim Jam Jems* (1920). He had even tried his hand at producing his own shows, first with the disastrous *Frank Fay's Fables* in 1922 and later with *Frank Fay Vaudeville* (1939), which featured Eva Le Gallienne and Elsie Janis. But after the divorce from Stanwyck, Fay retired to his $250,000 Hollywood estate and did little. He had no servants and no water in his swimming pool, having failed to pay the water bill. However, he did give up alcohol, and became addicted to coffee instead, drinking as many as seventy-seven cups in a five-hour period.

That might have been the end of the career of Frank Fay—and good riddance, quite a few would have said—had it not been for a six-foot, one-and-a-half-inch rabbit named Harvey, the subject of a play by Mary Chase. Brock Pemberton was casting the leading role of Elwood P. Dowd, and wanted Harold Lloyd for the part. But Lloyd did not find the play remotely funny and turned it down. While Frank Fay was in New York for one of his occasional night club appearances, Pemberton met with him and decided immediately that here was the perfect Elwood P. Dowd. *Harvey* opened at New York's Forty-eighth Street Theatre in November of 1944, and Frank Fay embarked on a new career which was to include more than 2,000 appearances in the play. It is not hard to understand why Frank Fay could be Elwood P. Dowd; his Irish ancestry and the years in vaudeville which taught him timing made him perfect for the role. "How could I help getting along with a rabbit," he told Maurice Zolotow, "when I was named after St. Francis of Assisi, who was brother to all the birds and beasts?"

"The gentle man of deadly humor," as *Time* magazine called Frank Fay, died in a Santa Monica, California, hospital on September 25, 1961.

Reference: "Frank Fay" by Maurice Zolotow in *Life* (January 8, 1945), pages 55–58, 60, and 63.

FEMALE IMPERSONATORS

Today, unfortunately, female impersonation usually means a garishly costumed and made-up male miming to a playback of a Judy Garland recording. With the honora-

Karyl Norman, The Creole Fashion Plate

ble exception of Danny La Rue in England and one or two other British impersonators, originality and talent has entirely disappeared from the art of female impersonation, which reached its zenith on the American vaudeville stage in the 1910s with such performers as Julian Eltinge, Bothwell Browne, Savoy and Brennan, Barbette, and others.

Female impersonation is as old as the theatre itself. Prior to 1660, it was normal and proper for women's roles to be portrayed by men. In the field of American popular entertainment, female impersonation began in the minstrel shows, where one of the most famous impersonators was Francis Leon (billed simply as "Leon"). One critic of the period wrote, "Just as a white man makes the best stage negro, so a man gives a more photographic interpretation of femininity than the average woman is able to give." In England, particularly in Christmas pantomimes, it was the norm to have buxom young ladies with beautiful legs playing principal boys while the leading comedians of the day—from Dan Leno to Arthur Askey—starred as the ladies. There was never anything improper in female impersonation, no hint of homosexuality or transvestism, as there is in much of female impersonation today.

In vaudeville, female impersonators were very careful to appear suitably manly offstage and, with the obvious exception of Bert Savoy, never "swished" around on stage. *Variety* was extremely antihomosexual and watchful of any hint of it in female impersonation. Frederick M. McCloy editorialized in the October 1, 1915, issue of the paper: "The offensive, disgusting, effeminate male or 'fairy' impersonator is now in line for expurgation. And the same influences that banish the 'cooch' [a suggestive

dance of the day and a predecessor to the shimmy] may be relied upon to kick this odious creature through the stage door into the gutter, where it belongs."

One of the earliest vaudeville female impersonators was Pete Shaw who, with his song "You May Look, But You Musn't Touch," was described as the prettiest "girl" of the nineties. There is no accurate count as to how many female impersonators played vaudeville. For example, on March 8, 1923, *Variety* reported, "There are more female impersonators in vaudeville this season than ever before. . . . Three impersonators on one bill at a split week house recently is viewed as a record."

Many of these impersonators are merely names, such as Balaban, Reine(?), Ray Lawrence, Auremia, Clemons and Rodgers, Dale and DeLane, Taciano (also known as Tacius), Tommy Martell, Francis Yates, George East, and Alvora. Most relied on gorgeous gowns and adequate "female" singing voices to put over their acts. The Divine Dodson in 1912 advertised that he wore $3,000 worth of costumes on stage. Also from 1912, Vardaman was, according to *Variety,* "probably the bulkiest of all the male impersonators of women." In 1911 Biscauex, as part of his act, played a female impersonating a male. From England, Herbert Clifton was billed as "The Male Soprano" and sang "One Fine Day" as part of his act in 1915; in 1922 he was headlining at the Palace. When he first came to America in 1910, *Variety* (January 22, 1910) commented,

Francis Renault as himself

"If an audience will applaud 'Love Me and the World Is Mine' and 'The Holy City' sung by a man in a soprano voice while dressed as a ragged urchin, managers are not to be blamed perhaps for the booking." In 1909 Stuart was

Francis Renault in drag

billed as "The Male Patti." Arthur Alexander performed his female impersonation act in 1922 in blackface. Reviewing Cecil Grey's act in 1921, *Variety* noted, "Mr. Grey presented an appearance that might easily excite the envy of the best-dressed society woman of America."

Typical of female impersonators was Du Nord, whose act *Variety* (March 12, 1920) caught at the State-Congress in Chicago: "Du Nord works in a neat eye, full stage, with transparent section which permits the audience to see the maid dressing him as he changes. He does three dances— a Spanish, a toe, and an Egyptian dance. Not using his voice, and giving the house a glimpse of the maid, has the tendency to heighten the surprise when he takes off his wig at the finish. The maid, rather, does this for him, which is an unusual twist, and then she takes off her wig." Presumably audiences could accept a man, dressed as a woman, dressing another man, dressed as a woman, but would they have been equally unconcerned if the maid was really a woman dressing and undressing a man on stage?

Bert Errol came to American vaudeville from England in November of 1913 and was soon considered a major rival to Julian Eltinge. He would occasionally drop the female mannerisms in the middle of his act to prove there was a man under the dress, and the high spot of his routine was a rendition of "My Hero" sung in mezzo-soprano. At the close of his act, Errol would introduce his wife as both his partner and his costume designer. It was a nice on-stage gimmick for proving his masculinity.

Francis Renault was as handsome in drag as he was out of it. His real name was Anthony Oriema, and so beautiful were his gowns that every Friday afternoon they would be

displayed on the stage of the theatre he was playing for the ladies to admire and envy. Karyl Norman (whose real name was George Paduzzi) was also noted for the splendor of his costumes and billed himself as "The Creole Fashion Plate." A rival, Francis Ryan, came along in 1919 and called himself "The Vaudeville Fashion Plate."

As far as this writer is concerned, the greatest of all female impersonators was the British Arthur Lucan, who played the character of Old Mother Riley on stage and in films but who, sadly, never made it to American vaudeville. Old Mother Riley was an elderly Irish washerwoman —"a Valkyrie of the back streets," as one critic described Lucan's character—who was endlessly having problems with her daughter, Kitty (played by Lucan's wife, Kitty McShane). A typical routine would begin:

McSHANE: Do you know where I went, mother? I went to a museum.
LUCAN: Went to a museum?
McSHANE: Yes, went into a museum.
LUCAN: What did you go into a museum for? Was it raining?
McSHANE: No, darling, it wasn't raining. I went to see an ancient curiosity.
LUCAN: An ancient curiosity?
McSHANE: An ancient curiosity.
LUCAN: You had to go into a museum to see an ancient curiosity? Why didn't you come home to see your mother?

Herbert Clifton in drag

One American female impersonator who predates Arthur Lucan but seems to come closest to him in style and mannerisms was Gilbert Sarony, who played a garrulous old woman who was forever exclaiming, "Goodness, girls, was I embarrassed." He died in Pittsburgh—of acute indigestion!—on December 15, 1910, and in its obituary *Variety* (December 24, 1910) wrote: "Sarony was one of the first female impersonators of the old maid type. He was considered one of the funniest men in the show business."

Reference: "Only Skin Deep" in *On with the Show* by Robert C. Toll (Oxford University Press, 1976), pages 239–263.

W. C. FIELDS

W. C. Fields

W. C. Fields (January 29, 1880–December 25, 1946) was one of the few vaudevillians who was able to transfer virtually all of his vaudeville routines to film, and by so doing not only create a new, financially successful career for himself but also ensure that his vaudeville act was preserved for posterity. To view the films of W. C. Fields today, particularly the Paramount features from the early and mid-thirties, is to understand the essence and creative comedy of Fields, the vaudevillian. His crooked poker game, with aces appearing like flies, may be seen in *Mississippi* (1935). The pool table sketch is preserved in *Six of a Kind* (1934); the juggling routine is there, cigar box by cigar box, in *The Old Fashioned Way* (1934); while classic visual and verbal gags are captured in *International House* (1933) and *It's a Gift* (1934), which is surely the finest of Fields's features. (The marvelous sequence in the film in which Fields is trying to sleep on the front porch in the early morning, disturbed by everyone from the milkman to an insurance salesman, was apparently based on an experience in his mother's home when, as a young vaudeville performer, he was trying to sleep late.)

William Claude Dukenfield was born in Philadelphia, about which he had much to say, all negative. At the age of fourteen he became entranced by the juggling of a circus clown and decided where his future lay. By 1900, W. C. Fields, "Eccentric Juggler," was a familiar figure on American vaudeville stages and within a few years he had been seen and lauded in Europe and South Africa. The *New York Telegraph* (October 24, 1901) reported that Fields's "comedy juggling is steadier now than when he first appeared in New York after his return from Europe. He makes few misses and his style, different from the others, amuses. His wife helps dress the stage and the black satin panties have not yet given way." Hattie, Fields's wife, remained as "window dressing" with his act until 1904, when she was replaced by liveried footmen on whom Fields could play such tricks as bouncing balls off their heads. For his costume, Fields appeared as a well-dressed tramp with a stubble of beard.

When Fields was starring at London's Palace Theatre in 1902 his act consisted simply of juggling, but when he returned to London in 1904 to star at the Hippodrome he had added the pool table. The program for the Hippodrome noted,

> Now the Philadelphian comique has come again among us, and the good opinion he then won is now not only maintained but strengthened, for his new billiard absurdity, in which he pockets no less than fifteen balls in one stroke, is one of those extremely clever things which would alone make the reputation of any juggler. His three chief moves on the green cloth are a trio of triumphs, and those interested in the art made famous by Roberts, Peall, and others, must make a point of seeing Fields "play the game." The fantastic way he handles his cue, the smart manner in which he pockets the balls, and his little bits of humor intervening all the while, make his turn the most lively and interesting juggling entertainment before the public.

Despite what one may have ascertained from some of his films, there was never anything vulgar in Fields's vaudeville act, so it was not surprising that in May of 1913 Sarah Bernhardt permitted him to appear on the same bill with her at the Palace. He was third on the program. *Variety* (May 23, 1913) reported, "The Palace Theatre maintains a certain atmosphere by the magnificence of its construction and appointments. Fields, with his high art pantomimic comedy juggling belonged to that atmosphere as much as the marble base of the box seats."

After many years on the vaudeville stage, Fields's career took a new turn in 1915 when he made his first appearance in one of Ziegfeld's *Follies;* Fields was to be part of the *Follies* through 1918 and again in 1920, 1921, and 1925. The last featured a drugstore sketch, which Fields transferred to film in *The Pharmacist* (1933), and "The Back Porch" sketch, which has already been mentioned, from *It's a Gift* (1934). When Fields starred in the

1927 edition of *The Earl Carroll Vanities,* he introduced the sketch of the prospector in the snow-bound cabin, with its famous line "It's not a night fit for man or beast" (the stagehand threw paper snow), which came to be filmed in 1933 as *The Fatal Glass of Beer.* From the same show came a dentist sketch which later appeared on film in *The Dentist* (1932). Fields's most important stage production of the twenties was the musical comedy *Poppy,* starring Madge Kennedy, which opened at the New Apollo Theatre on September 3, 1923. He filmed it twice, in 1925 as *Sally of the Sawdust* and in 1936 as *Poppy.*

W. C. Fields had made his first film, a short titled *Pool Sharks,* in 1915. In 1924 he appeared in a cameo, as a drunken British soldier, in the Marion Davies vehicle *Janice Meredith.* His film career began in earnest in 1925 with *Sally of the Sawdust,* followed by *That Royle Girl* (1926), *It's the Old Army Game* (1926), *Tillie's Punctured Romance* (1928), *Her Majesty Love* (1931), *Tillie and Gus* (1933), *Mrs. Wiggs of the Cabbage Patch* (1934), *You Can't Cheat an Honest Man* (1939), *My Little Chickadee* (1940), *Bank Dick* (1940), and *Never Give a Sucker an Even Break* (1941), among many others. Once he was ensconced as a film star in Los Angeles, there was to be no return for Fields to the vaudeville and revue stage.

Fields was, without question, a complex man—intelligent and perhaps introspective, but certainly not the drunken child-hater that he is often depicted to have been. Perhaps the best description of the comedian was given by the program writer for the London Hippodrome in 1904: "He is a twentieth-century man, devotes himself entirely to his work, and is satisfied to live on the earth without wanting to own it." Surely the world of entertainment has benefited much from Fields's participation.

Reference: *W. C. Fields by Himself,* edited by Ronald J. Fields (Prentice-Hall, 1973).

FILM STARS

With the coming of sound to the motion picture, silent movie stars by the dozen tried to become vaudeville stars overnight. There were two reasons for the movie invasion of the vaudeville stage; first, it offered film celebrities an opportunity to prove to their studio heads that they could speak, sing, and dance, and thus were prime material for talkies, and second, it was a means of bolstering a sagging —and in many cases, a doomed—career.

Yet even before the premiere of *The Jazz Singer* in 1927, with its ramifications for the film industry, an occasional silent star had tried his or her hand at vaudeville. As early as December of 1914, Crane Wilbur, who had been serial queen Pearl White's leading man, appeared on the stage of Poli's Theatre in Springfield, Massachusetts, to tell of the trials and tribulations of a picture hero. In the summer of 1923, Crane Wilbur returned again to vaudeville. Francis X. Bushman and Beverly Bayne, a romantic screen duo of the 1910s, appeared in the comedy sketch *Poor Rich Man* at the Palace in February of 1921. In January of 1922, Flora Finch, who had partnered comedian John Bunny in the early 1910s, tried her hand

at vaudeville but *Variety* (January 27, 1922) thought her act slovenly. Henry B. Walthall, one of the stars of *The Birth of a Nation,* made his vaudeville debut at the Hill Streeet Theatre in Los Angeles in May of 1922 in a twenty-minute playlet, *The Unknown,* in which he played the dual role of father and son. Child star Wesley Barry made his vaudeville debut in September of 1922 at the Orpheum Theatre in San Francisco, in a sketch titled "Welcome Home." As he toured the country with the sketch, he tried to dispel rumors of moral laxity in the film industry, brought on by the William Desmond Taylor murder, the Fatty Arbuckle rape scandal, and Wallace Reid's death from drug addiction, claiming "Hollywood is so tame that wild flowers won't grow there."

Dorothy Gish turned down an offer to appear in vaudeville in 1921 at $2,500 weekly—she would apparently have accepted $5,000—but Bebe Daniels, a major Paramount star, did play vaudeville dates in Buffalo and Detroit in the summer of 1923 at a reported salary of $3,000 a week— she had asked for $4,500. She sang, danced, and told stories of the "How To Get into the Movies" type. *Variety* found her act condescending and patronizing, and wondered why vaudeville audiences would sit through such performances with polite tolerance. Baby Peggy, a typical child star of the movies, headlined at the Hippodrome in February of 1925 with an eighteen-minute revue titled "From Hollywood to Hippodrome." The child actress proved remarkably self-assured in this and future vaudeville engagements and her voice apparently carried, without the aid of microphones, to all parts of the house. In March of the same year, Louise Glaum, a screen vamp, made her vaudeville debut at the Eighty-first Street Theatre with a telephone monolog titled "The Web." "Miss Glaum is not impossible to vaudeville if her name means anything, but she does need assistance," reported *Variety* (April 1, 1925). Betty Blythe, whose film career was already slipping, headlined at the Palace in August of 1926 with songs and impressions. Abel Green reported in *Variety* (August 25, 1926), "Fair voice and okay considering she is Betty Blythe of the silent drama."

Anita Stewart, a popular film favorite of the 1910s, was scheduled to tour in the vaudeville sketch "Modes of the Moment," but it closed in November of 1923 after a ten-day run. Another early favorite, Clara Kimball Young (who, like Anita Stewart, had starred for the Vitagraph Company) had better luck with a sketch titled "The Adorable Wife," in which she headlined at the Palace in April of 1925.

There was a disastrous vaudeville tour by silent movie stars in the spring of 1925. Bryant Washburn, Cullen Landis, Ruth Stonehouse, Phyllis Haver, Anna May Wong, Helen Holmes, and one or two other stars of the same magnitude—second class—were booked to appear at the Kansas City Convention Hall. Seats were two dollars each and the audience was promised the opportunity to dance with the stars after the show. On opening night the company drove to the Hall, accompanied by a police escort and a marching band, only to be confronted with 18,000 empty seats. There was an immediate display of temperament until the stars realized that reporters were present, at which point they decided to present their show anyway. However, their misfortunes had only begun, for before they could leave town for their next booking, in Atchison, Kansas, the local agent for the show filed an attachment on the admittedly very small box office receipts. After that was straightened out, the troupe left for Atchison and Omaha, where the final blow was struck. The orchestra conductor's check bounced and he attached the receipts. Discouraged, the stars returned to the safety of Hollywood, where such dramas were played out only on the screen.

When the talkies hit, the silent stars panicked. On February 1, 1928, *Variety* carried headlines announcing "Film Names Stampede Towards Vaudeville," including in that number George Walsh, Ben Turpin, Ian Keith, Ethel Clayton, Irene Rich, and Renée Adorée. On April 1, 1928, *Variety* listed Ralph Graves, Viola Dana, Shirley Mason, Ruth Clifford, Cullen Landis, Snub Pollard, Agnes Ayres, Lila Lee, William Desmond, and Hank Mann among the "25 Film Players on Coast Available as Vaude Acts." *Variety* also announced the death knell for silent stars anxious to embrace vaudeville in its issue of December 4, 1929, with the headline, "Fading Stars Not Wanted by Keith's." One star who did make it big in vaudeville was Tom Mix, who broke the attendance records at the Hippodrome. *Variety* (May 23, 1928) hailed him as "the one man who can do more for vaudeville than vaudeville has done, or could do, by itself for itself."

Silent serial queen Ruth Roland had a pleasant singing voice and became a popular favorite in vaudeville. *The Billboard* (January 24, 1931), noting she had "a sweet personality that immediately ingratiates her with the audience," saw her at the New Palace in Chicago, where she gave an impersonation of Ted Lewis impersonating Ruth Roland inpersonating Ted Lewis singing "Me and My Shadow." Ricardo Cortez appeared at the Palace in March of 1930 in the playlet *Wanted* by Edwin Burke. *The Billboard* (March 22, 1930) reported: "The screen 'name' scored a personal hit, and not only was his choice of vehicle a smart one, but good taste was also used in the selection of a supporting cast." Even animal stars went into vaudeville, with Rin Tin Tin playing the Palace in May of 1930 at $1,200 a week.

Viola Dana is both atypical and untypical of silent film stars who appeared in vaudeville. She is untypical in that prior to entering films in 1910 she had worked extensively on the stage and, in fact, left films after a year to star in *The Poor Little Rich Girl* on Broadway. When talkies appeared, she was surprised that producers failed to recognize that she was perfectly equipped for the new medium. "To tell the truth," she recalls, "I was fed up with this town. There was a different element coming in." Her vaudeville debut was in June of 1928 in a playlet titled *There Goes the Bride* at Proctor's Eighty-sixth Street Theatre. *Variety* (June 27, 1928), unaware of Miss Dana's earlier stage experience, commented unkindly: "As a line reader, Miss Dana does as well as might be expected from a death—and dumb—racket alumna." Viola Dana remembers, "Oh God, that was a terrible thing with an awful leading man. On opening night the audience roared with laughter. The leading man had come on with his fly open!"

The actress was more successful with her second vaudeville offering, *The Inkwell,* a sketch written by Anita Loos, in which Miss Dana was supported by Edward Arnold. It was, recalls Viola Dana, "a cute sketch suitable for the kind of things I had been doing," and she toured in it for forty weeks playing three shows a day and four on Saturdays and Sundays, except at the notorious Harris Theatre in Pittsburgh, where five shows a day were demanded. Viola Dana and *The Inkwell* were successful, although it must be reported that *The Billboard's* Cincinnati critic called it—when the sketch opened in that town at the Albee Theatre on April 13, 1930—"about the weakest and most inane piece of business we have looked at in this house in a long, long time."

Viola Dana experienced no unpleasantness or animosity from her fellow performers because of her movie star status and has nothing but praise for vaudevillians. She did run into one problem in that she worked full stage, which annoyed magician Fred Keating, one of whose tricks was to swallow needles and pull them, threaded, out of his mouth. Keating would not talk to Miss Dana, so she gathered together a dozen large darning needles, stuck them into a card, and had her maid deliver them to Keating's dressing room with a note asking if he would care to swallow these.

Nor was it just in the early days of the sound motion picture that film stars took to the vaudeville stage. As late as December of 1933, Gary Cooper, supported by Sari Maritza and Raquel Torres, played a week at the Paramount in New York. He was paid $4,000, far less than Lou Holtz could have demanded, to appear in a sketch titled "The Eternal Triangle," which had the two female stars battling over Cooper, who eventually walks off with the maid. That same month, Bela Lugosi played the State Theatre in an eighteen-minute version of *Dracula*.

If that was not enough entertainment by live film stars in vaudeville during December of 1933, Christmas week saw Mary Pickford appear at the Paramount in the nineteen-minute playlet *The Church Mouse* by Ladislaus Fodor. It was Miss Pickford's first formal stage appearance since performing in David Belasco's *The Good Little Devil* twenty-five years earlier; for her trouble the actress was paid $10,000 and a percentage of the gross. Mary Pickford was well worth the money, as standing-room-only crowds gathered to see her as a poor little stenographer who melts the stony heart of a big banker. *Variety* thought her performance a combination of Pickford's roles in *Tess of the Storm Country, Kiki,* and *Daddy-Long-Legs,* and hailed the vaudeville debut of a national institution as an occasion, if not an event.

Reference: "12 Film Stars in Bloomer" in *Variety,* Vol. 78, No. 3 (March 4, 1925), pages 1 and 34.

FINK'S MULES

Fink's Mules is probably the most famous opening act in the history of vaudeville, an act which has taken on almost mythological proportions. It is recalled with fondness by every vaudevillian, although almost nothing has been recorded concerning Mr. Fink or his animals. Despite the name, Fink's Mules was not an act entirely made up of mules; supporting the mules were ponies, dogs, and monkeys. Nor was it the first act of this type, having been preceded by Cliff Berzac's animals.

It was a comedy act, complete with a stereotypical stupid Negro trying to ride a mule, and first came to attention when it played the opening ten minutes of the Palace bill in April, 1918. Why do people remember Fink's Mules? Perhaps because, as Ken Murray recalls, it is quite a task to train a mule. Or perhaps because, as Sime Silverman wrote in *Variety* (April 19, 1918), "The trainer is middle-aged, the setting and apparatus are bright looking, also clean, with the animals the same, and the act may be counted upon as a comedy number in any program."

EDDIE FOY

Eddie Foy in 1910

Eddie Foy came to vaudeville somewhat late in his career, but when he arrived on the vaudeville scene he was welcomed and loved by audiences and management alike. After Foy's death, E. F. Albee wrote of him in *Vaudeville News and New York Star* (February 25, 1928):

There is no doubt that Eddie Foy brought as much wholesome happiness to the American public as any artist of the stage. With his humorous and witty clowning throughout his long career, literally he made millions laugh without ever affronting the good taste or sensibilities of anyone in his audience. Unlike most comedians, Eddie Foy's droll antics, absurd pantomime, and farcical singing and dancing captured and kept the young as well as the old, the innocent as well as the wise. Probably he was the favorite of more entire American families than any other stage artist. His last vehicle, a sketch called "The Fallen Star," booked as his farewell tour as a fitting climax to his fifty-six years on the stage, was a complete success from its start but when Eddie Foy looked over the long itinerary ahead of him he said with his quaint smile, "That is certainly the longest continuous tour that I ever started on. I doubt if I will live to finish it." Well it is finished, sooner than anyone could guess, but probably in the manner he might have chosen—in working to the last, happy in his beloved profession, and giving of his best to make others happy. He was an inspiration to all his countrymen and an honor to the N.V.A. and to his profession. . . . I shall miss his hearty salutation whenever he left. I shall always remember his kindly and humane qualities. I have lost a real friend.

The comedian was born Edward Fitzgerald in New York's Greenwich Village on March 9, 1856, the son of an Irish tailor from Dublin. When his father died in 1862, the young Eddie took to singing and dancing and performing acrobatics in local saloons to help his impoverished family. Sometimes he would appear in blackface, singing:

I'm happy little Ned;
I earn my daily bread
By doing chores for white folks' round this town.
I was never known to shirk
From any kind of work,
At blacking boots there's none can take me down.

In 1865 the family moved to Chicago, just in time for the great fire. At the age of sixteen Eddie teamed up with another boy, Jack Finnegan, and because Finnegan and Foy sounded too Irish, they called the act Edwards and Foy. The two played beer halls, singing and dancing and appearing in blackface. Later, Eddie Foy teamed with Ben Collins in a similar act, and he also began to work as a "super" at McVicker's Theatre and the Academy of Music in Chicago. Circuses and minstrel shows followed, and it was a tough uphill climb until Foy became known as "a Western variety artist," playing everywhere in the West from Butte to Denver and from Dodge City to San Francisco. From 1888 through 1894, Foy appeared under the management of David Henderson in fantasies such as *Cinderella, Sinbad the Sailor,* and *Ali Baba,* performing in Chicago and on tour. As Foy recalled them, they were "years of unqualified success, even of triumph; years of freedom from business or financial worry."

Eddie Foy became a Broadway star, thanks to his mimicry, pantomime clowning, and eccentric dancing in *The Strollers* in 1901. His greatest stage success was as Sister Anne, singing "I'm a Poor, Unhappy Maid" and "Hamlet

Was a Melancholy Dane" in *Mr. Bluebeard* which opened at the Iroquois Theatre, Chicago, on November 23, 1903. Foy was appearing in *Mr. Bluebeard* (which had originally been a Theatre Royal, Drury Lane, London, production) at the Iroquois Theatre on the afternoon of Wednesday, December 30, 1903. An audience of 1,800 people, chiefly children, was present when the stage curtain caught fire. Despite Foy's appearance on stage to try to calm the audience, there was panic in the theatre and more than 600 persons, half of them children, perished in the disaster, the worst theatre fire of all time.

There was a natural Irish complexion to Foy's features but in most of his stage productions he appeared in eccentric costumes or, as in the case of *Mr. Bluebeard,* in drag. In 1903 *Vanity Fair* wrote of him, "Every movement of his facial muscles tells a complete story of his prevailing emotions." Off stage he was apparently very different, according to *The Billboard* in 1911. "Eddie Foy, who is so dry, arch, and ludicrous on the stage, is rather quiet in private life and converses in a low tone with little laughter. He has, however, a kindly smile which flickers across his face when something amusing occurs to him." He was married four times. In 1879 Foy wed an actress named Rose Holland, by whom he had two children, both of whom died. After Rose Holland's death, he married another actress, Lola Sefton, and when she died in 1896, he married Madeline Morande, a member of the Chicago Opera House ballet. Madeline Morande died in 1918, and in 1923 Eddie Foy married Marie Reilly. By Madeline Morande, Foy had eleven children, of whom only seven lived. But those seven—Charles, Richard, Irving, Bryan, Madeline, Mary, and Eddie, Jr.—were to play an important part in the comedian's career after 1910.

Eddie Foy had played major vaudeville in the early years of this century, giving impersonations of President Theodore Roosevelt, John D. Rockefeller, and Elsie Janis. "He is one of the funniest acts in vaudeville at the present time," commented Sime Silverman in *Variety* (May 19, 1906). On August 12, 1910, Eddie Foy made his first appearance with his children, the Seven Little Foys, at a Lambs Club picnic. Within two years, Eddie Foy and the Seven Little Foys were established vaudevillians, and Eddie never really returned to the legitimate stage, content with his "happy family and happy act," as *Variety* (August 23, 1912) described them. They appeared in sketches titled "Fun in the Foy Family," "The Old Woman Who Lived in a Shoe," and "Slumwhere in New York," most of them written by Will Jerome. In any town where Foy was appearing, he would joke that if he and his family lived there it would be a city. Eddie Foy, Jr. would imitate his father and there would be dialogs like the one where Madeline Foy asked her father, "Bring me home a doll." Foy would respond, "What kind of a doll?" "Oh, mamma says you know all about dolls," answered Madeline. "I know enough about them not to bring them home," retorted Foy. At the end of the act, Mrs. Foy would often appear and take—in view of the number of offspring—a well-deserved bow.

Madeline Foy recalls, "We had a private tutor and our aunt. We had a lot of people taking care of us. We sang and danced. We all had very good voices. We'd come out all in a line, and my father would bring out a little suitcase in which was my brother, Irving, who was two years old. Then we'd sing a medley; each one would step down and sing a song. Then Eddie, Charlie, and Mary would dance. We used to do a march at the finish of the act. Old-fashioned and corny I guess, but it was cute." Madeline Foy doubts the story that her father went into vaudeville because of a fight with theatrical entrepreneur Lee Shubert which resulted in Foy's punching Shubert into a theatre pit and the latter banning Foy from Shubert theatres for all time.

The B. F. Keith's *Theatre News* in Washington, D.C., commented on September 15, 1919: "The Foy family in vaudeville presents a simple problem in arithmetic. If one Foy is funny, how funny are eight Foys? Those who have followed Eddie Foy and the younger Foys throughout their stage career know the answer. Eddie Foy has been and still is one of the brightest spots in American amusement. His peculiar methods have set a fashion in humor these many years, and his family is each and every one a chip of the old block. The family has been working together in a humanitarian effort to bring more cheer into the world for several years. In stature, one of the elder Foys is larger than his pater. But the stature has nothing whatever to do with fun, as shown by the fact that the smallest of the Foy progeny is generally conceded the best comedian of them all, not even excluding poppa Foy."

As the children grew, the act split up. Bryan went into the film industry, becoming one of the pioneers of the sound motion picture at Warner Bros. After Eddie Foy's 1923 marriage there was a brief period of animosity between father and children. In time, the Foy youngsters developed their own vaudeville act. Eddie Foy died in Kansas City on Thursday, February 16, 1928, while appearing on the Orpheum circuit in the title role of the sketch "The Fallen Star" by Tom Barry. He signed himself off, "On the whole, life has been a pretty jolly affair. I have no complaints to make, and few regrets."

Reference: *Clowning through Life* by Eddie Foy and Alvin F. Harlow (E. P. Dutton and Company, 1928).

IRENE FRANKLIN

Almost totally forgotten today, Irene Franklin, with her songs and impersonations, was once one of vaudeville's most popular entertainers, adored by critics and public alike. In 1908, in a popularity contest organized by Percy Williams to find the Most Popular Woman Vaudeville Artist, she came in first, easily beating Eva Tanguay, Vesta Victoria, and Marie Dressler. Reviewing her act in the *New York Dramatic Mirror* (May 12, 1915), Frederick James Smith wrote: "She injects so much humor, she touches such a vibrant note of pathos that she is quite irresistible. Her 'kid' songs are unforgettable, and her slangy dissertation of a chorus girl invading the Great White Way was a little masterpiece of characterization." A year later—on April 29, 1916—Smith wrote: "She combines an almost O. Henry understanding of everyday life

Irene Franklin in 1921

with a Eugene Field sense of childhood. And, aside from her creation of lyrics, as Will Cressy has said, she can tell a story with a single movement of her hands."

Irene Franklin was born in St. Louis on June 13, 1876, and claimed to have made her stage debut at the age of six months. She certainly played all the usual child roles of the period, from *Shore Acres* to *Editha's Burglar*, before embarking on a vaudeville tour of Australia at the age of fifteen. In 1894 she appeared in London variety theatres and the following year she made her American vaudeville debut. At the age of twenty, Irene Franklin was an established vaudeville performer, usually providing her own material which consisted of such kiddie songs as "I'm Nobody's Baby Now" and satires on such social phenomena as the feminist movement, which she lampooned in "The Woman Policeman." She sang of the plight of the unmarried woman in "If I Don't Lock My Family Up, It's the Old Maid's Home for Me." With the advent of Prohibition, Irene Franklin sang of the man who didn't carry a hip flask in the risqué number "What Have You Got on Your Hip? You Don't Seem to Bulge Where a Gentleman Ought to." The 1910s craze of the *thé dansant* was parodied in "At the Dansant."

In the brilliant 1907 song "Expression," Miss Franklin illustrated all the human emotions by facial expressions. A year later she introduced "The Red Head," in which she portrayed a little red-headed girl who tells of the names the other children call her. Sime Silverman wrote in *Variety* (October 10, 1908), "It is a work of art in character study, and Miss Franklin's delivery could not be improved upon." "The Red Head" was composed by Burton Green

who was for many years Irene Franklin's pianist, filling in on stage while she executed costume changes. The couple first met when the singer played Tony Pastor's, where Burt Green was the resident pianist at seventy-five dollars a week. Green divorced his wife, writer Helen Van Campen, and he and Irene Franklin became a team in private life and in vaudeville until Green's death on November 17, 1922. The couple entertained the troops in France during the First World War and were the first vaudeville artists to have a paid advertisement on the front cover of *Variety,* in its December 19, 1913, issue.

After Green's death Miss Franklin married another pianist, Jerry Jarnagan, who died in 1934. She continued in vaudeville and also returned to the legitimate stage, appearing in shows in New York, Los Angeles, and San Francisco. (She had made her legitimate stage debut as Josephine Zaccary in *The Orchid* at New York's Herald Square Theatre in 1907. Irene Franklin's other nonvaudeville shows included *Hands Up* [1915] and *The Passing Show of 1917* [1917].) With the demise of vaudeville, Miss Franklin entered films in 1933, appearing in *Lazy River* (1934), *Change of Heart* (1934), *The President Vanishes* (1934), *Timothy's Quest* (1936), *Song and Dance Man* (1936), *Midnight Madonna* (1937), *Married before Breakfast* (1937), and *Fixer Dugan* (1939), among others. She died in poverty at the Actors Fund Home in Englewood, New Jersey, on June 16, 1941. Only three days earlier she had celebrated her sixty-fifth birthday and the *New York Times* reported she had written a friend, "Another of my Friday the Thirteenth birthdays is upon me, but I don't think there are many who will remember me or who care."

It is hard to analyze or describe the work of this red-headed comedienne. At the time of her death some writers compared her to Beatrice Lillie, but it is clear that Irene Franklin's songs and impersonations were less subtle, less sophisticated than Miss Lillie's.

Take, for example, the tale of a passenger asking the conductor to put him off at Watt Street, as quoted by Douglas Gilbert in *American Vaudeville*. "The play on the word Watt—What Street? Yes, Watt Street, etc.—is amusing but hardly original." Perhaps the best comment on her art comes from Rush in *Variety* (February 9, 1907): "a style that is smooth and quiet but which baffles accurate description." One thing is clear; in an era when vaudeville performers generally impersonated other celebrities, Irene Franklin impersonated the ordinary working woman and child—in other words her audience—and in this her comic style is most closely approximated today by that of Lily Tomlin.

Reference: "How Not to Write Lyrics—Being an Exposition of Curious Phenomena, as Observed by a Collector of Crippled and Destitute Story Compositions" by Irene Franklin in *Variety,* Vol. 9, No. 1 (December 14, 1907), pages 20 and 65.

FREAK ACTS

So-called freak acts were popular during the entire history of vaudeville, and some of them, such as the Cherry Sisters (see their entry), remained headliners for years. These acts grew out of the freak museums of the 1880s, and despite their name were not usually freaks in the sense of being bearded ladies or Siamese twins. Rather they were unusual in that they owed their fame to a freak of publicity or a freak event. The greatest entrepreneur of freak acts was Willie Hammerstein, whose Victoria Theatre, at the junction of Seventh Avenue and Forty-second Street, almost always included at least one freak act on its bill, usually a newspaper headliner—a showgirl who had shot a wealthy lover or something of that kind.

Hammerstein was always on the lookout for new freak acts, and there is a story that he was approached by a vaudevillian down on his luck who offered to come on stage with a rope, some poison, a knife, and a gun, and ask the audience how they wished to see him kill himself. There are two versions of Hammerstein's reply. One was, "Not bad. Come to see me after you break in the act out of town." The other was, "Great. What do you do for an encore?" Funny as this story may be, there is some truth to it, for in the 1910s Hammerstein did offer an act in which the audience was invited to come on stage and participate in the simulated execution of a performer sitting in an electric chair.

Willie Hammerstein quarreled with his father Oscar, in the summer of 1912 and Oscar, who owned the Victoria, temporarily removed him from management of the theatre. When the family argument was resolved in November of that year and Willie returned to the Victoria, there was great rejoicing. *Variety* even published a poem, "Willie's on the Job Again," by Thomas J. Gray in its November 29, 1912 issue. The chorus went:

Willie's on the job again, and Hammerstein's looks great,
All of Huber's old time freaks are goin' to celebrate,
To show that he was still there, and that the news was real,
He rushed to the U.B.O. and booked "The Diving Seal."
Willie's on the job again, there's joy along Broadway.

Of the genuine freak acts, one of the most revolting, but popular, was Willard, the Man Who Grows. Billed as "the star attraction of the Wintergarten, Berlin," Clarence E. Willard was featured in vaudeville during 1913 and 1914, and could add 7½ inches to his height of 5 feet, 9¾ inches. He could extend his arms to anywhere from 8 to 15 inches, and could make one leg 4 inches longer than the other. As Wynn noted in *Variety* (October 17, 1914), "Willard is one of that strange species of novelty that one must see to appreciate."

However, if Willard sounds disgusting, consider Doss, who was similarly billed as "The Man That Grows." *Variety's* Wynn also reported on his act at the American Roof on December 8, 1916:

Entirely devoid of personality, appearance or general stage ability and entirely valueless for entertaining, since there is not even an atom of mystery surrounding his specialty, "Major" Doss, billed at Loew's American as "The Man That Grows" comes under the natural classification of a museum act. Doss is introduced by an announcer who gives a brief history of his life. Among other things he explained that during an attempted balloon ascension some years ago Doss suffered a fall which resulted in curvature of the spine. Doss is a hunchback and the disfiguration naturally leads one to the solution of the growth mystery. During the turn Doss squirms the hunch around from his back to his chest, one of the most disgusting "bits" ever shown on a stage, and any manager who would permit the exhibition before an audience of women should have his brain examined.

There was a very popular talking dog act by the name of Don that played the vaudeville circuits in 1912. The one problem with Don's act was that he spoke only German! Dog acts, however, were fairly common. A little more out of the ordinary was Rahlander's Pigs, which played Hammerstein's in September of 1912. The pigs performed an act similar to the regulation dog act, except that their trainer was dressed as a butcher, and would use a carving knife to direct the pigs' movements. Jolo in *Variety* (September 6, 1912) was not impressed: "Just another of the Hammerstein freak acts," was his comment.

Other animal acts included "The Sheik," a white horse that would strike various poses. He appeared in neighborhood vaudeville houses in the mid-twenties. In the summer of 1921 the Palace featured an elderly lady named Mrs. E. Hathaway Turnbull, who spent twenty-three minutes talking to the audience about "our animals and how they help us." *Variety* (August 1, 1921) found her "as pulsating as a rainy afternoon in Kenosha." There was even a monkey impersonator named Nathal, who, in the late twenties, clambered over the backs of seats and along the balcony railings of vaudeville houses.

From the world of fashion came Lucile, otherwise known as Lady Duff Gordon, who presented her fashion show at the Palace in December of 1917 and proved so popular that she was held over for a second week. Another member of the British aristocracy who tried vaudeville was Lady Aberdeen, who was assured of success by ending her act with the singing of "America." From the world of the criminal came Al Jennings, the famed outlaw, who talked to vaudeville audiences in 1921. Reviewing his act, *Variety* (February 11, 1921) wrote, "His monolog is a preachment against outlawry.... As it stands, it is rather dull and Jennings falls into the freak class."

Paul Swan was a somewhat effeminate classical dancer, of the Isadora Duncan school, who billed himself as "The Most Beautiful Man in the World." He played Hammerstein's Victoria Theatre in October of 1914 and was subjected to a certain amount of ribaldry and jeering from the audience. As Sime Silverman noted in *Variety* (November 1, 1914), "He died in the final dance, and it's tough to die at Hammerstein's." It was Silverman who made the pertinent comment about Albertina Rasch and her troupe of classical dancers (in the June 29, 1917, issue of *Variety*):

"To vaudeville 'classical dancing' is a matter of clothes—how little clothes." Although active for many years in vaudeville, and perhaps unfairly classified here as a freak act, Albertina Rasch went on to greater fame as a choreographer and leader of a troupe of dancers in many famous Hollywood films of the thirties, including *The Hollywood Review of 1929*, *The Merry Widow* (1934), and *The Great Waltz* (1938).

In the fall of 1912, the Women's Suffrage Party of Greater New York gave a seventeen-minute performance at Hammerstein's. *Variety* reported that their reception was cool, largely because too many of their sisters were where they should be, at home taking care of the laundry and the kids. If the Women's Suffrage Party received a disappointing response from the audience, it was as nothing compared to the downright antagonism of the audience drawn by Carrie Nation in February of 1909 when she lectured on the dangers of drink.

An unusual freak act which appeared at the Eighty-sixth Street Theatre in October of 1928 was a group of Hopi Indians, who performed a snake dance and other tribal dances. Again the audience was unenthusiastic.

The sports world provided many freak acts. In the fall of 1926, Babe Ruth played vaudeville houses in San Francisco and Minneapolis as a monologist. Gertrude Ederle, the first woman to swim the English Channel, proved fairly popular in vaudeville houses in the same year. She earned $1,000 a day at Brooklyn's Mark Strand Theatre, with an act similar to that of Annette Kellermann, which included waltzing underwater, etc. One of the most popular sporting acts playing vaudeville was Jack Dempsey; in February and March of 1922 he played the Hippodrome for four weeks at a guarantee of $5,000 per week, and in the first week he earned $7,000 as his percentage of the gross. Dempsey's act consisted chiefly of a dialog with his manager, Jack Kearns, with jokes such as "They (the girls) call me honey; I get stung so often." With reference to his knocking out Frenchman Georges Carpentier in the fourth round, he talked about the French and American national holidays and punned. "But we Americans all celebrate the Fourth." So popular did Jack Dempsey prove to be in vaudeville that he returned to play the Loew circuit in October of 1924.

One of the most extraordinary, and certainly most moving, of freak acts was Helen Keller, who played the Palace in February of 1920. With her mentor, Anne Sullivan, she demonstrated lip reading and answered questions from the audience. When a member of the audience asked Sullivan to ask Helen Keller what she thought of her instructor, the girl did not reply, but placed her head on Anne Sullivan's shoulder and gave her a hug. To quote *Variety* (February 27, 1920), "It was a throb scene."

The freak act of all time came in September of 1933, when evangelist Aimee Semple MacPherson played the Capitol. For $5,000 a week, Mrs. MacPherson, wearing a white dress and with a large cross dangling in front of her bosom, told the audience about her life and her religion. When she thanked God for His kindness in providing her with a steady income there were hoots of derision from the audience, but nothing disturbed the evangelist. What dis-turbed the management was the scarcity of people in the audience for, as *Variety* (September 26, 1933) pointed out, "As a box office attraction it looked like the founder and general manager of 226 churches was a washout."

TRIXIE FRIGANZA

Trixie Friganza

Trixie Friganza was credited with having a unique comic sense and a gentle humor that she used chiefly on herself. She was a large woman, made even larger by her innumerable costumes which she would discard one at a time during a performance, and her weight was one source of her humor. Trixie described herself as a "perfect forty-six," sang songs like 'I'm Not Having Birthdays Any More," and told 1920 audiences that "the way for a fat woman to do the shimmy is to walk fast and stop short." She announced that her favorite stone was a brick and told of the village belle who spurned the livery stable keeper in favor of the greenhouse keeper because of atmospheric reasons. She was always on the lookout for a suitor, be it only "my garbage man," who she sang about in 1918; in 1915 she had been lamenting "Won't Someone Kindly Stake Me to a Man?"

She was born Delia O'Callahan in Grenola, Kansas, on November 29, 1870, and took her mother's maiden name of Friganza for her first stage appearance, in the chorus of *The Pearl of Pekin* on October 23, 1889. In 1892 she was introduced to audiences in *The Mascot,* starring Henry E. Dixey, and by the mid-1890s Trixie Friganza had become a popular star performer, making her London debut in *The Belle of Bohemia* in 1901. Her first vaudeville appearance was at Hammerstein's in the summer of 1906. Sime Silverman reported in *Variety* (June 2, 1906): "In the imitations Miss Friganza did, the most pronounced and important of which was that of Marie Dressler, there is really nothing discernible showing a studied effort in preparation. . . . There is no reason why Miss Friganza, with a well laid out offering, should not become a valuable attraction in vaudeville. She has the requisites otherwise. With her present material it will be a gamble."

Among Trixie Friganza's many early stage successes were *The Girl from Paris* (1901), *Sally in Our Alley* (1902), *The Prince of Pilsen* (1904), *Twiddle Twaddle* (1906), *The Orchid* (1908), *The American Idea* (1908), and *The Passing Show of 1912,* after which she began her vaudeville career in earnest. She headlined frequently at the Palace, and was always, as *Variety* noted of her March 1920 appearance there, "a riotous hit." Trixie Friganza labelled her act "My Little Bag o' Trix."

She alternated vaudeville appearances with featured roles in musical comedies and reviews. In the early twenties she embarked on an additional career as a character actress in films, which continued through 1940 and included roles in *The Coming of Amos* (1925), *The Road to Yesterday* (1925), *Monte Carlo* (1926), *Gentlemen Prefer Blondes* (1928), *Free and Easy* (1930), *Myrt and Marge* (1934), *Wanderer of the Wasteland* (1935), and *If I Had My Way* (1940). However, "the Perpetual Flapper," as

Trixie Friganza

The Billboard dubbed her in 1931, was beginning to suffer more and more from arthritis. In 1940 she turned over her considerable fortune to the Flintridge (California)

Academy of the Sacred Heart, and (despite some opposition from convent authorities) made her home there, occupying a room from which she could watch the Rose Bowl games in Pasadena at the foot of the hill. She taught a drama class for the girls at the convent school until she became totally bedridden.

The champagne girl, as Trixie Friganza was sometimes called, died on February 27, 1955. In an interview on the occasion of her seventy-ninth birthday, Trixie told the *Los Angeles Times* of her delight in watching television. "You should hear me talk back to those actors. 'You still telling those old jokes and getting by with it?' I ask 'em. But they keep right on and pay no attention to me at all. Say, that's where vaudeville has gone—into television."

GALLAGHER AND SHEAN

Gallagher and Shean

In the annals of vaudeville, Gallagher and Shean are probably unique in being known for one song, and one song alone: "Absolutely, Mr. Gallagher? Positively, Mr. Shean." Through the years it has been the subject of endless parodies, a song for which any number of topical lyrics are available. Because Ed Gallagher and Al Shean had first appeared together in a sketch titled "Mr. Gallagher and Mr. Shean in Egypt," the song was always performed with Gallagher wearing a straw hat and Mr. Shean wearing a fez, with the Egyptian pyramids as a painted backdrop. It was first introduced by Gallagher and Shean in vaudeville in 1921 and was the hit number in the 1922 edition of *The Ziegfeld Follies.*

The origins of "Absolutely, Mr. Gallagher? Positively, Mr. Shean" are somewhat obscure. The words and music are generally credited to Gallagher and Shean, although

The Manhattan
Company Four in 1896:
Sam Curtis, Arthur
Williams, Al Shean, and
Ed C. Mack

in June of 1922 Bryan Foy filed a lawsuit claiming that he wrote the song in May of 1921, while Gallagher and Shean and Eddie Foy and the Seven Little Foys were appearing at Keith's, Indianapolis. Foy argued, " 'Mr. Gallagher and Mr. Shean' is unique in that it has done the unusual of elevating a two-man song act into one of vaudeville's greatest drawing cards and from there into the acme of production aspirations, a feature in a Ziegfeld *Follies* on the strength of that one song alone." Gallagher and Shean were quick to point out that others had used the idea of a "Mister" song before they did, particularly Major J. Orrin Donovan, who performed a "Mister Dooley" routine from 1903 on. In fact, the song obviously has its beginnings in the Minstrel Shows and their "Mister Bones" routines. Ed Gallagher revealed that the music, which is credited to him, was "doctored" by Ernest R. Ball and adapted from "old familiar strains." The truth appears to be that Eddie Foy did come up with the basic idea for the song and that Gallagher and Shean purchased the idea from him outright for an undisclosed sum of money.

Edward Gallagher was known as one of the best straight men in vaudeville and burlesque. For fifteen years he had a partnership with Joe Barrett. Gallagher and Barrett were known for a series of sketches of military travesties, the best known of which was "The Battle of Too Soon." Al Shean began his vaudeville career in 1890 with the Manhattan Comedy Four—the other three members of the act were Sam Curtis, Arthur Williams, and Ed Mack—which was noted for its knockabout comedy and harmonizing in such songs as "It Isn't What You Used to Be, It's What You are Today." When the Manhattan Comedy Four disbanded in 1900, Al Shean teamed up with Charles L. Warren in a sketch titled "Crovadus Upside Down" (a parody on the popular stage melodrama,

Quo Vadis?). Shean and Warren split up in July of 1904.

In the early 1910s, Al Shean and Ed Gallagher decided to join forces, first for the operetta *The Rose Maid,* which opened at the Globe Theatre, New York, on April 22, 1912, and ran for 176 performances. Then in 1914, for reasons unknown, the two split up and did not speak to each other for six years. Gallagher continued in vaudeville, while Shean appeared in a couple of musical shows, *The Princess Pat* (1915) and *Flo-Flo* (1917). One day Al Shean casually mentioned to his sister Minnie, mother of the Marx brothers, that "Al and I could do a great act together, only he won't talk to me." Minnie set about getting the two back together, and in April of 1920 the new Gallagher and Shean vaudeville act opened at the Fox Crotona Theatre on Long Island. They appear to have sung "Positively, Mr. Gallagher? Absolutely, Mr. Shean" for the first time on the New York stage at the Fifth Avenue Theatre in August of 1921. *Variety* (August 12, 1921) described them as "one of the strongest two-man comedy acts in vaudeville," and continued: "The dialog is all timely, and was good for a continuous roll of staccato laughs that punctuated the pauses like machine gun fire. . . . These youngsters look set for anything short of a typhoon."

Gallagher and Shean billed their act as "By, About and for Themselves," but the title was short-lived. After their hit in the 1922 *Follies,* they signed with the Shuberts, with whom they soon quarrelled. They decided not to work at all rather than tour for the Shuberts, but when Jones and Green purchased their contract Gallagher and Shean went into the 1924 edition of *The Greenwich Village Follies.* While appearing in a 1925 touring edition of that show, Gallagher and Shean had another difference of opinion. Again, history does not record the cause of the dispute. Al Shean announced he would continue with *The Greenwich*

Village Follies, while Gallagher said he would return to vaudeville with a new partner, Fifi Lussier, who had been a chorus girl in the show and who later became known as Fifi D'Orsay (see her entry).

At the height of his career, Ed Gallagher suffered a nervous breakdown, brought on by the legal dispute concerning the "Positively, Mr. Gallagher? Absolutely, Mr. Shean" song, the breakup with Al Shean, and maritial problems with his fourth wife, Ann Luther, who divorced him. In 1927 he was committed to the Rivercrest Sanitarium in Astoria, where he died on May 28, 1929, at the age of fifty-six.

Al Shean continued as a solo act on stage and later in films. Among his many screen appearances were roles in *Music in the Air* (1934), *Page Miss Glory* (1935), *San Francisco* (1936), *It Could Happen to You* (1937), *The Prisoner of Zenda* (1937), *Too Hot To Handle* (1938), *The Great Waltz* (1938), *Joe and Ethel Turp Call on the President* (1939), *The Blue Bird* (1940), *Atlantic City* (1944), and *People Are Funny* (1946). Al Shean's biggest critical success on the stage was in the title role of Brian Doherty's comedy *Father Malachy's Miracle,* which opened at New York's St. James Theatre on November 17, 1937.

In later years he would still perform "Positively, Mr. Gallagher? Absolutely, Mr. Shean," playing both himself and Ed Gallagher and changing hats and voices for each character. Al Shean died at the age of eighty-one in New York City on August 12, 1949.

LOTTIE GILSON

The big star at Tony Pastor's Fourteenth Street Theatre in the late 1800's was Lottie Gilson (described as "America's greatest seriocomic") who was billed as "The Little Magnet" because she was such a draw. Douglas Gilbert called her "one of the greatest soubrettes in show business," noted for her rendering of such tear-jerkers as "The Old Turnkey," "The Old Sexton," and "The Little Lost Child." Later, as the nineteenth century ended, she performed risqué numbers like "She's Such a Nice Girl, Too" and "The Sunshine of Paradise Alley." Lottie Gilson has two claims to fame; as the first singer to accept money to "plug" a song, and as the woman who introduced the idea of having a stooge planted in the balcony to sing and talk back to her. Lottie Gilson died in her home town of New York on July 10, 1912, at the age of forty-three.

NAT C. GOODWIN

One of the most popular actors of his day (the 1870s through the late 1910s) who, according to contemporary critics, was at his best in comedy roles. Nat C. Goodwin began his career in vaudeville and made three later forays into vaudeville in 1909, 1911, and 1916. He was born on July 25, 1857, in Boston and made his first stage appearance in that city, at Howard's Athenaeum in 1874. Goodwin's New York debut, and his first major success, was at Tony Pastor's Broadway Theatre in December of 1875 in a vaudeville sketch titled "Ned Stryker," with the billing of "actor, author, and mimic."

Nat C. Goodwin

On the legitimate stage, Nat C. Goodwin played almost everything, from *An American Citizen* (first performed in 1897) and *The Cowboy and The Lady* (1899) to *Nathan Hale* (1899) and *Cameo Kirby* (1908). He starred with one of his wives, Maxine Elliott, in *When We Were Twenty-One* in 1900, but his best-known role was that of Fagin in a 1912 stage adaptation of Charles Dickens's *Oliver Twist,* which also featured Marie Doro and Constance Collier. Reviewing his career in 1919, the *New York Dramatic Mirror* commented, "The range of his parts ran the entire gamut of dramatic construction. His greatest ambition was to play Shakespeare and he made productions of *The Merchant of Venice* and *A Midsummer Night's Dream,* but Shylock and Bottom did not bring him the fame he received in modern roles."

In the fall of 1916 Nat C. Goodwin was a headliner at the Palace, billed as a monologist; he told stories to the audience with a gentle and quiet humor. *Variety* (October 6, 1916) thought that as a vaudevillian he was "a glittering entertainer." Critics at Goodwin's theatrical performances were sometimes harsher.

Nat C. Goodwin died in New York on January 31, 1919, after leaving the touring company of *Why Marry?* prematurely in Philadelphia.

CHARLOTTE GREENWOOD

Tall, long-legged, and awkwardly graceful, Charlotte Greenwood is remembered mainly as a character actress in films such as *Palmy Days* (1931), *Down Argentine Way*

Charlotte Greenwood

(1940), *The Gang's All Here* (1943), and, of course, *Oklahoma!* (1955). (The role of Aunt Eller was written with her in mind by Rodgers and Hammerstein, but she never got to play it in the original Broadway production of the musical.) However, it was as a vaudeville performer that Charlotte Greenwood first came to prominence, with an act entitled "Two Girls and a Piano."

The two girls in question were Miss Greenwood and Eunice Burnham. They toured America together between 1909 and 1912, delighting vaudeville audiences everywhere and earning salaries as low as twenty-five dollars a week. The svelte Miss Greenwood was an excellent foil for the plump Miss Burnham; while the latter performed at the piano, Charlotte Greenwood did comic dances and sang about her "girlish laughter":

I may not be so pretty,
And I don't dress like a queen.
I may not be so witty;
I am over sweet sixteen.
My face is not my fortune
(It looks like the morning after),
But I still maintain
That I retain
(Bing! Bing!)
My girlish laughter!

"Miss Greenwood is the tall, awkward girl whose limbs seemed to take involuntary excursions to all portions of the stage, and who is described as being loose jointed as the latest toy from the toy factory," wrote one critic.

Another, somewhat unkindly and unfairly, wrote, "Her face is nearly as ugly as that of Polaire [see her entry]" Alan Dale, in 1913, summed up the secret of Charlotte Greenwood's success through the years: "Miss Greenwood is undiluted joy. She is funny all over. Her face is a comic mirror for every laugh."

Charlotte Greenwood was born in Philadelphia on June 25, 1893, and made her first stage appearance at the New Amsterdam Theatre in New York on November 2, 1905, in the chorus of *The White Cat.* As Lottie Greenwood, she received her first featured role—albeit very minor—as Lola in *The Rogers Brothers in Panama,* which played the Casino in 1908. After her years of touring with Eunice Burnham (years during which she was more and more frequently billed over her partner), the performer was invited to appear in *The Passing Show of 1912,* which featured Willie and Eugene Howard and Trixie Friganza. *The Passing Show of 1913, The Tik-Tok Man of Oz,* and *Town Topics* followed before Charlotte Greenwood gained her most famous stage role in 1915, that of Letty in *So Long Letty* (in which she costarred with Walter Catlett). This was followed by a series of "Letty" shows: *Linger Longer Letty* (1919), *Let 'er Go Letty* (1921), *Letty Pepper* (1922), and *Leaning on Letty* (1935). Actually, Letitia Proudfoot was first introduced in *Pretty Mrs. Smith* (1914), but it was not until *So Long Letty* and the Earl Carroll tune of the same name that Charlotte Greenwood became permanently identified with the character.

Throughout the twenties and thirties, Charlotte Greenwood was very much in demand for musicals and revues, including *The Music Box Revue* (1922), *Hazzard Short's Ritz Revue* (1924), with songs by Martin Brooner whom Greenwood married on December 22, 1924, and Rufus LeMaire's *Affairs* (1927). In 1930 Miss Greenwood appeared in her first nonmusical comedy, *Mebbe,* and in 1932 she made her London debut in *Wild Violets* at the Theatre Royal, Drury Lane. Between stage appearances, she worked as a solo turn in vaudeville in the twenties, embarked on a lengthy film career—which had actually begun in 1915 with *Jane*—and made many radio broadcasts. Her stage career continued through the fifties, and from 1947 through 1949 Charlotte Greenwood toured as Mama in *I Remember Mama.*

After an absence of twenty-three years, she made a triumphant return to the Broadway stage as Juno in Cole Porter's *Out of This World,* which opened at the Century Theatre in December of 1950. As an ardent Christian Scientist, Miss Greenwood objected strenuously to the risqué lyrics of the show. Charlotte Greenwood made her last screen appearance in 1956, in *The Opposite Sex,* and died in her Beverly Hills home on January 18, 1978.

When Charlotte Greenwood appeared with Eunice Burnham at Hammerstein's Victoria Theatre the week of September 26, 1909, she was billed as "The Laughing Hit of the Season." It was a description that could have been applied to her for the next forty years.

Reference: "The Secret of the Greenwood Kick" by Ralph E. Renaud in the *San Francisco Chronicle,* Vol. 100, No. 41 (February 25, 1912), page 21.

TEXAS GUINAN

Texas Guinan

If one person symbolizes the prohibition era in American history, that person is Texas Guinan, whose nightclubs were the only places to be if one wanted to enjoy life in New York City in the late twenties. Americans were willing to spend money as if there were no tomorrows, and Texas Guinan, with her famous cry of "Hello, Sucker!," was there to take it. However, many forget that Texas Guinan first came to fame in vaudeville, and it was in vaudeville that she ended her all-too-brief life.

Born Mary Louise Cecilia Guinan, Texas, as the name suggests, began her show business career as a rodeo driver. In fact, as a sort of female William S. Hart, she starred in a number of films in the late 1910s. In his 1927 book *Behind the Curtains of the Broadway Beauty Trust,* Will A. Page wrote, "When I first met her she was the prima donna of a touring musical comedy company in Little Rock, Arkansas. The manager of the company, the late John Slocum, told me that some day she would be a big star on Broadway. He was right. She is; not in musical comedy but in the night clubs." In May of 1909 Texas Guinan was performing sixteen minutes of song at the Fifth Avenue Theatre, where *Variety* (May 29, 1909) saw her and commented, "Miss Guinan has looks, and dresses well. Her well-trained soprano does the rest."

Within a year she had become a popular singer of popular songs in vaudeville, and it is claimed she was the first songstress to deliver her numbers from a swing suspended over the stage. Texas Guinan was featured in *The Passing Show of 1913,* and in 1916 she was touring in vaudeville

with musical comedy star Billy Gibson, performing a comedy sketch and singing songs like "Do What Your Mother Did, I'll Do the Same as Your Dad." Besides "Hello, Sucker!," Texas Guinan's other famous catch phrase was "Give the little girl a big hand." This she probably learned from vaudevillian Jack Osterman (the author of *We're Glad We've Got You, Mr. Wilson*), who died in 1937.

In the twenties the first New York night spot with which Texas Guinan was associated was the El Fay Club, backed by former taxi operator Larry Fay. The El Fay was followed by the Club Moritz and the Three Hundred Club. As Page wrote, "In a few weeks Texas had them standing in line, because she inaugurated the novel idea of the personal hostess sitting down at the table and even bringing over her little cuties to be introduced to the rich patrons of the place. But though she introduced the girls to the patrons, she had one invariable rule; the girls always had to leave her place alone and were never allowed to go on to 'parties' under penalty of losing their engagements."

In each of her clubs, Texas acted as hostess and mistress of ceremonies for the entertainment, which was often produced by Nils T. Granlund. She was also a born press agent, constantly inventing stories and promoting herself. She had Harry K. Thaw engaged to one of her dancers at one point, and even had a reconciliation between him and Evelyn Nesbit to be announced at one of her clubs.

When her clubs were shuttered by prohibition law enforcement officers, Texas Guinan put together a forty-one-minute vaudeville routine, Texas Guinan and Her Mob, which opened at the Hippodrome in May of 1925. The act featured a jazz sextet, a group of singers billed as the Texas Strollers, and, of course, her famous showgirls, including Ruby Keeler and Peggy Shannon, both of whom were to make names for themselves in the film industry. At this stage of her vaudeville career, Texas Guinan did nothing except introduce the members of her company, the female members of which she described as "glorious girls who don't need glorifying," an obvious dig at Florenz Ziegfeld. The entire company joined in the song "Oh, Mr. Buckner," an unflattering tribute to the U.S. Attorney General responsible for carrying out the edicts of the Volstead Act.

Texas Guinan was eventually arrested in February of 1927 for violation of the prohibition laws at her Three Hundred Club at 151 West 54th Street. She protested she was merely the club's hostess, helping everyone have a good time, and apparently the jury agreed with her for she was acquitted. After her brush with the law, Guinan appeared on Broadway in what has been described as an awful Shubert revue, *Padlocks of 1927.* (At least the title sounds funny!) With the end of prohibition, Texas Guinan returned to vaudeville, touring with her own company in a show titled *Too Hot for Paris.* While playing the Beacon Theatre, Vancouver, and, incidentally, establishing a new house record for attendance, she collapsed backstage after the fourth show on Saturday, November 4, 1933. She died the following morning.

The last word on Texas Guinan should be left to Will A. Page, who described her as "a breezy blonde and entertaining hostess; a good fellow, with a smile and a joke for everyone and a glad handshake. She made everyone feel at home whether they had ever met her or not."

References: *Behind the Curtains of Broadway's Beauty Trust* by Will A. Page, (The Edward A. Miller Publishing Company, 1927), pages 182–186. "Texas Guinan, Queen of Whoopee!" by James Doherty in *Chicago Sunday Tribune* (March 4, 1951), pages 4–6. "Texas Guinan Helped Make B'way History During the Volstead Era" by Abel Green in *Variety,* Vol. 201, No. 5 (January 4, 1956), page 423.

JANETTE HACKETT

Janette Hackett

Janette (sometimes billed as Jeanette) Hackett came from a well-known theatrical family, her brothers being Raymond and Albert Hackett and her mother Florence Hackett. (Raymond Hackett's wife, silent screen actress Blanche Sweet, also played vaudeville briefly with an act titled "Sweet and Lovely.") Janette had always been interested in dancing and after stints in the chorus of *The Passing Show* and as a solo dancer in a night club, she replaced Billie Shaw in the vaudeville act of Seabury and Shaw in the late 1910s.

When Seabury and Shaw decided to retire, they gave their act to Janette Hackett. She teamed up with Harry Delmar—whom she was later to marry—and formed Hackett and Delmar. The act made its New York debut at the 125th Street Theatre in March of 1919, and based on contemporary reviews it is surprising that the couple went any further. *Variety* (March 7, 1919) noted that

Delmar could neither sing nor dance and seemed lost in handling jazz and eccentric dances. The newspaper concluded, "The act is splendidly set, nicely costumed and splendidly routined. The girl looks big time."

Hackett and Delmar persevered and each year produced a new dance revue for vaudeville, which was unquestionably the creative work of Janette Hackett. The twenty minute act would feature chorus girls, a variety of dance routines, including an acrobatic number by Delmar, and Miss Hackett in a scanty costume. ("Most all of Miss Hackett's frocks are designed to show a good deal of bare skin," reported *Variety.*) Reviewing the fourth Hackett and Delmar Dance Revue, titled "Dance Madness," *Variety* (September 6, 1923) wrote, "It is . . . one that cannot fail to carry them far along the brightest lanes in vaudeville."

In the late twenties Hackett and Delmar split, both on and off stage, and Janette Hackett went solo with a fifteen-minute act featuring dramatic dance numbers in which she was supported by three male dancers, Jose Shalitta, Dan Hurwyn, and Wally Davis. *Variety*'s Abel Green saw Janette at the Eighty-first Street Theatre in February of 1929 and, after comparing her looks to Garbo's, reported, "She can take this act into anybody's playhouse and click." The climax of the act had Janette Hackett tear off her partner's mask and discover he was Death. Whereupon she would rush to the top of a flight of stairs, pull down a drape, and topple down the stairs, dragging the drape behind her while Death looked on triumphantly. In its dramatic choreography, it has the same shock effect as Busby Berkeley's "Lullaby of Broadway" routine from *Gold Diggers of 1935.*

In 1930 Janette Hackett married John Steel (who had introduced "A Pretty Girl Is Like a Melody" in the 1919 edition of *The Ziegfeld Follies* and was also a regular on the vaudeville stage). She continued to work as a dancer and choreographer; among her dancing partners were Cesar Romero and Ivan Triesault. She died in New York, at the age of eighty-one, on August 16, 1979.

Reference: "Janette Hackett" in *The Vaudevillians* by Bill Smith (Macmillan, 1976), pages 182–187.

JACK HALEY

Never was the continual crossover between vaudeville, musical comedy, and revue more apparent than in the case of Jack Haley. An actor-singer and comedian who began his career in vaudeville, he was to rise to fame in musical comedies and revues such as *Gay Paree* (1925), *Follow Thru* (1929), *Free for All* (1931), and *Take a Chance* (1932). His trademark of popping his eyes and gazing around in simple wonder as if to ask "what's funny?" later became as famous in films as it had become on the stage.

Jack Haley was born in Boston on August 10, 1899. He was encouraged by his parents to be an electrician, but as soon as he had sufficient funds he ran away to Philadelphia to enter vaudeville. Instead of headlining in vaudeville, Haley became a song plugger at twenty-five dollars a week for McCarty-Fischer Music Publishing Company. "Every job was temporary until I got the one I wanted," he once said, and the one he wanted was as a vaudevillian. Finally Haley did get into vaudeville in partnership with another young man, Charlie Crafts. Haley has compared Crafts and Haley to Dean Martin and Jerry Lewis, and, certainly there is a vague resemblance in style between Lewis and Jack Haley. In the mid-twenties Haley formed a partnership with William Rock's widow, Helen Eby Rock, who played a dumb straight woman to his comedy. The two appeared at the Palace in April of 1925, opening the second half of the show, and *Variety* (April 15, 1925) wrote, "The gags and laugh material are ideally bunched to make for spontaneous comedy throughout and is spaced by songs which also help nicely." While in vaudeville, Haley met his wife of fifty-two years, Flo McFadden.

Jack Haley came to films in 1930 with *Follow Thru,* singing with Zelma O'Neal the song that he had made famous in the stage production "Button Up Your Overcoat." Other films followed, including *Sitting Pretty* (1933), *Poor Little Rich Girl* (1936), *Alexander's Ragtime Band* (1938), *Moon over Miami* (1941), and *George White's Scandals* (1945). And, of course, Haley gained screen immortality as the Tin Woodsman in the 1939 film version of *The Wizard of Oz.* Haley's last great stage success was as Zachary Ash in the 1940 production of *Higher and Higher,* a role which he recreated in the 1943 film version. In 1972 the actor came out of retirement to appear in *Norwood,* a film directed by his son, Jack Haley, Jr. In addition to film work, Haley was also featured frequently on the radio in the thirties and had his own show from 1937 through 1939.

In the forties, Jack Haley announced his retirement from show business and devoted himself to his real estate interests. He explained, "Fortunately I never had to perform; I was not one of those extroverts who needed to have an audience. I found I could get just as much enjoyment from a real estate deal. I also found that you couldn't take your reviews to the grocery store."

By a happy coincidence, Jack Haley made his last public appearance in company with Ray Bolger (his costar in *The Wizard of Oz*) at the April 9, 1979, Academy Awards Presentation, produced by his son. He died in Los Angeles on June 6, 1979. Penny Singleton, who had worked with Haley in the touring versions of *Good News* and *Follow Thru* and who, like Haley, was a past president of the American Guild of Variety Artists (AGVA), paid tribute to the likeable comedian: "I learned so much from Jack Haley, about acting, about presence, and about getting laughs."

Reference: "Jack Haley" in *The Vaudevillians* by Bill Smith (Macmillan, 1976), pages 129–134.

ADELAIDE HALL

Adelaide Hall was far more than a great black jazz singer; she is best described as a diva, a songstress with a voice both operatic and modernistic, as exemplified by her 1927 recording of "Creole Love Call" with Duke Ellington. She is best remembered in America for featured roles in

Shuffle Along (1921), *Runnin' Wild* (1923), and *Black-birds of 1928*, but Adelaide Hall also had a brief career as a vaudeville headliner in the early thirties.

Brooklyn-born Adelaide Hall made her Broadway debut in 1921 in the Miller and Lyles musical *Shuffle Along.* She was the star, along with Bill Robinson, of Lew Leslie's *Blackbirds of 1928*, which opened at the Liberty Theatre on May 9, 1928, but ran for a mere forty-three performances. In this show she introduced "Digga Digga Do" and "I Can't Give You Anything but Love Baby." From *Blackbirds of 1928* Adelaide Hall went into vaudeville, although Lew Leslie refused to allow her to sing any of the songs that she had performed in *Blackbirds.* She made her vaudeville debut in February of 1930 at the Palace with an act titled "Singing Songs—and How," conceived by Cecil Mack and with Messrs. Dandridge and Tate at two pianos. On a bill which also included Fannie Brice and Phil Baker, she made a considerable impact (of course, she was helped at the Monday matinée by having Bill Robinson join her on-stage.) *Variety* (February 12, 1930) hailed her as "a bet for vaudeville," noting that "the colored singer and dancer had poise, appearance, and ability." Adelaide Hall successfully toured as a vaudeville headliner; seeing her at the E. F. Albee Theatre in Cincinnati, *The Billboard* (March 7, 1931) reported, "She has heaps of personality, a fair enough repertoire of song numbers, and sells it all with a bang." She is delightful in a 1935 film short singing "To Love You Again."

(*Variety*, in its issue of September 22, 1916, carried a report on a young dancer named Adelaide Hall, whose "good looks and youth help her other accomplishments." She was appearing at Rector's, but his does not appear to have been the same Adelaide Hall.)

In 1938 Adelaide Hall settled permanently in England where she has had her own clubs, the Floridan and the Calypso. In addition, she appeared in a couple of films, notably the 1940 version of *The Thief of Bagdad*, and a number of musical shows. In May of 1980 Adelaide Hall returned to the New York stage in *Black Broadway*, a splendid re-creation of the great black revues of the twenties which also featured Elizabeth Welch (who had been with Hall in *Blackbirds of 1928*), John Bubbles, and Edith Wilson. She had put on a few pounds since the twenties, but there was little doubt that Adelaide Hall was still a great singer and a great entertainer.

NAN HALPERIN

Nan Halperin was a singing comedienne who became known as America's Famous Satirist. What she satirized was never politics or religion or those genres so popular with satirists today, but rather the behavior and life styles of ordinary Americans. In a typical Nan Halperin vaudeville routine—from 1918—she presented the epochal periods in a girl's life. She appeared first in pigtails and a calico dress, bemoaning the arrival of a new baby in the household and her sudden drop from her special place as youngest in the family. She was next seen as a young woman attending her first ball and asking, "Why must I have so many clothes to capture just one man?" On her

Nan Halperin in 1922

wedding eve, Nan Halperin was busily disposing of the photographs and letters that reminded her of other romances. Finally, she appeared as a military bride, awaiting the return of her aviator husband from war triumphs.

Aside from vaudeville, Nan Halperin is best known for her appearance, along with Miriam Hopkins, in the musical farce *Little Jessie James*, which opened at the Longacre Theatre on August 15, 1923. She died at her Long Island home on May 30, 1963, at the reported age of sixty-five. Two brothers were also active in vaudeville: Hal as manager of the Chicago office of *Variety* and Max as a vaudeville agent in the same city.

POODLES HANNEFORD

Edwin "Poodles" Hanneford was one of the circus's great clowns and bareback riders who appeared occasionally in vaudeville (usually whenever the stage was large enough to accommodate his act). His favorite vaudeville venue was the Hippodrome, to which he returned many times in company with his wife, Grace, who acted as ring mistress. From all accounts, Hanneford's act was quite spectacularly—and dangerously—funny. He would pretend to fall off the horse's back, ending up on the ground directly beneath the animal; he would then proceed to climb back on the horse through its back legs, prying them apart with his head. The Hippodrome was the site of *Billy Rose's Jumbo*, which opened on November 16, 1935, and ran for 233 performances with Poodles Hanneford as one of the principals.

Hanneford was born into a famous British circus family

in Barnsley, in the north of England. He learned to ride at the age of five, blindfolded by his father to teach him reliance on the horse's instinct rather than his sight. In 1915 Hanneford emigrated to the United States, where he was to remain active through the sixties, appearing on television, on "The Ed Sullivan Show," and at the Hollywood Palace. For more years than most people can remember, he was a beloved member of the Ringling Brothers and Barnum and Bailey circuses. Poodles Hanneford died at the reported age of seventy-five at Kattskill Bay, New York, on December 9, 1967.

Poodles Hanneford

Despite his comic attire and his clowning, such as having his suspenders loose and flap in his face, resulting in his trousers falling down, there was never any question about Hanneford's brilliant trick riding. As Sime Silverman wrote in *Variety* in 1924, Poodles Hanneford was "an act for vaudeville, just built for the Hip."

PAUL AND GRACE HARTMAN

The greatest comedy dance team in vaudeville was that of Paul and Grace Hartman, who described themselves as "satirists of the dance" and combined a mixture of pantomine and first-class ballroom dancing. Unlike other dancers, they made facial expression equally important in their act, for as Paul Hartman once explained; "Many people think that to mug all you have to do is make faces, cross your eyes, wiggle your ears, or do something equally obvious and ridiculous. But mugging is a gentle art. The version which pays off for us is just a thought or an idea projected from the mugger to the audience with only a slightly exaggerated expression. If this exaggeration is

Paul and Grace Hartman

minutely overdone, the expression becomes a grimace. There is nothing grimmer in show business than a grimace."

Paul Hartman was the son of actress Josie Hart and producer-director-actor Ferris Hartman, a theatrical entrepreneur of the old school who was known as "The Ziegfeld of the West." He allowed his son to make his first stage appearance at the age of six weeks at the Tivoli Opera House in San Francisco. Paul and Grace Hartman were married when she was fifteen and he was seventeen. At that time they were billed as Hartman and Barrett, touring throughout the West Coast—"We were never able to get east of the Rockies, " explained Paul Hartman— and embarking on an extended tour of the Middle East and Asia before becoming national vaudeville favorites in the late twenties. Broadway audiences got to know the Hartmans in *Red, Hot and Blue*, the Cole Porter musical which opened at the Alvin Theatre on October 29, 1936, and which also featured Jimmy Durante, Ethel Merman, Vivian Vance, and Bob Hope. Their style of dancing was farcical but at the same time it was meticulously conceived and executed.

The Hartmans made their film debut in *Forty-Five Fathers* in 1937 and were also featured in *Sunny* (1941) and *Higher and Higher* (1943). They were also to be seen on NBC television in 1949 in the early situation comedy series "The Hartmans at Home." Presumably some of the trials and tribulations they suffered in this program as a suburban New York couple spilled over into their private lives, for Paul and Grace were divorced in 1951 after twenty-eight years of marriage. Grace Hartman remarried and retired. She died in Van Nuys, California, on August 8, 1955.

Paul Hartman continued to work in such films as *Inherit the Wind* (1960), *Soldier in the Rain* (1963), *Inside Daisy Clover* (1965), *Luv* (1967), and *How to Succeed in Business Without Really Trying* (1967). He was also seen in a continuing role as Emmett Clark on CBS television's "Mayberry RFD" from 1968 through 1971. Paul Hartman died in Los Angeles, on October 2, 1973, at the age of sixty-nine.

Reference: "The Hartman Mugs" by Robert Copeland in *Liberty* (June 15, 1946), pages 20–21 and 73–74.

TED HEALY

Ted Healy presents an interesting case of a vaudeville comic who entered films with his supporting company and saw those players rise to stardom while his fame slipped away. He was born in Houston, Texas, on October 1, 1896, and first succeeded in show business as a blackface comic in burlesque. In the summer of 1922, he broke into big-time vaudeville with his wife, Betty, telling jokes and singing a couple of songs in the style of Al Jolson and Eddie Cantor. Reviewing his act at Shea's, Buffalo, *Variety* (September 1, 1922) commented, "He shows himself possessed of a nimble wit and carries himself with the confidence and poise of a veteran."

A year or so later, Ted Healy invited two brothers who were childhood friends of his, Moe and Shemp Howard, to join the act as his stooges. In 1925 Larry Fine, from the vaudeville act of the Haney Sisters and Fine, was also invited to join Healy. The act became known as Ted Healy and His Racketeers, and later as Ted Healy and His Stooges. The group's knockabout humor came to the at-

Ted Healy

tention of the William Fox Company, and in 1930 they were starred in the feature film *Soup to Nuts*. "Not only is Healy, a comedian whom the New York Palace pays $6,000 a week for headlining in that ace vaude house, made a straight man, but he is turned into a flip romantic juvenile with a girl as unfunny as he is here hanging onto his neck all the while," complained Sime Silverman in *Variety* (October 29, 1930). Interestingly, Healy received the billing and the critical attention while his stooges were ignored.

Shemp Howard left the act shortly thereafter and was replaced by Jerry "Curly" Howard when the group was signed up by M-G-M for cameo roles in a number of features. In 1934 Jules White invited the three stooges to come to Columbia and star in a series of comedies he was producing. It was widely rumored that Ted Healy thought it beneath him to leave a prestigious studio like M-G-M for the Poverty Row Columbia outfit. The rest, of course, is history, for The Three Stooges became one of the most famous comedy acts to appear in film shorts. "Curly" Howard died in 1952; Shemp died in 1955; Larry Fine and Moe Howard died in 1975.

There were reports that Ted Healy had suffered internal injuries in one of his knockabout routines, and that these injuries brought about his death on December 21, 1937.

Ken Murray remembers Ted Healy as his favorite comedian and as his idol. he recalls:

He was a master of throwing things away. I remember one time he was playing the Keith's in Philadelphia, and he followed Vincent Lopez and His

Orchestra. Vincent Lopez had about a fifty-piece orchestra on stage, and they used rear projection even in those days. The finish of his act, the lights would dim down and, using the screen, it was as if you were on an airplane coming down the Hudson and circling the Statue of Liberty. The music is playing "The Stars and Stripes" and it was thrilling. A big finish with tremendous applause. Next act, Ted Healy, and he walks out, as he used to, in corduroy pants, old jacket, and the oddest kinda tie. He walks out on stage and says, "Wasn't that a great act with those fellows sitting there in their tuxedos? Look at me, I look like a bum, but what the hell, it's only a week." He was the throwaway master of them all. He was a great comedian.

ANNA HELD

Thanks to Luise Rainer's portrayal of her in *The Great Ziegfeld* (1936), an image was created of Anna Held as a slight, ethereal vision of dark loveliness. In reality, Miss Held was slightly buxom except for an eighteen-inch waist (which had expanded considerably by the mid 1910s). She was not beautiful in the modern sense; her face was plump and fringed with abundant red-brown hair. Her brown eyes, large and expressive, were her most striking feature. It is no wonder that her theme song was "I Just Can't Make My Eyes Behave" (written by Will D. Cobb and Gus Edwards), with its famous chorus:

> For I just can't make my eyes behave
> Two bad brown eyes I am their slave,
> My lips may say run away from me
> But my eyes say come and play with me.
> And you won't blame poor little me, I'm sure,
> Cuz I just can't make my eyes behave.

There is little question that much of Anna Held's success was thanks to the energetic efforts of her husband, Florenz Ziegfeld, who produced many of the shows in which she starred. He also handled her publicity, circulating the famous story of Anna Held's milk baths and setting her up in an apartment at New York's Ansonia Hotel, "heavy with the scent of one thousand American beauty roses." Held first aroused Ziegfeld's interest when he saw her on stage at London's Palace Theatre in 1895, with an act which featured a saucy number sung in halting English, "Won't You Come and Play Wiz Me?" That was precisely what Ziegfeld had in mind. He brought her to New York where she made her debut at the Herald Square Theatre on September 21, 1896, in *A Parlor Match*, again singing "Won't You Come and Play Wiz Me?"

A year later Anna Held and Ziegfeld were married, and the producer starred her in *Papa's Wife, The Little Duchess, Mlle. Napoleon,* and *The Parisien Model.* The last opened at the Broadway Theatre on November 26, 1906, and introduced "I Just Can't Make My Eyes Behave." Ziegfeld also arranged for his wife to appear successfully on the stage of Koster and Bial's Music Hall for several seasons in the late 1890s. Anna Held is often credited with

Anna Held

giving Ziegfeld the idea for his *Follies*, with their emphasis on beautiful girls, but Ziegfeld featured his wife in only one of his *Follies* revues, the 1910 edition, and then she was seen only as a film interlude. In fact, by that time relations were severely strained between the two. In 1908 Ziegfeld had forced his wife to submit to an abortion rather than allow her pregnancy to delay the opening of *Miss Innocence*, and there were also reports that Miss Held was becoming more and more agitated by her husband's extra marital activities. Finally they were divorced in 1912.

Anna Held had begun life in Paris on March 18, 1873, the daughter of a Polish mother and a French glovemaker. When Anna was nine her father opened a restaurant where she sang to entertain the customers. After his death Anna and her mother went to England and Anna Held made her show business debut in the chorus at the Princess Theatre. After minor engagements in Holland and Germany, she returned to France a successful chanteuse.

In November of 1910 she returned to London's Palace Theatre at a salary of $2,500 a week, proving that even without Ziegfeld's aid she was a star. When she had first played the Palace fifteen years earlier, Anna Held had been helped in her act by W. E. Ritchie, an American "tramp" bicyclist who added humor to her numbers by riding around the stage, but now she did not need anyone to sell her to an audience. In the spring of 1912, the star toured vaudeville in a skit, again drawing $2,500 a week. A year later she was starring in *Mlle. Baby,* singing "Roll Those Eyes," "Je Suis Grise," and "Buzzing Time in Beetown."

After a successful European tour, Anna Held returned to American vaudeville and the Palace in October of 1915. Jolo in *Variety* (October 29, 1915) reported, "She is still utilizing her talents in projecting rolling eyes, rhapsodic warbling, and exaggerated Frenchy hip-strolling back and forth. After three brief numbers and the passing of flowers across the footlights, Miss Held obliged with one verse of 'I Just Can't Make My Eyes Behave.' It was all very well received."

Anna Held starred in one feature-length film, *Madame La President,* produced by the Oliver Morosco Company in 1916 and based on the play *Madam President* which had starred Fannie Ward when it opened at the Garrick Theatre on September 15, 1913. As Mlle. Gobette, Anna Held seemed very much at home in this French farce of mistaken identities. Despite advancing plumpness and a face which was showing signs of Gallic homeliness, she was totally the star. Her large, expressive eyes made Anna Held totally suited to silent films, and it is unfortunate that she was not allowed to appear in more of them; before *Madame La Presidente* she was featured in a 1913 Kinemacolor short.

As her contribution to the war effort, Anna Held, in the summer of 1917, created but did not star in "Anna Held's Visions— Military Tableaux," a vaudeville sketch glorifying the gallant French, British, and American allies, for which *Variety* did not care. Miss Held died, relatively young, on August 13, 1918. Her daughter had appeared in vaudeville while Anna Held was still alive under the name of Liane Carrera; after her mother's death she billed herself as Anna Held, Jr.

VIOLET AND DAISY HILTON

Violet and Daisy Hilton were Siamese twins joined at the base of the spine. They started as a freak act exhibited in circuses and fairgrounds in both Europe and America and developed into serviceable vaudeville performers. The twins relied on talent rather than sympathy from their audience. Some sources indicate that they were born in England but it seems more than likely they were from San Antonio, Texas. Vaudeville manager Terry Turner realized they had more potential than mere sideshow attractions and brought the Hiltons into vaudeville, in which they made their debut at Loew's State, Newark, in February of 1925.

In vaudeville, the twins played the clarinet and saxophone and gave a reasonable impersonation of the Duncan Sisters. To close the act, two youths appeared on stage and danced with them. They were an immediate hit, with long lines waiting outside the theatre. *Variety* (February 25, 1925) reported, "The girls are pretty brunettes, tastefully dressed. Their motivation is as natural and easy as two people strolling arm in arm. One sister walks backward then the other walks forward. . . . It could be played in any vaudeville theatre in the country regardless of the clientele and will duplicate its pulling power in any spot on any bill in America. . . . The act contains nothing repellant or gruesome."

Billed as "The 8th Wonder of the World," Violet and Daisy Hilton tried to live normal lives despite their physical handicap. They reported that when one had a date, the other would sleep or read. There were problems in getting permission to marry, but in 1936 Violet married dancer James Moore; the marriage was later annulled. Then Daisy married vaudevillian Buddy Sawyer. In 1951 the girls were starred in a very low-budget feature film, *Chained for Life,* which purported to be loosely based on the Hilton's own life story. The high spot of the film was a dream sequence in which each picture life without the other, accomplished by one sister bending down to be hidden by a strategically placed bush. (In 1932 the sisters had been one of the acts featured in M-G-M's production of *Freaks.*)

After retiring from show business, Violet and Daisy Hilton managed a fruit stand in Florida, later working at a supermarket in Charlotte, North Carolina. There they died on January 4, 1969, at the reported age of sixty, of complications brought on by the Hong Kong flu. The only other Siamese twins to have any major success in vaudeville were the Gibb Twins, who made their debut in 1927 and were also managed by Terry Turner.

RAYMOND HITCHCOCK

Raymond Hitchcock's vaudeville career was less notable than his successes on the musical comedy and revue stage, as both singer and comedian, but nonetheless he should not be overlooked in the vaudeville field. He was born on October 22, 1871, in Auburn, New York, and after some success in amateur theatricals he was engaged by a road show company in 1890. However, audiences and manage-ment found Hitchcock unsatisfactory, and he ended the tour in Philadelphia where he spent a year as a shoe salesman at Wanamaker's Department Store. Eventually Hitchcock returned to the stage, singing in the chorus of *The Brigand* at sixteen dollars a week. When the show's star, Charles A. Bigelow, fell ill in Montreal, Hitchcock was given the opportunity to take over the leading role. Other engagements followed in such productions as *The Golden Wedding* (1893), *Charley's Aunt* (1894), *The Night Clerk* (1895), *Paul Jones* (1898), *A Dangerous Maid* (1899), *The Belle of Bridgeport* (1900), and *Vienna Life* (1901). He became a star under the management of Henry W. Savage in *King Dodo,* which opened in Chicago in 1902 and subsequently transferred to the Daly Theatre in New York.

The star's greatest success in the early years of this century was in *The Yankee Consul,* a comic opera by Henry M. Blossom, Jr. and Alfred G. Robyn. It opened at the Tremont Theatre, Boston, on September 21, 1903, and subsequently transferred to the Broadway Theatre, New York, on February 27, 1904. Many "hit" shows followed, including *Easy Dawson* (1904), *The Man Who Owns Broadway* (1909), *The Red Widow* (1911), *The Beauty Shop* (1913), and *Betty* (1916). In 1916 Raymond Hitchcock also made his English debut, in *Mr. Manhattan.*

Hitchy, as he was affectionately known, had his greatest triumph with *Hitchy-Koo,* which he both produced and starred in, and which opened at the Cohan and Harris Theatre, New York, in June of 1917. It was little short of a glorified vaudeville show, featuring Frances White and William Rock, Grace La Rue, Irene Bordoni, and Leon Errol. It contained comedy sketches, including a satire on Billy Sunday, and songs by the three female stars of the show. Hitchcock acted as a master of ceremonies, sometimes introducing the acts from the stage and sometimes from the front row of the orchestra seats; he even took time out to greet his friends in the audience personally. The comedian had a George M. Cohan song in the show, "Since I Became a Manager," in which he promised never again to criticize his manager. As Sime Silverman wrote in *Variety* (June 15, 1917), "It's not the kind of show you expect but it's the kind you like." Not unexpectedly, *Hitchy-Koo* was followed by a number of sequels, *Hitchy-Koo 1918, Hitchy-Koo 1919,* and *Hitchy-Koo 1920.*

Raymond Hitchcock continued to star in musicals and revues throughout the twenties, including *The Ziegfeld Follies* (1921), *Raymond Hitchcock's Pinwheel* (1922), *The Old Soak* (1923), *The Caliph* (1924), *The Ritz Revue* (1924), and *Just Fancy* (1927). He also appeared in a number of films through the years, including *My Valet* (1915, produced by Mack Sennett and his most famous screen appearance), *The Beauty Shop* (1922), *Broadway After Dark* (1924), *Redheads Preferred* (1926), and *The Money Talks* (1927). He was not always entirely successful. *Variety* (December 15, 1922) reviewed him at the Palace and commented, "Hitchy is a natural comedian and a natural monologist, but like others he is likely to be dull at times."

While appearing in *Your Uncle Dudley* in Chicago in

May of 1929, Raymond Hitchcock suffered a heart attack. He died in his Beverly Hills, California home on November 24, 1929. At his side was his wife, Flor Zabelle, who had appeared with Hitchcock in many of his shows from *The Yankee Consul* onward.

LOU HOLTZ

Lou Holtz

Probably the best way to describe Lou Holtz is as the Myron Cohen of his day. He could tell a good Jewish joke like no one else, and he was known for his singing of jokes to songs, such as "O Sole Mio," with which he ended his act. A typical verse was:

A fat lady tried to get on a streetcar.
She didn't know whether to get in front or behind.
The conductor said, "Which end will you get in, madam?"
She said, "I'll get them both in at the same time if you don't mind."
O sole mio. . . .

In some ways, Lou Holtz represented the stereotype Jew. When he was in someone else's office and saw a telephone he would ask, "Who can I call long distance?" If told by a gentile comedian, many of his jokes would have been offensive but from Holtz they were a delight to hear.

Lou Holtz was born in San Francisco on April 11, 1898, and after a variety of jobs he took to singing in the style of entertainer Gus Chandler. He worked as a double act with Fred Weiss and as part of the trio of Boland, Holtz,

and Harris. While playing at a popular San Francisco night spot, the Crest, Boland, Holtz, and Harris were spotted by Elsie Janis's mother who brought them East to work with her daughter as the Elsie Janis Trio. In time, Holtz married Rita Boland, but they were divorced and with the breakup of his marriage Lou Holtz became a single act in more ways than one.

As a single, Holtz did not become a success until he performed his act in blackface. Presumably he was taking after Al Jolson (for whom Holtz was once an understudy) and Eddie Cantor, both of whom he resembled in the 1910s according to *Variety.* The November 30, 1917, issue commented, "It looks as though Holtz with his present material could hold a big-time spot and improve." He did both, and by April of 1919 Holtz was holding his own on a Palace Theatre bill which included Van and Schenck and Jack Norworth. *Variety* (April 4, 1919) reported, "Lou Holtz in blackface was somewhat of a surprise. Holtz has some excellent material, and while without a positive individual style, his delivery is natural and the impression scored is due solely to his own personality. His gestures are not unlike [Frank] Fay, and the interrupted sentences unmistakably those of Jolson, but Holtz has original material, and were he to eradicate his style, his personality would suffer. His closing number makes a capital finish to the act and he was voted a genuine hit. This chap, industrious to an unusual degree, has been striving for some time to connect, and with this act he seems to have landed. He is ready for any big-time program."

As early as 1915 Holtz had appeared on the musical comedy stage in *A World of Pleasure,* with music by Sigmund Romberg, which opened at the Winter Garden Theatre on October 14, 1915. However, his career took a new turn in 1919 when he was featured with comic Lester Allen supporting Ann Pennington and Yvette Rugel in the first edition of *George White's Scandals.* The show opened at the Liberty Theatre on June 2, 1919, and ran for 128 performances. Holtz also appeared in the 1920 and 1921 editions of the *Scandals;* no doubt it was in one of those shows that he uttered the memorable question—to a mother whose daughter wished to go on the stage— "Would she like to be glorified by Ziegfeld or scandalized by White?" The comedian was also to be seen in three revues at the Winder Garden, along with *Tell Me More* (1925), written especially for him by Buddy DeSylva and the Gershwins, *Manhattan Mary* (1927), and *You Said It* (1931).

By the mid-twenties Lou Holtz had come to be recognized as the greatest dialect comedian on the vaudeville stage, although his humor at that time was apparently too New York-oriented. When he played a presentation house, the Chicago, in June of 1928, Windy City audiences were only polite in their enthusiasm. *Variety* (June 6, 1928) described him as "too smart for the families. Holtz is unknown to the majority at the Chicago. Drawing power dubious." Also in the twenties, Lou Holtz developed into a fine master of ceremonies for vaudeville. Douglas Gilbert wrote of him, "He was an extraordinary comic with immediate reactions that made him superb as a master of ceremonies, but he continually stepped over the blue line into vulgarity that often destroyed his effectiveness." Holtz was popular as a master of ceremonies at the Palace, and also gave that theatre plenty to worry about in 1932 when he opened in a vaudeville revue at the Hollywood Theatre which easily outgrossed the Palace, where the master of ceremonies at that time was Frank Fay. At the Palace in 1930, Lou Holtz had introduced Benny Baker as his stooge.

Holtz made his screen debut in 1930 in *Follow the Leader* with Ed Wynn, but some years later he reminisced that the experience had not been a happy one, with Wynn ordering most of his scenes deleted from the film. With Belle Baker and Block and Sully, Holtz was held over—an unprecedented move—at Loew's State in September of 1935. In 1936 he starred in two London revues, *Transatlantic Rhythm* at the Adelphi and *Laughter over London* at the Palace. With the demise of vaudeville, Lou Holtz appeared in night clubs and on radio and television. Lou Holtz died in his Beverly Hills, California, home on September 22, 1980. When told of his death, George Burns commented, "In vaudeville, they cancel you and give back your publicity pictures. I guess it was Lou's turn to get back his pictures."

Reference: "Lou Holtz" in *The Vaudevillians* by Bill Smith (Macmillan, 1976), pages 121–128.

HARRY HOUDINI

Houdini in 1918

"Houdini is a showman of the old school. He does baffling things and he gets every ounce of value out of them," wrote Frederick James Smith in the *New York Dramatic Mirror* (April 8, 1916). That statement probably best explains why Houdini is as well known today as he was in the early years of this century, and still the subject of film and television biographies. All of his exploits, escaping from strait jackets, chains, manacles, jails, barrels of water, and the like—off stage and on—were heavily publicized, as were his numerous exposés of fake spiritualism. In the late 1910s he also got into films, forming Houdini's Film Development Corporation to assure lasting records of his exploits.

Harry Houdini was born Erik Weisz in Budapest, Hungary, on March 24, 1874. His parents soon emigrated to America and eventually settled in Appleton, Wisconsin, where Houdini's father became a rabbi. Houdini's stage career began in 1891, first with a friend, Jacob Hyman, in an act called "The Brothers Houdini." The name Houdini had been chosen out of an early admiration for the French magician and illusionist Robert Houdin. By 1900 Houdini had become an established vaudeville star, billed as "The Undisputed King of Handcuffs," "Monarch of Leg Shackles," and "Champion Jail Breaker." From a $15-a-week dime museum attraction, Houdini became a $2,500-a-week vaudeville star, although *Variety* pointed out that he was worth and could have demanded far more had he ever been able to forget his humble beginnings in show business. When the Keith circuit raised his salary to $1,500 a week, he was quoted as saying, "I feel as though I'm stealing something. Think of $1,500 a week for me and the time when I got $15 a week for playing twenty shows a day." Houdini was certainly not the highest-paid magician of his day, for Howard Thurston, who was considered a more commercially successful magician than Houdini, earned considerably more.

In 1900 Houdini went to England, and his biographer notes that within a year of that trip he was the strongest vaudeville attraction in Europe. He performed every type of escapology on stage. He was tied to a ladder. He was sealed in a galvanized iron boiler. He was handcuffed inside a rolltop desk. He escaped from all the best jails. One of his most famous tricks involved pushing a long steel needle through his cheek without drawing blood. On January 7, 1918, on the stage of the Hippodrome, he made a live, 10,000-pound elephant disappear. "Mr. Houdini has provided a headache for every child in New York," wrote Sime Silverman in *Variety.* "The matinee crowds will worry themselves into sleep nightly wondering what Houdini did with his elephant."

In January and February of 1925, Houdini was to establish a record for being held over for six weeks at the Hippodrome, in an act which consisted chiefly of exposing fake spiritualists and explaining how they could make spirits materialize at Séances. Spiritualism became a fixation with Houdini in the early twenties, and after his death there were endless attempts to make contact with him in the spirit world. Houdini's wife, Bess, who had worked with him in the early days of vaudeville, participated in many of these.

At the time of his 1925 Hippodrome appearance Sime Silverman wrote in *Variety,* "Houdini is an intellectual and, besides that, among showmen he is the peer of all actor-showmen everywhere. Houdini as an actor is a showman on and off—more so, perhaps off than on. As an intellectual Houdini should be an educator upon the stage, for he has dove into the ultra-gullible—the thing that has made monkeys of wise men and fools—spiritualism."

Despite his frequent posing in the near nude—admittedly necessary to prove he had no keys or other means of escape hidden about his person—Houdini was not a handsome or imposing figure, yet was the idol of millions of his generation and of generations to come. There was little question that Houdini welcomed the adulation, for he was, in some ways, arrogant and egotistical. It was these failings that were, indirectly, to cause his death. On October 22, 1926, in his dressing room at the Princess Theatre in Montreal, Houdini was asked by a student visitor if it was true that he could sustain heavy punches on his abdomen without injury. Houdini agreed, but before he could brace himself for the blows, the student hit him hard three times. Houdini carried on valiantly as if nothing had happened, but he was in excruciating pain. His appendix became inflamed, poison entered his blood stream, and a few days later, on October 31, the magician died in a Detroit hospital after two operations for peritonitis.

Variety explained his unique appeal by noting: "It's not the tricks, illusions, or disappearances that make a successful magician outstanding; it's showmanship, personality, and oftimes creation. . . . For a magical act, tricks and apparatus may be purchased, but the requisite attributes are not on sale anywhere."

References: "Afterthoughts on Houdini" in *Variety,* Vol. 85, No. 4 (November 10, 1926), page 20. *Houdini: The Untold Story* by Milbourne Christopher (Thomas Y. Crowell Company, 1969).

JOSEPH E. HOWARD

Joe Howard's chief claim to fame is as a songwriter. Working usually with Will Hough, he wrote the music for such perennial favorites as "Hello My Baby," "Goodbye, My Lady Love," and "I Wonder Who's Kissing Her Now." In addition to his songs, Howard wrote the music for a number of early Broadway shows, including *The Time, the Place and the Girl* (1907), *The Land of Nod* (1907), *A Stubborn Cinderella* (1909), and *The Goddess of Liberty* (1909). He was born in New York on February 12, 1878, and at the age of eleven was appearing in vaudeville as a boy soprano. He returned to vaudeville in the early 1910s singing his own songs, and was always elegantly dressed and very much the ladies' man. In 1947 George Jessel produced a glamorized version of his life titled *I Wonder Who's Kissing Her Now* for 20th Century-Fox, starring Mark Stevens as Howard. Joe Howard died in Chicago on May 19, 1961.

WILLIE AND EUGENE HOWARD

Eugene was the straight man and Willie was the comic, and as a Jewish comedy team they were regarded by their contemporaries and their audiences as the best. Sime Silverman wrote in *Variety* (May 16, 1913), "If there is a Hebrew comedian in the world who can touch Willie Howard, trot him out. And Willie can give his challenger all those things a Hebrew comedian is supposed to have, including crepe hair, for Willie has none of these, nor does he need them." George Jessel simply commented, "Willie Howard was the best of all the revue comics, bar none." (In the thirties Willie Howard would often imitate Jessel singing "My Mother's Eyes.")

Willie and Eugene
Howard

Willie Howard and
Sophie Tucker in 1938

The brothers were as much at home on the vaudeville stage as they were in *George White's Scandals* or *The Passing Show*. There would be rapid-fire comedy cross-talk, often followed by a travesty of an operatic medley, and, of course, Willie Howard's impressions of Harry Lauder, Eddie Cantor, or Al Jolson. The classic Willie Howard line was "Comes the revolution, we'll all be eating strawberries." Willie would often parody a popular song; for example, in 1913 he sang "Snooky Ookums" with the line "All night long he's smoking opum." One of the secrets of the success of the act was that Willie Howard possessed a good baritone voice, which always added to the operatic travesties.

Willie and Eugene Howard were born in Nuestadt, Germany, Eugene in 1880 and Willie in 1883. They grew up on New York's Lower East Side after the family emigrated to the United States. The boys began their show business careers separately; Eugene made his first appearance on the stage at the Casino Theatre on September 28, 1897, in the chorus of *The Belle of New York,* while Willie made his debut as a boy soprano at Proctor's 125th Street Theatre, also in 1897. Willie first came to attention as the boy singing in the gallery to Anna Held in *The Little Duchess* in the autumn of 1901.

In 1902 the brothers joined forces with a vaudeville act titled "The Messenger Boy (Willie) and the Thespian (Eugene)." At approximately the same time, Willie began doing his impressions. The boys toured in vaudeville through 1912, when they were signed by the Shuberts to star in the first edition of *The Passing Show* at the Winter Garden Theatre. Willie and Eugene Howard were to be regulars in *The Passing Show* almost without a break until 1922. Sime Silverman of *Variety* (May 16, 1913) noted, "The Howards never fail to become a riot at the Garden.

They were that in vaudeville before entering musical comedy, and can go back to vaudeville with this act, duplicating their former successes here." Audiences loved their send-up of the Metropolitan opera star in "The Galli-Curci Rag" and their travesty of *Rigoletto.*

"The Howard Brothers, Gene and Willie, have long been missing from vaudeville," sighed the *New York Dramatic Mirror* (January 1, 1920), "and oh, what joy there would be if they only returned to the varieties." Eventually the Howards left *The Passing Show,* in 1922, and returned to vaudeville for a couple of years. In October of 1924 they headlined at the Palace, and *Variety* (October 22, 1924) reported, "The Howards now wear evening clothes with Eugene's the last word in sartorial elegance. Willie's is a comedy assortment of near misfits topped by a high hat. The Howards open with crossfire in which there is never a dull moment. Eugene's straighting in this portion is flawless. Willie's snappy retorts have the laughs popping like machine guns. Some of the gags will no doubt be heard around from now on for they are 'naturals.' " The brothers earned $2,500 a week in vaudeville at this time.

In 1926 it was back to the revue stage with *George White's Scandals,* in which the Howards appeared through 1929. They also returned for the 1935 edition of the *Scandals*. From this point on, the Howards were almost exclusively on the musical comedy stage, appearing in *Girl Crazy* (1930, Eugene only); *Ballyhoo of 1932*; *The Ziegfeld Follies* (1933, at the Winter Garden, which must have made them feel at home); *The Show Is On* (1937); and *Crazy with the Heat* (1941, Willie only). Willie and Eugene were also performing in films from 1927 through 1938, chiefly as the stars of short subjects.

In 1940 Eugene Howard retired from the act, concentrating on writing material and acting as manager for his brother. Al Kelly replaced him as Willie's stooge. Eugene Howard died in New York City on August 1, 1965. Willie Howard continued to be active almost until the day he died, featured in night clubs, on radio, and in the occasional revue. On December 8, 1948, Willie was forced to leave the cast of the revue *Along Fifth Avenue* during its Philadelphia tryout. He died in New York City on January 13, 1949, the same day that *Along Fifth Avenue* opened on Broadway. He was, as one obituary writer commented, "one of the great comedians of this generation."

MAY IRWIN

May Irwin

"Though a great portion of her career was spent in musical and farce comedy, it is as a vaudevillian that she will be remembered," wrote Robert Grau of May Irwin in his 1910 book *The Business Man in the Amusement World.* A legend of the legitimate stage and vaudeville, May Irwin was known as "the dean of comediennes." During the First World War, when she gave a solo command performance before President Wilson—to give him a good laugh and take his mind off war worries—she was created unofficial Secretary of Laughter.

May Irwin was born in Whitby, Ontario, on June 27, 1862; her first stage appearances were with her sister Flo in the mid-1870s. The sisters were "coon shouters," meaning they sang Negro melodies such as "Don't You Hear dem Bells?" By 1877 they were playing with Tony Pastor's company at the Metropolitan Theatre in New York, and

they did not split up until May was offered a job with Augustin Daly's company in 1883. May Irwin's first starring role was as Beatrice Byke in *The Widow Jones,* opposite John Rice, in 1895. The kissing scene from this play was filmed by the Edison Company and known as *The Kiss* it has become one of the most famous early film clips in the history of the cinema. In its review of *The Widow Jones,* the *New York Times* (September 17, 1895) said of May Irwin, "She is as round, as blonde, as innocent looking—when her mood is not reckless—as pink and white and as blue-eyed as ever.... Her fund of personal humour is prodigious."

It was not until November of 1907 that May Irwin made her New York vaudeville debut at the Orpheum Theatre. She had put on some weight—*Variety* unkindly said that at her entrance she looked like a sister team—and began her act by describing the pathos of becoming fat and bemoaning the fact that she no longer had a visible waistline. Throughout the 1910s May Irwin alternated vaudeville appearances with stage roles in *She Knows No Better* (1911), *A Widow by Proxy* (1913), and *Number 13 Washington Square* (1915), among others. Reviewing her 1917 Palace appearance, Sime Silverman wrote in *Variety* (April 6, 1917), "As often as May Irwin may wish to return to vaudeville just so often will vaudeville always welcome her with open arms, for vaudeville audiences, regardless of what else may be said of them, never fail to recognize an artist."

Sime Silverman was at the Palace in February of 1915 when May Irwin topped the bill, singing "Kentucky Home" and "Those Were the Happy Days," and reciting "Father's Old Red Beard," written for her by Irving Berlin. She closed her act with a recitation complaining that her "waistline will never be what it uster [sic]."

May Irwin retired in 1920 to her farm in the Thousand Islands section of New York State with her second husband and manager, Kurt Eisfeldt. She died on October 26, 1938. It is perhaps a sad reflection on our times that if May Irwin is remembered at all it is not as a vaudevillian or even as a star of the legitimate stage and musical comedy, but as a plump, somewhat unattractive actress, bestowing an amorous kiss in a flickering silent film from the cinema's infancy.

ELSIE JANIS

"Elsie Janis!" wrote Sime Silverman in *Variety* (September 22, 1922). "What Bernhardt is to all of the stage, Elsie Janis is to vaudeville. They like her in musical comedy, and they have liked her on two continents, but to vaudeville she is its queen.... Miss Janis in vaudeville is the most natural person in vaudeville." Elsie Janis, with her songs, her pep, her personality, and her general affability, was up there with Eva Tanguay and Nora Bayes as one of vaudeville's greatest stars. She was loved by audiences in America and Europe, and the darling of the society of two continents.

She was born Elsie Bierbower in Columbus, Ohio, on March 16, 1889, and owed her fame and her success to one person—her mother. A stage mother to upstage all stage

Elsie Janis

mothers, she may not have always worried about financial trusts for the future, as her daughter recalled in her autobiography, but she did ensure that Elsie Janis (a name suggested by a theatrical photographer) had a good time while embarking on a stage career second to none in the history of vaudeville and revue. Little Elsie made her stage debut on December 24, 1897, in Columbus, Ohio, as Cain in *The Charity Ball,* and she rarely stopped working from that day on. Elsie Janis claimed to have started at the age of three the imitations which were her greatest claim to fame; "I began imitating everything from animals to railroad trains," she recalled in 1908. As a child, she presented her impersonations before President McKinley, who was duly impressed. In the summer of 1900, the actress made her New York debut at the Casino Roof Garden, giving impersonations of Weber and Fields, Fay Templeton, and Lillian Russell.

That was the start of a vaudeville career that was to last through the twenties and to garner for Elsie Janis such titles as "America's Wonder Child," "The Cleverest Girl in the World," and "The Princess Royal of Vaudeville." In a 1916 interview Miss Janis explained, "I loved vaudeville. Of course, that sounds trite and conventional, but while two performances each day are hard, the response of the variety audience is an electrical encouragement." The Elsie Janis vaudeville routine remained basically the same, with impersonations and comic songs, but those whom she impersonated (always without the use of makeup or accessories) did vary. In 1907 at the Colonial Theatre, she was impersonating Vesta Victoria singing "Poor John," Eddie Foy, Eva Tanguay, Ethel Barrymore, and Anna Held. (Reviewing that act, Sime Silverman wrote in

Variety [April 27, 1907], "Miss Janis, taken by herself and considering her youth, pleases any number of people with her impressions.") In 1911 she introduced her own composition "I'd Rather Love What I Cannot Have than Have What I Cannot Love," and gave impersonations of Irene Franklin, Pat Rooney, Anna Held, Ethel Barrymore, Eddie Foy, and Harry Lauder.

Elsie Janis made her first appearance at the Palace on January 3, 1916; reviewing her act, Frederick James Smith wrote in the *New York Dramatic Mirror* (January 15, 1916), "Miss Janis offers little caricatures, vividly drawn with a keen and intelligent sense of humor and deftly exaggerating just a few of a player's peculiarities of style and personality." At that time the star was offering glimpses of Ethel Barrymore, Frank Tinney, Nazimova singing "I Didn't Raise My Boy to Be a Soldier," Eddie Foy, Harry Lauder, George M. Cohan, and Sarah Bernhardt singing "Tipperary." "You caught a splendid semblance of the divine fire—enough to truly thrill you," wrote Smith of the last impersonation. In 1916 Elsie Janis drew the Palace Theatre's first Monday night capacity crowd in months, causing *Variety* (January 7, 1916) to comment, "Elsie Janis in vaudeville evidently means something substantial." In September of 1922 she was back at the Palace with impersonations of Bert Williams, Ethel Barrymore as Fannie Brice, and George M. Cohan. One impersonation which Elsie Janis enjoyed giving through the years and which delighted audiences in both America and Europe was that of Will Rogers with his lariat.

In 1924 Elsie Janis, or rather her mother, had a dispute over billing at the Palace. Janis threatened to walk out if the name of comedian James Barton continued to be billed beside hers in front of the theatre. Barton's name remained, and Janis did indeed walk out. In her autobiography she claims the fault was not that of E. F. Albee, who was sick at the time, and that when Albee learned of it he insisted on paying her in full for the uncompleted engagement. However, Elsie Janis was banned from working at the Palace again until the late twenties.

Elsie Janis was vaudeville, but she was also of musical comedy and revue, and in both of those media she was tremendously popular with London and Paris audiences. Janis's first Broadway success was in *The Vanderbilt Cup* in 1906 which made her a star. It was followed through the years by *The Fair Co-ed* (1908), *The Slim Princess* (1910), *The Lady of the Slipper* (1912), *The Passing Show* (which opened on April 20, 1914, at London's Palace Theatre and made Elsie Janis a British star), *Miss Information* (1915), *The Century Girl* (1917), *Puzzles of 1925, Oh, Kay!* (1927), and many others. In shows such as these, Elsie Janis introduced many popular songs, including "Fo' de Lawd's Sake, Play a Waltz" (from *The Slim Princess*) and "Florrie Was a Flapper" (from *The Passing Show*).

Volumes could be written about Elsie Janis's work entertaining the troops during the First World War, which won her the title of Sweetheart of the A.E.F. (the American Expeditionary Force). On May 31, 1918, *Variety* reviewed her act, "Elsie Janis over There," as if it were a regular theatrical event rather than a makeshift show for the troops sponsored by the Y.M.C.A. "Wherever she may go," wrote *Variety,* "Miss Janis scores her usual knockout, and from the soldiers' point of view is the biggest thing that ever came down the pike. . . . Elsie Janis may be cited as having done her bit." After the war Elsie Janis came to the George M. Cohan Theatre on Broadway with her revue *Elsie Janis and Her Gang,* which opened on December 1, 1919, and featured a number of exservicemen plus several of the women who had worked with her during the war, including Eva Le Gallienne.

The cinema had played a small part in Eslie Janis's life in the 1910s. She had starred in four features, produced by the Bosworth Company for release by Paramount in 1915: *The Caprices of Kitty, Betty in Search of a Thrill, Nearly a Lady,* and *'Twas Ever Thus,* and in 1919 Selznick starred her in *A Regular Girl* and *The Imp.* However, as Miss Janis's stage career came to a halt in the late twenties, the actress turned again to the cinema, not for an acting job but to work behind the camera. She adapted *Oh, Kay!* for Colleen Moore in 1928. In 1929 she provided a story, *Close Harmony,* for two of Paramount's top musical stars, Buddy Rogers and Nancy Carroll. Also for Paramount, Elsie Janis came up with the idea of a revue, *Paramount on Parade,* which she also supervised and for which she provided song lyrics. For *Paramount on Parade,* she persuaded the studio to sign a young vaudevillian named Mitzi Green, with a talent for mimicry which reminded Elsie Janis of her own.

Cecil B. DeMille hired Miss Janis in 1930 to provide dialogue and lyrics for his feature *Madam Satan.* She also wrote lyrics for a song from Paramount's *Slightly Scarlet* (1930) and, with Edmund Goulding, provided the lyrics for Gloria Swanson's big hit "Love, Your Magic Spell Is Everywhere" in *The Trespasser* (1929). In 1939 Elsie Janis was starred by Republic Pictures in *Women in War,* but by that time she considered war far from the exciting experience it had been for her in 1917, and she agreed to appear in the production only on the understanding she was allowed to remark frequently on the horrors of war.

Elsie Janis's career ended to all intents and purposes with the death of her mother in 1932. The two had been inseparable and had lived for each other. "There are Elsie Janises born every day, but not mothers to give up their whole lives to them," said Mrs. Bierbower in 1916:

I can understand how many girls of cleverness, or real ability, never find their way to light. Opportunity is necessary, of course. But behind all success are years of hard work and self-sacrifice. Without understanding care a wonderful plant will fade and its beautiful fruit will be lost. I know people say that I keep Elsie from love and companionship. But they don't guess our closeness and devotion. They don't realize how we fought our way through the years. That's why we are inseparable, and that's why we go everywhere together. But the world doesn't understand.

Elsie Janis did not marry until after her mother's death:

then, within a matter of months, she married an actor sixteen years her junior, Gilbert Wilson. The couple was soon separated. In her charming and literate autobiography, *So Far, So Good!,* Elsie Janis suggested that her epitaph might read, "Here lies Elsie Janis, still sleeping alone." When death came on February 26, 1956, at Elsie Janis's bedside was Mary Pickford who had known the star since they were both children on the stage in the late 1890s. It was Mary Pickford who pronounced the perfect epitaph for Elsie Janis: "This ends the vaudeville era."

References: "Our Elsie's Own Story" by Frederick James Smith in the *New York Dramatic Mirror,* Vol. 75, No. 1936 (January 29, 1916), page 27. *So Far, So Good!* by Elsie Janis (E. P. Dutton, 1932).

GEORGE JESSEL

George Jessel

George Jessel is a man of many parts. He is a vaudevillian, an actor on both stage and screen, and a television personality whose years have not diminished his appeal to talk show hosts. He is America's Toastmaster General, an appointment given him by President Roosevelt. He is the master of the eulogy. (There is a story, probably apocryphal, that Jessel delivered a eulogy for James Mason's cat, and after the funeral a sobbing Jack Benny said, "I never knew cats were so good to Israel.") He is a humanitarian and a recipient of the 1969 Jean Hershot Humanitarian Award from the Academy of Motion Picture Arts and Sciences. He has been a film producer, responsible for *The Dolly Sisters* (1945), *I Wonder Who's Kissing Her Now* (1947), *Oh, You Beautiful Doll* (1949), and *Tonight We*

Sing (1953), among others. He has been an ardent supporter of Jewish charities and Israeli rights. He is a staunch conservative. Above all, George Jessel is a personality. You may hate him, hate what he has to say, hate his politics, but you have to admit that George Jessel is a unique human being who may be exasperating but never boring. When Groucho Marx said, "Jessel is the only man I would rather listen to than myself," he had a point.

Jessel is not a stereotype vaudeville performer, but his beginnings are typical of most Jewish vaudevillians. Born on April 1, 1898, in the Bronx, he took to entertaining in 1907 to raise money for the family when his father became sick. With two other boys Jack Wiener (who later became a Hollywood agent), and Walter Winchell, he formed the Imperial Trio to accompany song slides at a local nickelodeon. With Walter Winchell, he joined Gus Edwards's Company as part of a vaudeville act titled "School Boys and Girls." Also in the Edwards Company was Eddie Cantor, and a friendship formed which endured through the years and culminated in an historic 1931 Cantor-Jessel engagement at the Palace.

After leaving Edwards Jessel put together an act called "Two Patches from a Crazy Quilt" with another Edwards alumnus, Lou Edwards. In 1914 they managed to get as far as England. Back in the States, Jessel appeared with an act titled "A Ray of Sunshine," written for him by Henry Bergman and Sam Lewis, in which he played a man who believed he was George Washington. He continued to build up a reputation in vaudeville which he actively promoted by taking out a full-page advertisement in the June 20, 1919 issue of Variety. The ad quoted Percy Hammond's statement that "Georgie Jessel is in the front ranks of America's lyric comedians," and that of a Detroit critic who compared him to Chaplin. Jessel also boasted that he was the author of the "big comedy song hit" titled "Oo La La, Oui, Oui." (He is, in fact, the author of many songs, including "Stop Kicking My Heart Around," "Rose in December," and "Oh How I Laugh When I Think How I Cried about You.")

In the summer of 1920 George Jessel put together his own revue complete with chorus girls and a vaudeville team called Holmes and Welles. Jessel supplied the songs, including "Oh How I Laugh When I Think How I Cried about You" and "I'm Satisfied To Be My Mother's Baby," and cowrote the script with Andy Lewis. The New York Dramatic Mirror (September 18, 1920), reporting on the Revue at the Palace, commented, "There are sections that amble along with others putting it in the tempo necessary to send a big act over. Jessel has tried hard. He works hard. . . . The act will set right anywhere 'big-time' vaudeville is played."

The twenties saw the emergence of George Jessel's classic monolog routine in which he talked to his mother on the phone, assuring her that he knew nothing about the money missing from the bureau or the cake from the cupboard. In The Passing Show of 1923 Jessel performed an act similar in style, with his old Jewish mother (played by Annie Lovenworth) sitting in a stage box and talking back to him.

Reviewing Jessel's act at the Palace, the New York Dramatic Mirror (September 25, 1920) had written, "It would not be surprising to see this kid climb into the Broadway spotlights of a musical show before he is many seasons older." Jessel did indeed move on from vaudeville to revues such as the Shubert's Troubles of 1922, but his greatest success in the twenties was in the musical play The Jazz Singer by Sampson Raphaelson, which opened in New York at the Fulton Theatre on September 14, 1925. George Jessel played Jack Robin in The Jazz Singer more than a thousand times in New York and on the road. In addition, he has appeared in The War Song (1928) which he cowrote, Sweet and Low (1930), and High Kickers (1931) which he cowrote and presented.

Because of what appears to have been a dispute over money, George Jessel was preempted by Al Jolson for the screen version of The Jazz Singer, which became a landmark in cinema history as the film which, more than any other, forced the changeover from silent to sound motion pictures. Jessel had already made some sound shorts for Warner Bros., the producers of The Jazz Singer, but for his talkie feature debut he went over to the Poverty Row studios of the Tiffany Company to star in Lucky Boy, which introduced one of Jessel's best-known songs, "My Mother's Eyes." The song, along with "When the Curtain Comes Down," was featured on his first Victor recording, about which Variety reported (February 29, 1929), "Jessel discloses a rich, vibrant baritone, clean and clear as to diction and replete with the necessary dramatic pathos for the proper interpretation of songs of this calibre." Jessel has appeared in other films as an actor, but his chief and more recent contribution to the film industry has been as a producer, often of films based on the lives of famous vaudevillians.

Vaudeville has gone but George Jessel has never ceased performing, "flitting casually about with easy adaptation" (as Douglas Gilbert wrote) through the various areas of show business. On the dust jacket for his first autobiograpy, So Help Me, George Jessel is described as "Master Showman, Raconteur, Movie Producer, T.V. and Radio Personality, Speechmaker and Toastmaster General of the United States." This was one dust jacket which did not exaggerate.

References: So Help Me by George Jessel (Random House, 1943). The World I Lived In by George Jessel, with John Austin (Henry Regnery Company, 1975).

AL JOLSON

It is problematic whether Al Jolson should be included in this volume, for he was never a vaudeville star per se, and his stage career was limited almost exclusively to the revue and musical comedy fields. He belongs to that small group of performers, which includes Will Rogers, George M. Cohan, and Harry Lauder, who never played the Palace, although in September of 1930 Jolson turned down $12,000 a week to headline there, the largest vaudeville salary offer on record. No, Al Jolson belongs in this book because, as Eddie Cantor wrote, "Al Jolson wasn't just a musical comedy star. The great Al was an American insti-

Al Jolson

tution. He was even more than that—he was what all other musical comedy stars thought they were." It is doubtful that any other performer has introduced so many songs which have become standards: "April Showers," "Rock-a-Bye Your Baby with a Dixie Melody," "You Are Too Beautiful," "Hallelujah! I'm a Bum," "Toot Toot Tootsie," "Where Did Robinson Crusoe Go with Friday on Saturday Night?," "Let Me Sing and I'm Happy," "There's a Rainbow 'round My Shoulder," "Sonny Boy," "When the Red, Red Robin," "Dirty Hands, Dirty Face," "Home in Pasadena," "I'm Just Wild about Harry," "Liza," and many, many more.

Jolson's date of birth is uncertain, but he selected May 26, 1886. He was born Asa Yoelson, the son of Cantor Yoelson, in Russia, from which his parents emigrated to America while Jolson was still a child. He became fascinated with the stage after hearing Fay Templeton sing "Rosie, You Are My Posie," and received encouragement from minstrel Eddie Leonard. Jolson's first stage appearance is generally thought to have been in *The Children of the Ghetto,* which opened at the Herald Square Theatre on October 16, 1899. For a while he worked in burlesque with his elder brother, Harry, with an act titled "The Hebrew and the Cadet" (Al was the latter). Then, in 1901, he and Harry teamed with an older vaudevillian named Joe Palmer. They were initially billed as Joelson, Palmer and Joelson, but because the name was so long the *e* was dropped and the act became Jolson, Palmer and Jolson. When Palmer became sick the act split up, and Jolson journeyed to San Francisco shortly after the 1906 earthquake and began to make a name for himself.

As a single, Jolson first appeared in whiteface. His rea-

sons for adopting blackface are given in the souvenir program for *The Jazz Singer,* and the story is so outrageous that it is worth repeating here:

The turning tide was a chance conversation one night with an old darky. The man was a Southern Negro who assisted the comedian when he dressed. Jolson was extremely fond of him and appreciative of his loyalty through the lean years of his vaudeville tours. In Washington, Al had acquired a sympathetic interest in Negro life and had learned to mimic the accent of the race. One night when the two were preparing for a performance in a small theatre in Brooklyn, the actor confided to his old dresser his misgivings as to the merits of his act. "How am I going to get them to laugh more?" he mused. The darky shook his head knowingly. "Boss, if yo' skin am black they always laugh." The idea struck Jolson as plausible and he decided to try it. He got some burnt cork, blacked up, and rehearsed before the Negro. When he finished he heard a chuckle followed by the verdict. "Mistah Jolson, yo' is just as funny as me."

He was signed to appear as a member of Lew Dockstader's Minstrels, and soon became the star of the show, supplanting even Dockstader in popularity with the audience. "As a singer of coon songs," reported *Variety* (March 6, 1909), "Jolson has a method of his own by which lyrics and melody are given their full value. Al Jolson would be welcome to vaudeville."

It was not vaudeville, however, that won Al Jolson, but musical comedy, and throughout the 1910s it was a bad year when Jolson was not to be seen on the stage of New York's Winter Garden Theatre in shows like *La Belle Paree* (1911), *Vera Violetta* (1911), *The Whirl of Society* (1912), *The Honeymoon Express* (1913), *Dancin' Around* (1914), *Robinson Crusoe, Jr.* (1916), and *Sinbad* (1918). In many ways, these musical comedies were part vaudeville show, for there was never a time when Jolson would not stop the proceedings to present a ten- or fifteen-minute solo vaudeville act. He would always assure his audience, "You ain't heard nothing yet," a phrase that became part of cinema history when he uttered it in *The Jazz Singer,* the first words spoken in a film which is—incorrectly—regarded as the screen's first talkie. By 1922 there was no one who would argue with Jolson's claim that he was "The World's Greatest Drawing Card." When *Bombo* opened in October of 1921, it was at Jolson's Fifty-ninth Street Theatre.

Reviewers were unanimous in their praise for Jolson's hold on an audience. Alexander Woolcott wrote, "There is no other performer who holds such an absolute dictatorship over his audience." "They call him the world's greatest entertainer," wrote Alan Dale. "It doesn't seem exaggerated." O. O. McIntyre commented that "Jolson has the same magnetic qualities that lifted Mansfield, Duse, Tree, and Jefferson to the heights," while George Jean Nathan noted, "The power of Jolson over an audience I have seldom seen equalled." In private life, Jolson was a curiously mixed personality. "He was really complex. He could be marvelous and he could be pretty terrible," remembers Mrs. Gus Kahn. George Jessel has written, "He was cruel most of the time.... But, God, what a great artist he was!"

In 1927 Warner Bros. decided to transfer Samson Raphaelson's popular Broadway play, *The Jazz Singer,* to the screen, utilizing its new Vitaphone sound-on-disc process. George Jessel had been the star of the stageplay and was initially signed for the role. But for reasons unclear, he was replaced by Al Jolson. As the storyline was supposedly based in part on Jolson's life, he would have seemed the logical choice for the lead. Writing in the old *Life* humor magazine, Robert Benchley noted, "When Jolson enters, it is as if an electric current had been run along the wires under the seats where the hats are stuck. The house comes to tumultuous attention. He speaks, rolls his eyes, compresses his lips, and it is all over.... He trembles under his lip, and your hearts break with a snap. He sings, and you totter out to send a night letter to your mother."

The Jazz Singer started Al Jolson on a new career as a film star. It was followed by *The Singing Fool* (1928), *Say It with Songs* (1929), *Sonny Boy* (1929), *Lucky Boy* (1929), *Mammy* (1930), *Hallelujah! I'm a Bum* (1933), *Wonder Bar* (1934), *The Singing Kid* (1936), *Rose of Washington Square* (1939), and many others. Jolson also became immensely popular on radio, first with *Presenting Al Jolson* in 1932, then with *Kraft Music Hall* in 1934, and later with *Shell Chateau* in 1935. As the career of his third wife, Ruby Keeler, grew, Al Jolson's fame began to diminish. However, his career was given a tremendous boost in 1946 when Columbia produced *The Jolson Story,* with Larry Parks playing Jolson and miming to a playback of Jolson's own voice for the songs. *The Jolson Story* was followed a year later by *Jolson Sings Again.* Al Jolson was back at the top of the heap when he died in San Francisco on October 23, 1950. Just before news of his death was made public, Danny Thomas had kidded on his television show, "Larry Parks would be buried in the event of Jolson's death."

References: *The Immortal Jolson: His Life and Times* by Pearl Sieben (Frederick Fell, 1962). "Al Jolson" in *As I Remember Them* by Eddie Cantor (Duell, Sloan and Pearch, 1963). *Jolson* by Michael Freedland (Stein and Day, 1972).

THE THREE KEATONS

While they toured the vaudeville circuits for years and were fairly popular with audiences—though never as major headliners—the chief interest in the Three Keatons lies in the fact that one of them was Buster Keaton. The other two Keatons were his parents, Joe and Myra, who entered vaudeville around 1890 with Joe performing as an eccentric dancer and acrobat and Myra dancing and playing the cornet. The two Keatons were best known for an act titled "The Man with the Table," which consisted of Joe performing strenuous and violent acrobatics on a kitchen table with Myra entertaining the audience during the intervals while he rested.

The Three Keatons

Within months of his birth in 1895, the young Buster was being carried on stage as part of the act. He became a permanent member of the company on October 23, 1900, when the Three Keatons came into being in Easton, Pennsylvania. At that time Keaton's contribution to the act consisted of imitations and burlesque dancing. The *New York Clipper* (July 20, 1901) reported, "The tiny comedian is perfectly at ease in his work, natural, finished, and artistic, and his specialties have proved a fetching addition to the favorite act of the Keatons." In time, the whirlwind comedy of the Three Keatons act became more violent, centering on a savage, knockabout sketch between a father and his rebellious son. A 1905 advertisement for the act read, "Maybe you think you were handled roughly when you were a kid. Watch the way they handle Buster!"

The Three Keatons toured the Kohl and Castle, Hopkins, Keith, and Proctor circuits. They wore grotesque costumes, with the men sporting baggy pants and coats, fuzzy black wigs with skin masks over the fronts of their heads, and a pasty face make-up. The Three Keatons were still touring when Keaton reached manhood, but in 1917 they came to Los Angeles and Buster left the act to enter films. The rest is history....

Reference: *My Wonderful World of Slapstick* by Buster Keaton, with Charles Samuels (Allen and Unwin, 1967). *Keaton* by Rudi Blesh (Macmillan, 1966). *Keaton: The Man Who Wouldn't Lie Down* by Tom Dardis (Charles Scribner's Sons, 1979).

ANNETTE KELLERMANN

Annette Kellermann

"Annette Kellermann's appearance in a vaudeville theatre at this time is an event of such importance that at the opening of the sale of seats in any auditorium where she is announced, one would suppose a Bernhardt or a Patti was scheduled to appear," wrote Robert Grau in 1910. "Either Annette Kellermann is the greatest box office attraction the stage has ever known, or else her manager is the most compelling genius of modern theatrical achievement, and the writer is inclined to the belief that both statements qualify." Certainly much of Kellermann's success must be attributed to her husband and manager, Jim Sullivan, who guided her career through vaudeville houses in England, Australia, and the United States, and also in films. But credit must also go to Annette Kellermann's father who ambitiously pushed his daughter into show business in the first place.

Dates differ but Annette Kellermann was definitely born in Sydney, Australia, on July 6, in either 1887 or 1888. Both her parents were musicians. As a child, she was crippled with what appears to have been polio.

As she recalled in a 1917 interview,

My baby-legs were badly deformed, and I had to wear leg-braces to correct the deformity. As I hobbled about—a frail and sickly child—no one thought that I would ever amount to anything, and even my fondest relations believed that I was not very long for this world. I gradually began to improve, however. The braces helped to straighten my crooked limbs, and I found I could get about more easily and more rapidly. At this point the family doctor recommended swimming exercises to develop my frail underpinnings and facilitate the cure he had started. On his advice I was taken to Cavell's Baths. Here, somehow or other, in the course of a few lessons I learned to swim. The limbs which had served me so ill on dry land found their true congenial element in the water. At the age of fifteen, I was the champion girl swimmer of Australia. I had attained a fine physical development, and I enjoyed the output of bodily energy with every fiber of my being. Yes, it is true that Mamma, devoted as she was to her artistic profession, wished to make a musician of me. I had a good singing voice, and I was an expert on the violin, having been brought up in the atmosphere of the conservatory, where musicianship was easy. Mother felt that I could win fame and fortune in the distant, more settled lands with the bow and strings. It was planned for me that I should go to Paris, her old home, and there be tutored to perfection by the best violin masters. But, almost before I knew it, I was doing professional swimming work in Sydney, Melbourne, and Adelaide. Such a demand rose for my exhibitions that, almost perforce, I cast aside the thought of musical fame.

Annette Kellermann's father took her on what can best be described as a swimming tour of European capitals; she swam down the Seine, the Rhine, and the Danube. After attracting attention by swimming down the River Thames from Putney Bridge to Blackwell, Annette Kellermann starred in the British music halls, doing an act in which she dived into a large glass-enclosed tank on stage and performed various water ballets. When she came to America she created an immediate sensation (presumably designed to win her still greater publicity) by appearing at Boston's Revere Beach in 1907 wearing a one-piece bathing costume. Her vaudeville career took off soon after that! Albee signed her up, and refurbished her British act by placing mirrors in strategic positions around her tank so that audiences were treated to multiviews of Miss Kellermann's body. At this point, it should be pointed out that it was the lady's body that was her chief attraction; she had a remarkably unappealing face.

(Incidentally, Douglas Gilbert notes that Annette Kellermann was long preceded by a freak act named "Blatz, the Human Fish" who spent long periods of time underwater, eating, reading a newspaper, and playing the trombone. In 1909 "Enoch, the Man Fish," smoked, played the trombone, and sang underwater. Those who saw Kellermann's act report that in later years she was to eat a banana underwater.)

By 1909 Annette Kellermann had added diabolo throwing to her act, and seven years later "The Divine Venus," as she was called, was starred in *The Big Show of 1916* at the Hippodrome, replacing Anna Pavlova. One of the show's big production numbers featured an enchanted waterfall, peopled by 200 mermaids, and Kellermann performing a sensational high dive. By this time, Miss Kellermann had also become a film star, playing in *Neptune's Daughter* (1914) and *A Daughter of the Gods* (1916). In 1952 Esther Williams played Kellermann in M-G-M's supposed film biography of the star *Million Dollar Mermaid*. Film footage of Kellermann diving and swimming was often screened as an introduction to her vaudeville act.

In January of 1918 Kellermann introduced "Annette Kellermann's Big Show," a forty-one-minute extravaganza in which she sang, danced, walked a tightrope, and changed her clothes often, at the Palace Theatre. Of her figure, Sime Silverman wrote in *Variety* (February 1, 1918), "It's worth looking at twice or more daily," but audiences were less than enthusiastic about her nonaquatic activities. She was back at the Palace in December of 1918 with another revue prior to a world tour. Ted Doner supported Kellermann with impersonations of Eddie Leonard and Pat Rooney, while the star tried her hand again at singing and other assorted activities. "While the revue does not move slowly, thanks to Miss Kellermann's assistants," wrote Frederick James Smith in the *New York Dramatic Mirror* (December 21, 1918), "there is too much of what the star does indifferently or fairly well and too little of what she does admirably. The diving exhibition is very brief."

Annette Kellermann officially retired in the thirties, but she continued to swim half a mile a day through her eightieth birthday. She died in Southport, Australia, on November 6, 1975. Inasmuch as her vaudeville career was an extremely prominent one, and so far removed in content from that of the established stars of the field like Tanguay, Bayes, and Janis, Annette Kellermann well deserves the title bestowed on her in 1910 by Robert Grau: "The Queen of Modern Vaudeville."

References: "Annette Kellermann" by Henry MacMahon in *Motion Picture Classic,* Vol. 3, No. 6 (February 1917), pages 17–19. "Neptune's Daughters" by DeWitt Bodeen and Larry L. Holland in *Films in Review,* Vol. 30, No. 2 (February, 1979), pages 73–88.

BERT LAHR

"His face appears to be composed of pouches, crevasses, and hummocks between two vast outcroppings of ear—a veritable terminal moraine of a face—and his pale blue eyes obviously mean a great deal to each other, since they are set close together," wrote Gilbert Millstein in a perfect description of Bert Lahr. One of the great comedians of burlesque and vaudeville, Lahr went on to prove himself a more than capable character actor in films and on the legitimate stage. He never retired and always gave his all to any performance. As early as September 8, 1922, *Variety* noted, "Lahr is a laugh-maker with the accent on the 'maker'.... Working single-handed, he mugs and gags and exhumes and originates until he reaches the point of exhaustion."

Bert Lahr was born in New York City, the son of German immigrants, on August 13, 1895. He entered burlesque as a member of a child act, "The Seven Frolics," in 1910 and might have sunk into obscurity had it not been for Billy K. Wells who wrote sketches for the major Columbia Burlesque Circuit and who spotted Lahr's act in

Bert Lahr with Mr. and Mrs. Jack Haley at the Stork Club

1915 and hired him for the Columbia Circuit. After the First World War, Lahr developed a vaudeville routine with his first wife, Mercedes Delpino, and the act of Lahr and Mercedes prospered. In their most famous sketch, Lahr was a drunken cop trying to arrest hootchy-kootchy dancer Mercedes. The latter would ask, "Are you speaking to me?" To which Lahr would respond, "Yeah to you and [looking at her breasts] to you too." (Lahr divorced Mercedes Delpino in 1939 and a year later married Mildred Schroeder Robinson; one of the children of that first marriage is theatre critic and scholar John Lahr.)

On November 28, 1927, Bert Lahr made his Broadway debut in *Harry Delmar's Revels*, but it was not until 1928 and *Hold Everything!* that Lahr established himself as a major musical comedy star. Interestingly, Lou Holtz claims that Bert Lahr was nothing as a single comic act in burlesque and vaudeville, but once he was playing a scene, with the aid of a good scriptwriter, he was unbeatable. This is confirmed by Lahr, who once commented, "My kind of comedian is more like an actor. I'm just playing situations and characters." Certainly, from all accounts, Lahr was not funny off stage, constantly worrying about his act and the future. "I am a sad man. A plumber doesn't go out without his tools. Does a comedian have to be funny on the street?" Lahr once asked.

Thanks to *Hold Everything!*, Bert Lahr headlined at the Palace on many occasions. Through the years, he was also kept busy in a number of Broadway productions, including *Flying High* (1930), *Hot-Cha!* (1932), *Life Begins at 8:40* (1934), *George White's Scandals* (1935), *The Show Is On* (1936), *DuBarry Was a Lady* (1939), *Seven Lively Arts* (1944), *Burlesque* (1946 revival), *Two on the Aisle* (1951), *The Beauty Part* (1962), and *Foxy* (1964). In 1956 Bert Lahr played Estragon in Beckett's *Waiting for Godot,* which introduced him to a new audience that may have been totally unaware of his early years in burlesque and vaudeville. The comedian's performance in *Waiting for Godot* showed the truth of Brooks Atkinson's remark that "on many occasions he proved that he was not merely a hired fool but a gifted actor."

Bert Lahr had made his first film, a Vitaphone short, in 1929 and between 1931 and 1967 was featured in sixteen productions, including *Flying High* (1931), *Zaza* (1939), *DuBarry Was a Lady* (1939), *Ship Ahoy* (1942), and *Rose Marie* (1954). Lahr's most famous screen appearance is of course, as the Cowardly Lion in M-G-M's 1939 production of *The Wizard of Oz.* During the shooting of *The Night They Raided Minsky's,* a film which pays generous and warm tribute to burlesque, Bert Lahr died on December 4, 1967. He had not filmed enough footage to make the film fitting tribute to his art and craft, but enough of Lahr's performance remains for the production to give us a glimpse of a comedian who helped make burlesque great.

References: "A Comic Discourses on Comedy" by Gilbert Millstein in the *New York Times* magazine (March 31, 1957), pages 27 and 62. "Bert Lahr, Comic Actor, Dies" by Alden Whitman in the *New York Times* (December 5, 1967), pages 1 and 51. *Notes on a Cowardly Lion* by John Lahr (Alfred A. Knopf, 1969).

LILLIE LANGTRY

Lillie Langtry

"Vaudeville," wrote Acton Davies in 1905, was "a place where a great many bad actors go before they die. A good variety show is one of the finest tonics in the world, but vaudeville when for the most part it consists of fallen stars in mediocre wishy washy one-act plays is one of the finest producers of mental dyspepsia that I know of." Davies's comments might seem to apply very well to Lillie Langtry (1852–1929), for by all accounts she was not a great actress, relying more on her fame, or infamy (as the mistress of King Edward VII when he was Prince of Wales) than on histrionic ability. And she did embark on a vaudeville career after nearly exhausting the possibilities held for her by the legitimate stage. Yet Mrs. Langtry, by the sheer magnetism of her personality, completely overwhelmed critics and public alike.

She had made her first stage appearance in London on December 15, 1881—"it was a great social event," reported one observer—and made her American stage debut in 1883. It was the distinguished manager H. B. Marinelli who persuaded Mrs. Langtry to make her vaudeville debut at the Fifth Avenue Theatre in October of 1906. The vehicle was a playlet, *Between the Nightfall and the Light* by Graham Hill, in which she was supported by Arthur Holmes-Gore and Hubert Carter. Rush in *Variety* (October 6, 1906) thought Mrs. Langtry "a finished artist" but found that although she "moved gracefully through the playlet," she "hardly reached the requirements of the strongly emotional scenes."

In 1912 Lillie Langtry toured the English music halls

in a twenty-two-minute comedy sketch titled *Helping the Cause,* which she brought to the New York Hippodrome in October of that same year. "Mrs. Langtry is sixty-three years old according to report. She's a wonder and didn't even begin to look old alongside the Doctor who appeared about twenty-two," noted Dash in *Variety* (October 4, 1912).

When Lillie Langtry's 1915 American tour of the legitimate play *Ashes* closed in Richmond, Virginia, the actress returned to vaudeville in a one-act play featuring only herself and her leading man, Lionel Atwill. E. F. Albee's booker, Edward Darling, had his doubts about the playlet, but Mrs. Langtry completely disarmed him with her charm, and Darling later commented that he would have paid her $2,500 a week had she been one of the Cherry Sisters. Leading man Atwill did not fare so well; he almost lost his job for refusing to take care of Mrs. Langtry's luggage.

Lillie Langtry was not kindly disposed toward many of the vaudeville managers with whom she was forced to deal. When one asked her what she did, Mrs. Langtry responded, "I ride a bicycle on a tight rope." "Aren't you afraid?" he asked. "Oh no," came the reply, "I have fallen so many times."

The dramatic sketch disappeared almost completely from the vaudeville stage in 1919, and by that time Mrs. Langtry's career had ended. But had it continued, who knows? Perhaps the dramatic sketch might have remained an integral part of vaudeville for years.

GRACE La RUE

Grace La Rue

Grace La Rue was a singer—perhaps prima donna is a better word—and actress, who was both a vaudeville star and a frequent object of parody in vaudeville. Born in Kansas City, Missouri, in 1882, Miss La Rue began her professional career in vaudeville with the team of Burke and La Rue. She later went into musical comedy, appearing in *The Blue Moon* (1906), *Molly May* (1910) *The Troubadour* (1910), *Betsy* (1911), and the 1907 and 1908 editions of *The Ziegfeld Follies*.

She made her vaudeville debut as a single (with three supporting players) in a fifteen-minute sketch, "The Record Breaker," by Hassard Short, at Poli's in Springfield, Missouri, in November of 1912. As part of the sketch, she sang an aria from *Madame Butterfly* and a duet with a phonograph recording of Caruso. *Variety* (November 29, 1912) thought it gave Miss La Rue "opportunity to display her Parisian cultivated voice, and her few nible steps." Grace La Rue made her Palace debut on August 4, 1913, and was a well-deserved hit with the song "You Made Me Love You."

During the 1910s and the twenties, Grace La Rue alternated vaudeville with appearances in musical comedy and revue. In the mid-twenties she began to appear with her second husband, actor Hale Hamilton. She died in San Francisco on March 13, 1956.

HARRY LAUDER

Harry Lauder's songs are as famous today as when he sang them sixty years ago and more. Melodies such as "I Love a Lassie," "She Is Ma Daisy," "Stop Yer Tickling, Jock," "Just a Wee Deoch-an-Doris," "Roamin' in the Gloamin'," "She Is My Rosie," and "The End of the Road" are probably some of the best known Scottish popular songs. Listeners may not know what a "deoch-an-Doris" is but it makes (and made) little difference. Unfortunately, while the songs may still be popular, Harry Lauder's appeal is harder to understand. Viewing him on film, one is aware only of a small, grouchy-looking Scotsman putting a lot of energy but little personality into his songs, and telling jokes that must have been corny when he first used them. The estimation is to some extent backed up by *Variety,* which, reviewing his act at the Garrick Theatre, Chicago, in February of 1930, noted that he was still a great entertainer for the Scotch "but today a little slow for the young folks."

As Joe Laurie, Jr. explained it, Lauder took Scottish wisdom and humor, threw in a few songs and homemade jokes, and combined it all with a good clean monolog. Lauder was born in Portobello, Scotland, on August 4, 1870, and worked in a flax mill and a coal mine before making his first public appearance in Arbroath, Scotland, on August 24, 1882. After years of touring in both professional and amateur engagements, he made his London debut at Gatti's Westminister Music Hall on March 19, 1900, singing, with great success, "Tobermory," "Callahan-Call Again," and "The Lass of Killiecrankie." He soon became one of the most popular and highly paid of British music hall artists, touring throughout the United Kingdom as well as South Africa and Australia.

Harry Lauder

Lauder became an international star in 1907 when he made his initial American appearance. Audiences simply would not let him leave the stage; at his first New York appearance, at the New York Theatre, he was held by the audience for more than an hour. After that, Joe Laurie, Jr. wrote in *Variety* (March 1, 1950), "He remained all through the years as one of the greatest, if not the greatest, one-man show that graced our shores and theatres." William Morris, at that time with Klaw and Erlanger, handled that and all of Lauder's subsequent American engagements until his twenty-fifth and last tour of the United States in 1934. The entertainer was extraordinarily loyal to Morris and to others with whom he worked. Martin Wagner was always the company manager and Jack Lait was always the publicist.

Just as Lauder was loyal to those who helped him, audiences were loyal to him. In 1911 he was booked into the Manhattan Opera House (the first vaudevillian to play there) and because of fog and quarantine problems he did not get to the theatre on opening night until 12:45 A.M. The audience had waited patiently for him since 8:15 P.M. Lauder's opening remark was, "Ha' ye no hame to go to?"

A typical Lauder vaudeville stage appearance would last for an hour and fifteen minutes. When he appeared at New York's Lincoln Theatre in 1908, audiences refused again to let him leave the stage, becoming unruly in their demands of "Give us another song, Harry." He sang everything from a drunken toastmaster's wedding song, "The Wedding Bells Were Ringing," to "Rocked in the Cradle of the Deep." "It is impossible to catch and analyze the peculiarly elusive charm of this great artist," wrote *Variety*. "It is a thing so subtle and indefinable it has not a name, and yet it exerts a force that cannot be escaped. . . . His every word and gesture gives a line or faithful touch of color to the picture he seeks to draw, and the whole is a vivid, forceful characterization."

During the First World War, Harry Lauder was tireless in entertaining the troops, for which he was knighted in 1919. Winston Churchill said of Lauder, "By his inspiring songs and valiant life he rendered measureless service to the Scottish race and to the British Empire." He also appeared in the United States selling Liberty Bonds. A reputation for stinginess was apparently without foundation, for Lauder was actually generous even returning $3,000 of his usual $5,000 a week salary to William Morris for performances that he had missed. His only fobile was that he would never play a Sunday performance, maintaining that, like him, his audience was deeply religious. Harry Lauder's philosophy was basically to be honest, to pay one's debts, to work hard and save. He never strayed from those simple beliefs.

After the death of his son, Captain John Lauder, on the battlefront Lauder returned to America in December of 1918, opening in New York's Lexington Theatre. There were tears in his eyes as he sang his son's favorite song, "Wee Hoose 'mang the Heather," and the keynote of his performance was a plea titled "Victory with Mercy" in which he asked "Don't let us sing any more about war; just let us sing of love." Lauder made a similar tour in 1928 after the death the previous year of his wife, Nancy. Beginning January 30, 1928, he played four weeks at New York's Knickerbocker Theatre. He sang all the old favorites, including the morale-boosting "The End of the Road." "Monday night, to a sold-out theatre, he was the rollicking comic, the comedian extraordinary," wrote *Variety* (February 1, 1928). "The Pagliacci in the flesh. He made them laugh; he wrung them dry after he had doused them with laughter. Then he drenched them again—with tears. A few well-chosen words, no reference by name or direct implication to his loss, and a song of courage—and he had a thousand people weeping."

Harry Lauder made many recordings of his songs and also appeared in a few unnoteworthy films, including some experimental sound films in 1914. Harry Lauder never played the Palace, but those early talkie shorts did. He eventually retired in 1949 at the age of seventy-eight. "Retirement is a word I've simply been far too busy to use, a word that I've avoided," he commented. "I've worked hard all my life and enjoyed every minute of it. Still, I suppose a man can't go on forever, although I'd be perfectly willing to. I daresay it's time I took a breather." He died at his London home on February 26, 1950. In an editorial the *Los Angeles Times* commented, "To a generation which never heard him, Harry Lauder was no more than a tradition. To their oldsters, however, Harry Lauder was the grandest of entertainers, a minstrel with a personality that won audiences wherever he appeared. There was nobody like him; nor is another such likely to appear soon."

JOE LAURIE, JR.

Joe Laurie, Jr. was a vaudeville performer, but he was also coauthor of one of the best overviews of American entertainment in the twentieth century, *Show Biz: From Vaude to Video*, plus one of the few major works on vaudeville, titled simply *Vaudeville*. After his death at age sixty-one, on April 29, 1954, Abel Green paid tribute to him in the May 5, 1954, issue of *Variety*. Inasmuch as Laurie was a prominent contributor to *Variety* for many years, it seems appropriate to reprint that tribute here:

Of all the historians of the theatre, none loved show biz with the ardor and affection as did "little Joe"— "the oldest junior this side of John D."—whose passion for things theatrical was the epitome of "there's no business like show business." It was a manifestation long before Irving Berlin gave the industry which he, too, loves, its fitting "theme song."

. . . Laurie knew more about show biz than perhaps any contemporary. His fund of knowledge was prodigious. Nobody needed any newspaper files when Joe was around; if lacking any exact date, he had it in his prodigious files or knew where to get it.

He had enough left from the 200,000 overmatter words of "Show Biz" which he coauthored for another book. His more recent solo-authored *"Vaudeville: Honkeytonks to the Palace"* is the definitive authority on the subject. His public performance achievements as a vaude and musical comedy star have been generously reprised in the dailies, as indicated below. He was working on a post-1950s updating of *Show Biz* along with other theatrical writings.

The magic of electronics, of course, projected Joe Laurie, Jr. into widest public recognition via the "Can You Top This?" package in a decade of association with "Senator" Ed Ford (owner of the show), Harry Hershfeld, Peter Donald, and Ward Wilson, both on radio and tv. Latterly, Ford continued the package on NBC radio sans Laurie.

Joe was a prolific after-dinner speaker and raconteur. He was the "literati circuit" and disc jockey's delight because, in the latterday orbit of "have written book, must travel," Joe's barnstorming appearances on sundry radio and video shows, panel programs, interviews, deejays, et al., he brought to each fifteen- or thirty-minute show a wealth of anecdotage, nostalgia, and reminiscence. Plus his own basic talents as a song-and-dance man, which made him a very "special" literati pitchman. He discovered that with *Show Biz*, but really did an intensive tour on behalf of his *"Vaudeville"* book.

The very "special" connotation probably sums up Joe. He was another of that great show biz tradition who did their soft deeds in the dark. A fast man with a buck, none knew the extent of Joe's personal pension list. He also knew the esprit that obtains among the show biz quick-givers. He had tremendous respect for certain personalities who, like him, were fast on the draw with a buck and "never expected it back." Yet when Joe was in need, he made it a credo to make sure he would not be on the "forget to give it back" list. And in the lean years when he needed it, and prospects were grim, "somehow I never had to ask anybody for anything; they'd always thrust it on," Joe confided. That was easy to understand with a guy like Joe Laurie, Jr.

. . . Joe's life was rich and colorful. He could have inspired the Joe-Miller about "burning the schoolhouse down to get him out of 3-B," excepting that Joe's career started when he wasn't quite ten. In a bio sketch which he characteristically captioned "Laurie on Laurie," prepared for Henry Holt and Co., his book publishers, he wrote:

I was born on the lower East Side of New York, on the same street as the late Al Smith; the resemblance ends right there.

The Chinatown bus used to go down that street but since I moved to Forest Hills there is nothing there to show the customers, so now they go down another street.

About the time I graduated from 3-B, I got a job in a florist shop. Would have stayed there but the boss of the place used to squirt insect powder all over the joint, so my life was continually in danger. I also was in love at that time with some gal and I spent most of my time tearing the daisies apart ("she loves me, she loves me not"). It came out "not" no matter where I started. I got a bad case of fallen arches from standing on my tiptoes trying to look a pansy in the face.

I couldn't stand the smell of the greenhouse so got a job in a stable—Newcastle Stable to be exact. I was exercise boy. Horses are pretty smart but they didn't know whether I was on their backs or not. I weigh about twenty-two pounds while walking the floor with the baby in my arms. The owner of the stable one night put rattraps all over the place. I got caught in one of 'em—it wouldn't have been so bad, but the owner came down and found I had eaten all the cheese, so they threw me out. After World War I the Kaiser went to Holland and I went to vaudeville. It was some years before anybody saw either of us.

I was billed in vaudeville as "the pint-sized comedian." I don't care to tire you with statistics but here are the facts: A pint is sixteen ounces; sixteen ounces is a pound; a pound is five dollars . . . and I am no five dollar comedian. I played vaudeville until they got smarted up.

Have been staff columnist for *Variety* for over twenty years, but those muggs can't wise up to anybody. I am prouder of them not catching up with me than anything I have ever done. I am one of the three stars on the "Can You Top This?" program. My other joke conspirators are Senator Ford and Harry Hershfeld. I hope they never catch up to me. They're nice guys.

I am always working on books about show business, besides writing for magazines, pictures, etc. Between times I play pool at the Lambs, which makes me enough money so I can afford to write. SEZ

Joe Laurie, Jr.

Altogether he held about eighty jobs from newsboy, messenger, exercise boy for Newcastle Stables, florist, copy boy for Dow, Jones Co., Sulka's, office boy for Street & Smith, shirtwaist factory, bookbinder, drugstore, petticoat biz, water boy for harvest hands, to running errands for lawyer, dentist, diamond setter, jewelry store, stationer's, made garters, dealt stuss in a gambling house, stickman in a dice game, hopped freights from Chicago to the Coast and back to New York.

His first professional appearance was in an act with Aleen Bronson at a Fireman's Benefit, Greenlawn, Long Island. It was a big hit and their self-written act thereafter toured every small-time vaudeville circuit in the land. They became headliners eventually and Joe was proud of the fact that "we played the Palace on Broadway over twenty times as a team." Laurie and Bronson were a man-and-wife as well as professional team until 1922 when he married Nellie Butcher (professionally June Tempest), who was in Harry Carroll's vaudeville flash act.

. . . The chronology of his show biz activities include his career as monologist after Laurie and Bronson split; he wrote ten scenes for "Over the Top," Broadway musical with Ed Wynn, T. Roy Barnes, Justine Johnstone, and Fred Astaire; a Laurie sketch gave the latter his first speaking lines. Laurie and Bronson were also featured in "Over the Top." He starred in "Gingham Girl" (Chicago), "Plain Jane," "Great Little Guy," "If I was Rich," "Weather Clear—Track Fast."

He owned and produced "Memory Lane," the biggest act of old-timers ever produced wherein a pseudo-Mr. and Mrs. Laurie, Sr. came on for a pleasantly polite song-and-dance finale. Laurie's basic cast included William C. Handy ("St. Louis Blues, " etc.) J. Rosamond Johnson ("Under the Bamboo Tree"), Gus Hill (Indian club swinger and onetime burlesque and "tab" show producer), Dave Genaro ("the original cakewalker"), Annie Hart, Emma Francis, Lizzie Wilson, et al. Laurie impersonated Chuck Connors and emceed.

He authored over 100 vaudeville sketches; play-doctored many Broadway legit and musical shows; wrote skits and blackouts for revues; was principal writer for Eddie Cantor and Al Jolson radio shows; has been staff columnist on *Variety* for over twenty years; wrote "Barbary Host" for Warner Bros. and other film originals; collaborated on plays with Ben Hecht, Gene Fowler, Paul Gerard Smith, Douglas Durkin, and Wallace Smith. He wrote "Union Depot" for Douglas Fairbanks Jr. and Loretta Young,

and collaborated on the pic version of "Babes in Arms."

Long billed as "the pint-sized author-comedian," Joe Laurie, Jr. was a giant in show biz and, even more importantly, loomed very large in the hearts of his fellow showmen.

JANE AND KATHERINE LEE

Jane and Katherine Lee

Jane and Katherine Lee were child actresses who first came to prominence in 1914 after successfully supporting Annette Kellermann in the film *Neptune's Daughter*. They were cute and winsome, and movie audiences liked them in such films as *Soul of Broadway* (1915) and *Swat the Spy* (1918). Between 1914 and 1919, the Lee Sisters were featured in a number of successful films, chiefly for the William Fox Company, and *Photoplay* (Many, 1916) went so far as to describe Jane as "one of the really great personalities of the screen."

It was natural that the girls should try vaudeville, which they did very successfully in the spring of 1920. They appeared in a skit by Tommy Gray, which was set in a movie studio and had them exchanging comic patter, impersonating a couple of old maids, and engaging in a spot of tragedy as Jane cried beside the bed of a dying Katherine. "The act was a riot at the Riverside Monday night, stopping the show cold for three or four minutes," reported *Variety* (April 2, 1920). "It's ready for the biggest and best of the big-time houses and should clean up everywhere."

In the twenties, the sisters toured in a version of the Duncan Sisters' *Topsy and Eva* and also played picture theatres. They returned to New York vaudeville in May of 1926 with a fifteen-minute act at Loew's State, which proved they were still appealing despite advancing years —by this time they were in their late teens. The sisters did a comic dialog, then sat on the stage with their feet in the footlights and sang "Tie Me to Your Apron Strings Again" and "When It's Onion Time in Bermuda." As *Variety* (May 26, 1926) reported, "The result was the girls winning the hit of the show." They continued together in vaudeville until 1932, when they split and Jane soloed in the Fanchon and Marco touring version of *Whoopee!* They reunited a year later and made their triumphant return to vaudeville at the RKO Theatre in Paterson, New Jersey, on November 21, 1933.

They appear to have retired in the mid-thirties. Jane Lee, the youngest of the two, died at the reported age of forty-five in New York on March 17, 1957. Katherine may well be still alive. Despite their billing as sisters in both films and vaudeville, this writer has the strong suspicion that they were not blood relatives at all but were simply teamed as a sister act by Jane's ambitious mother.

EDDIE LEONARD

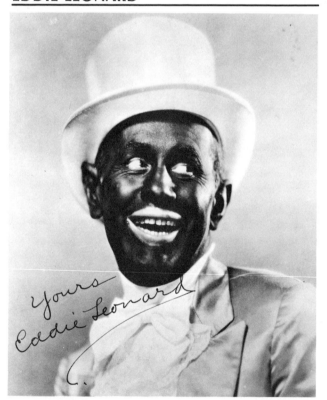

Eddie Leonard

The phrase "blackface minstrels" instantly brings to mind images of Al Jolson or perhaps Eddie Cantor, but the greatest of all minstrel showmen was neither of these men but Eddie Leonard, whose career spanned the years from the 1890s through the mid-thirties. In 1927 *Billboard* wrote of him, "Eddie Leonard is a great showman; he knows minstrelsy to the last lilt; his graceful stepping equals any of the former masters of the art, and he deserves every favor extended to him by his audience. He is indeed the minstrel of the hour."

"The Minstrel of the Hour," as Leonard came to be known, was born in Richmond, Virginia, on October 18, 1875. He had no time for a formal education, as he had to support his mother, so he became an apprentice at a Richmond rolling mill. James Decker, the agent for Lew Dockstader's Minstrels, heard of Leonard's rich singing voice, with which he used to entertain his fellow workers, and invited the boy to join Dockstader in the early 1890s. From Dockstader's Minstrels, Eddie Leonard joined the Haverly Minstrel Troupe and by 1902 was one of the stars of the company.

With his wife, Mabel Russell, Eddie Leonard soon became a favorite of the vaudeville halls. In 1909 *Variety* hailed him as "easily up with the leaders in modern minstrelsy." His song and dance act would usually include "coon" songs such as "Wha, Wha Coon" (performed by Mrs. Leonard) and a number of songs composed by Leonard, the most famous of which were "Ida, Sweet as Apple Cider," "Roly Boly Eyes," and "Just Because She Made Them Goo-Goo Eyes." Leonard was a great believer in publicity. In 1928 he took three pages of advertising in one issue of *Variety,* pointing out that he was as good as , if not better than Jolson. He was the last of a line of minstrels which could be traced back to the Southern plantations.

Of course, blackface minstrelsy died out in the thirties, and Eddie Leonard's fame and career disappeared. On Friday, July 29, 1941, he checked into the Imperial Hotel in the Herald Square section of New York, close to the sites of his many successes. A few hours later, he was found dead in his room, apparently of natural causes. Critics thought Leonard a gentle minstrel performer, with an appealing voice which did not hide a slight Irish brogue. He was equally at home with Negro spirituals and with comedy songs. His act was not racially insulting, but rather, as one critic had remarked, he transformed burnt cork into a thing of beauty. He was graceful and he was tender. A critic wrote, "Here is a rare performer, one with the discernment to see the vast wealth that is the heritage of the millions of Negroes in America. Much great art is naive, simple and unaffected—and this is the quality of Negro art. Leonard is a Southerner, is deeply in sympathy with the Negro, and as faithful as (Stephen) Foster in his depiction of the spirtitual qualities of the race."

ETHEL LEVEY

Variety's Sime Silverman described Ethel Levey as "always the perfect song deliverer," but she was more than a songstress; she was also an accomplished dancer and comedian with a vibrant and exuberant personality. Ethel Levey was born Ethelia Fowler in San Francisco on November 22, 1881, and took the name of Levey from her Jewish stepfather. She appeared in amateur theatricals as a child, and by the age of eight was recognized as an accomplished pianist and elocutionist. The performer made her professional debut, with a coon song specialty,

Ethel Levey in 1921

at San Francisco's Columbia Theatre on December 31, 1897, in *A Milk White Flag*. Her New York debut came at the Weber and Field's Music Hall, which led to a twenty-week engagement at Koster and Bial's Music Hall.

In 1898 Ethel Levey met George M. Cohan and they were married the following year. For the next seven years Ethel Levey was to play in all of Cohan's productions, including *The Governor's Son* (1901), *Running for Office* (1903), *Little Johnny Jones* (1904), and *George Washington, Jr.* (1906). However, both Cohan and his wife were strong-willed, individual personalities, too much so to co-exist for any length of time, and they were divorced on February 18, 1907.

After the divorce Ethel Levey returned to vaudeville, with an initial engagement at the Harlem Opera House. There was no question about her popularity; every seat in the house was sold, and standing patrons were lined up four deep behind the orchestra rail. Miss Levey sang four songs, including her big hit from *George Washington, Jr.* "I Was Born in Virginia." As *Variety* noted, she "scored a great bit solid hit."

In 1909 Ethel Levey was in London, where she had first appeared in 1900. She returned to London in 1912 to appear in *Hullo, Ragtime!*, followed by *Hullo, Tango!* in 1913. In those years Ethel Levey's biggest successes were in London, with shows such as *Follow the Crowd* (1916), *Three Cheers* (1917), and *Oh! Julie* (1920). She was in demand on both sides of the Atlantic. As early as 1911 she had delighted audiences at Hammerstein's Roof with such songs as "Pride of the Prairie" and "Dear Old Broadway," —above all, with her dancing, which apparently was the

high spot of her vaudeville appearances. In January of 1921 Miss Levey returned to New York and to the Palace, following years of success in London, and audiences here were just as enthusiastic as their European colleagues.

Ethel Levey continued to appear on stage through the fifties; she died on February 27, 1955.

TED LEWIS

Ted Lewis

With his battered top hat, his clarinet, and his greeting, "Is *ev'*rybody happy?" Ted Lewis became an American institution, billed as "The Jazz King" quite erroneously, because he did not play jazz as we know it today. That croaky voice of Ted Lewis's introduced such songs as "When My Baby Smiles at Me" and "Me and My Shadow," from which he extracted an element of drama as well as an element of jazz. He was a showman as much as he was a musician; he came on stage twirling a cane and let his hat roll down his arm before catching it—a gag he claimed to have learned from W. C. Fields.

Ted Lewis was born Theodore Leopold Friedman in Circleville, Ohio, on June 6, 1890. His first professional engagement was singing in a Circleville nickelodeon, and he learned to play the clarinet in the public school band. In New York a few years later, he changed his name to one that would fit a theatre marquee and formed the Ted Lewis Nut Band. He acquired the battered top hat from a hack driver named "Mississippi" in a dice game at Rector's Restaurant in 1917, and it was at Rector's that he first made his famous introduction. In 1918 Lewis opened his own cabaret in New York, the Bal Tabarin, which was to be followed later by the Montmartre Club and the Ted Lewis Club.

He had, of course, played small-time vaudeville prior to coming to New York in the early 1910s, but his first major New York vaudeville appearance came in September of 1919 at the Palace. The *New York Dramatic Mirror* (September 4, 1919) reported, "He made his entry at the Palace with a bang and kept on banging clean through his exit to a curtain speech. There are few who would dare dispute his title of 'Jazz King.' His middle name is rhythm and he fingers a wicked clarinet not to mention a mean shimmy. His four abettors, togged out like the clown dog in an animal act, give valuable assistance. The laughing trombone is a wonder. Altogether, Ted and the boys make a prize bunch of Jazz banditti."

Lewis was to return to the Palace many times in the future. In May of 1922 he was back with the same routine, except that the members of his band (five brasses, a drummer, and a pianist) were now dressed in tuxedos rather than clown costumes. The big number was "You've Made a Dr. Jekyll and Mr. Hyde Out of Me." Later that year Lewis was to introduce "Me and My Shadow," with Eddie Chester as the first and most famous shadow. In 1924 Ted Lewis was back at the Palace with an act which included comedy sketches and a much bigger band. His showmanship paid off as he played a jazz preacher uniting the trombonist and the cornet player, and the baton-twirling leader of a small town band, using an effect which appears to have been similar to the flickering lights so popular in today's discos. "Lewis is in a class by himself as an entertainer," wrote *Variety* (September 10, 1924). "He is the John Henry of the band leaders."

Aside from vaudeville, Ted Lewis was featured in revues such as the Ziegfeld *Midnight Frolic* (1919), *The Greenwich Village Follies* (1921), and *Artists and Models* (1927). In the summer of 1925, he and the Dolly Sisters were a big hit at London's Kit-Kat Club.

"My shows were always clean and always entertaining to the masses," Ted Lewis recalled in 1970. "What most people want are lyrics that come straight from the heart." Rock and roll put an end to lyrics straight from the heart, and also to Ted Lewis's career. He retired at the age of seventy-seven, declaring "They think Ted Lewis is too corny." He died in his New York apartment on August 25, 1971, with his wife of fifty-six years, Adah Becker, at his side. She had appeared in burlesque prior to their marriage and had been his secretary and business manager. In 1977 Mrs. Lewis created the Ted Lewis Museum in Circleville, Ohio, as a permanent memorial to the man who for more than fifty years did make *ev*-'rybody happy.

WINNIE LIGHTNER

Winnie Lightner's loud voice and comic features delighted vaudeville and film audiences for a good many years. One has only to see and hear her in Warner Bros. 1929 all-star revue *Show of Shows* performing "Singin' in the Bath Tub" (supported by a male chorus in female attire) to recognize the qualities that made her so popular. In vaudeville, Winnie Lightner sang many of her numbers so

Winnie Lightner

quickly and performed with such zest—preferring a hasty exist without an encore, to leave the audience wanting more—that she became known as "The Song-a-Minute Girl."

She was born Winnifred Hanson in Greenport, Long Island, on September 17, 1901, and made her vaudeville debut in the late 1910s with an act titled "The Lightner Girls and Newton Alexander." Sometimes the act was billed as "The Lightner Sisters and Newton Alexander," although the other girl in the act was not Winnie's sister but Alexander's wife. The *New York Dramatic Mirror* saw the trio perform at the Alhambra in August of 1920 and commented, "The Lightner Girls and Newton Alexander, featuring that inimitable facial contortionist, Winnie Lightner, dispensed patter, ditties, and puns that would have died an early death had it not been for Winnie's face comedy.' " In October of 1920 the act was at the Palace, and the *New York Dramatic Mirror* noted that Winnie Lightner was a show in herself. For the first time, besides the zippy comedy numbers of "Since that Jazz Has Gone to China Town" and "Tric-Tric-Tricoline," Winnie Lightner showed a serious side by performing a ballad, "Wonderful Eyes," with great success. From vaudeville, Winnie Lightner (minus sister and Newton Alexander) went into *George White's Scandals*. In the 1923 edition she was an immediate hit, singing George Gershwin's "I'll Build a Stairway to Paradise" backed by Paul Whiteman and His Orchestra. The following year she scored another success with Gershwin's "Somebody Loves Me." In many ways it was remarkable how this rough and rowdy woman could put across a gentle ballad with feeling. She was back at the Palace in June of 1927 showing what she could do with a variety of songs. *Variety* (June 15, 1927) wrote, "This girl can stay in vaudeville for so long as she wills," describing her act as "Fast, furious, and always to the point."

However, as vaudeville died Winnie Lightner was able to embark on a new career—in films. She made her first screen appearance in 1928 and, thanks to her success in th 1929 production of *Gold Diggers of Broadway*, she was signed to a Warner Bros. contract. Winnie was featured in *She Couldn't Say No* (1930), *Life of the Party* (1930), *Gold Dust Gertie* (1931), *Manhattan Parade* (1932), and *Eight to Five* (1932) among others, many of which were directed by her second husband, Roy Del Ruth. Winnie Lightner's last film was *I'll Fix It* in 1934, after which she decided to settle down to life as a housewife. She died at her home in Sherman Oaks, California, on March 5, 1971. A brother, Fred Lightner, was a fairly popular comedian in vaudeville.

ALICE LLOYD

Alice Lloyd

Marie Lloyd may be the best known and most popular member of the Lloyd family as far as the English are concerned, but it was her sister, Alice, who was far better known and liked in America. Her career in America spanned the years from 1906 to 1927. Unlike her older sister, Alice was pretty and appealing; her songs lacked the caustic and raucous quality of Marie's. She was billed as "The Ideal Daintee Chanteuse." Douglas Gilbert, in

American Vaudeville, goes so far as to claim she was nothing more than a pretty face, helped along by a good press agent.

Alice Lloyd was born in London on October 20, 1873, and made her first stage appearance with her sister Grace, as "The Sisters Lloyd," at the Forester's Music Hall on February 20, 1888. She continued to appear with her sister until the latter married, and Alice embarked on a solo act. Alice Lloyd made her American debut at the Colonial Theatre in February of 1907, and proved so popular she was selected to headline the bill for the second week of her engagement. On March 23, 1907, she was featured on the front cover of *Variety*. On that first American engagement she sang "May," "Stockings on the Line," "The Tourist and the Maid," "Never Introduce Your Bloke to Your Lady Friend," and "Who Are You Looking At?" It was the last song which the audiences loved, and *Variety* (March 2, 1907) wrote, "No more dainty, artistic bit of song acting has been given on the American stage and there is not an American actress who could not benefit by listening to this number."

The singer quickly became almost a resident of the American vaudeville stage. At the Majestic Theatre, Chicago, in June of 1908 she proved the proverbial knockout, reported *Variety*, and was retained to headline for a second week. In 1913 she had a new hit song "Who Are You Getting At, Eh?" In *Variety* (October 31, 1913), Sime Silverman wrote, "There's only one Alice Lloyd. There's something about that English girl, and she's a great little girl, Alice, on or off the stage." The following year she and Marie Lloyd were playing on opposite sides of Times Square, Alice at the Palace and Marie at Hammerstein's. There was little question as far as critics and audiences were concerned as to who was the bigger draw.

In September of 1925 Alice Lloyd was at the Palace again after a three-year tour of the world. She was plumper than she had been ten years before, but audiences were just as enthusiastic about her songs which included "Naughty but Nice," "Have a Little Dip with Me," and "The Older the Fiddle the Sweeter the Tune." In 1927 Alice Lloyd toured the Pantages western circuit at $1,250 a week—"the cheapest act for drawing power Pan had had in months," according to *Variety* (January 18, 1928). She turned down an offer to appear on an all-English bill at the Palace for the week of January 23, 1928, but instead returned to England, ending her years on the American stage. Strangely enough, she was not acclaimed as a legitimate successor to her sister until January of 1927, but, of course, she was not imitative of Marie Lloyd and was a star performer in her own right.

Alice Lloyd died at her home in Banstead on the outskirts of London on November 16, 1949. Reporting her death, the *London Times* recalled her last famous song from the late twenties, "Good Old Iron—Never Been Known to Rust," and remembered her as "a pleasant-faced, buxom, middle-aged woman, a good deal like her more famous sister in feature."

Reference: "Why I Am So Grateful" by Alice Lloyd in *Variety* Vol. 42, No.1 (December 11, 1909), page 32.

MARIE LLOYD

Marie Lloyd

"Marie Lloyd is more than a dissipation," said one wit. "She's a beloved 'abit, which grows on you just like your mustache." She was the most famous performer in British music hall, yet she was eclipsed in American vaudeville by her sister, Alice, and never achieved lasting popularity here, making only two visits to these shores. Perhaps her songs were simply too English for American tastes and audiences failed to get the nuances of her risqué lyrics.

The woman who was to become a national institution in England was born Matilda Alice Victoria Wood in the London slum neighborhood of Hoxton on February 12, 1870. She made her first stage appearance as Bella Delmere, at London's Eagle Assembly Rooms on May 9, 1885; six months later she had become Marie Lloyd, taking the last name from the popular newspaper *Lloyd's News*. Shortly thereafter Marie Lloyd had her first big success at the Middlesex Theatre in Drury Lane, singing a song first introduced by Nelly Power, "The Boy that I Love Sits up in the Balcony." She quickly became known for raunchy songs like "She'd Never Had the Ticket Punched Before" and "Johnny Jones," which went like this:

What's that for, eh! Oh tell me Ma.
If you won't tell me, I'll ask Pa.
But Ma said, Oh it's nothing, hold your row.
Well, I've asked Johnny Jones see,
So I know now!

The earliest great song identified with Marie Lloyd was "Oh, Mr. Porter," the tale of a girl who took the wrong train, which she first sang at the Royal Theatre, Holborn, in 1893. British audiences loved the plump little girl with her cheeky songs, many of which have been classics in England, songs like "A Little of What You Fancy Does You Good" and "My Old Man Said Follow the Van." She had a unique knack for dealing with her audience. When a galleryite shouted "Marie, give us a dirty look!" she retorted, "No need, you've got one."

Marie Lloyd gave of herself wholeheartedly, both physically and financially. However tired she might be, she always appeared before an audience full of energy. Her generosity was boundless. She once took over a shop in London's East End and handed over its stock to the poor; when nothing was left she proceeded to hand out money to latecomers. Many liberal show business personalities today could learn much about charity and humility from Marie Lloyd.

In October of 1907 Marie Lloyd made her first New York appearance but failed to appeal. She returned to America in the fall of 1913 and her arrival caused a considerable stir because the immigration authorities refused to allow her to leave the S.S. *Olympic* on which she was traveling; the man with whom she was sharing a cabin, Bernard Dillon, was not her husband—they were subsequently married in February of 1914—and Miss Lloyd used a few too many four letter words to the immigration officers. Eventually, E. F. Albee and various major vaudeville performers intervened on her behalf, and she was allowed to enter the country. She appeared at the Palace in early October singing "Something on His Mind," "Woman Knows How Far She Can Go," and "A Little of What You Fancy Does You Good," among others. *Variety* thought her songs and jokes too mild for her reputation, but the audience apparently loved her; she had the biggest crowd seen at the Palace on opening night since Sarah Bernhardt played there.

The distinguished dramatic critic Acton Davies reviewed her performance in the *New York Evening Sun* on October 16, 1913, and wrote, "Marie Lloyd is a wonder. More than that, she is consummate artist. . . . This woman with a few notes of music to help her out could make the City Directory sound like the bluest of Blue Books, and she would achieve her purpose not with her voice, which may be regarded as a strictly limited asset, but by a mere glance of the eye."

Marie Lloyd once said, "I seem to have had a busy life, eh? Wonderful constitution they must think I have." The life she led gradually took its toll. Early in October of 1922 she appeared at the Edmonton Empire Theatre in London closing her act with another of her famous cockney songs, "One of the Ruins that Cromwell Knocked About a Bit." The audience roared at her imitation of a drunken woman staggering around the stage, little realizing they were watching an actress so sick she could hardly stand. Three days after that performance, on October 7, 1922, Marie Lloyd died at her home in Golders Green, London. Ten thousand people attended her funeral and another one hundred thousand visited the graveside that first weekend.

She was indeed, as Sarah Bernhardt said, "the most artistic comedienne of the English stage," and, as T. S. Eliot wrote, she expressed the soul of the people.

Besides Alice and Marie, other members of the Lloyd family appeared on the stage. Daisy Wood, a sister, played vaudeville, as did Marie's daughter, first as Marie Courtney and later as Marie Lloyd, Jr. Rose Lloyd appeared with Alice as "The Sisters Lloyd." As early as September 21, 1908, *Variety* reported, "The record of the Lloyds to date in point of merit and public appreciation now stands Alice, Marie, Daisy, and Rosie."

CISSIE (CECILIA) LOFTUS

Cissie Loftus

"The Queen of Mimics" and "That Incomparable Mimic" were just two of the titles bestowed on Cissie Loftus, one of the greatest impressionists of the vaudeville stage. Born in Glasgow, Scotland, on October 22, 1876, Cissie Loftus carried on the show business tradition set by her mother, Marie Loftus, who had been a popular performer in American burlesque. (Her songs included "And She Lisped When She Said 'Yes,'" "One Touch of Nature Makes the Whole World Kin," "Don't You Believe It, Dear Boys," "She Wore a Little Safety Pin Behind," and "To Err Is Human, To Forgive, Divine.") Cissie Loftus made her first stage appearance at the Alhambra Theatre, Belfast, in October of 1892, singing a ballad entitled "Molly Darling." Less than a year later she made her London debut at the Oxford Music Hall, on July 15, 1893.

Cissie Loftus made her American debut at Koster and Bial's Music Hall on January 21, 1895, and for the rest of her life she traveled constantly between London and New York. Aside from vaudeville, she was in great demand on the legitimate stage. In 1900 she appeared with Madame Modjeska's Company; in 1901 she became E. H. Sothern's leading lady; in 1903 she played Marguerite opposite Sir Henry Irving in *Faust;* in 1905 she played Peter Pan in a revival of the J. M. Barrie play at London's Duke of York's Theatre; during 1913 and 1914 she toured with William Faversham in *Romeo and Juliet* and *Othello,* etc. In other words, Cissie Loftus was a uniquely talented lady.

Her impersonations in vaudeville were highly regarded, and included Bert Williams, Nazimova, Caruso, Sir Harry Lauder, Nora Bayes, and Irene Franklin. Her vaudeville tours across America, whether on stage with her impersonations or in one-act plays such as *The Diamond Express* in 1906, were immensely successful. In September of 1909 she broke the attendance records at the Masonic Temple in Chicago. In 1915 she appeared with Marie Dressler at the Palace and did a "sister" act, with gags like "She never married, did she?" "No, her children wouldn't let her." After several years of absence from American vaudeville, Cissie Loftus came back to the Palace to top the bill in November of 1923. She was scheduled to appear on stage for twenty minutes but the audience simply would not let her go; she remained and performed for them for over an hour. At that time, *Variety* noted she could entertain both the masses and the classes with her impersonations of Harry Lauder, Ethel Barrymore, Alice Delysia, and others. In April of 1925 she was one of the stars appearing in the old-timers week at the Palace, and despite the presence of Weber and Fields and Marie Cahill there was no question that Cissie Loftus was *the* star old-timer.

Although she continued acting almost continually through the thirties, both on the stage and in films, and apparently never missed a performance, alcoholism became more and more of a problem for her. In addition, she was hauled into a London court on charges of possessing narcotics. Despite these setbacks, Cissie Loftus continued to give her impersonations in a series of summer concerts and Sunday night performances at New York's Vanderbilt Theatre during 1938; that year she also appeared in Noel Coward's *Tonight at 8:30* at the Vanderbilt. A year before she died, she toured in *Arsenic and Old Lace.*

Death came to Cissie Loftus on July 12, 1943, in her room at the Lincoln Hotel in New York. Few who had the privilege of seeing her on stage would disagree with *Variety's* summation of her as "one of the most versatile women on the stage."

NICK LUCAS

Writing of a typical Nick Lucas performance in the late thirties, *The Billboard* (May 27, 1939) commented that his "voice is very soothing to the ears." That was the secret of Lucas's success through the years; he always gave a relaxed and relaxing performance, singing his songs in a gentle manner entirely devoid of gimmickry. The songs and the way in which he put them over were his act. He never told jokes or conversed with his audience, and his

Nick Lucas

act has not fundamentally changed in more than fifty years—except that today he will offer a mild wisecrack about his age. "I had to create a style that was accepted by the general public," says Lucas. "When you play the theatre, you play to all age brackets and all different types of people who like simple music that they can understand. I adopted a style of singing and playing my guitar that became successful, and that's all that matters."

Nick Lucas's philosophy has always been that audiences were paying to hear good singing of attractive songs. "Singers with gimmicks leave me cold," he once wrote. "There's no substitute for a good voice, singing a good song with good accompaniment. If a singer can do that he doesn't have to wiggle his ears, cry, whisper, groan, or grovel in the orchestra pit."

Lucas was born Dominic Lucanese in Newark, New Jersey, on August 22, 1897, the son of poor Italian immigrants. His brother was a musician—he played the accordian—and he taught the young Lucas to play the mandolin and guitar. Together the two would perform at local saloons. "It was practically a necessity that I got started in the music business," recalls Lucas. Later, around 1915, Nick Lucas began to work as a solo performer in cabarets, singing and playing the banjo. Lucas remembers, "I was working as a musician at the Edgewater Beach Hotel in Chicago with Ted Fio Rito's Orchestra, and I was on the radio a lot, when radio was practically in its infancy. I gained popularity unbeknownst to me, and then Brunswick asked me to do a recording—the band used to record for Brunswick. And the record was so big that immediately I left the band and went on my own."

In fact, Lucas had made a recording of himself playing the guitar as early as 1922, but it was with his 1924 recordings of "My Best Girl" and "Dreamer of Dreams" that he was able to establish himself as a major vaudeville entertainer, often appearing in the guise of a Venetian troubador, accompanying himself on the mandolin. Lucas's big vaudeville break came in December of 1924 when he appeared as one of the acts prior to the film at a major presentation house, the Chicago Theatre. *Variety* (December 17, 1924) reported, "Lucas has a soft sweet tenor, particularly suited to such songs as he uses in this appearance. His voice and the remarkably fine setting made the picture a memorable one." When he first started in vaudeville, Lucas never used a microphone; they were unnecessary because the acoustics of theatres such as the Palace were superb. Lucas recalls, "I think the first time I had a microphone was when I played the Roxy Theatre in New York. They had them in the footlights. They wouldn't dare put them on the stage—the audience wouldn't accept them. But then eventually they put the microphone on the stage. Sometimes I wonder how I did it, singing to 3,000 people without a microphone, but then, of course, I studied voice for two years in Chicago while I was appearing at the Edgewater Beach Hotel."

Between 1924 and 1934 Nick Lucas recorded more than a hundred songs, but there is no question that the best known and the one which became most associated with him was "Tip-Toe thru the Tulips." " 'Tip-Toe thru the Tulips' found me," comments Nick.

Back here in Los Angeles in 1929 I was appearing at the Orpheum Theatre on Broadway and Ninth Street, and one night there was a talent scout there from Warner Bros. who was making a picture called *Gold Diggers of Broadway.* And after the show, this chap came backstage and asked me if I would be interested in making a picture. I said, "Why not?" So the next day I went up to the studios and Mr. Zanuck heard me and said, "Hire him." They had only one song written for me in the film, "Painting the Clouds with Sunshine," and so the writers, Joe Burke and Al Dubin, were requested to write some more songs for me. And they wrote this song "Tip-Toe thru the Tulips," and when Zanuck heard this song he turned it into a big production number. That's how I latched onto 'Tip-Toe thru the Tulips,' which became synonymous with me.

Although Lucas was also featured in Warner Bros. all-star revue *Show of Shows* (1929), he turned down a career in films for one on the stage and in recording. Curiously, motion pictures and recording came back into his life in 1974 when his voice was heard on the soundtrack and the record album for *The Great Gatsby,* singing "When You and I Were Seventeen," "Five Foot Two, Eyes of Blue," and "I'm Gonna Charleston Back to Charleston." He received no credit for his work on either the film or the album.

Nick Lucas was the headliner on the last all-vaudeville bill at the Palace Theatre for the week of November 12,

Nick Lucas today

1932. (Others on that bill were Hal Le Roy, Giovanni, the Honey Family, Ross and Edwards, Ola Lilith, and Sid Marion, whom Lucas remembers as a particularly fine comedian.) He was not particularly aware that he was participating in the end of an era. "The wane was coming, I could see it, but I was surprised to find that was the last big-time vaudeville show," he comments.

Since 1937 Nick Lucas has been based in Los Angeles; from there he made an extensive tour of Australia on the Tivoli circuit (also in 1937) and, of course, worked for the U.S.O. during the Second World War. "I'm practically on the retired list," he says. "I don't seek work, but if it comes I grab it. I would like to work three days a week for the rest of my life." As a vaudevillian, Nick Lucas was a curiosity in that his style of singing was an intimate one and yet he was able to project that intimacy to an audience of thousands. It was a successful style and one that still appeals. As he notes, "Every song tells a story, and if you get them to listen to you from the beginning to the end, then you're a hit." For almost sixty years audiences have been listening with pleasure to Nick Lucas.

MAGICIANS

Magicians were a staple vaudeville act, particularly in the early years of this century when audiences were less sophisticated and more gullible. The most famous magician on the vaudeville stage was Houdini (see his entry), and his closest rival was Howard Thurston (1869–1936), famous for his card tricks including the rising card. He was, apparently, somewhat arrogant toward his audience and

his fellow performers. Reviewing Thurston's two-hour show at the New National Theatre on New York's Second Avenue in 1913, *Variety* (May 16, 1913) wrote, "Thurston has developed into a magician of much expertness, some originality, and considerable showmanship. Neither of these things was predicted for him upon the Great Kellar, when retiring a few years ago, placing his Kingly Magical mantle upon Thurston."

Harry Kellar (1849–1922) was one of the first great vaudeville magicians, noted for his sleight-of-hand and his atrocious English. It was claimed that he was such a perfectionist that if he so much as stepped on stage on the wrong foot, he would return to the wings and begin his act again. On a par with Kellar was Alexander Herrmann (1843–1896), billed as "Herrmann the Great," who worked with his wife, Adelaide, and included jugglers in

ful in America and Europe; because he appeared before many of the crowned heads of Europe, he billed himself as "The Royal Illusionist." Goldin's most famous illusion was sawing a woman in half, which was accomplished by using two women, one hidden in the box who thrust her feet out and kept her head down between her knees, and the other was seen getting into the box, then poked her head out and drew her knees up under her chin. Simple, but very effective in 1921, when it was first introduced to American audiences.

Ching Ling Foo (1854–1918) was the greatest of Chinese magicians. He earned $2,000 a week in 1913 touring the Loew's circuit, and even had an imitator, Houang Yuen (who was actually an American disguised as an Oriental). From under his flowing mandarin robe, Ching Ling Foo would produce goldfish bowls, a garbage can filled with milk, and a tub of live ducks. In 1933 an acrobatic act titled "Ching Ling Foo, Jr." toured the vaudeville circuits, but it appears to have had no connection with the famous magician.

Not to be confused with Ching Ling Foo was Chung Ling Soo, in reality an American, William Ellsworth Robinson (1861–1918). He had been an assistant to the Great Herrmann and Harry Kellar and in 1899, while Ching Ling Foo was appearing at the Union Square Theatre, he had accepted a challenge to duplicate the Chinese magician's tricks. Unfortunately, when Chung Ling Soo was given such an opportunity at the Folies Bergère in Paris in 1900, a goldfish bowl slipped from beneath his gown and shattered on stage, completely breaking up the act.

Chung Ling Soo's most famous trick was borrowed from Herrmann the Great, and that was catching a bullet between his teeth. It was a trick which cost him his life. It was performed by hiding a flattened bullet in the magician's hand and having the gun fire blanks. On the night of March 23, 1918, Chung Ling Soo was appearing with his bullet-catching act at London's Wood Green Empire. Somehow—it has never been fully explained—a live bullet was placed in the trick muzzle-loading rifle and fired; presumably the live bullets shown to members of the audience were not correctly palmed by Chung Ling Soo's assistant, who then failed to replace them with the blank cartridges.

Other magicians active on the American vaudeville stage included Harry Blackstone (1885–1965), famous for his dancing handkerchief trick; Charles J. Carter (1874–1936); Lafayette (1872–1911); Eugene Laurant (1875–1944); John Mulholland (1898–1970); Nicola the Great (1880–1946); Frederick Eugene Powell (1857–1938), known as the Dean of American Magicians; and John Wyman (1816–1881).

References: "Magic, Mental Acts" in *American Vaudeville* by Douglas Gilbert (Whittlesey House, 1940), pages 306–320. *Cyclopedia of Magic,* edited by Henry Hay (David McKay Company, 1949).

WILL MAHONEY

Will Mahoney

Will Mahoney's biggest claim to fame was that he played the xylophone, but while others played the xylophone with their hands, Mahoney played the instrument with hammers attached to his feet. He was what was known as a "nut" comedian, for obvious reasons. Prior to the xylophone act, Mahoney performed with a live duck and executed various comedy dance routines. He once summed up the secret of his success by noting, "It's not how old the joke is. It's the confidence you put into it."

Although often referred to as an Australian comedian, Mahoney was born William James Fitzpatrick Mahoney in Helena, Montana, and made his first public appearance as a dancer at the age of eight in Spokane, Washington. He toured the Western vaudeville circuits before coming to New York in the early twenties, when *Variety* (October 28, 1921) called him "another 'nut' single from the West that impresses as being not above the ordinary." By the mid-twenties *Variety* had improved its opinion of Mahoney, just as Mahoney himself had improved his act. When the comedian headlined at the Palace, the *New York Times* (January 11, 1927) commented, "Mahoney employs a disarmingly joyous insouciance and gusto in putting over his songs and does his tap-and-clog dances with the tireless precision of an automaton."

Mahoney introduced his xylophone dance in the spring of 1930 in *Earl Carroll's Sketch Book.* Sime Silverman reviewed the dance in *Variety* (April 2, 1930) as a favor to Mahoney, who wished to ensure his claim to the creation of the routine. Silverman wrote, "The specially built xylophone is of the usual style but quite long. Mahoney, with a hammer attached to each shoe, steps upon the instrument without his shoes causing a sound. He had just finished his 'Mammy' song on the stage, and went upon the instrument when urged back to finish his act after he had sobbingly said he couldn't do any more (business). With the music starting Mahoney commences to dance, the hammers hitting the keys to perfect rhythm. It's a complete surprise, and when the dancer did his third and last number, Sousa's 'Stars and Stripes,' the house burst into heavy plaudits. The idea is magnificent in it's originality, and Mahoney is splendid in the execution." Mahoney brought his new speciality to vaudeville and the Palace, beginning June 14, 1930, under the title of "Glorifying Feet, Falls, and Foolishness."

In addition to *Earl Carroll's Sketch Book,* Mahoney also appeared in the 1924 edition of *George White's Scandals,* the 1931 edition of *Earl Carroll's Vanities* and *Take the Air* (1928). He was also fairly popular in England in the thirties. In 1935 he starred in *Radio New York* at London's Holborn Empire, and the *Daily Telegraph* (April 16, 1935) wrote, "He is perhaps the most good-humored comedian in variety and the secret of his success is that he infects the whole audience with his own sense of the ridiculous. It is impossible not to laugh at him."

Will Mahoney remained a popular star until his death in Melbourne, Australia, on February 9, 1967, at the age of seventy-three. In 1955 he had starred as Finian McLanergan in the New York revival of *Finian's Rainbow.* Mahoney exemplified the originality and talent of comedians on the vaudeville stage.

FAY MARBE

Fay Marbe was beautiful, young, and full of vitality. An accomplished singer and dancer on the vaudeville stage in the late 1910s, she made her "big-time" vaudeville debut at the Palace Theatre in September of 1920, with Jerry White at the piano, singing "The Kiss," "Tra Tra La," "The Jazz Vampire," "Sweet Daddies," and "Mexico." She wore a stunning array of gowns designed by her and her mother. The *New York Dramatic Mirror* (September 18, 1920) reported, "She got along swimmingly with the vocal numbers assigned and then cavorted in the style of pep and animation that established her in big favor." Prior to entering vaudeville, Fay Marbe had been seen on the

Fay Marbe in 1932

THE MARX BROTHERS

Chico, Harpo, Groucho, and Zeppo Marx

Broadway stage in Victor Herbert's *The Velvet Lady* and Sigmund Romberg's *The Magic Melody.*

In the early twenties Fay Marbe went to Europe, appearing on the stage in London and starring in eight films for the Ufa Company in Germany. She returned to the States later in the decade billed as "The Magnetic International Star," and toured in a one-girl show, "A Continental Revue," featuring dances and songs from Europe sung in various languages. She was also seen on the vaudeville stage again performing "The Blue Danube Waltz" with her brother, Gilbert. Critics compared her to London's Beatrice Lillie, Madrid's Raquel Meller, Paris's Yvette Guilbert, and Vienna's Fritzi Scheff. In 1929 Fay Marbe starred in a "Poverty Row" film production, *The Talk of Hollywood,* which also featured her brother. She faded from the show business scene in the early thirties.

MARCELLE AND SEA LION

An English importation into American vaudeville in the mid-twenties, "Marcelle and Sea Lion" was considered one of the better sea lion acts, because the animal did not appear to be getting any visible cues from Marcelle. It performed tricks such as picking up objects to perform balancing and juggling feats, singing, laughing, mimicking a cat, applauding, and shaking hands. While the sea lion performed, Marcelle would chat with the animal and with the audience, which, incidentally, was invited to shout instructions to the sea lion, all of which it obeyed. On a January 1925 bill at the Hippodrome, *Variety* thought the sea lion shared top honors with Vincent Lopez and His Orchestra.

Audiences enjoying the Marx Brothers' antics, as they have for the past fifty years in classic screen comedies such as *Animal Crackers* (1930), *Monkey Business* (1931), *Duck Soup* (1933), and *A Night at the Opera* (1935), should not forget that the clowning and, above all, the timing of the gags were worked out in vaudeville and revue years before the Marx Brothers' screen debut. The brothers themselves recognized the value of vaudeville and would even try out some of the routines for their films before live audiences prior to including them in their productions.

Groucho (1890–1977) was the first of the Marx Brothers to enter vaudeville, in 1905, as a member of the Leroy Trio. Groucho recalled that the trio sang a song titled "I Wonder What's the Matter with the Mail," which sounds as if it might be quite appropriate today. Later, Groucho, Gummo, Lou Levy, and Mabel O'Donnell formed the Four Nightingales, which Harpo joined after Mabel O'Donnell's departure in 1910.

The first four Marx brothers in show business were Groucho/Julius, Gummo/Milton (1897–1977), Harpo/Arthur (1888–1964), and Chico/Leonard (1886–1961). They joined together as an act when their uncle, Al Shean, later of Gallagher and Shean, wrote a sketch for them titled "Fun in Hi Skool." The act, which also included three other members, was favorably reviewed by Sime Silverman in *Variety* when it first came to New York in February of 1912. The sketch was quite obviously based on Gus Edwards's "School Boys and Girls" routine, and Silverman was quick to point out that the Marx Brothers sketch was superior. Groucho played the schoolteacher in the then-popular style of a Dutch comedian, while Harpo had an opportunity to play his harp halfway through the twenty-seven-minute routine. The dialogue went something like this:

GROUCHO: What is the shape of the world?
HARPO: I don't know.
GROUCHO: Well, what shape are my cufflinks?
HARPO: Square.
GROUCHO: Not my weekday cufflinks, the ones I wear on Sundays.
HARPO: Oh, round.
GROUCHO: All right, what is the shape of the world?
HARPO: Square on weekdays, round on Sundays.

Al Shean helped the Marx Brothers again in 1914 when he provided them with a second sketch, "Home Again," which their mother, Minnie Palmer, directed. Harpo was featured in another harp solo, while Chico did a piano solo. The sketch kept the Marx Brothers busy during the war years, with Zeppo/Herbert (1901–1979) replacing Gummo when the latter was drafted. Amusingly, the Marx Brothers' dealings with the draft board sounds like one of their routines. In September of 1917 they appeared en masse at the Chicago recruiting station and were promptly rejected, one for defective eyes, one for flat feet, one because of physical disability due to an operation, and one for general reasons.

Songwriter Gus Kahn's widow, Grace, recalls her first meeting with Groucho Marx:

Gus had a song that he wrote with a man called Van Alstyne. I was working for Remick and Company, that was a big music publisher, and they sent me as a songplugger to Grand Rapids to get Groucho to sing this song when he came into Chicago. You see, they always tried to get 'em out of town so they would know the song when they got to Chicago. That was the funniest meeting you ever heard of. I rapped at the door, and Groucho said, "Come in." He said, "Sit down." I said, "I'm from a publisher and I'm here about a song." He said, "Have a cigar." I said, "No thank you." We started to talk about the song, and he said, "You want to take a shower?" After that we became close friends. In fact, my daughter, Irene, married his son. Anyway, he put the song in the act, and I think we paid him twenty-five dollars a week to sing it.

The Marx Brothers appeared at the Palace in January of 1917 with "Home Again," and *Variety* (February 2, 1917) thought it was "the best tabloid for value in vaudeville." The magazine continued, "Mrs. Minnie Palmer, their mother, can feel that mother's pride that she brought up four good boys who have made good as well." In 1919 the brothers were appearing in a sketch titled " 'N Everything," again written by Al Shean. The *New York Dramatic Mirror* (October 23, 1919) reported that the part which seemed to please the most was Arthur Marx's harp playing, and then embarked on a discourse on harp playing in vaudeville: "As we have said many times before there is not enough harping on the vaudeville stage. About the only harping we get is the harping some acts do on old jokes. The harp is especially suited for syncopated ballads, and although good harpists are hard to get, it can be done. The trouble it takes would be amply rewarded by the way an act is built up which has an harpist."

When the Marx Brothers headlined again at the Palace in August of 1920, the *New York Dramatic Mirror* (August 21, 1920) wrote of "the Marx family using its familiar roughhouse antics and coarse idioms of speech, with the musical specialities by the comedy of the troupe proving the big feature." Incidentally, the Marx Bros.—as they were billed in vaudeville, comparable to Warner Bros. rather than Warner Brothers—made their first appearance at the Palace in Christmas week of 1915.

However, by 1920 the Marx Brothers' vaudeville career was coming to a close. As Groucho recalled in his autobiography, the brothers were discontended. There were new worlds to conquer. There was a prestige attached to being a Broadway star that they could never attain in vaudeville. The brothers had already appeared in a 1919 musical comedy, *The Cinderella Girl*, with lyrics by Gus Kahn, and in 1924 they were to star in a revue which assured them a permanent place on the legitimate stage. Titled *I'll Say She Is*, the revue was almost universally hailed by the critics as one of the worst ever staged, but it was also, thanks to the ad-libbing antics of the Marx Brothers, one of the funniest. Robert Benchley's comment in the humor magazine *Life* was to be echoed by critics and public alike in the years to come: "Not since sin laid its heavy hand on our spirit have we laughed so loud and so offensively."

References: *The Marx Brothers* by Kyle Crichton (Doubleday and Company, 1950). *Groucho and Me* by Groucho Marx (Bernard Geis Associates/Random House, 1959). *Groucho, Harpo, Chico—and Sometimes Zeppo* by Joe Adamson (Simon and Schuster, 1973). *The Marx Brothers Scrapbook* by Groucho Marx and Richard J. Anobile (A Darien House Book/W. W. Norton, 1973). *The Grouchofile* by Groucho Marx (Bobbs-Merrill, 1976).

OWEN McGIVENEY

Owen McGiveney was the greatest exponent of a forgotten vaudeville art, that of the fast-change artist. In a ten-minute act, he would play as many as five roles. McGiveney's greatest triumph was an excerpt from Charles Dickens's *Oliver Twist*, in which he appeared as both Bill and Nancy Sikes. His success lay in the speed of his changes and in the characterizations that he obtained through make-up. McGiveney was not a great actor in the accepted sense; audiences would often complain that they could not hear what he was saying, and *Variety* once commented that watching McGiveney was like seeing a play in a foreign tongue after having read the book in English.

McGiveney recalled that "when vaudeville was at its peak, there were as many as twenty quick-change acts, most of them Italians who did quick versions of operas." Second to McGiveney as far as both critics and public were concerned was Mark Linder, who played four types of prisoners about to be released from jail, ending with a Hebrew and a Chinaman.

The performer began as a music hall artist in his native England in 1904. "I was playing in the legit," he recalled, "and we came to a town where a man owned a legit house and a music hall next door to each other. He told me he paid $150 for the entire legit troupe, but next door he paid as much as $500 for a single performer. I decided I was in the wrong end of the business." McGiveney came to the States around 1910 and soon became a headliner. In May of 1913 he was one of the acts supporting Sarah Bernhardt at the Palace and almost stole the show from its star. He closed the first half of the bill and received a tremendous ovation. *Variety* (May 23, 1913) wrote, "McGiveney and his act are of the sort that create talk, and his Bill Sikes easily takes rank with R. A. Roberts's Dick Turpin in the protean class." (It should be noted that McGiveney was billed not as a fast-change artist, but as a protean performer, a term which, although it indicates change, was used to describe most male actors appearing in vaudeville playlets.)

With the demise of vaudeville in the thirties, Owen McGiveney returned to England. It was Ken Murray who brought the performer back to America in 1946 to appear in his *Blackouts* in Los Angeles. "I had played the Palace with Owen McGiveney in 1927," Murray told me. "He was one of the great vaudeville headliners, a great act, the only one of its kind. And I had the idea to use his act as part of a dramatic sketch that I had developed for *Blackouts*. He was tickled to death to come back to America. And the interesting thing about *Blackouts,* of course, is that our contracts were not for a few weeks but for months or years. So when Owen McGiveney and his family came to Los Angeles, they were able to buy a house here from what they made with me."

The move to Los Angeles gave Owen McGiveney a new career as a character actor in films; among the features in which he appeared are *If Winter Comes* (1948), *Showboat* (1951), *Pat and Mike* (1952), *Brigadoon* (1954), *Snow White and the Three Stooges* (1961), and *My Fair Lady* (1964). It also gave his son, Owen McGiveney, Jr., an opportunity to continue his father's fast-change art on television. Owen McGiveney died in Woodland Hills, California, on July 31, 1967, at the reported age of eighty-three.

McINTYRE AND HEATH

In the annals of blackface minstrelsy, McIntyre and Heath was probably the most famous partnership, dating from 1874 through 1924. James McIntyre was born in Kenosha, Wisconsin, in 1857, and Thomas Heath was born in Philadelphia in 1852. As one 1908 biographer noted, "As children living in the South, the boys studied the language and characteristics of the Negro 'befo' de war.' " They

McIntyre and Heath in 1910

joined forces in San Antonio, Texas, in 1874 and became headliners at the Theatre Comique in St. Louis in 1876. Prior to the partnership, McIntyre had toured the South with Kate Pullman, performing clog dances and playing Little Willie in *East Lynne;* in 1869 he joined a circus and sang and danced his way through the mountains of Alabama.

Heath was the straight man of the team and, as *Variety* noted, he was the perfect feeder for McIntyre. The couple was famous for a number of classic minstrel sketches, including "The Georgia Minstrels," "The Man from Montana," "The Ham Tree" (which was adapted into play form and in which they toured for Klaw and Erlanger for a number of years), "Chickens" (in which McIntyre appeared in drag), and "Back to the Stable" (a sequel to "Georgia Minstrels," which McIntyre and Heath introduced in 1918). A fairly good description of this sketch survives. It opened with Otto T. Johnston pasting up a three-sheet poster announcing the coming of a minstrel show, at which point Alexander (McIntyre) sauntered on stage leading a small white donkey. Alexander sells the donkey to Johnston for twenty-five dollars and an I.O.U., which McIntyre insists on calling a U.O.I. Heath then enters, in the guise of the owner of the minstrel show, and separates Alexander from the twenty-five dollars. It may not sound very funny, and perhaps it was not, for by 1916 Frederick James Smith was complaining in the *New York Dramatic Mirror* that ninety percent of the McIntyre and Heath act was tedium, with only ten percent laughs.

In *American Vaudeville* Douglas Gilbert remembers a typical slice of McIntyre and Heath dialogue:

HEATH: Well, didn't that train stop?
McINTYRE: No, it didn't stop. It didn't even hesitate.
HEATH: You got egg on your chin.
McINTYRE: Thas jes clay from the ditch where I slep' last night.
HEATH: Well, didn't that woman at the house where I sent you up give you something to eat?
McINTYRE: No, she didn't. I saw she looked kinda hard and I thought of the old minstrel joke so I got down and started to eat the grass thinkin' that might touch her. An' she said to me—"you poor man, you must be starvin', come around to the back yard an' I'll show you where the grass is longer."

McIntyre claimed that the team originated ragtime, in the form of a buck and wing dance accompanied by clapping hands to the tune of an old "Rabbit" song which McIntyre had learned from Southern Negroes and introduced to New York at Tony Pastor's Theatre in 1879. This claim was disputed by Ben Harney who said he originated ragtime with two of his songs, "Mr. Johnson Turn Me Loose" and "You've Been a Good Old Wagon, But You've Done Broken Down."

After an enthusiastic farewell tour in 1924, McIntyre and Heath retired. They did make one final, farewell appearance in 1929, on radio with Rudy Vallee. The pair remained friends and lived close to each other, denying rumors that they had not spoken for a twenty-five-year period. McIntyre died in Noyack, Long Island, on August 18, 1937. Exactly a year later, August 18, 1938, Thomas Heath died in Setauket, Long Island; he had never been told of his partner's death.

RAQUEL MELLER

Raquel Meller

Raquel Meller's name has not weathered the years and, to a large extent, the passage of time has not helped in the appreciation of her own peculiar appeal. On viewing a film of Miss Meller performing one of her celebrated chansons, one is aware only of a somewhat overweight, dowdy woman singing a monotonous song in an unmelodious manner.

Yet in the twenties Raquel Meller was the darling of the intellectuals of the world. Sarah Bernhardt said, "If there is one woman in the world who possesses genius, it is Raquel Meller." Chaplin adored her and planned to costar with her in a film on the life of Napoleon and Josephine. Arthur Hopkins, in "An Appreciation of Raquel Meller," wrote, "To the question 'Is acting an art?' the best answer I know is Raquel Meller." George Jean Nathan wrote of her performance, "She creeps over the footlights like an odourless incense, hypnotically, alluringly. She is like a convent on fire."

Born Francesca Marques, in Aragon, Spain, in 1888, Raquel Meller became a Spanish music hall star in the early years of this century. From Spain she went on to conquer the world, starring at the Olympia Music Hall in

Paris in 1919, taking top billing in Alfred de Courville's *Joy Bells* at the London Hippodrome in 1920, appearing in several European films (the most famous of which was *Carmen* in 1926), and embarking on a successful year-long tour of South America. Raquel Meller continued to appear on stage until 1946; she died in Barcelona on July 26, 1962.

Raquel Meller first came to the United States in the spring of 1926 for a four-week engagement at the Empire Theatre in New York. Her New York appearance, which began on April 14, 1926 and in which she was assisted by a symphonic orchestra selected from the Philharmonic Society of New York under the direction of Victor Baravelle, was cosponsored by a Committee of Patrons and a Committee of the Theatre. Patrons included Otto Kahn, Mrs. Anthony J. Drexel Biddle, Sr., Howard Chandler Christy, and Charles Dana Gibson, and the Committee of the Theatre included Ethel Barrymore, Irving Berlin, Lynn Fontanne, Otis Skinner, Eva Le Gallienne, and David Belasco. In connection with her appearance, a lavish souvenir program was published, featuring a poem to her art by Robert Underwood Johnson and a critical appraisal by Randolph Bartlett which described Miss Meller as "El Alma Que Canta—The Soul That Sings."

The diseuse sang from twelve to fifteen songs at each performance. The songs, many of which were featured on the twenty-three phonograph records by Raquel Meller available in the United States in the twenties, included "El Relicario" (The Charm), "El Peligro de las Rosas" (The Treachery of the Roses), "Besos Frios" (Kisses of Marble), and "Diguili que Vingui" (Tell Him To Come). A description of each song appeared in the program. For example, one of her songs, "Mariana," was described thus: "Mariana is the loveliest girl in all Andalusia. She is carrying on a flirtation with a village boy and her cousin. Her friends all warn her not to whisper, by mistake, the name of her cousin in the ear of his rival."

There were those, of course, who were not transported into ecstasy by Miss Meller's performance. One such person was humorist Robert Benchley, who published his own versions of her songs, complete with synopses. A typical Benchley parody was "Camisetas de Flanela" (Flannel Vests): "Princess Rosamonda goes nightly to the Puerta del Sol to see if the early morning edition of the papers is out yet. If it isn't, she hangs around humming to herself. If it is, she hangs around humming just the same. One night she encounters a young matador who is returning from dancing school. The finches are singing and there is Love in the air. Princess Rosamonda ends up in the police station."

However, most critics at the time agreed with Arthur Hopkins's description of a Meller song.

In Raquel Meller we find the artist freed. Her every song seems a fine flight away from mundane reality into a new and blazing reality which somehow seems a part of all time and place. And the flight seems to be into herself. The beautiful, graceful woman fades away and one feels only the embodiment of gay, poignant, sullen, grieving, tragic emotions. And the body thus abandoned finds a new and glorious grace. Its motions are effortless. The face looks far, far away. The hands are like faces. And Raquel Meller finally drifts back to her body. The song is over, but you feel you never again will get quite back to the same place you were when the flight began.

Raquel Meller returned to New York, to the Henry Miller Theatre, for thirteen more performances beginning on October 25, 1926; then she embarked on a reasonably successful American vaudeville tour. She also appeared in two of the first Fox Movietone sound shorts to be released.

As a performer, Raquel Meller belongs to another time and place; her songs of tragedy and joy seem somewhat out of style in contemporary Spain. However, although she, and her followers, would undoubtedly have misgivings about it, she is noteworthy in a dictionary of vaudeville performers, not only because of her American stage appearances but because of the unique position she held in the realm of European music hall.

Reference: "Raquel Meller" by Liam O'Leary in *Cinema Studies,* Volume 2, Number 4 (June, 1967), pages 61–64.

FLORENCE MILLS

Florence Mills

A dainty, elfin black girl, Florence Mills brightened the twenties with her sweet voice and vivacious personality. Thanks to her performances in *Shuffle Along* (1921), *The Plantation Revue* (1922), *The Greenwich Village Follies* (1923), *Dixie to Broadway* (1924), and *Blackbirds* (1926), she became an international star, as popular with revue audiences in Paris as she was with Broadway audiences in America. As delicately beautiful as Josephine Baker was grotesquely attractive, Florence Mills was the first of the American Negro performers to take Paris by storm, paving the way for Josephine Baker and others.

Born in 1899 or 1901, Florence Mills began her career in vaudeville appearing with an act titled Tennessee Ten which included a dancing trap drummer named U. S. Thompson whom she later married. In the 1910s she played the Pantages circuit as a member of a trio called The Panama Girls. After *Dixie to Broadway* closed, Florence Mills returned to vaudeville, headlining the act Florence Mills and Company, which opened at the Hippodrome in late April of 1925. The twenty-six-minute act, which was described as one of the first "colored productions" to play big-time vaudeville, featured Will Vodery and His Orchestra, which had accompanied Florence Mills on the road in *Dixie to Broadway,* blues trumpeter Johnny Dunn, and Johnny Nit, "the brown skin dancer with the pearly teeth." Florence Mills sang (from *Dixie to Broadway*) "Bamboula" and "Back to Dixie," plus the number with which she will always be associated, "I'm a Little Blackbird Looking for a Bluebird, Too."

In a somewhat patronizing review of her act, Ibee wrote in *Variety* (April 29, 1925), "Florence Mills has been a name along Broadway and in Broadway's night places for seasons. There is no reason why the Mills turn should not get the best of the big-time bookings for it is understood the salary is not exorbitant."

Florence Mills died, after an operation for appendicitis, on November 1, 1927. Her death was a tragic loss to the world of black entertainment. Had she lived, there can be little question that "the pride of Harlem" would have been as popular and remembered with as much affection as is Josephine Baker today.

BORRAH MINEVITCH

Variety's Abel Green described Borrah Minevitch as "a Continental personality of stature." This is as may be, but as a vaudeville performer in America from the late twenties through the fifties, Borrah Minevitch and His Harmonica Rascals was an act which seemed both dreary and sickeningly unfunny. It is hard to understand why the sight of Minevitch and his men romping around playing mouth organs of various sizes should have aroused any interest in a vaudeville audience. Yet Minevitch was an exceedingly popular entertainer in this country, not only in vaudeville but also on radio, and he certainly popularized the harmonica, going so far as to create the Harmonica Institute of America.

Borrah Minevitch was born in Kiev, Russia, circa 1904; he died while honeymooning with his second wife in Neuilly-sur-Seine, France, on June 26, 1955. He became interested in the harmonica as a youth and played his first solo number with the orchestra of Hugo Riesenfeld at the Tivoli Theatre.

Variety (May 13, 1925) caught his act at the Palace and commented,

Coincident with what seems to be a growing fad for mouth organs comes this youthful harmonica soloist, who seemingly floored the house with his appearance and then went on to render four selections

**Borrah Minevitch and
His Harmonica Rascals**

to much approval. Minevitch, as to the front he presents dressed in a dinner jacket, begins where most of the dance orchestra boys proverbially end. For that reason he's a cinch with the feminine patrons before starting. His playing sounds intricate and smacks of expert technique during the manifold variations of the theme melody, whatever it may be. The repertoire is away from "blues," and mainly confines itself to popular dance selections of the semi-classical type. Minevitch seemingly depends upon his manipulation for effects to get the numbers across.

According to another harmonica-playing vaudevillian, Ted Waldman, Minevitch was temperamental. He recalls one theatre manager who did not understand why Minevitch was screaming at him, when his name was at the top of the bill on the theatre marquee. Minevitch yelled at him, "You've got too many *M*'s and no *V*!"

Minevitch conceived the idea of harmonica orchestra which became the Rascals, whom Minevitch owned but who also appeared without their leader, as at the Palace in April of 1952 when Borrah Minevitch's Harmonica Rascals supported Betty Hutton. In addition to touring with his Rascals, he operated a bistro in Paris, was involved in film and television productions, and owned harmonica factories.

MORAN AND MACK

After the days of McIntyre and Heath, one blackface comedy team was left to carry on the tradition that those

two preeminent minstrels had established. Moran and Mack, also known as The Two Black Crows, had first become partners in the late 1910s, but it was not until 1927 that they became major stars, thanks largely to their recording of a sketch titled "The Early Bird Catches the Worm." It was, and still is, a classic routine, with Mack as the stereotypical lazy black, shuffling around the stage, speaking his lines slowly, much as Stepin' Fetchit was to do in the movies a few years later. Mack would explain to Moran, "I would go to work, if I could find any pleasure in it." When asked to spell Ohio he replied, "Capital O-H-Ten." When Moran asked Mack to explain why the white horses on the farm ate more than the black horses, Mack responded, "We never could find out, unless it was because we had more of the white horses than black horses." It doesn't sound funny in print, but on film and record, with Moran and Mack's perfect timing, it was—and is—hilarious.

Kansas-born Charles Mack entered show business as a stage electrician after serving as a catcher on the Olympia (Washington) baseball team. Because his jokes and stories went over so well with vaudevillians, Alexander Pantages (of the West Coast-based Pantages circuit) suggested that Mack go on stage as a single comedian. As a single, he played on the same bill with a blackface act called Garvin and Moran, and at Mack's suggestion George Moran (also from Kansas) joined him in a blackface double act. One of the pair's first major appearances was in the Sigmund Romberg revue *Over the Top,* which opened at the Forty-fourth Street Roof Theatre on November 28, 1917, with a cast that included Justine Johnstone, Fred and Adele Astaire, and Mary Eaton. In the twenties Moran and

Moran and Mack with writer Roy Octavus Cohen

Mack were perhaps more popular on the revue stage than in vaudeville; they were to be seen in the 1920 edition of *The Ziegfeld Follies,* the 1924 edition of *The Greenwich Village Follies,* and the 1927 edition of *Earl Carroll's Vanities.* In the last, Moran and Mack introduced another classic routine, "The Rock Pile," in which they appeared as two convicts and engaged in the following dialoque:

MORAN: Man, is it hot.
MACK: Sho, nuff. Wish I had an ice-cold water-
        melon.
MORAN: Oh, lawdy. Me, too.
MACK: Wish I had a hundred ice-cold watermel-
        ons.
MORAN: Hm, huh.
MACK: Wish I had a thousand ice-cold watermel-
        ons.
MORAN: Glory be. I bet if you had a thousand ice-
        cold watermelons you'd give me one.
MACK: Oh, naw! No siree. If you are too lazy to
        wish for your own watermelons, you ain't
        gonna get none of mine.

In 1927 Moran and Mack recorded "The Early Bird Catches the Worm" for Columbia, and it became an immediate best-seller. So popular were Moran and Mack that in 1928 a black act, Moss and Frye, tried to cash in on their success by calling themselves The Two Black Crows.

With their popularity in revue and vaudeville, it was natural that Moran and Mack should try films, which they did in 1929 with the Paramount feature *Why Bring That Up?,* written by the popular Jewish writer of black stories, Octavus Roy Cohen, and directed by Broadway producer George Abbott. Moran and Mack was an unusual act off stage in that it was owned exclusively by Charlie Mack— he owned Moran and Mack as a registered, copyrighted trademark. Mack wrote most of the material and took the lion's share of the team's salary. When Moran demanded an equal portion of the pair's earnings Mack refused, and Moran walked out on the act.

Mack replaced him with Bert Swor, who had been half of the blackface act of the Swor Bros. and who had appeared in *Why Bring That Up?* With Swor, Mack starred in a second Paramount feature, *Anybody's War,* released in the summer of 1930. Despite the change in personnel, the film's stars were still billed as Moran and Mack. The two appeared in blackface throughout but the production was not a success, with Sime Silverman writing in *Variety* (July 16, 1930), "Story itself is silly without being laughable." After release of *Anybody's War,* George Moran returned to the act in time for the team to play the RKO circuit in September of 1930 at a weekly salary of $5,000.

While driving to New York with George Moran and Mack Sennett, with plans to appear in a series of comedy shorts for the producer, Charles Mack was killed in an automobile accident near Mesa, Arizona, on January 11, 1934. He was forty-six years old. After Mack's death, Moran continued with the act for a few years but the popularity of blackface acts declined rapidly in the thir-

ties. During the Second World War Moran toured with the USO. He died in the charity ward of an Oakland, California, hospital on August 2, 1949. It should be stressed that there was never any deliberate racism in the Moran and Mack routines; in their time, the pair was never criticized, and *Variety* noted at one point that they probably had as many black fans as white ones.

Reference: "Moran and Mack: The Two Black Crows" by Teet Carle in *Hollywood Studio Magazine* (June, 1972).

HELEN MORGAN

Helen Morgan

Helen Morgan's name brings back memories of a small woman with a hauntingly beautiful face perched on top of a grand piano, singing a lament about her lost man. The artist James Montgomery Flagg thought her singing "a composite of all the ruined women in the world," while one critic described her as "Camille on a piano." No one, and I mean no one, could ever sing the songs that she made famous with the same feeling and the same emotional tug at the heartstrings. Those songs—"Bill," "Can't Help Lovin' Dat Man," "Why Was I Born?," "What Wouldn't I Do for That Man?," and "Body and Soul"— are exclusively Helen Morgan's property and Helen Morgan's bequest to the world.

She was born in either Danville, Illinois, or Toronto, Canada (nobody really seems to know), of French Canadian parents, in the autumn of 1900. Before making her stage debut she was to work in the Chicago area as a lingerie model, as a clerk at Marshall Field's, and as a packer at the National Biscuit Company. She once claimed that she always perched on a piano during her act because "I had to stand up twelve hours a day for years, boxing crackers, and I made a vow to sit down forever if I got the chance." Helen Morgan came to New York in 1918 after winning a couple of beauty contests and was eventually hired by Florenz Ziegfeld to appear in the chorus of *Sally,* which opened at the New Amsterdam Theatre on December 21, 1920. It ran for two years, and when it closed Helen Morgan went to Chicago for an engagement at the Cafe Montmartre.

The singer returned to New York late in 1922 and appears to have accepted various night club engagements and performed in extremely minor roles in several shows, although it seems impossible to discover which ones. She was probably in the 1925 edition of *George White's Scandals* and, although she received no billing, she was definitely in *Americana* in 1926, in which she sang "Nobody Wants Me." By the late twenties Helen Morgan was also appearing in various night clubs which bore her name: Helen Morgan's Fifty-fourth Street Club, Chez Helen Morgan, Helen Morgan's Summer House, and The House of Morgan. (In 1928 she was arrested for violation of the prohibition laws.) In these clubs Helen Morgan developed the technique of delivering her song perched on a grand piano. Another story about the origin of this device (probably erroneous) is that there was so little room for Helen Morgan to stand and deliver her numbers that Ring Lardner picked her up and placed her on the piano. It's a nice story, even if it isn't true, but one thing is certain: by January of 1927 that had become her trademark.

Variety mentions it when reviewing her first appearance in vaudeville at the Palace in January of 1927. With Joe Santley at the piano, she sang four numbers and *Variety* described her as "an exotic brunette [who] would be a find for vaudeville ordinarily. She is a treat optically and a talented entertainer."

The one role with which Helen Morgan will always be associated is that of Julie in *Showboat,* which opened at the Ziegfeld Theatre on December 26, 1927, after tryouts in Washington, D.C., Philadelphia, Pittsburgh, and Cleveland. Legend has it that the show's composer, Jerome Kern, saw her sing "Nobody Wants Me" in *Americana* and declared that he had found his Julie. Certainly she *was* Julie, and no one could sing "Bill" and "Can't Help Lovin' Dat Man" as she did. Fortunately, a record of her performance exists in the 1936 film version of *Showboat,* one of a half a dozen features in which Helen Morgan appeared in the thirties. She had entered films in 1929 in Rouben Mamoulian's *Applause,* in which she gives an extraordinary performance as the boozy burlesque queen, Kitty Darling. This film, incidentally, provides a perfect recreation of a 1910 burlesque show.

But by 1929 the boozy Kitty Darling was beginning to resemble the real life Helen Morgan a little too closely. Liquor was taking its toll of the singer, as her face clearly indicated. She continued to appear in vaudeville, night spots, and musical comedy, but not always to enthusiastic audiences. On April 5, 1930, *The Billboard* complained that all her songs were the same; she was always crooning about her man and plaintively melodizing about her "chronic melancholy." In September of 1941 she came to Chicago to appear in a version of *George White's Scandals* at the State Lake Theatre. She became seriously ill with a liver complaint brought on by her drinking and died in Chicago on October 8, 1941. Perhaps ironically, it was in Chicago that her career had begun.

Since her death, there have been at least two versions of her life story, the first on CBS's "Playhouse 90" in 1957, starring Polly Bergen. The second, filmed by M-G-M, featured Ann Blyth (with songs dubbed by Gogi Grant) in *The Helen Morgan Story,* also from 1957. Neither did justice to a unique show business personality.

References: "The Girl on the Piano" by Tim Taylor in *Cue* (May 4, 1957), pages 17 and 55. *Helen Morgan: Her Life and Legend* by Gilbert Maxwell (Hawthorn Books, 1974).

J. HAROLD MURRAY

J. Harold Murray

Best known for his role as Jim in the original stage production of *Rio Rita,* which he played for two years from 1927 through 1929, J. Harold Murray had an attractive, virile voice and a pleasing personality. It is unfortunate that John Boles and not he was asked to star in RKO's 1929 film version of *Rio Rita;* Murray's rendition of "The Ranger's Song" has far more bite to it than Boles's.

Born in South Berwick, Maine, on February 17, 1891, J. Harold Murray began his career as a song plugger for publisher Leo Feist. He entered vaudeville in 1918 and was kept busy in that medium until 1920, when he made his Broadway debut in *The Passing Show of 1921* at the Winter Garden Theatre. For the rest of the twenties he was active on the Broadway stage, starring in *Vogues of 1924, China Rose* (1925), *Captain Jinks* (1925), and *Castles in the Air* (1926), among others.

Murray also found time for the occasional vaudeville appearance; in November of 1924 he appeared in the number-four position on the bill at the Palace Theatre in a fourteen-minute act with Leo Feiner at the piano. He sang "On the Road to Mandalay," "Dear One," and "Falling in Love with Someone." Con in *Variety* hailed him as "the singing find of the season for vaudeville. . . . He has everything—appearance, good rangey singing voice, and more personality than any singer of this type usually allows himself." A few years later, in its March 27, 1929, issue, *Variety* was dubbing J. Harold Murray "a natural for vaudeville or the picture palaces." He chose the latter, signed a contract with Fox, and starred in *Happy Days* (1929), *Married in Hollywood* (1929), *Cameo Kirby* (1930), *Women Everywhere* (1930), and *Under Suspicion* (1931), among others. Reviewing *Women Everywhere, Photoplay* (July 1930) noted that "J. Harold Murray has a voice that can't fail to charm you."

The singer's last major stage role was in *Venus in Silk* in 1935, which closed in Pittsburgh before reaching Broadway. Murray gradually drifted away from show business (although he did star in the late thirties on a radio show out of Hartford, Connecticut) and devoted his time to the New England Brewing Comapny, of which he was president and whose product was known as Murray's Beer. The genial baritone died a wealthy man at his home in Killingworth, Connecticut, on December 11, 1940.

KEN MURRAY

What can one say about Ken Murray and his fifty and more years in show business? He was a vaudeville star in the twenties and thirties and boasted Bob Hope as his understudy. He became a leading man in films in 1929. He had his own radio show in the thirties and his own television show in the fifties. He headlined for an unprecedented twenty-five straight weeks in Las Vegas. He is the author of innumerable articles, not to mention his autobiography, *Life on a Pogo Stick,* and a biography of Earl Carroll, in whose *Vanities* Ken starred in 1935 and 1936. He received a special Academy Award in 1947 for his extraordinary feature *Bill and Coo.* Then, of course, there was *Ken Murray's Blackouts* which ran for seven-and-a-half years from 1942 through 1949, played to five million paying customers, and was known as Hollywood's most popular show—and it was. If all that is not enough, Ken Murray has been taking home movies of the stars for many years and has put those "movies" together into compilations for television and theatrical release, the most recent being *Ken Murray Shooting Stars,* first shown in 1978. In other words, Ken Murray is a show business phenomenon.

Ken Murray was born Kenneth Abner Doncourt in New York City on July 14, 1903. He made his stage debut with the Pete Curly Trio in vaudeville, in Huntington, Long Island, in 1922, and that same year changed his

Ken Murray

name to Ken Murray. A fellow named Morey left the act of Morey, Senna, and Dean, and Charles Senna invited Ken to join the act, which would change its name to Murray, Senna, and Dean (close enough to the original for bookers to be unaware of any change in the group's personnel).

With his first wife, Charlotte, Ken Murray began to develop quite a successful vaudeville routine. *Variety* (April 14, 1926) reviewed the act at the Broadway and commented, "Ken Murray is one of those swift-talking nut comics who runs from one gag into another with lightning rapidity. . . . He has a good sense of pacing the act and when he comes to the end, he gives a climax and gets off—commendable." *Variety* liked Murray's clarinet playing, which he did very well and which became a staple of his act through the years, but found Charlotte meant nothing to the act, a comment with which Ken Murray obviously agreed because he divorced her shortly thereafter.

Variety also questioned the risqué nature of some of Murray's jokes, but these were the performer's stock in trade during his vaudeville days—a typical one-liner was "Two old maids took a tramp in the woods. The tramp died." It was because of these jokes that Ken Murray gained his most famous prop, the cigar. As he recalls it, he was playing Proctor's Newark and read a write-up of his act the next day in which the reviewer complained that Ken's countenance, his cherubic face, belied the type of risqué material he performed. "So what I did," says Murray, "was take the cigar merely to put some miles on my countenance. There were many comedians in those days who had a cigar. While George Burns gets credit for the cigar today, he didn't even start in as early as I did. There was a fellow named Al Herman, who did blackface, who used a cigar." Ken Murray's other trademark, the crewcut, dates not from his vaudeville years but from the forties when he was in *Blackouts.* Taking a vacation in the Canadian backwoods one year, he asked his barber to give him a crewcut so he would not have to worry about his long hair. Murray liked the convenience of the crewcut so much he decided to retain it.

By April of 1928 Murray was headlining at the Palace and, according to *Variety,* he was carrying the show. He had reached the top of one profession, and so, unlike many of his fellow vaudevillians, Murray decided to try something new. He became a movie star, playing lead roles in *Half Marriage* and *Leathernecking* for RKO in 1929 and 1930 respectively. Next it was radio, on which he made his debut in 1932 as a guest of Rudy Vallee on "The Fleischmann Hour," followed in the same year by his own short-lived "The Ken Murray Show." In 1935 Ken Murray starred in *Earl Carroll's Sketch Book,* his debut in a Broadway musical. Television was a natural challenge for Ken Murray, one that he readily accepted with "The Ken Murray Show," a comedy variety series featuring Darla Hood, Tony Labriola (who had also been with Murray on radio), and Jack Mulhall. It ran on CBS from January 7, 1950 through June 21, 1953. In between, Ken Murray found time to produce *Bill and Coo,* an extraordinary feature film of 1947 with a cast comprised entirely of birds; it received a special Academy Award.

Bill and Coo developed from one of the acts—George Burton's Birds—featured in Ken Murray's long-running variety show *Blackouts.* It opened at Hollywood's El Capitan Theatre on June 24, 1942, and finally closed some seven years later on April 28, 1949. *Blackouts* featured Marie Wilson (into whose cleavage Murray was forever peering) along with Daisy the Dog, Jack Mulhall, and the Hollywood Elderlovelies, nine senior citizens who proved as talented and as vivacious as the showgirls known in *Blackouts* as the Glamourlovelies. *Blackouts* was very much in the vaudeville tradition with its comedy poker game—a standout feature in which many famous Hollywood personalities participated—and its gags along the same risqué lines as Murray's act from the twenties. A typical routine might open with Murray asking Marie Wilson, "Do you have a fairy Godmother?," to which Wilson would reply, "No, but I have an uncle we're not too sure about." *Blackouts* had a brief New York run, opening at the Ziegfeld Theatre on September 6, 1949, and closing fifty-one performances later on October 15 of the same year.

The key to Ken Murray's success through the years is not hard to discover. Of course, talent and old-fashioned showmanship had a lot to do with it, but it was also his willingness to get involved. He did not merely introduce other acts in vaudeville, television, or *Blackouts,* he participated in those acts, whether doing acrobatics, playing his clarinet with Louis Armstrong, or performing a buck and wing or a soft shoe with Pat Rooney. Ken Murray was an all-round entertainer in an age of one-dimensional performers.

References: *Life on a Pogo Stick* by Ken Murray (John C. Winston Company, 1960). "Ken Murray" in *The Vaudevillians* by Bill Smith (Macmillan, 1976), pages 195–202.

CARRIE NATION

It may come as a surprise but Carrie Nation (1846–1911), who came to fame as a temperance advocate in Kansas in 1900, enjoyed a brief vogue as a vaudeville performer between 1901 and 1909. The hatchet-swinging, six-foot, heavyset Mrs. Nation appeared anywhere from county fairs to English music halls to preach her message of temperance. In December of 1903 she starred in *Ten Nights in a Bar Room* at New York's Third Avenue Theatre, provided her own lines, wrecked the bar scene at every performance, passed through the audience selling miniature hatchets, and also talked back to hecklers in the crowd. Her reception was less than friendly when Mrs. Nation played the London music halls in February of 1909; eggs were thrown at her, there were shouts of "get off," and a voice from the gallery suggested, " 'ave a drop o' gin, old dear." Mrs. Nation was willing to continue and even managed to tell a few members of the audience in the front rows what she thought of them, but the management of London's Canterbury Music Hall decided it was safer to cancel her contract. "She simply wasn't popular," commented *Variety* (February 13, 1909), somewhat understating the case.

THE NICHOLAS BROTHERS

Fayard and Harold Nicholas—Harold was the shorter of the two—were the most explosive tap dancers on the vaudeville stage, performing acrobatic leaps and splits so astounding in their vigor that they were painful to watch. Their speed, polish, and inexhaustible energy were unmatched. As *The Billboard* commented on April 22, 1939, "Style is fast, showy, with eccentric and acro interspersed thruout the tap routines." Along with Fannie Brice, Josephine Baker, Gertrude Niesen, Eve Arden, Judy Canova, and Bob Hope—all of whom admittedly received higher billing—the Nicholas Brothers were featured in the 1936 edition of *The Ziegfeld Follies* which opened at the Winter Garden Theatre on January 30, 1936. *Variety* (February 5, 1936) described them, patronizingly, as simply "two colored lads," but did admit that they delivered "exceptional tap dancing." As Ivor and Irving DeQuincy, the Nicholas Brothers were one of the highlights of the Rodgers and Hart musical *Babes in Arms,* which opened at the Shubert Theatre on April 14, 1937.

The Nicholas Brothers are still with us, happily, and although age may have slowed down their act somewhat, they continue to be two of the greatest exponents of acrobatic tap dancing around. Fortunately, some of their most spectacular routines have been captured on film, in Vitaphone shorts from the mid-thirties, *Sun Valley Serenade* (1941), *Orchestra Wives* (1942), *Stormy Weather*

The Nicholas Brothers

(1943), and the "Be a Clown" number with Gene Kelly from *The Pirate* (1948).

BOBBY NORTH

Although his name means little today, Robert (Bobby) North was quite a talented man, rising from the ranks of vaudeville and the legitimate stage to be one of the film industry's leading producers. He was responsible for many major films at First National and Warner Bros., including the 1930 feature *The Dawn Patrol.* "I started in show business when I was twelve-and-a-half years old," North recalled:

I left New York and joined a company, and at that time there was a vogue of a soubrette, as we called her, singing on the stage, and a kid would get up from the gallery and sing the chorus. The Gallery Gods, of course, thought he was one of them and applauded loudly, and she made a big hit. I was the kid in the gallery. I had the voice and I could sing. From that I graduated into little shows, one night stands, and so on. In those days you had a lot of companies which traveled all over the country, playing little towns with ten and fifteen thousand populations. Every little town had an opera house or a theatre, and they might be open one or two days a week. What we called number-two or number-three shows of a New York success would play through the country in these one- and two-night stands. I did a lot of that. In these theatres you *did* learn your trade, because you were an amateur; you learned to

communicate with an audience; you learned to feel what an audience wanted; and it gave you a great education in how to play a part.

In his early twenties Bobby North was involved in various aspects of show business. He appeared in the 1909 Emerich Kalman operetta *The Gay Hussars.* He was a straight actor in the 1910 play *Just a Wife,* and a comedian in the 1912 "jumble of jollification," *Hanky Panky.* In 1910 North and Cliff Gordon coproduced *The Merry Whirl,* which ran for a mere twenty-four performances. Bobby North was one of the stars, along with Fanny Brice and Bert Williams, of the 1910 *Ziegfeld Follies.* He recalled singing and dancing in the *Follies,* but it was as a monologist, telling Jewish stories, that North headlined at the Palace in 1914, having appeared in vaudeville in this capacity as early as 1909.

In January of 1909 Bobby North dropped his song-and-dance act to play the Colonial as a "Hebrew Impersonator," a strange title for an act which involved telling gently humorous stories with a Yiddish accent. His delivery was similar in style to that of another great vaudeville monologist, Julian Rose, and included parodies of popular songs and typical Yiddish patter. Sime Silverman reviewed the act in *Variety* (January 23, 1909), found it too long—it ran eighteen minutes—and thought North was a better singer than monologist.

Robert North entered films because he found touring the halls with a pregnant wife and a young son (who grew up to be Edmund H. North, the screenwriter) too exhausting. His film career began in 1915 with Popular Plays and Players, for whom he produced the films of vaudeville star

Olga Petrova (see her entry). Robert North devoted the rest of his life to the cinema. He died in Los Angeles on August 13, 1976, at the age of ninety-two.

OLSEN AND JOHNSON

Ole Olsen and Chic Johnson were unlike other comedy teams in that there was no sharp dividing line between the straight-man/stooge and the funny man. Each was equally funny in his own right, although perhaps Chic Johnson with his shrill, high-pitched laughter was the more outrageous of the two. As early as 1918, when they were playing the Royal Theatre with a ten-minute act of comedy and songs and accompanying themselves on the piano and violin, *Variety* (September 13, 1918) commented, "It's the way they do their act that counts." And the way they pursued their act was sheer lunacy, which reached its climax with the greatest vaudeville revue of all time, *Hellzapoppin*. Just as *Billy Rose's Jumbo* was the ultimate in sophisticated vaudeville-style revues, *Hellzapoppin* was the ultimate in comic vaudeville revues, taking the best—or the worst, depending on your point of view—from vaudeville and burlesque routines of the past and adding more than a touch of Olsen and Johnson mayhem.

John Sigvard Olsen and Harold Ogden Johnson met in 1914 when the pianist in Olsen's quartet, The College Four, quit the group and Johnson became his replacement. The two began to throw in comedy ad libs to help the vaudeville routine, and out of this developed their comic style. By the thirties Olsen and Johnson were fairly well known on the vaudeville and Broadway stage, and

had even appeared in a few films, none of which do them justice: *Oh! Sailor Behave!* (1931), *Gold Dust Gertie* (1931), *Country Gentleman* (1936), and *All over the Town* (1937).

However, it is *Hellzapoppin* for which Olsen and Johnson will always be remembered, and which was their greatest single achievement. "Assembled and produced" by Ole Olsen and Chic Johnson, *Hellzapoppin* opened at the Forty-sixth Street Theatre on September 22, 1938 and closed 1,404 performances later, (after transferring to the Winter Garden Theatre) on December 17, 1941. It was comedy of the lowest type, totally devoid of intellect, and it was hated by all the New York critics with the exception of Walter Winchell who constantly plugged it in his column. "We try to devise situations which are so sure fire that you or Bill Jones or John Smith could step into them and get laughs," explained Olsen. Those situations might include throwing plastic or rubber snakes and spiders into the audience, someone walking up and down the aisles selling tickets for a rival show, or a gift night sketch in which the duo gave away anything from a washtub to a live chicken. A fruit-laden girl would be asked where she was going and respond, "Orange, New Jersey." A famous running gag in *Hellzapoppin* was to have a stooge in the audience shout out, "Hey . . . which of you mugs is Johnson?" At the conclusion of each performance Olsen would turn to Johnson and say, "May you live as long as you want," to which Johnson would reply, "And may you laugh as long as you live."

Two comments sum up *Hellzapoppin*. The first is from *Variety's* review: "It's an object lesson in how entertaining vaude can be." The other is by newspaper columnist H.

Olsen and Johnson

I. Phillips: "Good old Olsen and Johnson. They are to be congratulated for one thing if for no other, and that is, they gave the boys of this war an opportunity to laugh at the same jokes their fathers did in World War One." As Olsen and Johnson proved, there's no joke like an old joke.

Unfortunately, after *Hellzapoppin* there was nothing left for Olsen and Johnson to do except recreate it, fairly successfully, in a film version for Universal in 1941, and in such Broadway shows as *Laffing Room Only* (1945), *Funzapoppin* (1949), and *Pardon My French* (1950).

Eventually the team split up, with Johnson touring in *The Chic Johnson Revue* and Olsen entertaining the troops abroad. Johnson died on February 25, 1962, in Las Vegas, at the age of sixty-six. He had been in Las Vegas checking out the possibility of opening a restaurant there. Olsen died in Albuquerque, New Mexico, on January 26, 1963, at the age of sixty-three. Just as they had been inseparable in life, so it was in death. Late in 1962 Olsen's body was shipped from Kansas, where it had been initially interred, to be buried beside Johnson in Las Vegas. That unique blend of Olsen and Johnson slapstick, which they called "gonk," meaning "hokum with raisins," has never been satisfactorily repeated since *Hellzapoppin,* and probably never will.

THE ON WAH TROUPE

A typical Chinese balancing and acrobatic act which came to prominence in 1930, the On Wah Troupe remained popular during the first half of that decade. The troupe consisted of three men and two women who engaged in contortions, balancing plates on the end of poles, and similar feats. Apparently, the On Wah Troupe consisted of a father, two sons, and two daughters. But as *The Billboard* (April 19, 1930), reviewing the act at Fox's Academy, so charmingly expressed it—"can't be sure, however, as all Chinese look alike."

ORCHESTRAS AND DANCE BANDS

It was not until the mid-twenties that orchestras and dance bands emerged from their then natural habitats of hotels and night spots to appear on a regular basis on the vaudeville circuits. Vaudeville offered a perfect winter booking for orchestras which had been kept busy all summer at resorts like Atlantic City's Million Dollar Pier and New York's Coney Island. By the mid-thirties there was hardly a vaudeville bill in the country which did not feature a popular orchestra.

One of the earliest bands to play vaudeville was the eleven-piece Alexander's Rag Time Band which also featured a company of five singers and dancers. It included marches and ragtime in its repertoire, and *Variety* (February 24, 1912) though that "the turn will rouse any small time audience it appears before." In 1923 dance bands appearing on the vaudeville circuit included Al Tucker and Band, Carl Shaw and Band, and Verne Buck and His Merry Garden Orchestra. The last was "void of all personality," according to *Variety*. Al Tucker was a trick fiddler who appeared in a tramp costume, and his band played jazz with a measure of opera and a Sousa march thrown in. Carl Shaw's band was a five-piece affair, and the highlight of its March 1923 appearance at the Twenty-third Street Theatre was a Gallagher and Shean routine between cornet and clarinet. Like most bands in vaudeville at this time, Carl Shaw was the closing act on the bill.

The Rhythm Boys: Harry Barris, Bing Crosby, and Al Rinker

In the mid-twenties the Ray Miller Band was popular in vaudeville; noted, but less popular, was the minor act of Tom Kerr and His Musical Kerriers. The California Collegiates, who began their career in Laguna Beach, California, in 1923, are of interest in that the group's saxophonist at one time was Fred MacMurray. Horace Heidt and His Orchestra successfully toured the western Fanchon and Marco circuit in the late twenties. Jan Garber and His Band featured a dance team. Most orchestras and dance bands found it necessary to include vocalists and dancers as part of their vaudeville acts.

Many bands had financial worries, but one that didn't was the Roger Wolfe Kahn company, not only because it was a successful orchestra but because Kahn was the son of millionaire steel magnate and art collector Otto Kahn. He headlined in a twenty-three-minute act at the Palace in February of 1929 with a program that included the two William Sisters. Kahn played dance music, and *Variety* complained that they did not dance in vaudeville houses. Al Rinker, the last surviving member of Paul Whiteman's famous Rhythm Boys, says there was no comparison between Kahn and Whiteman, either in their approach to music or in personality. "Roger Wolf Kahn, actually I think he played the piano, and he played well. I remember we used to go down to hear him at the Pennsylvania Hotel, and we all thought he had a hell of a band."

Vincent Lopez (December 30, 1894–September 20, 1975) was a favorite on radio, in vaudeville, and, from 1949, on television with his theme song, "Nola," and his greeting, "Hello, everybody, Lopez speaking." He came to fame in 1921 when he broadcast live from New York's Pennsylvania Hotel, and his success on radio led to vaudeville engagements throughout the twenties and thirties. In 1939 Lopez was to be found touring the vaudeville circuits with Betty Hutton and Abbott and Costello.

Most people believe that all-girl orchestras started with Phil Spitalny or with Ina Ray Hutton and Her Melodears, billed as "The glamorous blonde bombshell of rhythm, with her swinging sweethearts." But all-girl orchestras were nothing new to vaudeville. In December of 1903 the Fadettes of Boston, a woman's orchestra under the direction of Caroline B. Nichols, was playing the Keith's Theatre in New York. As early as 1918 the Rita Mario Orchestra, consisting of ten young ladies each wearing an evening gown of different style and color, was enchanting vaudeville audiences. Sime Silverman, writing in *Variety* (May 13, 1918), called it "a turn that will grace any bill." Silverman was not so impressed by Frankie Cramer and Her Melody Bandits, an eight-piece, all-girl orchestra that was little more than a novelty act in the late twenties. Eva Shirley and her five-piece jazz band delighted audiences at the Palace in May of 1919. *Variety* hailed them as the best of the jazz combinations playing around the New York area. As part of the act, the group featured a male shimmy dancer who made the Palace audience regulars sit up and take notice! For the record, the first "all-colored," all-girl orchestra was the Harlem Playgirls, which came on the vaudeville scene in 1937.

Phil Spitalny, who was a popular leader of all-male orchestras in the late twenties and thirties, got his idea for

Vincent Lopez

an all-girl orchestra in the early thirties after witnessing a performance by a teenage violinist named Evelyn Kaye Klein. He signed her to an exclusive contract, hired twenty-seven other female musicians, and in 1934, at the Capitol Theatre, Phil Spitalny and His All-Girl Orchestra made its debut. Evelyn Kaye Klein was the featured soloist, billed as "Evelyn and Her Magic Violin."

Phil Spitalny and His All-Girl Orchestra made its radio debut on "The Hour of Charm" in January of 1935 and was heard almost continuously on that program through 1948. In a 1942 issue of *Radio Life*, Evelyn talked of life in the all-girl orchestra:

Associations in the all-girl orchestra are much like sorority like. We room together, share our recreations, and even our sorrows. As for temperament, Mr. Spitalny won't tolerate it, so all of us are very evenly dispositioned. Whenever a girl wants to go out, she goes to the committee and says, "I want a date with Mr. So-and-So." They ask her who the man is, what he does, and for references. If he passes muster, she gets her date. But if the committee feels that it would hurt the orchestra for a member to be seen with the man, the engagement doesn't materialize.

Spitalny and Evelyn were married in 1946 and made their home in Florida, where Spitalny died in 1970.

The biggest orchestra name in vaudeville was undoubtedly Paul Whiteman (March 28, 1891–December 29, 1967). Once a dominant force in modern American music,

Paul Whiteman introduced "symphonic jazz" in 1919, with which he had first come in contact around 1915 on San Francisco's Barbary Coast. Along the way he was also responsible for the introduction of George Gershwin's "Rhapsody in Blue" and Ferde Grofe's "Grand Canyon Suite"—Grofe had once been a member of his band. In 1925 Whiteman was known as vaudeville's most expensive headliner, being paid an unprecedented $7,000 a week to headline at the Hippodrome. Four years earlier he had been willing to play the Palace for a mere $2,500 a week. Reviewing his Hippodrome appearance, *Variety* (May 13, 1925) wrote, "Whiteman's program is a happy medium. It is not musical hoke. It does not resort to moron appeal with blatant jazz, or so-called popular appeal with scenic back-ups, but gets to both, and beyond that, with a study in syncopation that distinguishes the orchestra as an individuality and not of a class."

Al Rinker recalls, "Whiteman was a marvelous personality. He wasn't a great band leader. He wasn't a great musician, like Tommy Dorsey; he played fiddle, but he gave that up and all he did was carry it, and it had nothing to do with leading the band. But he was a marvelous personality. He paid big salaries. In those days, a top lead in that orchestra, a sax player, would make three hundred dollars a week. No one else paid three hundred dollars a week."

Aside from working with Whiteman, Al Rinker, Harry Barris, and Bing Crosby, as the Rhythm Boys, toured the vaudeville circuits in 1928. Rinker remembers the problems that they encountered. "The younger people knew who we were, because they bought our records, but the average person who went to vaudeville was not used to seeing such a type of act as ours. We didn't go over at all at the Palace. We'd sing 'Mississippi Mud' and all these things, and the audience didn't know what the hell we were doing. They were probably waiting for Sophie Tucker to come on and sing 'Some of These Days.' We were too modern."

The Rhythm Boys would parody the old type of vaudeville entertainer with a dance performed to the tune of "Baby Face." They engaged in comedy patter, and, of course, they harmonized. *The Billboard* (August 18, 1928) saw them at Keith's Eighty-first Street Theatre and commented: "The Paul Whiteman Rhythm Boys have personality, good voices and a way of putting their song numbers over effectively. . . . They have the art of rhythm perfected to a stellar degree."

After completing *The King of Jazz* for Universal Pictures in 1930, Paul Whiteman prophesied that "within two years you will see the bands and orchestras back in the picture houses again. The talkies drove them out, but they will make the people so music loving that they will have to put the bands back. I think that pictures with music will make the people demand big bands and good bands. They won't stand for four- and five-piece affairs again. They will be educated up to the big band class. And watch big bands come back to the theatres. A good band can make a house pay even if the picture is bad." Whiteman was correct; with the changeover of cinemas to presentation houses featuring both movies and vaudeville shows, the big bands did become a staple of the new vaudeville bills.

It would be impossible to mention all the orchestras featured on vaudeville bills and in presentation houses in the late thirties, but notable were Ben Bernie's Band, Mike Riley's Band, Joe Venuti's Band, Teddy King's Band, the Abe Lyman Band, Tommy Dorsey and His Orchestra, Henry Busse and His Band, Isham Jones and His Orchestra, Lou Breese's Band, Anson Weeks's Orchestra, Glenn Miller and His Orchestra, Frankie Masters and His Orchestra, Al Donahue and His Orchestra, and Eddie Delange and His Band. It speaks volumes for the importance of orchestras and dance bands in vaudeville that only after vaudeville was stricken, and generally nothing more than half of a cinema program, did orchestras find a permanent place on the vaudeville stage.

References: *The Wonderful Era of the Great Dance Bands* by Leo Walker (Howell-North Books, 1964). "Evelyn and Her Magic Violin" in *Whatever Became of . . . ?* (Fourth Series) by Richard Lamparski (Crown, 1973).

MISS PATRICOLA

Just as Giselle MacKenzie delighted television audiences in the fifties on "Your Hit Parade" with her violin playing and singing, so did Miss Patricola in the late teens and twenties with a similar act. "Patricola is such a personable young woman that she could entertain almost any audience," reported the *New York Dramatic Mirror* (March 1, 1919). At an early vaudeville performance she won over the audience with her first number, "Sweet Adeline," and by the second chorus even the orchestra was joining in with enthusiasm.

In her early career Miss Patricola was the opening spot on the bill, but by October of 1923 she was headlining at the Palace. A brother, Tom, was also on the vaudeville stage as a first-rate comedian. Isabelle Patricola died in Manhasset, Long Island, on May 23, 1965, at the age of seventy-nine.

OLGA PETROVA

Classifying Olga Petrova's vaudeville act is not easy, perhaps because Madame Petrova was in a class all her own. She was a patrician of the stage in the manner of Ethel Barrymore. She gave recitations and she sang, and sometimes she merely stood there and cried, and audiences knew they were in the presence of someone unique. She was exceptional, and as the *New York Dramatic Mirror* (March 1, 1919) described her, "a rare trinity of emotional actress, screen star, and vaudeville artist."

Madame Petrova's whole life was an act, carefully stage-managed and never underrehearsed. The writer had the good fortune to know her well in her last years, and the closest she came to intimacy was allowing me to address her as Petrova rather than Madame Petrova. Although born in England and a resident of the U.S. for more than sixty years, she insisted on speaking with a Russian accent, which occasionally would be forgotten—

Olga Petrova

obviously due only to advancing years. Robert North, who was an associate of the actress during her screen career, told me: "She had a Russian accent. Always. She never, never forgot that. Of course, we all knew she was an English girl, but she never lost that Russian accent. Day or night, the accent was there—off stage or on stage. I don't think she ever spoke without that accent, even to her husband at home. That was part of her personality, and, of course, she capitalized on it."

Aside from being a star—and a major one—of vaudeville and film, Petrova was also an ardent feminist. North recalled, "She wouldn't listen to any talk about women being inferior at all. She raised hell about it." In stage plays and in films Petrova always portrayed women with strong personalities and minds of their own. In a 1918 film, *The Light Within,* for example, she played a doctor of bacteriology who discovers a cure for meningitis and anthrax. She told *Motion Picture Classic* (September 1918), "I do want to bring a message to women—a message of encouragement. The only women I want to play are women who do things. I want to encourage women to do things—to take their rightful place in life." She even wrote poetry on women's rights, such as "Thus Speaks Woman," published in 1919.

Madame Petrova's life was a struggle for independence, for herself and for her sex, and much of that struggle is recorded in her autobiography, *Butter with My Bread,* which tells of her early life in England and of her fight to find freedom from a tyrannical father. Her autobiography, as Petrova told me, is "a tale of my struggle as a female child to break away from that life, a struggle to obtain by

devious means—the screen happening to be one of them —a home, bread, and butter of my own." After amateur theatricals and minor stage roles, Petrova came to London at the age of twenty and within four years, through hard work and talent, she had become a prominent stage actress.

Although Petrova vehemently denied it, she apparently was born Muriel Harding and under that name had started her stage career. Leon Zeitlin, a London theatrical booker, suggested she change her name because it did not suit her looks—red-haired and regal—or her temperament. Thinking of her one-time husband, Boris Petroff, the actress suggested Olga Petrova. Zeitlin added the "Madame" and liked the name because it was reminiscent of Anna Pavlova. The latter was starring at the London Palace, and Petrova was about to become a star at the London Pavilion—to be precise, on April 5, 1911.

As a result of her successful appearance at the Pavilion and other British music halls, Petrova was signed by Jesse L. Lasky and Henry B. Harris to star in a new type of vaudeville entertainment, a supper club, to be called the Folies Bergere. It was located at the Fulton Theatre in New York, and opened in the summer of 1911. She was not a success, nor for that matter was the Folies Bergere. Madame Petrova sang a few songs and gave an impersonation of dramatic actress Jane Hading (assisted by comedian and master of ceremonies James J. Morton, who was a hit). Sime Silverman in *Variety* (August 5, 1911) described Petrova's act as "very light, in texture and execution," and ended his review by writing, "Petrova should go in for the dramatic matter or employ other numbers, and change her name back to where it was." Petrova did neither, but instead accepted the role of Diane in Henry B. Harris's production of the Lionel Monckton musical comedy *The Quaker Girl* which opened at the Park Theatre on October 23, 1911, and was to run for 240 performances.

From *The Quaker Girl* Petrova went back into vaudeville. She refined and perfected her act, adding an impersonation of Lena Ashwell in her 1906 hit *The Shulamite* and singing a French translation of "Oh, You Beautiful Doll." Eddie Darling wanted to book her into the Fifth Avenue Theatre, which Petrova agreed to under certain conditions—she wanted no money and no billing for the first week. Darling agreed, of course, and Petrova was a success; the theatre was flooded with inquiries about the unbilled performer who cried real tears during the scene from *The Shulamite.* Petrova played a second successful week, but the third week she demanded billing as the headliner. Darling consented and the English actor R. A. Roberts (noted on the American vaudeville stage for his characterizations from the novels of Charles Dickens) who was supposed to have been the headliner agreed to take second billing. What happened next is unclear, except that when Roberts discovered who had preempted his headliner status, he walked out of the show. Some claim that Petrova had sought revenge against Roberts who had treated her badly when she toured, as Muriel Harding, in his company in South Africa. Madame Petrova denied to me that this was so. In fact, she claims she did not know

Olga Petrova

among others. Petrova later signed with Famous Players-Lasky for *The Undying Flame, The Exile,* and *The Law of the Land,* all released in 1917, and then formed her own Petrova Picture Company which released five features through First Naitonal. Besides starring in films, Petrova later found time to write articles and interviews for a number of film periodicals, including *Shadowland, Motion Picture Magazine,* and *Photoplay Journal.*

In 1919 Petrova returned to vaudeville, making her first appearance at the Orpheum in New York in February. She recited an original verse titled "There, Little Girl, Don't Cry," sang songs in four different voices, gave an excerpt again from *The Shulamite,* and performed "My Hero." The *New York Dramatic Mirror* (March 1, 1919) commented, "Few actresses have caused editorial pens so much perplexity as to the proper classifying of her particular style of work. Some of the scribes have got real mad about the difficulty and others have used excessive flattery as the easiest way to untie the knot. Such a state of editorial indecision makes her a distinct novelty." After six weeks at the Orpheum, Petrova set out on an extended tour which included twenty-two different theatres in as many cities. In eighteen of these she broke the records for attendance—a feat previously accomplished only by Sarah Bernhardt. As Madame Petrova's act would sometimes include an impersonation of Bernhardt fainting, the performer must have achieved a great deal of satisfaction in seeing her success compared to that of the great French actress.

Petrova's debut at the Palace came in 1919 at which time she performed a recitation of her own authorship titled "To a Child That Enquires," which is so wonderful and became so popular that it is worth reprinting here, although the full dramatic impact is somewhat lacking without Petrova's voice and inflections:

How did you come to me, my sweet?
From the land that no man knows?
Did Mr. Stork bring you here on his wings?
Were you born in the heart of a rose?
Did an angel fly with you down from the sky?
Were you found in a gooseberry patch?
Did a fairy bring you from fairyland
To my door—that was left on the latch?
No—my darling was born of a wonderful love,
A love that was Daddy's and mine.
A love that was human, but deep and profound,
A love that was almost divine.
Do you remember, sweetheart, when we went to the Zoo?
And we saw that big bear, with a grouch?
And the tigers and lions, and that tall kangaroo
That carried her babes in a pouch?
Do you remember I told you she kept them there safe
From the cold and the wind, till they grew
Big enough to take care of themselves,
Well, dear heart, that's just how I first cared for you.
I carried you under my heart, my sweet,
And I sheltered you, safe from alarms,

that Roberts, whom she described as "a very clever protean performer," was the headliner. One thing is certain, and it is that Petrova was tremendously successful. *Variety* (April 6, 1912), seeing her at the Fifth Avenue Theatre, described her as "one of the cleverest, classiest, and most attractive of turns." Edward Darling wrote to her, "I am quite sure that anything I was able to do for you has been warranted by your own talent. It is so seldom one meets with originality that to have given you the opportunity at a New York theatre was as much a pleasure to me as it was to you."

Petrova's salary at this time was $125 a week. The salary increased when she decided to try the legitimate stage, starring in Monckton Hoffe's play *Panthea* which opened at the Booth Theatre on March 23, 1914, with Milton Sills playing the male lead. *Variety* (April 3, 1914) did not care for the play but its critic, Jolo, was bemused by Petrova: "Zat Madame Petrova is ze most exotic figure on ze New York stage zere can be little doubt. Her full white zroat has ze lines zat Praxicles molded in Aphrodite —her ruby lips retain zere poster redness even though Pantzea (as she pronounces it) makes her entrance rescued from the sea, and her Burne-Jones hair is given an extra marcel or two by the waves of the Northumberland Coast."

While appearing on tour in *Panthea* in Chicago, Petrova was offered a film contract. Her first feature, *The Tigress,* released in December of 1914, was a success, and she subsequently signed a two-year contract with Popular Plays and Players for whom she starred in *The Heart of a Painted Woman* (1915) and *The Black Butterfly* (1916),

Till one wonderful day the dear God looked down—
And I cuddled you tight in my arms.

E. F. Albee apparently found the verse indecent.

In the twenties Petrova was chiefly preoccupied with three plays: *The White Peacock, Hurricane,* and *What Do We Know?* The last two dealt with birth control and spiritualism respectively, and like most of Petrova's activities they were controversial. After a three-year absence Petrova returned to the vaudeville stage at the Palace Theatre in Chicago in May of 1923 with a thirty-four-minute act, which included all her earlier songs and recitations. She even moved the piano when she found it was not in exactly the right position, telling the audience, "If you want anything done right. . . ." *Variety* (May 24, 1923) reported that as usual she was dramatic in all she did, and, as usual, she was a great success with the audience. In 1925 Petrova starred at the Hippodrome singing a French and a Spanish number and closing her act with "Carry Me Back to Old Virginny" sung in three different voices: baritone, soprano, and a very high falsetto. "With Petrova," commented *Variety* (October 21, 1925), "the secret is charm, showmanship, dry European wit, and a startlingly different way of doing things."

Petrova invested her money well and retired to the south of France in the late twenties. At the outbreak of the Second World War she returned to America and settled in Clearwater, Florida, where she died on November 30, 1977, at the age of ninety. In the course of writing a piece on her screen career I asked her to define her greatness, and she replied, "What is little? What is Great? Let me put it this way. I did achieve what I set out as a child to get, my own bread, my own butter, my own house in which to enjoy it. That—to me—is the height of what I will accept and acknowledge as greatness."

References: *Butter with My Bread* by Olga Petrova (The Bobbs-Merrill Company, 1942). "Olga Petrova" in *The Idols of Silence* by Anthony Slide (A. S. Barnes and Company, 1976), pages 47–55.

MOLLY PICON

Molly Picon, the great star of the Yiddish theatre, was born in New York on June 1, 1898. She began her career at the age of five in vaudeville and burlesque. As a child she would introduce herself to theatrical producers with the words, "I sing, dance, play the piano and ukelele, and do somersaults." Between 1915 and 1918 she toured with an act called The Four Seasons, singing and dancing on the Gus Sun and other small-time vaudeville circuits.

After becoming a leading lady in the Yiddish theatre, which was centered on New York's Second Avenue, Molly Picon was invited to headline at the Palace in the spring of 1929 at a salary of $2,500 a week. She took some of the Yiddish numbers she had performed on Second Avenue and translated them into English for her vaudeville debut. Sophie Tucker, who was on the same bill, did the reverse and performed half of her act in Yiddish,

Molly Picon

causing *Variety* to comment, "The Broadway actress did a Second Avenue show and the Second Avenue actress did a Broadway show."

Her success at the Palace led Molly Picon to appear in vaudeville elsewhere, including a 1932 stint at the London Palladium. She was a regular at the Palace, with her salary soon rising to $3,000 a week. In July of 1930 Miss Picon's Palace act included an interview with "Mister Ziegenfeld," in which she tried to put Fatima Goldberg in the glorifying business, together with songs such as "The Immigrant Boy," "Kiss Me Again," and "Temperamental Tillie," composed by Joseph Rumshinsky, known as the Second Avenue Irving Berlin. *Variety* (July 16, 1930) noted, "A clever artiste, that Picon girl. The favorite Yiddish soubrette on the East Side, her transition to Broadway and Forty-seventh is heightened, if anything, by her Broadway material and further presented in cameo relief by her own charming personality and style."

Vaudeville was, however, nothing more than a side venture for the tiny and effervescent Molly Picon who is still entertaining Yiddish and Gentile audiences today as much as she did fifty and more years ago.

Reference: *Molly!* by Molly Picon with Jean Grillo (Simon and Schuster, 1980).

POLAIRE

Mlle. Polaire had a strange—and short—career in American vaudeville. She was one of the darlings of the Parisian music halls in the early years of this century, famed for her

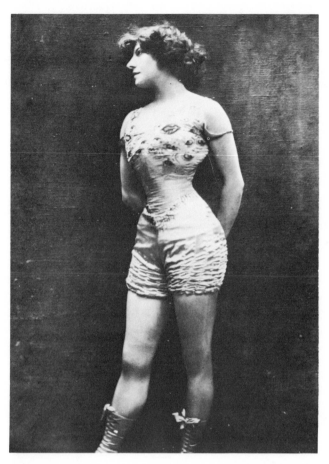

Polaire

stage. She was fairly popular for the first two weeks of her engagement, but then audience attendance dropped, and, apparently, there was more applause for Bedini and Arthur's burlesque of her act on the same bill than there was for Polaire herself. Out-of-town managers were unwilling to meet Polaire's high salary so in July of 1910 the star returned to France.

Much of the credit for Polaire's initial American success must go to Hammerstein's press agent, Nellie Revel, who thought up "The Ugliest Woman in the World" title, which, incidentally, Polaire subsequently ordered removed from outside the theatre along with pictures of herself which she claimed were not good likenesses. Nellie Revel had the idea of photographing Lillian Russell with Polaire and captioning the result as "The Ugliest and Handsomest Women in the World," but she was beaten out by Morris Gest. In anger, Miss Revel punched Gest in the nose and quit her job with Hammerstein.

An Algerian by birth, Mlle. Polaire was christened Emile Bouchaud, but was renamed by her brother who brought her to Paris and first obtained engagements for her singing in boulevard cafes. She died at the reported age of fifty-nine in Champigny-sur-Marne, France, on October 14, 1939. Long retired, she had relied on old friends like Colette for financial support, for, as one writer noted, Polaire had become as outdated as the corset which had made her fifteen-inch waist famous.

POWER'S DANCING ELEPHANTS

There were four elephants in the act, which was an attraction for many years in the late teens and early twenties at the New York Hippodrome. They played a baseball game and fenced with their trainer. In May of 1923 Power's Dancing Elephants had the distinction of being the first elephant act to play the Palace.

EVA PUCK

Eva Puck was a bright dancing and singing comedienne in vaudeville's halcyon days. With her husband, Sammy White, she went on to play the comedy lead in Rodgers and Hart's *The Girl Friend* (which opened at New York's Vanderbilt Theatre on March 17, 1926) and in Kern and Hammerstein's *Showboat* (which opened at New York's Ziegfeld Theatre on December 27, 1927).

Prior to their joining up as a team, Eva Puck had worked with her brother, Harry, in an act titled—you guessed it—Puck and Puck, while Sammy White was half of the team of Clayton and White. The couple's vaudeville routine was titled "Opera versus Jazz." In it White portrayed a dancing teacher trying to instruct a stupid Miss Puck, followed by a burlesque of grand opera and classical dancing. Reviewing their act at the Palace, Abel wrote in *Variety* (December 27, 1923), "Both go in for comedy in a broad vein, but it is judiciously counterbalanced by the other when each is featuring a speciality." *Variety's* Chicago critic, Loop, caught the couple's act at the Chicago Theatre and declared them "ideal entertainers whether in revue, vaudeville, or picture houses."

beauty (although she did have a rather sharp, pointed nose which was often caricatured) and for her extraordinary fifteen-inch waist. She had neither a great voice nor great acting ability, apparently, but she was a passionate and intense performer, who one critic noted, "shook like an infuriated wasp" while she was on stage. Polaire portrayed Claudine when Colette's books on that character were transferred to the stage, and the writer described Polaire as "a strange young woman who had no need of true beauty to put all other women in the shade, an inspired actress to whom training and study were equally unnecessary." She was a temperamental star, concerned only with her performance. When Colette told her to sleep well, the actress replied, "Oh, I don't sleep much, you know. I lie and wait." When Colette asked for whom, her star replied, "Nobody! I wait and wait for tomorrow's performance."

Willie Hammerstein brought Polaire to America in June of 1910 as a freak act at his Victoria Theatre for the staggering salary of $2,800 a week. Hammerstein billed her, very unfairly and inaccurately, as "The Ugliest Woman in the World" and offered prizes to women who, with the aid of corsets, could beat Polaire's fifteen-inch waist. Polaire appeared in a twenty-minute, French-language playlet, *Le Visiteur,* the high spot of which was an apache dance, then still a novelty to American audiences who were not used to seeing women knocked around on

Harry and Eva Puck

Eva Puck died in Granada Hills, California, on October 24, 1979, at the reported age of eighty-seven. During her life she had proved, contrary to the song she introduced in *Showboat,* that "Life on the Wicked Stage" could have its rewards.

SALLY RAND

Sally Rand's place in the history of show business is secure not because of what she did, but because she did it for so long—from the early thirties through the seventies and almost up to the day she died, in Glendora, California, on August 31, 1979. What Sally Rand did, as if anyone did not know, was a famous fan dance involving two ostrich plumes which she moved with perfect precision to cover and uncover certain parts of her naked body, usually to the accompaniment of Debussy's "Clair de Lune." When not using her fans, Sally Rand was dancing around with a large balloon in the glare of a pink spotlight.

She was born Hazel Beck in Hickory County, Missouri, on April 3, 1904, and selected the name Rand from the Rand McNally Atlas. Why she picked Rand rather than McNally is unclear, perhaps because it enabled her to pun "The Rand is quicker than the eye." Sally Rand worked as an acrobat in carnivals and circuses before coming to Los Angeles in the mid-twenties, at which time she gained bit parts in Hal Roach comedies followed by small roles in a number of features. These included *Man Bait* (1926), *Night of Love* (1927), *His Dog* (1927), *Getting Gertie's Garter* (1927), *Galloping Fury* (1927), *Heroes in Blue* (1927), *Crashing Through* (1928), *A Girl in Every Port*

(1928), *Woman Against the World* (1928), *Nameless Men* (1928), *Golf Widows* (1928), *Black Feather* (1928), and Cecil B. DeMille's *King of Kings* (1927) in which she played Mary Magdalene's handmaiden. A 1925 publicity handout from DeMille's P. D. C. studios described Sally Rand as "saucy, piquant—your eye just naturally goes to her. She's a cute, lithesome charmer, whether as a blonde or a brunette—and above all she radiates personality."

Following her initial screen career (she was back at Paramount in 1934 with a featured role in *Bolero*), Sally Rand toured the vaudeville circuits and even headlined at the Palace in September of 1928 with a twenty-minute act titled "Sally's Boy Friends." With the aid of three male dancers and an octet of male singers, Sally Rand did an adagio act plus a spot of tap dancing. Her reception at the Palace was "indifferently pleasant" according to Abel in *Variety* (September 26, 1928).

Sally Rand

The fan dance was first performed, according to legend, in a Chicago night club in 1932. The following year Sally Rand gained nationwide fame as an attraction at the "Streets of Paris" section of the Chicago World's Fair; on the opening night of the Fair she appeared as Lady Godiva complete with a white horse. Sally Rand worked continuously in burlesque and night clubs from then on, and in 1965 she replaced Ann Corio as mistress of ceremonies for *This Was Burlesque* on Broadway. She always refused to allow herself to be termed an exotic dancer, claiming, "The dictionary defines 'exotic' as that which is strange and foreign. I am not 'strange'; I like boys. I am not foreign; I was born in Hickory County, Missouri."

HARRY RICHMAN

Harry Richman with Irving Berlin

"When the Red, Red Robin," "On the Sunny Side of the Street," "This Is My Lucky Day," "It All Depends on You," and "Puttin' on the Ritz" are just a few of the songs associated with Harry Richman, a song-and-dance man whose top hat or straw hat, tails, and cane were his trademarks. He composed many of his own hits, including "Shake Hands with a Millionaire," "Singing a Vagabond Song," and "Walking My Baby Back Home." His colorful career embraced vaudeville, films, radio, night clubs, musical comedy and revue. It included three marriages and romantic affairs with innumerable women, including—according to Richman's autobiography—Mae West, Clara Bow, and Nora Bayes. (For his second marriage, to showgirl Hazel Forbes, Harry Richman spent $30,000, with $5,000 going for flowers alone.) He was involved with gangsters and with payola in the early days of radio. Bob Hope recalled costarring with Richman in *Say When* (1934). When he asked "Who let those mugs in?" referring to Lucky Luciano and his mob, Richman replied, "They're the backers and you better be funny—or you get a concrete overcoat." He claimed to have earned and lost thirteen million dollars, although most of his colleagues put the amount closer to seven million. His Club Richman on Park Avenue was one of New York's top night spots in the twenties, and he even played the Palace with an act titled "A Night at Club Richman."

Harry Richman was born in Cincinnati, Ohio, on August 10, 1895; his mother came from Germany and his father, Harry Reichman, from Russia. As early as 1907 he became an entertainer in Cincinnati, playing piano in cafes and honky tonks. In his autobiography, Richman recalls that Sophie Tucker came to the city, heard him play, and told his mother that he had talent and a great future. At the age of fourteen he teamed up with a violin player named Bud Remington, and they formed an act called Remington and Reichman. By the time he played San Francisco in 1914 Remington had disappeared, and Harry Reichman was now billing himself as "The English Comedian."

The first big break came in the late 1910s when Harry Richman became a piano accompanist for Mae West and later the Dolly Sisters. As Miss West recalled at a 1962 Friars Club testimonial to Richman, "I don't remember if I discovered you or if you discovered me, Harry. But I do remember you had a great touch—even with a piano." In the early twenties Richman started singing on Nils T. Granlund's WHN, one of New York's two radio stations. "I was on from noon till midnight," Richman recalled. "Nils T. Granlund would get on the air and recite something like 'Boots, Boots, Boots!' and then I would sing. We didn't get paid anything because they didn't know whether anyone was listening. Those were the days of crystal sets, when you had to listen with earphones. I went around to song publishers and made deals where if I sang a song on the air, they'd give me a dollar. I was the first nationally known radio performer." Thus was payola created!

In 1923 Richman put together a new vaudeville act in which he appeared with a midget, sang a "mammy" song, and gave impersonations of Al Jolson and David Warfield. Reviewing his act at the Fifth Avenue Theatre, *Variety* (March 29, 1923) wrote, "Richman makes a good appearance, and his turn is made different. On second (place on the bill) he served well enough. The numbers may be new, though they did not impress for melody values. Richman's ability to put 'stuff' into their rendition counted." In 1925 he was appearing at the Palace with Eddie Elkins and His Band, and his way of putting over a song with a rich voice, a slight lisp, and mannerisms reminiscent of Al Jolson and Ted Lewis, had been perfected. The secret of Richman's success was not his face, not even the manner in which he held his body, but rather the simple fact that he had personality in his voice. As *Variety* (February 4, 1925) noted, "Richman now struts himself without a blush and takes on all the mannerisms of a star."

Harry Richman's career was further enhanced by appearances in the 1926 and 1928 editions of *George White's Scandals,* and by an appearance as the master of ceremonies in *The Ziegfeld follies of 1931.* He claimed to be earning between $25,000 and $30,000 a week, a staggering amount in those days of little or no income tax. In 1937 Richman appeared before England's King George VI and Queen Elizabeth, sang "The Birth of the Blues," and ended his act by telling them, "May God bless and keep you. I wish I could afford to!"

In 1947, Richman recalled, "My voice was beginning to

go—I was having more and more trouble hitting the big ones," and as his voice went so did his career. (Of course, Richman hastened to add that every other part of him was in excellent shape, and that he could still satisfy two ladies a day.) In August of 1963 Richman tried a comeback at New York's Latin Quarter, where, as the *New York Times* (August 24, 1963) noted, "Most of the patrons are old enough to remember the days when he was one of the biggest names in town." But to most people, the man whose suave and debonair manner personified Broadway —Beau Broadway, as he liked to be called—was an unknown entity.

Harry Richman died in Los Angeles on November 3, 1972. George Jessel delivered the eulogy at his funeral and might well have quoted the title of Richman's autobiography as the singer's epitaph: "A hell of a life."

References: *A Hell of a Life* by Harry Richman, with Richard Gehman (Duell, Sloan, and Pearce, 1966). "The Richman Era" by Helen Lawrenson in *Show* (June 1962), pages 75–6, 106, and 107.

LIEUTENANT GITZ RICE

Gitz Ingraham Rice was a Canadian who served with that country's armed forces during the First World War, organizing entertainment for the soldiers and writing a number of popular war-time songs. Among the best known are "Dear Old Pal of Mine" and "Keep Your Head Down, Fritzi Boy" (based on the music hall number "Hold Your Hand Out Naughty Boy"). After the end of hostilities, Lieutenant Gitz Rice was much in demand as a vaudeville performer, usually accompanying other entertainers at the piano.

In 1919 he toured the country with Irene Bordoni in an act which had the chanteuse singing in French "Over There" and "Dear Old Pal of Mine." The *New York Dramatic Mirror* (May 6, 1919) prophesied that they could become "the classiest song team in vaudeville." A year later Gitz Rice was touring vaudeville with Frank Fay in an act titled "Bits of Hits of Their Own Conception." After Gitz Rice's entrance, the telephone on his piano would ring and the soldier-composer would supposedly talk to Fay, inviting him to come down and play a little vaudeville. Frank Fay would appear, and between Rice's piano solos he would provide some comedy patter and songs, including an imitation of John Charles Thomas— the opera star—singing "Darktown Strutter's Ball." While doubting Gitz Rice's ability to hold down the stage without Frank Fay, *Variety* (March 12, 1920) thought the act "a valuable addition to any bill."

By 1923 Lieutenant Gitz Rice had a new partner in the rather large form of Blanche Ring. He played and sang "Dear Old Pal of Mine," engaged in some comedy chatter with his costar, and joined Blanche in singing "Rings on My Fingers," "Yip-I-Addy-I-Ay," and "Bedelia." The act appears to have opened first at the Palace Theatre, Chicago, on September 12, 1923, and, as *Variety* noted, it sounds "a happy combination for vaudeville."

Of course, Gitz Rice also worked as a solo act in vaude-

ville and with other lesser-known performers. In the late twenties he put together an act with a group of male singers billed and dressed as members of the Royal Canadian Mounted Police. Again, Gitz Rice's own compositions were featured, and when the act played the number-two spot at the Palace in October of 1927, *Variety* (October 12, 1927) thought "The costuming is effective and the harmony gets the act over."

Gitz Rice was born in New Glasgow, Nova Scotia, on March 5, 1891; he died in New York City on October 16, 1947. After retirement from vaudeville he went into public relations, but at the outbreak of the Second World War he returned to the stage to entertain Canadian troops. Among the Lieutenant's other compositions are "Mother, I Love You," "Under the Roof Where Laughter Rings," "Because You're Here," "By My Fireside," "Waiting for You," and "I Have Forgotten You Almost."

BLANCHE RING

Blanche Ring

Blanche Ring was one of the great names of musical comedy and vaudeville. Her infectious way of putting over a song was unsurpassed in the history of twentieth century entertainment. She was credited with being the first person in vaudeville to get an audience to sing along with her, and the songs which she made famous were definitely audience participation numbers: "In the Good Old Summertime," which she introduced in *The Defender* (1902); "Waltz Me Around Again, Willie,"; "When Ireland Comes into Her Own," "Yip-I-Addy-I-Ay" (with a "Yip" that demanded an audience yell its head off; when Blanche Ring introduced the song to vaudeville in 1913 she was forced to reprise it five times); and, of course, "I've Got Rings on My Fingers," from *The Midnight Sons* (1909). The last became her theme song, performed, as were all her numbers, in a jovial Irish brogue (not so Irish as to be incomprehensible but sufficiently reminiscent of the old country to send all Irish-Americans into spasms of ecstasy).

Reviewing her vaudeville act in 1919, the *New York Dramatic Mirror* commented, "Not every actress can include the audience in her cast and still retain the footlight illusion." In addition to her songs, Blanche Ring would include character studies of an Irish hotel maid, a manicurist, and a telephone operator, and she would also call on the audience to shout out topics for her to discuss. "Of course she must have had plants to shout out those parties or topics which would dovetail into her song material," wrote the *New York Dramatic Mirror,* "but what of that, it was such a merry program and she cheered the blues out of all present, so thanks to her for being the jolly comedienne she always was and is."

Blanche Ring was born in Boston on April 24, 1876. Her father and her grandfather, both named James Ring, were actors. Early in her career she appeared on stage with Nat C. Goodwin (see his entry) and Chauncey Olcott, but it was not until 1902 when she appeared in the musical comedy *The Defender,* that she came to prominence. Among her many hits were *The Jewel of Asia* (1903), *The Jersey Lily* (1903), *About Town* (1906), *The Wall Street Girl* (1911), *When Claudia Smiles* (1913), and *The Passing Show of 1919.* Blanche Ring made her London debut in a vaudeville act at the Palace Theatre on November 16, 1903. In 1908 she toured with Joe Weber in his burlesque

of *The Merry Widow,* and in 1909 she made her first appearance as *The Yankee Girl,* her most famous stage role, which she filmed in 1915. (Blanche Ring appeared in two other feature films, *It's the Old Army Game* in 1926 and *If I Had My Way* in 1940.)

The actress was married four times. Her last husband was character actor Charles Winninger who she married in 1912, separated from in 1928, and eventually divorced in 1952. Blanche Ring died in Santa Monica, California, on January 13, 1961.

Blanche Ring was always a favorite with vaudeville audiences; she was the hit of the show when she appeared on an old-timers' bill at the Palace in 1925. When she appeared at the Colonial in February of 1913, Dash in *Variety* (February 6, 1913) wrote, "It has ever been a question whether a singer made a song or a song the singer. With Ring and her record of song hits, she seems entitled to any doubt." There was, and is, no doubt that Blanche Ring was one of the great purveyors of hearty songs, and one of the few songstresses from this era whose personality still comes across on primitive phonograph recordings.

Reference: "Blanche Ring on Vaudeville" in *Variety,* Vol. 42, No. 1 (December 11, 1909), page 47.

THE RITZ BROTHERS

The Ritz Brothers exemplify a certain type of trio or quartet act popular in vaudeville in the late twenties and early thirties which combined slapstick and acrobatic comedy, rowdy and robust. Similar acts include The

The Ritz Brothers

Three Jolly Tars (Eddie Mills, Joe Kirk, and Harry Martin), the Slate Brothers, and the Runaway Four. The Runaway Four would combine their bodies to form a camel, with the lead performer spouting water from his mouth. It was vulgar, but it was also clever. So popular and so similar were these acts that they could never play the same bill.

Al was the first of the Ritz Brothers (from Newark, New Jersey) to enter vaudeville as a song-and-dance man, followed some years later by Jim and Harry. They claimed to have inherited their clowning from their father, Max Ritz, an actor and dancer. The brothers' first appearance together was at the Albee in Brooklyn in September of 1925, dressed in oversize baggy pants, red ties, and socks in a parody of the fashions favored by college youths. (A year later, in the 1926 edition of *George White's Scandals,* the Ritz Brothers were to introduce the song "Collegiate.") They danced, clowned around, and played the ukelele at their debut as a brother act, and the trio followed that formula pretty much without change in subsequent years.

Their broad humor and clowning made the Ritz Brothers equally at home in vaudeville or burlesque. You could perhaps compare them to the Marx Brothers, but they lacked the subtlety of the latter's humor, for everthing the Ritz Brothers did was loud. One favorite antic of the Ritz Brothers was to dress in grotesque female clothing, with rolled-up trousers clearly visible peeping out from under the dresses. The Marx Brothers would never have stooped this low, nor, would Ritz Brothers aficionados cry, could they have gotten away with it.

In a 1937 interview the Ritz Brothers jokingly recalled that they played the best vaudeville houses for two weeks. "Then they all closed down. We played Shubert shows, Carroll revues. Then we played for two years in revolving doors. That's where we got dizzy." The demise of vaudeville was, as it happened, their salvation—a means to immortality for the Ritz Brothers. In 1936 they entered the movies and thanks to films such as *One in a Million* (1937), *On the Avenue* (1937), and *The Three Musketeers* (1939) they will always be remembered, just as surely as the Slate Brothers and the Runaway Four are forgotten.

Reference: "Harry Ritz" in *The Vaudevillians* by Bill Smith (Macmillan, 1976), pages 179–181.

A. ROBBINS

A. Robbins was a clown with a novelty act in which he would pull every known musical instrument from his clothing. "He was so great he could pull out a grand piano," recalls Ted Waldman. Ken Murray remembers that Robbins would also change outfits and begin taking a seemingly endless number of bananas from his pockets. It was, as *The Billboard* (April 19, 1930) noted, "a sure-fire act."

Variety (September 3, 1920) gives a fairly detailed account of the act A. Robbins was performing at the time at the Fifth Avenue Theatre. For his backdrop, Robbins had cardboard representations of musicians which he worked mechanically to give the impression that they were performing. From his clothing, he took cups and saucers, ending by pouring coffee and milk from his sleeves. "It's ready for the big-time bills as it stands" was *Variety's* estimation.

Little is known of Robbins's background, or even if he is still living. According to a program from the Palace Theatre, on whose stage he was popular from the late teens through the early thirties, Robbins was born in Vienna and had been Imperial Jester at the Court of the Czar of Russia—an appointment which sounds suspiciously like a publicist's invention. Aside from vaudeville A. Robbins appeared in a number of revues, particularly *Billy Rose's Jumbo,* and he was even to be seen on television in the early fifties.

BILL ROBINSON

Bill Robinson

There can be little argument that the greatest tap dancer in vaudeville was Bill "Bojangles" Robinson. The Nicholas Brothers might have been more athletic, but there was a relaxed assurance to Bill Robinson's dancing that vaudeville and later film audiences came to admire and appreciate. When he appeared in his most famous film, the 1935 Twentieth Century-Fox production of *The Little Colonel,* he explained to star Shirley Temple, "All you gotta do is listen with your feet." There was a joyousness to Robinson's dancing style that infected not only his fellow blacks but white audiences as well. Even his nackname "Bojangles"—nobody knows what it means but it has a happy sound—was given to him by a fellow black as an expression of delight and admiration on seeing Robinson dance. Fred Astaire paid his own tribute to Bill Robinson with the "Bojangles of Harlem" number in the 1936 film *Swing Time.* Robinson invented the word "copacetic" to express his pleasure with the world in which he danced, a world far removed from that into which he was born in Richmond, Virginia, on December 14, 1878. (Some sources give May 25, 1878, as his date of birth.)

Both of his parents died when Robinson was still a child, and he was brought up by his grandmother, a former slave. "I had to shell peas to make a living," he once recalled. Other odd jobs followed, after he ran away from home to Washington, D.C., menial tasks such as selling newspapers and shining shoes, while dancing at night for pennies in club and beer halls. At the age of seventeen he formed a partnership with an older black vaudeville dancer, George Cooper. An agent named Marty Forkins (who was married to revue star Rae Samuels) saw the two and signed them; later he persuaded Robinson to go solo, and Forkins remained Robinson's agent for the rest of his life. Robinson rose gradually from playing exclusively black vaudeville to being accepted in national vaudeville. In July of 1915 he was featured at Henderson's in Coney Island, not only dancing but singing and imitating musical instruments. "Bill dances," reported *Variety* (July 2, 1915), "and it will be a hard audience that will not take kindly to his work along this line. Bill Robinson is a clever entertainer who can hold down an early spot on a big-time program."

By the twenties Bill Robinson had become a regular at the Palace and had taken to billing himself as "The Dark Cloud of Joy." He would usually appear in the number-two spot on the bill, a spot often occupied by a song-and-dance man, but Douglas Gilbert recalls that Robinson's position in the program would often have to be changed because no one could go on after him; he invariably closed the show.

Because of the color of his skin, Bill Robinson did suffer from racial prejudice. While appearing at the Maryland Theatre in Baltimore on August 21, 1922—in the usual number-two spot—he was hissed by a group of women, "apparently refined, and certainly well-dressed, of middle age" (according to *Variety*). However, after the women were asked to leave, the audience applauded Robinson's act enthusiastically. *Variety* (August 25, 1922) reported, "He said that in thirty years in the show business such a thing had never happened to him before, and that he had been taught that, should it ever happen, to ignore it. He did and won his house by the neat way he turned the tide."

Eleanor Powell recalls that in 1928 she and Bill Robinson devised a dance routine together in which they would challenge each other, and they performed at private parties organized by the Vanderbilts, the Rockefellers, and others. They were paid $500 an evening. Miss Powell remembers:

> Although he was a big star, they would not allow him to ride up in the front elevator, so I always used to ride up in the service elevator with Bill. And we would wait in the butler's pantry to go on. After we were finished, we were perspiring and waiting to dry off, and invariably they would ask me if I would like a glass of water, and I would say yes if Mr. Robinson could have one. And they would give him one. And each time he would break the glass and pay for it— crystal glass. I said to him the first time, "What did you do that for?" He said, "Well I'm just beating them to the punch. I know no one will drink out of that glass." It was sort of a revenge kind of thing. It was very difficult, because a white person was not allowed on the stage with what we called coloreds.

In time, Bill Robinson became a spokesman for blacks, but he stayed clear of ideologies and most black militants today would have questioned his attitude. Robinson's acceptance of himself as a black in a white world was pleasing to white audiences. It was a "white" organization, the New York League of Locality Mayors, which named him Honorary Mayor of Harlem in 1934, and it was not until 1948 that a group of blacks organized an election whereby Harlem residents could select a Mayor. Their choice was not Robinson, but the owner of a chain of barbecue restaurants. However, one should not denigrate Robinson for he was the most generous of men when it came to his own race, giving away literally millions of dollars to worthy causes and individuals. He gave much to his home city of Richmond, where he is honored with a life-size statue on whose base Robinson is described as "Dancer, Actor, Humanitarian."

During the twenties Bill Robinson expanded his career. He was a big hit at London's Holborn Empire in July of 1926. He starred in two revues, *Blackbirds of 1928* (in which he introduced "Doin' the New Low-Down") and the 1930 production of *Brown Buddies.* In the thirties Bill Robinson embarked on a new career in such films as *Dixiana* (1930 and his first), *The Little Colonel* (1935), *The Littlest Rebel* (1935), *Dimples* (1936), and *Rebecca of Sunnybrook Farm* (1938). He and Shirley Temple made an ideal team, and in *The Little Colonel* the two of them danced Robinson's famous stair dance which Eleanor Powell says he taught only to her and Shirley Temple— Miss Powell danced it in *Honolulu* (1939). One of Robinson's best films was *The Hot Mikado.* Earlier he had played the Mikado in the original stage production which opened at the Broadhurst Theatre on March 23, 1939. Reviewing him in this show, *The Billboard* (April 1, 1939) described Robinson: "One of the world's greatest living actors, he delivers a concert in taps that stand sole and heels above anything else of its type in the known world."

Bill Robinson remained active as he grew older and never lost his youthful vitality. Perhaps it was because of his dancing, or perhaps because he neither smoked nor drank alcohol; Eleanor Powell recalls that his one big vice was ice cream, but it never seemed to affect his weight. On his sixty-second birthday Bill Robinson danced for fifty-two blocks up Broadway. He was honored by New York City on April 29, 1946, when Mayor William O'Dwyer proclaimed Bill Robinson Day.

He died in New York on November 26, 1949. Forty-five thousand people stood in line and filed by his casket. More than one-and-a-half million lined the funeral route from Times Square to Harlem. Over the Palace Theatre was hung a banner with the legend, in black letters, "So Long, Bill Robinson. His Dancing Feet Brought Joy to the World." In Times Square, a thirty-piece band played "Give My Regards to Broadway," and in his eulogy Mayor Dwyer said, "Without money, just good manners and decency, you got into places no money can buy. You got into the hearts of all America." "Bill was the first one to do intimate tap dancing, a slow, confined type of dancing," remembers Eleanor Powell of the man who was, indeed, the King of the Tap Dancers.

References: "How To Keep Fit" by Bill "Bojangles" Robinson with Roy Barclay Hodges in *American Magazine* (October, 1946), pages 48–9, 154–56. "At 70, Still Head Hoofer" by Richard Strouse in the *New York Times Magazine* (May 23, 1948), pages 17, 48–51.

WILLIAM ROCK AND FRANCES WHITE

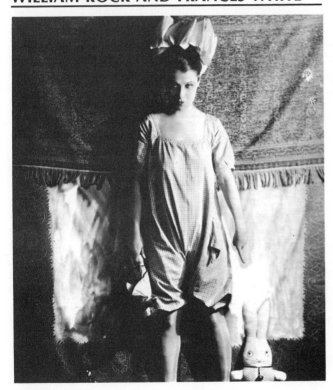

Frances White in 1924

William Rock was dubbed a character dancer in vaudeville, in that he would appear in the guise of anything from an old man to a roué, characterizations which he claimed drew the audience's attention away from his feet. For as *Variety* (June 30, 1922) noted, "He was a better showman and producer than dancer." After an early career in musical comedy, Rock teamed with Maude Fulton in vaudeville. He was credited with being the first vaudevillian to have a band, which accompanied his act, appear on stage with him, and also one of the first to condense a Broadway play for the vaudeville circuits.

In 1916 Maude Fulton decided to go solo again and dissolved the partnership with Rock. At that time he was on the West Coast, and in San Francisco he spotted a chorus girl named Frances White, who he felt had talent. (Frances White had begun her career singing "Splash Me" at the Bristol Cafe on the Santa Monica Pier in Los Angeles.) Thus the team of Rock and White came into being. The couple made their New York debut at the Palace in May of 1916 in an act titled "Dansant Characteristique," and Sime Silverman reported in *Variety* (May 5, 1916) that Frances White was "very young, of considerable personality, a pleasant singer, an excellent and graceful dancer, besides being good-looking and able to deliver dialogue." Soon it was Frances White who was the star attraction of the act. She closed the 1916 *Ziegfeld Follies* by singing "The Midnight Frolic Rag." In March of 1917 Rock and White were forced to perform a fifty-five-minute act at the Royal Theatre in the Bronx because of the audience's enthusiasm for Miss White, particularly when she sang, in a lisping, childlike voice, "M-i-s-s-i-s-s-i-p-p-i," spelling out each of the letters. Another hit song from this period had Frances White complaining, "Six times six is thirty-six and six is forty-two, and as the rabbits multiply, why can't I?"

In December of 1917 Rock and White were signed at $2,000 a week to appear in the *Ziegfeld Revue* at the Amsterdam Roof. All went well until April of 1918 when Ziegfeld brought in Ann Pennington to strengthen the bill. Miss White walked out, disliking the attention her costar was receiving from the audience. Ziegfeld made no effort to encourage Frances White to change her mind, probably because of an incident that had occurred a few days earlier when Miss White appeared in court for driving the wrong way down a one-way street and for calling a police officer —in the words of *Variety*—"what the officer knew he was not."

Rock and White were not husband and wife in private life. Rock was married to Helen Eby, while Frances White was the wife of Frank Fay. The Fays were separated in June of 1917, after which *Variety* noted Rock and White gave a noticeably smoother performance. Frank Fay's only comment was, "It cost me $3,800 to be known as Frances White's Husband." It was said that after the divorce Miss White would purchase front row seats at Frank Fay's shows in order to make faces at him.

In September of 1919, shortly after returning from a starring engagement in *Hullo America* at London's Palace Theatre, Rock and White announced that the act was splitting up. White went into Ziegfeld's *Midnight Frolic* and Rock was starred in *What's the Odds.* Later, William Rock played in vaudeville with his wife; he died in Philadelphia at the age of forty-seven on June 27, 1922.

Frances White continued in vaudeville as a solo performer, but as the years went by engagements became fewer and fewer. In September of 1930 she was arrested in New York for failure to pay a $3.50 taxi fare. With only thirty cents to her name, Miss White was thrown in jail until eventually Frank Fay came to her aid. A couple of years later, Frances White repaid Fay by demanding thirteen years of back alimony from him. Frances White died in Los Angeles on February 24, 1969, at the age of seventy-one; she had been retired for more than thirty years.

DR. ROCKWELL

George L. Rockwell, better known as Dr. Rockwell, was what was known in vaudeville as a nut act. His billing was "Dr. Rockwell, Quack, Quack, Quack," and his specialty was a lecture on the human anatomy using a banana stalk as a skeleton. It was an act which stood him in good stead for thirty years until the early forties when he retired. He was a regular at the Palace, and one of the acts on the opening bill at Radio City Music Hall on November 27, 1932. He was a close friend of Fred Allen, and was frequently featured on the latter's radio show. Unfortunately, he is perhaps best known as the father of the one-time leader of the American Nazi Party, George Lincoln Rockwell. Dr. Rockwell died in Brunswick, Maine, on March 2, 1978, at the age of eighty-nine.

WILL ROGERS

Will Rogers (1879–1935) wore many caps—journalist, humorist, columnist, film star, trick roper, and, of course, America's homespun philosopher-hero—but it was as a vaudevillian that he first came to fame. And it was in vaudeville that he developed his technique of simply talking casually to an audience, a technique which he was to use to advantage in his later careers as a newspaper columnist and as an easy-going star of sound films. The Oklahoma cowboy entered show business in Wild West Shows,

Will Rogers

and it was in Chicago—at the Cleveland Theatre—that Will Rogers first appeared before a vaudeville audience in 1904. On April 27, 1905, he made his New York debut with Colonel Mulhall's troupe of trick ropers and riders at Madison Square Garden.

From the Garden, Rogers went to Keith's Union Square Theatre where he opened on June 12, 1905; vaudeville engagements followed elsewhere in New York and also in Boston and Philadelphia. He would appear with his pony and with a rider, Buck McKee, and perform various roping tricks, but he never spoke to the audience. Then a fellow performer told him that one trick, in which Rogers threw two ropes and caught the horse and rider separately, was so good that he should announce it. According to Rogers's autobiography, he had no idea what he was going to say to the audience; he simply stopped the orchestra and began to talk. At first he was horrified when the audience began to laugh at him, but he soon realized his potential as a comedian with lines like "A rope ain't bad to get tangled up in if it ain't around your neck." His understatement, his Oklahoma drawl, and his slow delivery of lines appealed to New York audiences, and in one year, 1905, his salary rose from $75 to $250 a week. (By 1921 Rogers was touring for the Shuberts at $3,000 a week.)

In 1906 Will Rogers visited Europe, playing vaudeville engagements in Paris, London, and Berlin. In the last city his performances at the Winter Garden proved a huge success. Less successful was a Wild West act which Rogers brought to London in 1907.

For the next few years Will Rogers went from success to success in vaudeville, taking time out in 1912 to appear with Blanche Ring in the musical production of *The Wall Street Girl* and in 1914 to play with Nora Bayes in London in *The Merry-Go-Round.* Rogers developed and perfected his vaudeville routine, including chewing gum while he roped and talked. He was totally unpretentious in explaining changes in the act; in 1911 he told the audience, "I've been getting away with this junk for so long that I thought you would get wise to me sooner or later so I went out and dug up a little new stuff with which to bunk you for a few more years." The new stuff included imitations of Fred Stone performing his lariat dance and of George M. Cohan if he had to throw a rope while dancing. As time passed, the rope tricks became almost incidental to Rogers's commentary, for as *Variety* (January 14, 1911) noted, "It is Rogers, though, who is liked. His personality, careless manner, and broad grin are worth more than the most intricate tricks that could be figured out."

Will Rogers's involvement with Florenz Ziegfeld began in 1915 when the showman hired him to appear in his *Midnight Frolic,* a revue-type entertainment which began precisely at the stroke of midnight on the roof of New York's New Amsterdam Theatre. Ziegfeld was apparently unimpressed by the cowboy star until he saw how popular he was with the audiences. It was the time of Henry Ford's attempts to stop the First World War on behalf of the pacifist movement, and Rogers joked, "If Mr. Ford had taken this bunch of girls in this show, and let 'em wear the same costumes they wear here, and marched them down between the trenches, believe me, the boys would have been out before Christmas!" Rogers claims that this was his first topical joke, and its success led him to bring more and more jokes about politics in general and Congress in particular into his act.

When Ziegfeld needed a headliner for his 1916 *Follies* it was small wonder he selected Rogers, still appearing in the *Midnight Frolic,* to join his cast, which included W. C. Fields, Fanny Brice, Bert Williams, and Ann Pennington. Will Rogers was subsequently to appear in the *Follies* of 1917, 1918, 1922, and 1924.

Between appearances in the *Follies,* Rogers was still to be seen on the vaudeville stage. *Variety* (November 4, 1921) reviewed his act at Washington's Belasco Theatre and noted, "His talk is right up to the minute as always, just full of honest-to-goodness laughs, and he is just as dexterous as ever with his ropes. He belittles the films as well as praising them, referring to himself as the homeliest man that ever appeared on the screen." (Rogers also commented that his chief distinction in the film industry was that after two and a half years in pictures, he came out with the same wife.) Will Rogers had entered films in 1918 and was to continue making them on and off through 1935; in 1922 he started his legendary newspaper column. These two circumstances, which offered him audiences far wider than he could possibly hope to reach on the stage, obviously led to Rogers's eventual retirement from vaudeville.

Rogers obtained much personal satisfaction and pleasure from his years in vaudeville, for, as he wrote in his autobiography:

> I did the old act with the horse for almost six years; then I tried the act without the horse, just doing tricks, and trying all the time to develop the comedy end of the act. I wasn't any headliner, but they played me steady all the time, and I kept practicing new tricks, as I love roping better than anything else in the world. I work out lots of tricks that I never do on the stage, but I have them for my personal satisfaction. And lots of days yet I go to the theatre and rope for six or eight hours just because I like to.

References: *Will Rogers: His Life and Times* by Richard M. Ketchum (American Heritage, 1973). *The Autobiography of Will Rogers,* selected and edited by Donald Day (Houghton Mifflin Company, 1949).

PAT ROONEY AND MARION BENT

There used to be an old vaudeville joke that went something like "Just because I'm a fool, don't think I'm Irish," but that was a gag that could never be applied to vaudeville's great Irish family of entertainers, the Rooneys. They took Irish performers away from the stereotype of the lowbrow comic to a new level of artistry. In the last century, Pat Rooney, Sr. was the most famous member of the Rooney family, but in the twentieth century it is his son and his son's wife, Marion Bent, who are remembered with glowing affection.

Pat Rooney

Despite his Irish name, Pat Rooney, Sr. was born in Birmingham, England, in 1844. He made famous songs like "The Old Dinner Pail," "Katy Is a Rogue," "Pretty Peggy," and "His Old High Hat." In the December 20, 1912, issue of *Variety,* his son reminisced, "His characterizations had that intimate touch of human reality without which no comic presentation of a type can be more than crude burlesque." Douglas Gilbert recalled that sometimes Rooney would appear on stage in knee pants, sack coat, ballet skirt, flowing tie, and a soft hat. At other times he would wear a cutaway coat with tight sleeves, a fancy waistcoat, large plaid check pants, and a plug hat to sing "Owen Riley," "The Day I Played Baseball," "The Sound Democratic," and "Biddy the Ballet Girl." The last has some similarity to Fannie Brice's "Becky Is Back in the Ballet;" during its chorus Rooney would perform a clog dance in ballet style:

> On the stage she is Mamselle La Shorty,
> Her right name is Bridget McCarthy.
> She comes at night and from matinées,
> With baskets of flowers and little bouquets . . .
> She's me only daughter,
> And I am the man that taught her,
> To wear spangled clothes
> And flip 'round on her toes,
> Oh, the pride of the ballet is Biddy.

Patrick James Rooney died of pneumonia in 1892, by which time his son Pat and daughter Mattie were already appearing on the vaudeville stage in a singing and dancing

Marion Bent

act titled "Two Chips off the Old Block." In 1900 Pat and Mattie Rooney advertised themselves as "The Premier Eccentric Dancing Act of the Business—Bar None."

Pat Rooney, Jr. was born in New York on July 4, 1880 (an interesting date in view of his father's most famous song, "Is That Mr. Riley?," in which he sang of the Irishman's dream, including having July the Fourth declared St. Patrick's Day). Pat Rooney, Jr. started dancing at the age of ten with his father and mother (Josie Granger). He once recalled, "When I was a kid in Baltimore, I'd go down to the corner grocery where they had one of those wooden cellar floors. On that I would practice tap dancing. It was fun because the floor had a nice hollow sound and, besides, I could attract a lot of attention before the grocer got fed up and chased me."

With his height of five feet, three inches and his pixieish face, it is not hard to describe Pat Rooney, Jr. as a leprechaun. His smile was devilish and his dancing divine. W. C. Fields once said, "If you didn't hear the taps you would think he was floating over the stage." Taking after his father, Rooney became a classic clog dancer whose best-known routine was "The Daughter of Rosie O'Grady" (written in 1918 by Monty C. Brice and Walter Donaldson) which he performed with his hands in his pockets hitching up his trousers, a grin on his face. Graceful as a ballet dancer, Rooney would waltz around, leap up in the air, click his feet together, and perform steps that dazzled because they appeared both simple and intricate. "A sort

of electrified hairpin" is how Frederick James Smith described Rooney in the *New York Dramatic Mirror* (May 20, 1916).

Marion Bent was the daughter of cornet soloist Arthur Bent. She and Pat Rooney met when they were both children and first appeared together professionally in *Mother Goose,* "a musical extravaganza" by J. Hickory Wood and Arthur Collins, starring Joseph Cawthorn, which opened at the New Amsterdam Theatre on December 2, 1903. Rooney and Bent were married shortly thereafter, and together they became vaudeville's best-loved couple. There was something about Pat Rooney and Marion Bent that made one feel they were Pa and Ma to the vaudeville family. Writing of Pat Rooney in *Variety* (November 2, 1917), Sime Silverman commented, "He and his wife are among the most popular of the big time faves."

On stage, Rooney and Bent would dance and sing. Sometimes, as in the thirty-three-minute revue "Dances of the Hour" at the Palace in May of 1925, their act would be augmented with a chorus of seven dancing girls, but it was always, as *Variety* (May 13, 1925) noted, "crammed with superlative action." The comedy crosstalk would be along the lines of:

ROONEY:	What's your favorite stone?
BENT:	Turquoise.
ROONEY:	Mine's a brick.

Marion Bent was forced to retire in 1932 because of arthritis, although she did come out of retirement on her wedding anniversary, April 10, 1935, to appear with Pat Rooney in a special program at the Capitol Theatre. Rooney never really retired; in 1950 he was featured in the original production of *Guys and Dolls* and he was also to be seen in many early television shows. Between 1915 and 1948 Rooney appeared in a dozen or so relatively unimportant films, and he was also a songwriter, responsible for "I Got a Gal for Every Day in the Week" and "You Be My Ootsie, I'll Be Your Tootsie," among others. The Rooney marriage was not a happy one toward the end, and a year before Marion Bent's death in New York, on July 28, 1940, she and her husband separated. Pat Rooney, Jr. died in New York on September 9, 1962, "a mite of a man who refused to grow old."

Carrying on the Rooney tradition was Pat Rooney III who was born in 1909, and, as a child was often carried on stage by his parents. After his mother's retirement Pat Rooney III would usually work in a double act with his father, performing a precision dance routine with the two men working back to back. It was quite extraordinary and has never been successfully copied. After the Second World War Pat Rooney III worked as a single act, although he and his father were reunited for a 1956 appearance at the Palace. And after retiring from show business the third Rooney ran a popular hot dog stand in Lake Blaisdell, New Hampshire. He died there on November 5, 1979.

In the annals of vaudeville, with the honorable exception of the Foys and the Cohans, there was never a family as talented or as popular as the Rooneys.

BABY ROSE MARIE

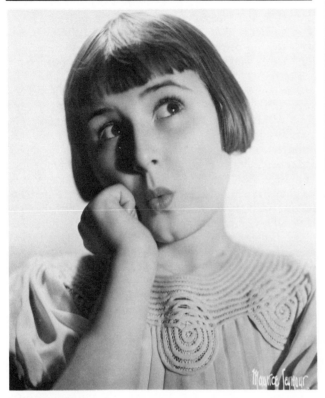

Baby Rose Marie

Gus Edwards's child stars were vaudeville's best-known celebrities in that category, but in vaudeville's last years a new child star entered the field. She was cute and cuddly with jet black hair, a toothy grin, and a deep, husky voice. Her name was Baby Rose Marie, and through the years she has developed into a television and stage personality of considerable verve and energy, with a quick wit that she is not reluctant to use against herself.

Born Rose Marie Curley in New York City on August 15, 1923, Rose Marie won a talent contest in New York at the age of three, the first prize of which was a trip to Atlantic City and a pair of Brocade and gold shoes. In Atlantic City she was "discovered" by the manager of radio station WPG, and he had her sing from a glass-enclosed studio booth on Atlantic City's famous Steel Pier. As a result of that Atlantic City engagement, Baby Rose Marie was signed by WMCA for "The Ohrbach Hour" which led to a contact with NBC and her own fifteen-minute show on its Blue Network in 1932. Baby Rose Marie's only rival on radio was Mary Small, a twelve-year-old who sang a good Blues number but lacked Rose Marie's punchy delivery.

From radio Baby Rose Marie—the "Baby" handle was given to her by Evelyn Nesbitt Thaw and was not entirely justified, for there was nothing babyish about Rose Marie except her age—went into vaudeville, not because she was a great entertainer (which she was) but because radio listeners had become suspicious. Audiences wondered how one so young could sing so old, and there were many

who claimed she was a forty-five-year-old midget. Whenever the Child Laws permitted, Baby Rose Marie sang and danced; where they did not permit, she mimed to recordings she had made for the Brunswick label. This probably makes her the first variety star to sing to a playback, something which is an accepted part of show business today.

At the age of twelve, Rose Marie jokingly recalls, "I became fat and ugly, so I retired from the stage." Happily, she returned to show business in 1947 and has been busy ever since. She started on television in the early fifties as a guest on the Milton Berle and Morey Amsterdam shows and on "Pantomine Quiz;" she has been a regular on "My Sister Eileen" (1960–1961), "The Dick Van Dyke Show" (1961–1966), "The Doris Day Show" (1969–1971), and "The Hollywood Squares" (1968 to date). For the last few years Rose Marie has helped to bring back the spirit of vaudeville with the variety show *4 Girls 4,* featuring herself along with Margaret Whiting, Rosemary Clooney, and Helen O'Connell. One critic of the show described her as a female Jimmy Durante, an affectionately perfect title for a performer who never seems to have lost the vitality and zest for living she had as one of vaudeville's youngest child stars.

Reference: "Rose Marie" in *The Vaudevillians* by Bill Smith (Macmillan, 1976), pages 260–266.

ROSE'S ROYAL MIDGETS

In no way as famous or as important as Singer's Midgets, Rose's Royal Midgets played neighbourhood vaudeville houses during the twenties; they arrived in the United States from Germany in July of 1922. Ike Rose, who was not a midget and, in fact, was apparently a rather large man, was the leader of the troupe, which originally consisted of nine female and fifteen male "little foreign folk" with "quaint Teutonic accents."

As the years rolled by, the original group of German midgets was augmented by two Americans: a Negro, and a Javanese woman, who, according to publicity, was of royal blood. The fast-paced act included dancing, acrobatics, juggling, a violin solo, and a spot of magic thrown in for good measure. *Variety* commented on the timing of the act, which it always reviewed favorably. On September 14, 1927, Meakin described the midgets as "a sure bet in vaude houses"; a year later, Bige, on November 28, 1928, called them "a fine turn."

BENNY RUBIN

Benny Rubin was a Jewish dialect comedian of considerable talent, who is undoubtedly better known for his work in films than for his early years in vaudeville. Born in Boston, Massachusetts, on February 2, 1899, Rubin was seventeen years old before he began to appear in tab shows in the Boston area. From Boston, Benny Rubin moved to New York and to burlesque, in which he worked for a couple of years before entering vaudeville in the early twenties in partnership with Charles Hall. Rubin made his

Benny Rubin in 1929

debut as a single in the fall of 1923 (although he did have a partner in the shape of child performer, Norman Gast, who exchanged some gags with the comedian and played the violin). Seeing Rubin at the Alhambra, *Variety* (November 29, 1923) wrote that he had the makings of another Fannie Brice, and continued, "Rubin is set for any kind of time with his present offering."

In addition to his comic Jewish monologs, Benny Rubin played the trombone and proved to be a skillful tap dancer. In July of 1930 he was appearing at the Palace with his own fourteen-minute act plus serving as the master of ceremonies. *Variety* (July 30, 1930) reported, "Rubin has jumped to the top flight of stage comics, with dancing and gag-writing ability added to his comic delivery. He's welcome anywhere vaude can play him."

Where Benny Rubin seemed most welcome was in the film industry, and between 1928 and 1969 he was to appear in more than forty features and shorts, including *Seven Minutes of Your Time* (1928), *Naughty Boy* (1929), *Marianne* (1929), *It's a Great Life* (1930), *George White's Scandals* (1935), *Sunny* (1941), *Here Comes Mr. Jordan* (1941), *Torch Song* (1953), *A Hole in the Head* (1959), *Pocketful of Miracles* (1961), *The Errand Boy* (1961), *The Patsy* (1964), *Thoroughly Modern Millie* (1967), and *Airport* (1969). One film which demonstrates Rubin's talents very clearly is a 1929 Universal short titled *The Delicatessen Kid* in which the comedian gives impersonations of Pat Rooney and Bill Robinson, and proves he is as good a dancer as a comedian.

Rubin interspersed film work with vaudeville appear-

ances during the thirties. In July of 1934 he was teamed in vaudeville with Max Baer. *Variety* (July 3, 1934) saw the act at the Paramount and commented, "Max Baer, without Benny Rubin, might have been catastrophic, but with the aid of the experienced comic he gets over.... Sufficiently well handled to serve, but Rubin is earning his salary."

The comedian's fall from grace—so to speak—was because of the ethnic nature of his humor. Pressure groups from within the various ethnic minorities have kept up a constant fight against what they, in this writer's opinion, wrongly consider racist humor. Television comedy shows today are totally devoid of any hint of ethnic humor, and because of this, comedy shows lack vitality and they lack laughter. Traditional butts of the comic's art, the mother-in-law, the homosexual, the Pole, the Negro, and the Jew, have all become forbidden territory to today's humorists —not because the humorists meant harm, but because minority groups have become more and more suspicious of possible hidden motivations of hatred behind such humor. This antiethnic humor crusade began in the thirties, brought on perhaps by the Nazi persecution of the Jews and the plight of the southern Negroes, and the feeling that humor, rather than lightening the situation, would add to the problems. On a 1961 television show Benny Rubin said, "It wasn't a case of my giving up the business, it was the business that gave me up. Dialect comics were considered out. This was announced at a meeting of the entertainment bigs back in 1938. Pressure within banished us, not the general public. Ethnic groups were becoming hypersensitive and a section of the industry thought it knew what was best for the nation."

Rubin quit show business for a while. He ran a dress shop on Hollywood Boulevard and managed the Victor Hugo Restaurant in Beverly Hills. He worked with Orson Welles on his Mercury Theatre, and later became a stockbroker. Eventually Rubin returned to films and has only recently retired.

Reference: *Come Backstage with Me* by Benny Rubin (Bowling Green University Popular Press, 1972).

LILLIAN RUSSELL

The phenomenon that was Lillian Russell is not easy to explain. She was described by her biographer as "the most gorgeous and desirable woman on the American stage." Her beauty was matchless from all accounts, and yet photographs of her do not show us a woman of stunning beauty. Similarly, her voice was said to make grown men cry, and yet extant recordings of her most famous song, "Come Down, My Evenin' Star," which she first sang in 1899 at the Weber and Fields Music Hall, are far from impressive. They give the impression of a somewhat cracked, semioperatic voice, far from lilting and far from emotionally enthralling. Perhaps it is as a 1915 magazine writer commented: "Lillian Russell's beauty is of our mother's generation and not ours." It was Mark Twain who wrote, "God has gifted only a choice few with literary talent to withstand the ravages of time," and perhaps the

"THIS IS PICTURE #1 OF A SERIES OF 6"

Lillian Russell

same applies to those whose voices are preserved on phonograph recordings. If it does, Lillian Russell is not among the choice few.

Lillian Russell was born Helen Louise Leonard in Clinton, Iowa, on December 4, 1861. With her mother, she came to New York and eventually obtained a position with the chorus of one of the pirated versions of Gilbert and Sullivan's *H.M.S. Pinafore*. (While appearing in this operetta at the Brooklyn Academy of Music, she met and married her first husband, Harry Braham, the company's conductor. There were to be two later marriages, to Don Giovanni Perigini in 1894 and to Alexander P. Moore in 1912.) In 1881 Lillian Russell played the role of Mabel in Tony Pastor's travesty on *The Pirates of Penzance*, entitled *The Pie Rats of Penn Yann;* she was later to star in straight versions of Gilbert and Sullivan's *Patience* and *The Sorcerer*. Russell remained with Tony Pastor through 1893 becoming, as *The Spirit of the Times* (October 29, 1881) noted, "a bright particular star of *opéra bouffe*."

From 1883 through 1885 Lillian Russell was in England, appearing in successful shows and in a few failures as well. In 1888 she signed a contract to appear at New York's Casino at a salary of $20,000 a year; her reputation was made, and the Casino was to be the scene of some of her greatest successes, including *The Princess Nicotine* (1893) and *An American Beauty* (1896), a title which was soon to become her soubriquet. During the 1890s Lillian Russell developed her famous—and apparently platonic—friendship with Diamond Jim Brady, and also began to

have weight problems which were to plague her for the rest of her life. When Fay Templeton quit the Weber and Fields Music Hall, Lillian Russell replaced her, making a courageous step from opera to burlesque. When Weber and Fields reunited in 1912 she happily joined them in their production of *Hokey-Pokey,* along with Fay Templeton and George Beban.

Lillian Russell's true vaudeville debut did not come until 1905, when she signed a contract with F. F. Proctor which called for her to be paid $100,000 for a thirty-three-week engagement. She opened with unqualified success at Proctor's Twenty-third Street Theatre on October 2, 1905, and Diamond Jim Brady bought a box for her entire run. Of Lillian Russell's first vaudeville appearance, Acton Davies wrote in the *New York Sun* (October 3, 1905), "Songs may come and songs may go, but age cannot wither nor variety custom stale Miss Russell. She is the same old Lillian, and her voice is the same old voice." From this point on, Lillian Russell alternated vaudeville appearances with legitimate stage performances and could do no wrong as far as the critics were concerned. When she played the Palace in 1915, *Variety* (November 12, 1915) commented, "What matters how she sings or why she sings, she's Lillian Russell, and there's only one," a statement which seems to imply that perhaps the lady was indeed past her prime and succeeding only because of the fond memory in which she was held. Back at the Palace in 1918, Sime Silverman hailed her as "a feminine freak of Loveliness," while the distinguished critic Alan Dale noted, "Lillian Russell is one of the very, very few women who never needed advertising."

The vaudeville act would, of course, include a rendition of "Come Down, My Evenin' Star," written by John Stromberg and Robert Smith, and Miss Russell was not above reminding herself and her audience of the era from which it came. In a 1919 Palace engagement she told the audience she had first introduced the song a hundred and fifty years ago. It is doubtful that Lillian Russell would have continued with such frequent stage appearances after her prime had it not been for financial problems, which she blithely told the *New York Dramatic Mirror* (November 23, 1918) were caused by her buying too many Liberty Bonds. However, she was still able to draw a four-figure salary, and that was all that mattered.

There was one feature film appearance by Lillian Russell, a 1915 World Film Production of *Wildfire* (which she had first played on the stage in 1907) in which she was partnered by Lionel Barrymore. When the film was released on January 25, 1915, the critics and public alike were only mildly exicted.

Lillian Russell's third husband, Alexander P. Moore, was an ardent Republican and presumably had something to do with his wife's becoming increasingly involved in political matters. In 1921 she was appointed by President Harding to investigate immigration problems, and her findings showed a markedly conservative viewpoint. Lillian Russell died in Pittsburgh on June 6, 1922; after her death, a daughter, Dorothy, had a brief fling in vaudeville.

There can be no question that Lillian Russell was much loved and admired in her day, and, in fact, had become a living legend. As one obituary noted, she was "a woman who left a trail of affection wherever she passed."

Reference: *Lillian Russell: The Era of Plush* by Parker Morrell (Random House, 1940).

THE RUSSIAN ART CHOIR

The Russian Art Choir was organized by Alexander U. Fine from the Otto Harbach and Oscar Hammerstein operetta *The Song of the Flame,* which opened at New York's Forty-fourth Street Theatre on December 30, 1925. The fifteen-man choir made its vaudeville debut in January of 1927 at the Hippodrome, closing the bill with a seventeen-minute Russian cabaret routine which was described as "A Human Pyramid of Voices." *Variety* (January 26, 1927) was not enthusiastic; its critic Fred wrote, "As it is, the act isn't there for vaudeville. As a concert attraction it would serve nicely, for the voices alone would satisfy."

In 1930 the Russian Art Choir had the dubious honor of appearing in a one-reel Vitaphone short with George Jessel. In between inane commentary by Jessel, (e.g., "I'll never forget how the Russians shot my Uncle Sol") the choir sang "Nightingale," "Cossack Farewell Song," "Down by the Nevia River," and "Schilnichky." The film ends with the choir performing a Negro spiritual which is unbelievably—and unintentionally—funny because of their mispronunciation of the English language plus Jessel's participation in the chorus.

CHIC SALE

Chic Sale, with his bucolic humor, was almost unique among vaudeville monologists. On the vaudeville stage he presented various kinds of country characters, as many as twenty-seven different types, from the head of a cultural group trying to bring little theatre to his small town, to the moronic yokel, the old maid, and the preacher. Sale's favorite character was Gran'pa Summerill, a testy old veteran of the Union army in the Civil War, who could supply both knee-slapping humor and heartrending pathos. If his characters had any common denominator it was that much of their humor was earthy, concerned with outside lavatories and old ladies who burned their bottoms on the church pipes bringing in the newfangled steam heat.

"I never try to be funny," said Chic Sale in 1931:

I present my types going seriously through their routines and the comedy takes care of itself. It would be fatal for me to think "Now I'm going to be funny." Golly, I just couldn't! I just act out familiar people—and there you are. Folks don't like exaggeration, and I'll tell you why. When you make fun of a person, you hurt his feelings, and you make the folks around you uncomfortable. I aim to offend nobody, at any time, in any way. As long as you're entertaining, as long as you can make people laugh

Chic Sale

without making them uncomfortable, you're sure to get ahead.

Chic Sale's comedy was wisecracking humor, and "wisecrack" was a term which he originated. The comedian's humor was aggressively down to earth; Sale always claimed to abhor sophistication.

Charles "Chic" Sale was born in Huron, South Dakota on August 25, 1885. Soon after his birth the family moved to Urbana, Illinois, and there Chic worked up an act with his brother Dwight. It was "home town stuff," and as part of the act Sale would often borrow a pair of false teeth from his dentist father's surgery. A flyer advertising a performance by Charles Patlow Sale, "reader and impersonator," survives from this period and indicates that as part of his burgeoning act Sale gave recitations on "The Village Gossip," "A District School Program," and "Saving a Seat for a Friend."

In 1907 Dwight Sale died, and Chic, who had been working as a mechanic, decided to leave Urbana and try his luck in Minneapolis. At first he worked as a waiter, but he was discharged after serving water in a cup. However, at the restaurant he met a waitress with whom he formed a comedy act; the couple tried it out in Lafayette, Indiana. The girl decided Chic Sale was better than she and joined a burlesque show, whereupon Sale changed his name to Chick Earle and played the lowest vaudeville circuit, Gus Sun, at twenty-five dollars a week.

Gradually, Chic Sale began to make a name for himself. In September of 1916 he headlined at the Palace with his "Rural Sunday School Benefit" sketch, in which he appeared as a rube preacher announcing an entertainment to celebrate the installation of "the steam heat." He also played the church janitor and various country entertainers. As a character comedian in vaudeville, Chic Sale was the greatest, and Sime Silverman suggested in *Variety* (September 15, 1916) that a play could be built around the performer. Sale stopped the show at the Palace; even the orchestra was whistling its appreciation. He paid so many visits to the stage of that theatre that by January of 1917 he was hailed as "almost a Palace permanency." Reviewing a 1920 appearance at the Palace, the *New York Dramatic Mirror* (August 21, 1920) wrote, "Sale is an artist to his fingertips and he strives to make natural the types he portrays. None is overdone. He characterizes types that are familiar to most Americans with telling realism and humor."

One staple Chic Sale prop was the organ, behind which he would hang the clothes for his various changes. Sale always maintained that a performer could make all the clothes changes he wanted on stage, provided the audience could see what he was doing. His timing was always perfect, something which his sister believes he learned from playing the drums.

Chic Sale usually wrote his own material and would often improvise during a performance. One character for whom he did not provide his own script was that of Billy Brown, a friend of President Lincoln, based on the Ida M. Tarbell story "He Knew Lincoln." Sale would tell of going to Washington to meet the President and talk about the Civil War. After he returns home he learns of the President's assassination, and says "I want to think of him as I knew him. The front door will open and in will walk Mr. Lincoln and say, 'Heard any new stories, Billy?' " In later years, Chic Sale was to play Abraham Lincoln in a vaudeville sketch and an early M-G-M talkie short.

From vaudeville Sale went into revues, and then moved on to films. He worked continuously in films from 1929, although he had made at least two earlier films in 1922 and 1924; among Sale's features were *The Star Witness* (1931), *The Gentleman from Louisiana* (1936), and *You Only Live Once* (1937). In Hollywood he was something of a curiosity, with his high-pitched rasping voice and his use of such phrases as "my gosh" and "land sakes." Equally unusual was his penchant for keeping a goat at his Beverly Hills mansion; "I like to have a little livestock around," he explained. "We always did have, back in Urbana."

In 1929 Chic Sale wrote and published his "masterpiece," a thirty-one-page pamphlet titled *The Specialist* which was the ostensible story of Lem Putt, "the champion privy builder of Sangamon County"; it sold more than two million copies. *The Specialist* was a classic of what is commonly referred to as "outhouse humor," with such lines as "I built fer him just the average eight-family three-holer" and "It's a mighty sight better to have a little privy over a big hole than a big privy over a little hole." Thanks to *The Specialist,* Chic Sale's own particular brand of rural comedy has been preserved for all time.

Chic Sale died in Los Angeles of pneumonia on November 7, 1936. I wonder if any of those comics of a few years ago who delighted in bathroom humor recalled their ancestry in Chic Sale, a comic who dealt with very earthy matters.

References: *The Specialist* by Charles (Chic) Sale (Specialist Publishing Company, 1929). "Chic Sale—The Actor Who's Never Himself" by Terrence Costello in *Motion Picture Magazine,* Vol. 42, No. 5 (December, 1931), pages 42 and 95.

RAE SAMUELS

Rae Samuels was billed as "The Blue Streak of Vaudeville" because she delivered her songs with such force and would often end her act by punching the scenery. She began her career in vaudeville and was one of the stars of the 1912 edition of *The Ziegfeld Follies,* singing "I Should Worry and Get a Wrinkle" and "Down in Dear Old New Orleans." She remained popular through the early thirties, and died in New York at the age of ninety-three on October 24, 1979.

JULIA SANDERSON see Frank Crumit and Julia Sanderson

EUGENE SANDOW

Sandow, courtesy of Harvard Theatre Collection

Eugene Sandow was not the only strongman to perform on the vaudeville circuit, but he was certainly the best known, although he was—and is—far more famous in England than in the United States. Born in Koenigsberg, Germany, Sandow made several American tours, first for Abbey, Shoeffel, and Grau and later under the management of Florenz Ziegfeld. He died in London, England, on October 14, 1925, at the age of fifty-eight. His death was caused by the rupture of a blood vessel in the brain, brought on by the lifting of automobile out of a ditch single-handed.

It was Ziegfeld who starred Sandow at the Chicago World's Fair in August of 1893, when the strongman was said to have held a grown man in the palm of his hand, lifted a piano with several men on it, and finally had three horses walk across a plank over his stomach. In addition, Ziegfeld had the idea of exploiting Sandow's body by having him appear in the briefest of shorts, thus creating a sensation with the ladies.

Sandow began his career at the age of twenty-two when he appeared at a London music hall and challenged the strongman on the bill, made a fool of him, and was almost instantaneously recognized by London audiences as the greatest of strongmen.

Later on came an act titled Young Sandow and Lambert that *Variety* described as "the regulation physical culture act," in which the two men used each other as weights. It played the Union Square Theatre in New York in October of 1906.

Retiring from the stage, Sandow's business interests, not always too successful, included the Sandow Corset and the Sandow Health Oil.

SAVOY AND BRENNAN

Aficionados of female impersonation still remember one act from the heyday of vaudeville with relish and affection, and that act is Savoy and Brennan. Jay Brennan was the straight—no pun intended—man dressed in dapper male attire, while Bert Savoy was the "female" member of the team. Unlike other female impersonators of the day, Bert Savoy was outrageously "camp" in his speech and mannerisms both on stage and off. He would refer to all effeminate men of his acquaintance as "she" while everyone else was "dearie." Bert Savoy's pet phrases were "You must come along," "I'm glad you asked me," "You don't know the half of it," and "You must come over." There are many who claim that Mae West borrowed not only her famous walk from Bert Savoy but also the last phrase, with all the insinuation that Savoy put into it, and it became of course, "Come up and see me sometime."

In the act, Bert Savoy was forever talking about his friend Margie and her gossip. It might be the one about the girl who took the man out to dinner where the lights were dim, the music soft, and the wine well-chilled. The man said, "I've never been in a place like this before," to which the girl answered, "My God! I'm out with an amateur." Or Bert might tell of the showgirl who, after seeing Douglas Fairbanks in *The Three Musketeers,* passed a shop with the Dumas novel in the window and commented, "Ain't the printing press wonderful—they've got the book out already." Margie's dialogue, as reported by Bert Savoy, would go something like this: "I'll never forget, dearie, the time a baroness or somethin' ast me if I

Savoy and Brennan

knew Sir Herbert Tree, an' I answered, 'No, but I knew his younger brother, Frank Bush.' "

Without his female wig Bert Savoy was slightly balding and might have been mistaken, provided he kept his mouth closed, for the president of a flourishing business. Unlike other female impersonators, Savoy did not remove his wig on stage, feeling it would ruin the audience's interest in the character. Jay Brennan was tall and good-looking, with blue eyes that he fluttered at his partner. In fact, theatre critic Ashton Stevens noted that Brennan would have made a more ladylike female impersonator.

Bert Savoy was born Everett McKenzie in Boston circa 1888; he claimed his first stage appearance was in a freak museum in Boston where he was paid six dollars a week to perform twelve times a day as a "cooch" dancer, alternating with a deaf mute. Savoy later teamed with the deaf mute girl and the two worked in a carnival until the owner left town without paying them. According to Savoy, this was so great a shock to the deaf mute that it restored her voice and she cried, "Oh, my Gawd!" After a term as a chorus boy, Savoy was stranded in Montana where he began to work as a female impersonator. After entertaining miners in the Yukon and Alaska he returned to the United States, and, in Chicago in 1904, met and married a showgirl named Ann, who was later to run a theatrical boarding house on New York's West Forty-nineth Street. According to *Variety* (July 16, 1930), the marriage was purely platonic and ended in 1922 when Bert returned home to find Ann and the furniture missing. The next day he telephoned the bank and found that, like the furniture, their joint account was gone. Ann Savoy was last heard of in Chicago in July of 1930 when she was arrested on a robbery charge.

Ann Savoy picked up the man who was her accomplice in robbery on a streetcar, and apparently, this is how Bert Savoy and Jay Brennan met in 1913, on a streetcar traveling down Broadway. Both were out-of-work chorus boys and they decided to put together new-style female impersonation acts for vaudeville.

By 1916 Savoy and Brennan were appearing at the Palace, and their salary quickly rose to $1,500 a week. In 1920 the two starred in the second edition of John Murray Anderson's *The Greenwich Village Follies;* they were to remain firm favorites in that revue for the next three years, performing everything from a Bohemian number with Savoy as Lady Nicotine and Brennan as a French apache to a "Naked Truth" routine with Savoy as the model for Inspiration and Brennan as a sculptor. Bert Savoy took great care with his dress, and employed a wardrobe mistress names Mrs. Jones. He explained, "They tell me Mary Garden's got a valet, but as for me, I contend it takes a woman to understand a woman's clothes. Mr. Eltinge had a Jap for years, but now that he's tried a woman he wouldn't have any other sex in his dressing room. Besides, you can't depend on a man. Just when you want him to lace you up he's out in the wings with the women. And why put temptation in the poor devil's way? Anyway, I always feel safer in a woman's hands."

Bert Savoy's end was as theatrical as his camping. On the sultry afternoon of Tuesday, June 26, 1923, Bert Savoy and a fellow vaudevillian, Jack Vincent, were walking on Long Beach, Long Island. A thunderstorm suddenly swept across that part of New York State, and after a particularly strong clap of thunder, Savoy supposedly said, "Mercy, ain't Miss God cutting up something awful?" Immediately, there was a lightning bolt from the sky and both Bert Savoy and Jack Vincent were killed instantly.

After Savoy's death Jay Brennan teamed up with Stanley Rogers, and they made their New York debut at the Palace in January of 1924 after six months of trying out their act on the road. Rogers adopted all of Savoy's mannerisms and catchphrases, while Brennan wrote the new dialogue, which, according to *Variety* (January 31, 1924), "fits Rogers just as smoothly as the new gown which drew gasps from the feminine portion of the audience." The review continued, "Jay Brennan as the same suave, sleek, straight man cuing his new partner admirably, feeding him at just the proper moments and regulating the tempo of the crossfire in his usual flawless manner." The seventeen-minute act ended with a song, "You Should Have Been with Us," and was a tremendous success.

Jay Brennan went solo in 1929, playing the role of Caponetti in the Earl Carroll musical revue *Fioreta,* which opened at the Earl Carroll Theatre on February 5, and ran for one hundred and eleven performances. Also in the cast were Fannie Brice, Leon Errol, Lionel Atwill, and Louise Brooks. Brennan and Rogers were reunited at the Palace Theatre in January of 1930. It is interesting to note that even seven years after his death, Bert Savoy was so well remembered that one vaudeville act, Ann Butler and Hal Parker, was having quite a success with impersonations of Savoy and Brennan.

In the mid-thirties Jay Brennan entered the film industry as a scriptwriter and dialogue director; the only film on which he appears to have received credit, as a coscriptwriter, is *Expensive Husbands,* released in 1937. Brennan continued to perform until his retirement in 1945. A bachelor all his life, Jay Brennan died at the reported age of seventy-eight in Brooklyn, where he had made his home, on January 14, 1961.

References: "The Mutterings of Margie" by Savoy and Brennan in *Variety,* Vol. 44, No. 5 (December 28, 1917), pages 13 and 40.
   "Consistently Savoy and Brennan" in *Actorviews* by Ashton Stevens (Covici-McGee, 1923).

FRITZI SCHEFF

Opera singers were no vaudeville novelty. Rosa Ponselle had begun her career in vaudeville with her sister, Carmella, in an act titled The Two Italian Girls, prior to reaching new heights and new audiences at the Met. Vinie Daly and Alice Zeppill—whom *Variety* thought the "prettiest of all the opera primas"—were regulars on the vaudeville stage. *Variety* (January 11, 1922) noted that one out of fifty opera singers made it in vaudeville, but one who definitely did, becoming a major headliner, was Fritzi Scheff.

"The Little Devil of Grand Opera," as Fritzi Scheff was

Fritzi Scheff

known when Charles Dillinger was her manager and building her as one of the biggest names on the American operatic stage, was born in Vienna, Austria, on August 30, 1879. She studied singing with her mother, prima donna Hortense Scheff Yarger. Fredericka Scheff Yarger was, by all accounts, a child prodigy. Maurice Grau heard her sing at the Munich Royal Opera and invited her to become a member of the Metropolitan Opera Company, with which Miss Scheff made her American debut in Beethoven's *Fidelio* on December 28, 1900. A contemporary critic wrote, "She was received with much warmth, not only for her pure, high soprano of birdlike brilliance, but because of her youthful vivacity and piquant beauty of face and form."

After three seasons with the Met, together with appearances at London's Covent Garden, Charles Dillingham persuaded his star to enter comic opera, which she did in 1903 in Victor Herbert's *Babette.* This was followed by *The Two Roses,* an operatic version of Oliver Goldsmith's *She Stoops To Conquer.* On October 7, 1905, Victor Herbert's *Mlle. Modiste* opened in Trenton, New Jersey, starring Fritzi Scheff in the role of Fifi. The role became Miss Scheff's best known, and the song "Kiss Me Again" almost her signature tune. "The singer's predominating trait is her vivacity, and innumerable adjectives have been applied to her in praise of her melodious, well-trained voice, her perfect figure, her piquancy and inexhaustible good humor," was a typical critical comment. "There is no other singer on the American stage today who ranks with her in the field of comic opera."

Although she was to overcome her temperament, it was

something for which Fritzi Scheff was noted in the early years of her career. In his 1927 book *Behind the Curtains of Broadway's Beauty Trust,* Will A. Page recalled:

> Miss Scheff was charming and unaffected at first, but as her name went up in electric letters and adulation was poured upon her, she became more and more temperamental. She surrounded herself with a retinue of servants and maids. She would not let the chorus girls walk across the stage while she was rehearsing. She made excessive demands on hotels for suites where her nerves could rest in absolute quiet. She carried her own cook to prepare her meals after declaring that hotel food was impossible. She once had her maid telephone to my room at the Congress Hotel in Chicago at three o'clock in the morning in great excitement. Johanna, the maid, said Madame insisted that I must come to her apartment. I awoke from a sound slumber, dressed, and responded to the call with the alacrity of a fireman sliding down the brass pole. Johanna met me at the door. "Madame says" (she spoke with a German accent) "will you be so good as to take the dog out for a walk?"

Fritzi Scheff's vaudeville debut came in September of 1913 at the Palace in an act in which she sang three numbers accompanied by Eugene Bernstein at the piano. Sime Silverman wrote in *Variety* (September 5, 1913), "To those who want to see Fritzi Scheff and pay vaudeville price, she's probably worth the money. Otherwise her act is a classy straight singing number." By October of 1913 Miss Scheff was announcing she was tired of vaudeville, but nonetheless she continued to be active on the vaudeville stage through the twenties. In July of 1918 she headlined at the Palace, billed as "The Brilliant Prima Donna." In fact, Fritzi Scheff was a regular at the Palace, making her last appearance there in April of 1930 in a twenty-minute revue-type act in which she was assisted by twelve male dancers and singers. Needless to say, she sang "Kiss Me Again." *Variety* (April 30, 1930) reported, "Her reception at the Palace was long and sincere, as her appearance was, in the language of the billing, 'ever glorious'. . . . Miss Scheff has a neat, pretty, and diverting turn. With her own presence and reputation to top it."

The petite singer was featured in later years in Billy Rose's Barbary Coast Show at the 1940 New York World's Fair and, in 1946, appeared at Rose's Diamond Horseshoe. She died in her New York apartment on April 8, 1954, within a month of being featured on television's "This Is Your Life."

Reference: "Fritzi Scheff" in *Musical Biographies,* compiled by Janet M. Green (Irving Squire, 1908), page 274.

BLOSSOM SEELEY AND BENNY FIELDS

They called her the Queen of Syncopation and the hottest gal in town, for Blossom Seeley could belt out a song like no one else. Sophie Tucker came close, and Mae West in

**Blossom Seeley and
Benny Fields**

the thirties adopted a style in her films similar to that of Blossom Seeley, but there was only one Blossom Seeley. As *Variety* commented back in 1911, "When Blossom starts those hands agoing, and begins to toddle, you just have to hold tight for fear of getting up and toddling right along with her." Her style of singing was brassy, earthy, and sexy without being crude, as she delivered, with smouldering but relaxed intensity, such numbers as "Somebody Loves Me," "Way Down Yonder in New Orleans," and "I Cried for You." As Ruth Etting once noted, "She had a way with a song." And from 1921 on she was backed up by Benny Fields, generally credited with being America's first crooner, whose easy style of delivery perfectly complemented that of his wife.

San Francisco-born Blossom Seeley was already a stage performer at the age of ten, billed as "The Little Blossom." She added sex appeal to song salesmanship, one reviewer wrote. *Variety* (October 1, 1910) saw her at the Washburton in Yonkers and predicted, "Miss Seeley ought to be a hit anywhere." After some success on the burlesque and vaudeville stages singing "Put Your Arms Around Me, Honey," and "Toddlin' the Todalo," she was spotted by Lew Fields who put her in the cast of his 1911 production, *The Henpecks*. She followed this with other shows, notably *Whirl of Society* (1912) with Al Jolson, *The Charity Girl* (1912), *Maid in America* (1915), and *Ned Wayburn's Town Topics* (1915). In 1913 Blossom Seeley made her first appearance at the Palace, supported on stage by her second husband, Rube Marquand, the baseball player. Late in 1916 she was working with Bill Baily and Lynn Cowan, the trio billed as Seeley's Sycnopated Studio.

Benny Fields was born in Milwaukee, Wisconsin, on June 14, 1894. He had been playing and singing with a trio in a small Chicago night spot when Blossom Seeley first saw him in 1921. She asked him to join her act, and a year later—in March of 1922—they were married; it was Miss Seeley's third marriage. As both were quick to admit, it was a very unequal partnership for there was little question that Miss Seeley was the star. Later, when Benny Fields worked solo, he once recalled, "When I arrived at the theatre there was the marquee. In tiny letters it said 'Benny Fields,' and below, in letters a foot high, it said, 'Formerly with Blossom Seeley.' "

Blossom Seeley and Benny Fields were popular headliners in the twenties. Benny Fields would handle the comedy and assist with the vocalizing, but Blossom Seeley was the main attraction, giving new life to such ballads as "You Left Me Out in the Rain" and "A New Kind of Man with a New Kind of Love for Me." Sime Silverman saw them at the Palace and reported in *Variety* (April 22, 1925), "The turn now has songs, speed, music, and comedy, well placed and timed. A review of it in *Variety* from out of town (Kansas City) a few weeks ago said it is the best act Blossom Seeley has ever had—it is all of that." The two were in the last (1928) edition of *The Greenwich Village Follies*. For the 1922 edition of *George White's Scandals,* George Gershwin composed a twenty-five-minute jazz opera, *Blue Monday,* which was pulled from the show after opening night. On December 29, 1925, the opera reappeared at Carnegie Hall under the title of *135th Street,* and the leading roles were sung by Blossom Seeley and Benny Fields, accompanied by Paul Whiteman and His Orchestra.

In 1936 Blossom Seeley decided to bow out of show business. "When Benny clicked," she wrote, "I went on being Mrs. Benny Fields, not Blossom Seeley. Singing was his career, and *he* was *my* career. That's the way it's got to be in any successful marriage. You don't have to be in show business to know that a husband must be the headliner. Second billing is good enough for the wife. And why not—as long as the act is a smash hit?" Fields was featured in two films, *Big Broadcast of 1937* and *Minstrel Man* (1944). Aside from a couple of shorts, Blossom Seeley appeared in only two films, *Blood Money* and *Broadway thru a Keyhole,* both released in 1933.

Blossom Seeley came out of retirement in 1952 when Paramount filmed the couple's life story under the title of *Somebody Loves Me,* with Betty Hutton as Seeley and Ralph Meeker as Fields. She recorded three long-players of her most famous songs for Mercury, M-G-M, and Decca, and she and Fields embarked on a successful engagement at the Cocoanut Grove in Los Angeles in November of 1952. Soon both became regulars on "The Ed Sullivan Show." Benny Fields died in New York on August 17, 1959, shortly after he and his wife had completed a successful engagement at the Sands in Las Vegas. Blossom Seeley made her last public appearance on "The Ed Sullivan Show" in 1966; she died in a New York nursing home on April 17, 1974.

Reference: "This Love of Ours" by Blossom Seeley, as told to Dan Senseney in *The American Weekly* (October 26, 1952) page 12.

ELLA SHIELDS

One of Britain's great male impersonators, Ella Shields, was, surprisingly, born in America, in Baltimore, on September 26, 1879. She had a brief career in this country as a singer of coon songs—making her debut in Altoona, Pennsylvania, on April 28, 1898—before making her English debut at London's Forester's Music Hall on October 10, 1904. She quickly acclimatized herself to the English music hall scene, and her soft Southern accent became indistinguishable from a British West Country accent. Her male impersonation closely followed that of Vesta Tilley's, relying on either evening dress or a military uniform to make, as one critic wrote with unconscious humor, "a charming and gay figure."

The one exception to her elegant dress was when she sang her most famous song, "Burlington Bertie from Bow" (written by her one-time husband, William Hargreaves, and not to be confused with an earlier Vesta Tilley song, "Burlington Bertie"). Ella Shields would appear on stage in tattered clothes, a worn top hat, and white gloves to sing of the starving, broken-down swell too proud to accept invitations to dine:

I'm Burlington Bertie,
I rise at ten-thirty and saunter along like a toff.
I walk down the Strand with my gloves on my hands,
Then I walk down again with them off.

Ella Shields

I'm all airs and graces, correct easy paces,
Without food so long, I've forgot where my face is.
I'm Bert, Bert, I haven't a shirt, but my people are well off, you know!
Nearly ev'ryone knows me, from Smith to Lord Roseb'ry,
I'm Burlington Bertie from Bow.

Ella Shields's first great triumph was her appearance at the opening of the London Palladium on December 26, 1910. Her second was surely her first American comeback, after the years in England, in January of 1920 at the Palace. The *New York Dramatic Mirror* (January 15, 1920) reported, "Miss Shields to most of that Palace crowd Monday was an unknown—a complete stranger—yet before she was half through the audience sat up and took notice of everything she did. It couldn't help it; Miss Shields was giving the folks an act worthy of their attention and appreciation. True, she reminded us of the days of Vesta Tilley when she sauntered on in male attire, but her style, voice, unaffected way of working and gracefulness when tripping a few steps a la light fantastic were such that she was accepted as an artist worth while." *Variety* (January 9, 1920) thought her "an artist through and through. . . . We haven't had anything like such a turn in America in years."

Other American engagements followed. In January of 1924 she was back at the Palace, again singing "Burlington Bertie from Bow," plus "I'm a Steward on an Ocean Liner" accompanied by a hornpipe.

"Before a discriminating audience she's a cinch," reported *Variety* (January 31, 1924). In January of 1928 Ella Shields appeared with Ada Reeve and Lily Morris on an all-English bill at the Palace, although it must be reported that it was Lily Morris who was the hit of the show.

Ella Shields officially retired in 1929, but she made endless returns to the stage. In fact, only days before her death on August 5, 1952, she was appearing at a holiday camp at Morecambe, a seaside resort in the north of England.

SINGER'S MIDGETS

They were certainly not the only troupe of midgets on the American vaudeville stage, but Singer's Midgets were the most popular and best known and are still remembered today. The troupe consisted of between eighteen and twenty midgets, all from Austria and Hungary, under the supervision of Leo Singer, an entrepreneur who died on March 5, 1951. Singer, his wife, and the midgets all lived together in a New York brownstone, and each midget was assigned a specific task; for example, Charlie Beeker was the cook and Emily Garanyi was the seamstress. (Other midgets in the troupe were Franz Steingruber; Christine, Lydia, and Eddie Buresh; Sandor Roka; Vincent and Fritz Tarabula; Gabor Bagi; and Hattie Angerer, who at three feet, one inch was said to be the smallest in the group.)

Singer brought his midgets over to America in the mid-teens, after they had already achieved fame in Europe. Marcus Loew booked them for his then minor vaudeville circuit, and the midgets were said to have been largely responsible for Loew's financial success, which eventually, of course, led to his controlling Metro-Goldwyn-Mayer. Who knows, perhaps that studio's production of *The Wizard of Oz*, with all those Munchkin midgets, was the company's way of saying thanks to Singer's Midgets? The midgets' act was a vaudeville show in itself, featuring baby elephants, ponies and dogs, a boxing match, the legend of Lady Godiva, and a musical playlet titled "A Little Touch of Paris." There was no question as to their success. In the summer of 1917 the little people played the Pantages circuit, and other acts cancelled rather than compete on the same bill with Singer's Midgets. In the twenties Singer split the troupe into two, with one group of "twelve midgets and two girls" presenting a revue titled "Toyland" and the other group a revue titled "Models and Music," featuring the Imperial Russian Balalaika Orchestra.

Despite the stereotyping of midgets as disagreeable, Singer's Midgets are remembered with affection. Marian Spitzer, who handled their publicity when they appeared at the Palace, found them agreeable and well-adjusted, while Nils T. Granlund, who handled them for Marcus Loew, described the group as "the most wonderful little people I ever met"; in his autobiography he recalls that the troupe's prima donna, Dora Vege, had a penchant for falling in love with every man over six feet tall.

After the demise of vaudeville, Singer's Midgets combined with Roper's Midgets of England to form "the world's greatest show of little people." They toured the circuses and fairgrounds of the world successfully until the Second World War.

Reference: "High-and-Low Hunt on for Vanished Little People" by Michael Mok in the *New York World-Telegram* (December 7, 1959), page 21.

KATE SMITH

Franklin Delano Roosevelt once introduced Kate Smith by saying: "This is Kate Smith. And Kate Smith is America." So it is appropriate that a performer who first introduced Irving Berlin's "God Bless America," on November 11, 1938, should have played a meaningful part in the history of that particularly American institution, vaudeville. She came to vaudeville late in its career but early in her own, making her first professional stage appearance at B. F. Keith's Theatre in Washington, D.C., in the mid-twenties, and her first New York vaudeville appearance in February of 1926, at which time *Variety* prophesied a bright future for her. In 1931 Kate Smith starred in the stage show at the Capitol Theatre, and later that same year she had her own revue at the Hippodrome. However, it was in the following year that she made vaudeville history by being the only performer to play ten consecutive weeks, from August 1 through October 9, at the Palace. Those Palace audiences never grew tired of hearing that familiar phrase which was to be part of show business for the next forty years, "Hello everybody, this is Kate Smith."

Kathryn Elizabeth Smith was born May 1, 1909, in Greenville, Virginia—hence the title "Songbird of the South"—and raised in Washington, D.C. As a child she won amateur contests and eventually persuaded her family to let her try for a career in show business. Her first break came when she was signed for a small part in the musical *Honeymoon Lane,* which opened in Atlantic City on August 29, 1926, and subsequently ran for two years on Broadway. When it closed in 1929 she went into the road company of *Hit the Deck,* playing the blackface "Mammy" role and singing "Hallelujah." From *Hit the Deck* Kate Smith went into *Flying High,* which opened on March 3, 1930. In all three productions she played a plump, jovial character, and in *Flying High,* as Pansy Sparks, she was the foil for Bert Lahr, the brunt of jokes such as "That girl is sitting on top of the world—nothing else could bear her weight."

Kate Smith became more and more self-conscious about her size—at the height of her fame she weighed 212 pounds—until she met a recording manager for Columbia Records named Ted Collins. Collins (who was born in New York City on October 12, 1900 and died at Lake Placid, New York, on May 27, 1964) taught Kate Smith self-confidence, became her manager in 1931, and was to be her lifelong friend and confidant. As Miss Smith wrote in her autobiography, "Ted was more than a manager, more even than a friend.... Without Ted there would have been no Kate Smith." Collins introduced Kate Smith to radio, and the singer made her first broadcast for CBS on May 1, 1931, singing "By the River St. Marie," "I Surrender Dear," "Please Don't Talk about Me When I'm Gone," "Dream a Little Dream of Me," and the number which was to become her theme song, "When the Moon

Kate Smith with Ted
Collins

Comes over the Mountain." It was Collins who suggested the simple self-introduction and her closing words, "Thanks for listening." Her radio show soon became one of the most popular on the air.

The singer never learned to read music. In 1938, when she sang with Leopold Stokowski and the Philadelphia Orchestra, she asked the maestro to whistle the music for her! He reportedly told Kate Smith, "Don't ever take a lesson. Your voice is a gift from God and should never be spoiled."

Kate Smith made her television debut on September 25, 1950, with "The Kate Smith Hour." By 1956 she claimed to have made 8,000 radio broadcasts, recorded 2,200 songs, and earned as much as $38,000 in a single week. She continued, "There's really nothing I've missed I'd care to do." Kate Smith officially retired in 1979, and now lives in Raleigh, North Carolina. Her happy, simplistic style of performing, coupled with the joviality which many plump people seem to radiate, made her a natural for all aspects of show business. She might well have become a joke from an earlier time to today's audiences, but Kate Smith was too good, too straightforward, and too honest ever to be sneered at.

References: *Living in a Big Way* by Kate Smith (Blue Ribbon Books, 1938). *Upon My Lips a Song* by Kate Smith (Funk & Wagnalls, 1960).

SMITH AND DALE

Thanks largely to Neil Simon's *The Sunshine Boys,* with its version of the classic "Dr. Kronkhite" sketch, Smith and Dale are as well known today as they were at the height of their fame. And, of course, for all those millions who saw Smith and Dale's comedy routines live or on television, the two have never been forgotten. Their timing was immaculate and the jokes, often corny by today's standards, were always funny. Joe Smith would ask Charlie Dale, "How could a low life like you have high blood pressure?" and the joke would become as classic— and certainly more amusing—than any line Shakespeare ever wrote.

Smith and Dale were both born in New York City, Joe Smith as Joe Sultzer on February 16, 1884, and Charlie Dale as Charles Marks on September 6, 1881. They met in December of 1898 while riding bicycles on New York's East Side. They got into an argument and were told that their verbal sparring was reminiscent of Weber and Fields, and that they should get together. Sultzer and Marks began to sing and dance in the saloons of the Bowery, working in blackface; during the day they would earn fifty cents working as waiters at Childs' Restaurant. Smith and Dale became their names when Joe Smith's brother found a printer who had made up calling cards for a vaudeville act of that name which had subsequently decided to change its billing. In 1900 they joined the Imperial Vaudeville and Comedy Company, which played the Catskills area of New York State around Roundout, and in which Smith and Dale first conceived one of their best-known sketches, "The New Schoolteacher." (Later the Catskills area was to become known as the Borscht circuit for vaudevillians.)

When the Imperial Vaudeville and Comedy Company ran out of funds, Smith and Dale returned to New York and decided to perfect the schoolteacher act with two new partners, Will Lester and Jack Coleman, who were working as singing waiters at the Avon Cafe on 116th Street. From the name of the saloon, the new partners took their new billing, the Avon Comedy Four. The group's sketch was set in a schoolroom and appears to have had various names through the years—in the early days of this century it was called "The Private Tutor"—but the characterizations always remained the same: a Hebrew-type, a German, a tough guy, and a sissy. "There are no dull moments during its presentation and numerous laughs accompany it from start to finish," reported the *New York Clipper* (August 20, 1904). In addition to appearing on the vaudeville stage, it should also be noted that the Avon Comedy Four made a number of phonograph recordings in the 1910s, not only of comedy sketches but also of songs.

Joe Smith often recounts the story of how vaudeville performers were first allowed to work on Sundays. Performers could entertain on the Sabbath, but the New York Blue Laws forbade make-up, talking, tumbling, or emoting. Despite the law, the Avon Comedy Four were told by Willie Hammerstein to go ahead with their usual act on a Sunday; they were promptly arrested. The next day, in court, the judge asked the arresting officer to describe the act. The detective explained, "This sissy comes out and says he is going to call the roll—all those who are absent say "absent." Then he asks the Yid to use the word "delight" in a sentence, and he hits him on the head with a stick." After listening to his account, the judge responded, "They don't have an act—case dismissed." From then on, performers were allowed to work unhindered on Sundays.

In time, the members of the comedy and singing quartet changed, with Irving Kaufman and Harry Goodwin replacing Lester and Coleman. Others who have been mem-

bers of the Avon Comedy Four include Charlie Adams, Eddie Rasch, Eddie Miller, Frank Corbett, Paul Maul, Lou Lawrence, Mario Palermo, Alan Chester, Al Evans, Eddie Nelson, Al Walden, Al Rauth, Al Greene, Fred E. Ahlert (the composer, for one day at the Palace), Ben Edwards, Mike Kelly, Tom Dillon, and Arthur Fields. In 1914 the Avon Comedy Four headlined the first All-American bill at London's Finsbury Park Empire. In the spring of 1929 Joe Smith and Charlie Dale, with Mario Palermo and Lou Lawrence, headlined at the London Palladium for the first time. In 1916 the group added a restaurant sketch, with Joe Smith playing the chef who feigns illness when he gets too many orders. The waiter would ask, "Where's the water?" and back would come the reply, "In the milk." "It's an elastic act that might be worked up to almost any limits," reported Sime Silverman in *Variety* (October 13, 1916). "While the new turn does not yet compare with the old one as a laugh maker, it may in time, and is at least a departure from a routine the Avons made very familiar to big-time audiences."

Irving Kaufman left the Avon Comedy Four in January of 1919 and was replaced by Charlie Dale's brother, Lou. The Avon Comedy Four was ending its comedy reign, to be replaced by Smith and Dale. The "Dr. Kronkhite" sketch—"kronk," of course, is both German and Yiddish for sick—had originated while the two were still billed as the Avon Comedy Four, but was perfected when Smith and Dale took top billing in the act now called Smith and Dale and Their Avon Comedy Four. Smith would ask, "Is this the doctor's office?" The nurse would reply, "Yes, I'm his nurse." Back would come Smith, "His nurse? Is the doctor sick too?" "No, I'm a trained nurse." "Oh, you do

Smith and Dale

tricks?" And so on. . . . Around 1926 Smith and Dale dropped "Dr. Kronkhite" from their vaudeville sketch, but they reintroduced it in 1928 and remained inseparable from it in the years to come.

One twenty-minute sketch which Smith and Dale featured, introduced at the Palace in September of 1925, was titled "Battery to the Bronx," in which they were supposedly on a subway train traveling the length of New York City. The sketch opened with a song, "Canal Street," and then moved into a scene in the office of lawyer U. R. Stuck (played by Dale). The next stop was Harlem, where Smith and Dale were two firemen, too busy playing pinochle to leave the station and respond to an alarm. "How big is your house?" they ask. "Three stories." "Is it brick?" "Yes." "Then you've got plenty of time. Brick takes longer to burn." (This sequence was later adapted into a full-length vaudeville sketch in its own right and also into a 1929 Paramount film short, *The False Alarm Fire Company.*) The Bronx sequence had the husband coming home to find his wife in the arms of his partner, Wolf, leading to the line, "While I'm down struggling to keep the wolf from the door, you let him come in the house." The husband shoots both his wife and Wolf and walks off with the maid. "The turn in its present shape is sure fire for anywhere," reported *Variety* (September 16, 1925).

Smith and Dale's continuing success was due in no small part to the constant changing of the dialogue and the endings of their sketches. As late as June 5, 1934, *Variety* was still reviewing them under the heading of "New Acts."

Aside from vaudeville, the pair appeared in a number of revues and in several short films and three features, *Manhattan Parade* (1931), *The Heart of New York* (1932), and *Two Tickets to Broadway* (1951). They made frequent television appearances, and participated in the fabulous Judy Garland show at the Palace which opened on October 16, 1951. Charlie Dale died in Teaneck, New Jersey, on November 16, 1971. Joe Smith was a resident of the Actors Fund Home in Englewood, New Jersey, and was quick to point out that despite the obvious similarities between Smith and Dale and the vaudeville partners in *The Sunshine Boys,* he and Charlie Dale only argued for the betterment of the act, never on a personal level. When Smith attended a Friars Club roast of Neil Simon, he commented, "Neil Simon didn't plagiarize Smith and Dale—he Simonized them."

Of Joe Smith's more recent years, his close friend Terry McGrath writes:

Eleven years ago I invited Joe to guest lecture at Hackensack High School. The lectures expanded into faculty variety shows, and before long other schools were asking for Joe to lecture. At the time Charlie was almost totally deaf, so I was doing his part. In 1971 the Hackensack Board of Education awarded Joe a high school diploma—he had only finished the fourth grade. We then began to perform at colleges. Drama departments go ape over Joe showing the students how to do a take or take a fall.

Last year one of the local colleges wanted to give Joe an honorary degree, but he turned it down out of loyalty to his alma mater, Hackensack.

For more than fifty years Smith and Dale ended their act with a verse:

Over fifty (sixty, seventy) years together,
With a bond that never tore,
And if somebody up there likes us,
We'll make it more and more.

After Charlie's death Joe Smith changed the ending:

Over seventy years together
As close as two peas in a pod,
And the only one that could
Separate us—(pause)—
Was God.

As Terry McGrath notes, it was a hell of an ending. But then Smith and Dale was a hell of an act. Joe Smith died on February 11, 1981.

References: "Spawned in the Catskills, Christened in Harlem" by Joe Smith and Charlie Dale in *The Spice of Variety,* edited by Abel Green (Henry Holt and Company, 1952), pages 252–258. "Joe Smith" in *The Vaudevillians* by Bill Smith (Macmillan, 1976), pages 239–251.

AILEEN STANLEY

To a generation of record collectors, Aileen Stanley was the Victrola Girl and her recordings are still prized by them today. Among her hits were "My Little Bimbo down on the Bamboo Isle," "Singin' the Blues," "Look What You've Done with Your Doggone Dangerous Eyes," "Whatcha Gonna Do When There Ain't No Jazz?," "I'm Looking for a Bluebird (To Chase the Blues Away)," "Bimini Bay," "Lovin' Sam (The Sheik of Alabam')," "You May Be Fast, But Mamma's Gonna Slow You Down," "Everybody Loves My Baby," "Ain't That a Grand and Glorious Feeling," "When My Sugar Walks Down the Street," and "Here am I—Broken Hearted."

From 1920 through the mid-thirties Aileen Stanley was also a vaudeville favorite, a torch singer par excellence whose handsome, aristocratic look and stance belied the songs she would sing. She was born in 1897 in Chicago where, in 1919, she won a contest organized by the *Chicago Herald and Examiner* to find the most beautiful bathing girl in the city. From that contest she went on to the vaudeville stage, and *Variety* (September 26, 1919) wrote of her (using a quaint spelling for jazz), "Aileen Stanley is the syncopated goddess of jass. Jass music originated as the expression of an impulse. Today it is a science. Miss Stanley is a post graduate and carries all the degrees. Her unique method of delivering syncopated melody is rendered most effective by a demure and sedate personality which offers a charming and unusual background for this school of song. There are scores of young women in

Aileen Stanley

vaudeville who sing jasual songs. Miss Stanley stands alone with her individual talent."

She came to New York in 1920, initially in vaudeville and then as one of the stars of *Silks and Satins* at the George M. Cohan Theatre. From *Silks and Satins* Aileen Stanley returned to vaudeville, making her Palace debut in October of 1920. She remained a firm favorite through the twenties. At the New Palace Theatre in Chicago in 1931 she sang "Just like Jimmy and Me," "Some Pigs, a Hen and a Cow," and "Walkin' My Baby Back Home," and at the time *The Billboard* (February 28, 1931) commented, "There's a graciousness and charm about Aileen Stanley that is hard to put into words, and it fits perfectly with the sort of heart-throb songs she sings." Aileen Stanley retired in 1936 and now lives in Los Angeles.

FRED STONE

Fred Stone was one of those all-around entertainers who no longer seem to exist in show business. Seemingly, he could do anything: acrobatics, tight rope walking, a song-and-dance act, and straight acting. One of the reasons for his versatility was that he started early, learning tightrope walking as a child in his mother's back yard, and touring in circuses with his younger brother, Eddie, before either of them were in their teens. Because of his expertise, Fred Stone worked in every area of show business: circuses, minstrel shows, burlesque, vaudeville, musical comedy, legitimate drama, and motion pictures.

Born in a log cabin in Valmont, Colorado, on August 19, 1873, Fred Stone was christened Val by his father

(until an angry grandmother changed the name to Frederick) and spent his early years traveling around with his father, an itinerant barber. At the age of eleven Fred Stone joined a traveling circus with his brother, and from that point on he seldom returned home. On April 19, 1894, he teamed up with a young man from St. Joseph, Missouri, named David Montgomery, who had previously appeared as Montgomery and Wilson in an act titled "Pullman Car Porters." Thus the team of Montgomery and Stone came into being. Working in blackface, the pair appeared on the vaudeville stage together for the first time at Keith's Theatre, Boston, and soon became headliners, earning $150 a week, and even appearing at the Palace Theatre, London, as early as 1900. Montgomery and Stone made their first musical comedy appearance together, under Charles Froman's management, in *The Girl from Up There,* which opened at the Herald Square Theatre on January 7, 1901.

Montgomery and Stone's greatest success was in *The Wizard of Oz,* with book and lyrics by L. Frank Baum and music by Paul Tietjens and A. Baldwin Sloane, which was first seen at the Grand Opera House in Chicago on June 16, 1902. Fred Stone appeared as the Scarecrow, and the cyclone scene in which the Straw Man is torn to bits was one of the most famous tricks of the legitimate stage. Dave Montgomery played the Tin Woodsman and introduced a popular song of the period, "Must You Have Meat with Your Mustard?" *The Wizard of Oz* eventually opened in New York at the Majestic Theatre on January 21, 1903, and ran for a magnificent 293 performances. Also in the production, playing Lady Lunatic, was Allene Crater, whom Fred Stone married in 1904, and by whom he had three daughters, Paula, Dorothy, and Carol, all of whom entered show business.

The Wizard of Oz was followed by the Victor Herbert operetta *The Red Mill,* which opened at the Knickerbocker Theatre in New York on September 24, 1906, and ran for 274 performances. In the role of Con Kidder, Fred Stone had another hit, and the show marked the beginning of his long association with Charles Dillingham. In 1909 Stone toured in the George Ade comedy *The Old Town,* in which he introduced his famous lariat dance. To teach him how to use a rope, Fred Stone looked for someone familiar with a lasso and found that person in Will Rogers. The two formed a close friendship which lasted until Rogers's death in 1935. It was the death of Dave Montgomery at the age of forty-seven on April 20, 1917, that was to break up one of this century's great theatrical partnerships and a friendship that was, as *Variety* commented, "firm and fast from the outset." "For twenty-five years we had been together," wrote Stone. "We had built our careers together, so closely that they seemed like one career. We had in common a whole lifetime of shared experiences, and deep-rooted friendship and trust. We supplemented each other, as is the case with all enduring partnerships. He had a gayety and sparkle and love of life that aroused a response in his audience and his friends. No one will ever know how I missed him. The most difficult thing I ever had to do was to go ahead alone. For one thing I decided —I would never take another partner. No one should have Dave's place."

Fred Stone with
daughters Dorothy and
Paula

Montgomery and Stone did more than entertain vaudeville audiences. On June 1, 1900 they were two of the seven original founders of the White Rats, an organization of vaudevillians dedicated to controlling the ferocious power of the vaudeville management led by B. F. Keith and E. F. Albee. They named themselves after the British Music Hall organization of Water Rats, rats being "star" spelt backward. The White Rats ultimately failed in their efforts to be a strong union and were superseded by the National Vaudeville Artists, created not by vaudevillians but by E. F. Albee.

After Montgomery's death Fred Stone appeared in the title role of *Jack o' Lantern,* which opened at the Globe Theatre on October 16, 1917. This "musical extravaganza" was claimed to be the most expensive production in terms of seat prices to play Broadway up to that time. A year later Fred Stone went to Hollywood to appear in his first film—for Famous Players-Lasky—*Under the Top,* directed by Donald Crisp and written by John Emerson and Anita Loos. Stone was advertised as "the marvel of musical comedy," and the film, set in a circus, gave him ample opportunities for wire walking and acrobatics. Stone appeared sporadically in films through the forties, and among his features are *Broadway after Dark* (1924), *Smiling Faces* (1932), *Alice Adams* (1935), and *The Trail of the Lonesome Pine* (1936). He also continued to appear on the stage, in *Tip-Top* (1920), *Stepping Stones* (1923), *Criss-cross* (1926), *Ripples* (1930), *Smiling Faces* (1932), and *Jayhawker* (1934). In 1928 Stone was about to go into rehearsals for a new show, *Three Cheers,* when he was involved in a plane crash and broke both legs; his friend

Will Rogers took over the part and would accept no salary, sending his weekly paycheck to Stone.

Fred Stone's last major stage appearance was as Grandpa Martin Vanderhof in *You Can't Take It With You* at New York's City Center in 1945; he also essayed the same role in a small 1950 Hollywood production at the Las Palmas Theatre. After a long illness, Fred Stone died at his North Hollywood, California, home on March 6, 1959. He had experienced a remarkable career and, as he wrote in his autobiography, "The world has been good to me. I have been a happy man."

Reference: *Rolling Stone* by Fred Stone (Whittlesey House, 1945).

STRONGMEN

Strongmen were fairly popular on vaudeville bills in the 1910s and the early 1920s, despite their being little better than freak attractions. Most would boast only one name, for example, Sandow, the most famous of all strongmen. His competitors included Kronas, Medevedeff, Bertische (who would hold three men on a bar with his teeth), and Breitbart (whose 1923 act at the Orpheum, Brooklyn, included immobilizing a miniature carousel with six horses on which sat six members of the audience). In 1924 Francisco Pantilon, known as "The Lion," was popular, and there was even one female "strongman," Mary Arniotis. In 1927 a strongman who wore a hood and was known as "The Masked Athlete" was touring the vaudeville circuits.

VALESKA SURATT

Just as Theda Bara exemplified exoticism in her role as the screen's most famous vamp, Valeska Suratt represented a similar quality in vaudeville. It is no coincidence that Miss Suratt had a brief, relatively unsuccessful film career between 1915 and 1917, playing parts similar to those of Theda Bara and trying to eclipse the cinema's reigning vampire (female variety).

Valeska Suratt was born in Terre Haute, Indiana, in 1882, and details of her early life are sketchy. Her first job was apparently as an assistant in a millinery shop at five dollars a week. Eventually she became an actress in Chicago and may also have appeared in vaudeville at the turn of the century, but it is not known in what capacity. She was spotted by song-and-dance-man Billy Gould shortly after he had broken up with his first partner, Nellie Burt, and he teamed up with her to form a highly successful act which included exotic dancing by Miss Suratt and an apache dance by the two of them. The couple split up in 1908, and Valeska Suratt embarked on a solo vaudeville career, singing, dancing, and displaying her figure in a variety of stunning costumes. By 1909 she was advertising herself as "Vaudeville's Greatest Star" and "The Biggest Drawing Card in New York." Sime Silverman wrote in *Variety* (November 20, 1909), "In the show world Valeska Suratt occupies a little niche all to herself. There is no one who can look as Miss Suratt does when costumed as only she can dress."

In December of 1910 Miss Suratt was starring in her own thirty-three-minute mini-revue at Hammerstein's, suitably titled "Bouffe Variety." Her leading man was Fletcher Norton (Suratt's one-time husband), and with him she had a brief romantic interlude on stage, performed a comedy routine which included her singing "When Broadway Was a Pasture," and closed with her as the bride. *Variety* doubted the piece was good enough for "The Belle of Broadway," Valeska Suratt's new title.

The chief importance of "Bouffe Variety" is that it appears to have been the first time Valeska Suratt performed any type of playlet on the vaudeville stage, and from this time on that was to be her chief claim to fame, as a sultry and exotic leading lady of generally tawdry vaudeville melodramas. Typical of the playlets in which she appeared was *The Purple Poppy* (1917) in which she portrayed a young lady of dubious background who lures a former Russian governor to a Greenwich Village cafe and then strangles him with the scarf with which he had strangled her brother. "She has now done everything in the acting line," was the comment from *Variety* (December 7, 1917).

Popular plays were condensed into forty minutes for Valeska Suratt's vaudeville act. Jack Lait adapted his successful *One of Us* for Miss Suratt, and retitled it, as befitted her image, *Scarlet*. Valeska Suratt played a cabaret singer loved by a Society type (Eugene Strong) who pretends to be a tough guy in order to win the singer. "Miss Suratt gives a subtle impersonation of a woman of the slums who feels the urge of finer things," commented the *New York Dramatic Mirror* (November 6, 1920).

Valeska Suratt reached the peak of her career in 1920 when, as "The Dynamic Force of Vaudeville," she headlined at the Palace, moving Sime Silverman to write in *Variety* (February 20, 1920), "There are two wonders in and of vaudeville. They are Eva Tanguay and Valeska

Valeska Suratt

Suratt." Just as her rise to fame had been sudden, so was Valeska Suratt's departure from vaudeville. By the end of the twenties, the woman who "wore her clothes as a flower its petals" had vanished from the scene.

In the thirties Suratt was living in one room in a shabby New York hotel. Fannie Hurst heard of her plight and arranged a benefit performance in her honor, which netted a couple of thousand dollars for Suratt. After receiving the money, the performer disappeared for a couple of weeks. Upon her return to the hotel room, she was carrying half-a-dozen eggs and a bouquet of red roses. She had lost the two thousand dollars gambling, and was back where she started. Valeska Suratt also tried to interest the Hearst newspapers in publishing her autobiography, but when a reporter finally read the lengthy manuscript he discovered that Suratt now believed herself to be the Virgin Mary, and what he was reading was the autobiography of the mother of God. "She was completely batty," remembers one newspaperman. Valeska Suratt died in Washington, D.C., on July 3, 1962.

SWAYNE'S RATS AND CATS

Swayne's Rats and Cats was a freak animal act from the 1910s, in which rats dressed in jockey outfits would ride around a miniature racetrack on the cats' backs. How Mr. Swayne trained these natural enemies to perform together is a mystery, and another mystery to this writer is how an animal as small as a rat could be clearly seen by everyone in the vaudeville audience. In one of his books Groucho Marx tells the story of Fannie Brice, who was appearing on the same bill as Swayne's Rats and Cats, finding a rat in her dressing room. She screamed and Swayne came in and retrieved the rat, which he declared was not one of his. Next year, the rat was the star of the show. (It should, perhaps, be noted that Fred Allen, in his autobiography *Much Ado about Me,* tells exactly the same story, but claims the act was Nelson's Cats and Rats.)

Lady Alice's Pets was a similar act in the late twenties that featured trained cats, mice, and dogs. *Variety* (January 18, 1928) reported, "a couple of these babies were accomplished wire-walkers."

EVA TANGUAY

To most people Eva Tanguay was American vaudeville; for almost vaudeville's entire existence, Eva Tanguay was its biggest female star. She was overweight and ugly and her dresses were deliberately outrageous—one was covered in memo pads and pencils—and yet Eva Tanguay was adored for more than twenty years by audiences and critics. The latter were constantly looking for new ways to describe her. In 1914 *Variety* wrote that she was "vaudeville's single greatest drawing card"; on December 25, 1914, she was on the front cover of *Variety* with the caption, "The Girl Who Made Vaudeville Famous"; in 1915 Tanguay was called "The Evangelist of Joy"; in 1920 she was "The Dynamic Force of Vaudeville"; and that same year the *New York Dramatic Mirror* hailed her as

Eva Tanguay

"Vaudeville's Greatest Box Office Attraction" and described her as "The Man-o-War of Vaudeville."

Eva Tanguay's appeal for those who never saw or heard her is, of course, difficult to explain. Phonograph recordings do not do her justice. Photographs seem to be deliberately posed to show her at her most repellant and outrageous, with bosoms bursting out of bras and thighs rippling with fat. Douglas Gilbert thought it easy to analyze her act: "It was assault and battery." And that, to a degree, does sum up the secret of Eva Tanguay's success. She did have boundless energy. She sang suggestive songs in an inimitable fashion, with a blatant delivery which proved the point of her most famous song, "I Don't Care." She really didn't care what people thought of her, be those people critics, audiences, or theatre managers.

Above all, Eva Tanguay was a perennial youngster; she was ever youthful, and audiences who had grown up with her could forget the passing years, watching her changeless, ageless, frantic gyrations. In her book on the Palace, Marian Spitzer wrote, "Eva had the fizz and taste of a not-very-good brand of champagne," but even mediocre champagne can seem good and fizz well to an unsophisticated taste, and that was what comprised much of vaudeville's audience. Cheap champagne she may have been, but she was never cold duck.

On October 6, 1915, the *New York Dramatic Mirror* reviewed her act and noted, "We can't imagine anyone sitting back in his theater chair and placidly observing Eva Tanguay. There's no passive way of watching the Cyclonic One. When the spotlight centers upon the corner of the stage and the trombones blare, as the Tanguay moment

Eva Tanguay

choir—one would never have guessed it from her later career—and appearing in amateur nights at Parson's Hall in Holyoke, Massachusetts, where her parents had moved from Canada. Later she played child parts in the Rose Stahl Repertoire Company, and for five years she toured as Cedric Errol in *Little Lord Fauntleroy.* On February 11, 1901, she opened at Hammerstein's Victoria Theatre in *My Lady,* and, as she recalled, "Several musical numbers were given me that had been promised a favorite chorus girl and that settled it. Obstacles of all sorts were put in my way to prevent my success, but I started to fight and discovered I had a temper that had been given me to carry me through life." By 1903 she was starring in the Eva Tanguay Comedy Company and was acclaimed as the youngest star on the American stage; she starred in *The Office Boy* (1903), *The Sambo Girl* (1904), and *A Good Fellow* (1906). Shortly after playing in *A Good Fellow,* Eva Tanguay entered vaudeville and almost never left it again for the next twenty-five years.

The mass of frizzy blond hair, animated arms and legs, and a big voice singing lyrics that no one would believe could be produced by a sane person was vaudeville's newest hit. In 1908 she introduced the story of Salome to vaudeville audiences and created a sensation, not to mention a host of imitators. By 1910 she was asking—and getting—$3,500 a week, making her the highest-salaried star in vaudeville, beating out Ethel Barrymore who could ask $3,000 for a week's engagement. There was more than a hint of truth to a song Eva Tanguay introduced in 1915:

Eva Tanguay

comes, you have such a feeling as we suspect a staid resident of London harbors when a Zeppelin hovers in the English evening mists. There's a tingling sensation of electrical expectancy.... If ever the United States becomes involved in war, we recommend Miss Tanguay as recruiting sergeant extraordinary." (The trombones, by the way, were always used by Tanguay to announce her entrance.)

Apart from "I Don't Care," none of Eva Tanguay's songs has achieved lasting fame, perhaps because no one could sing them the way she did. One might listen in vain today to hear "I'd Rather Be a Booster Than a Knocker" (1916), "Tune in on Eva" (1921), "I May Be a Nut, But I'm Not a Crossword Fan" (1921), "I Want Somebody to Go Wild with Me" (1913), "It's All Been Done Before, But Not the Way I Do It" (1913), and "Go as Far as You Like" (1913). As the *New York Dramatic Mirror* noted in 1915, all her numbers were Tanguayesque, distinctly and thunderously personal.

Off stage, Eva Tanguay was apparently as tempestuous as she was on. She argued with everyone, totally ignored E. F. Albee's puritanical dictates on type of material that could be used in his theatres, constantly walked out on engagements because of imagined or actual slights, and once even threw a stagehand down a flight of stairs because he was in her way. In a 1908 article in *Variety,* Eva Tanguay admitted that her success relied in part on the fact that she did behave in a crazy fashion, and because she was a terrible and crazy actress, who acted like an insane person, audiences flocked to see her.

Eva Tanguay was born in Marbleton, Canada, on August 1, 1878. By the age of ten she was singing in a church

There's method in my madness,
There's a meaning for my style;
The more they raise my salary,
The crazier I'll be.

In 1916 she demanded a weekly salary of $10,000 and a guarantee of three years work before she would agree to star in films. It was claimed that Tanguay earned more than two million dollars in vaudeville, all of which she lost in the Wall Street crash.

Ted Waldman worked with Eva Tanguay in her early days, playing his harmonica while she changed clothes and exchanging crosstalk with her from the stage box. He remembers her as a complex personality, a mixture of eccentricity and warmth. Often she would send him across the street to take a hundred-dollar bill to a beggar, with instructions not to divulge from where the money came. As part of her act Tanguay used a pet monkey, and when it died in San Francisco, she had Waldman bury it in Golden Gate Park. That night, she worried that the monkey would be cold and ordered Ted to return and dig it up.

The years did not dim Eva Tanguay's popularity. When she appeared at the Palace in January of 1921, she had to admit that she was not the Eva of her prime—Tanguay never lied about her age—but a year earlier, on December 13, 1920, she had appeared at the Coliseum Theatre and played to the biggest matinée audience since the theatre opened. Reviewing Tanguay's January 1924 Palace appearance, *Variety* (January 17, 1924) wrote, "What Ruth is to baseball, Dempsey to pugilism and Chaplin to pic-tures, Tanguay is to vaudeville. She embodies the spirit of youth in her work, her personality is elusive and baffling as ever, and she has the color that penetrates beyond the four walls of a theatre and cashes in at the box office."

Eva Tanguay returned to vaudeville in 1930 after a three-year absence. For an opening number to her act, she sang, "Back Doing Business at the Same Old Stand," followed by "Mae West, Texas, and Me," a comedy number about the mob having dubbed her, Miss West, and Texas Guinan as "The Unholy Three." In 1931 Tanguay was touring with the Fanchon and Marco unit.

As the years went by, vaudeville died and Eva Tanguay dropped from the public eye, becoming more and more reclusive in her Hollywood, California, home. (She had announced in March of 1917 that henceforth she would make her home and her headquarters in Los Angeles.) On her sixty-eighth birthday, she gave an interview through the screen of her bedroom window to a reporter from the *Los Angeles Times,* and told of her hopes for a film based on her life. This was to come to reality after her death in the dismal 1952 George Jessel production of *The I Don't Care Girl,* starring Mitzi Gaynor in the title role. "The I Don't Care Girl" died, after years of ill health, on January 11, 1947. Her last years were in pitiful contrast to the fabulous era of vaudeville through which she had lived and with which her name was synonymous.

Reference: "Success" by Eva Tanguay in *Variety,* Vol. 13, No. 1 (December 12, 1908), page 34.

FAY TEMPLETON

Eva Tanguay as Salome

Fay Templeton

Fay Templeton

One of the truly old-time favorites of the legitimate and vaudeville stages, actress, singer, and comedienne Fay Templeton had a career which was crammed with excitement even before this century began. She was born on December 25, 1865, in Little Rock, Arkansas, the daughter of theatrical manager and former editor of the *Tammany Times* John Templeton, in whose Templeton Opera Company she was to tour as a child. Before that, however, Fay Templeton made her first stage appearance, as a cupid singing fairy songs, on August 16, 1869. On August 19, 1873, she first appeared as Puck in Augustus Daly's production of *A Midsummer Night's Dream* at New York's Grand Opera House.

By the age of fifteen Fay Templeton had a national reputation as a light opera singer; she had also eloped with and separated from minstrel singer Billy West. In 1886 Miss Templeton made her first appearance in London, at the Gaiety Theatre, in *Monte Cristo, Junior.* It was in this production that she sang "I Like It, I Do" in a daring costume. The Lord Chamberlain, the English theatrical censor, objected to both the song and the clothing, and Fay Templeton fought his decision in the courts. Her second marriage was to Howell Osborn, known as "The King of the Dudes," a marriage which was kept secret until his death in 1895, when he bequeathed $100,000 to his wife.

After a number of successful stage performances in, among others, *Madame Favart* (1893) and *Excelsior, Jr.* (1895), Fay Templeton joined the Weber and Fields Music Hall Company for the season of 1898/99. Felix Isman

described her as "the finest feminine talent ever given to American burlesque," and with such songs as "Keep Away from Emmeline" and "What? Marry Dat Gal?," not to mention parodies of actress Ada Rehan, she took New York by storm. Fay Templeton reached even greater heights in 1905 by starring in George M. Cohan's *Forty-Five Minutes from Broadway,* and singing "Mary's a Grand Old Name."

On August 1, 1906, Fay Templeton made her third and final marriage, to the wealthy Pennsylvania industrialist William Patterson and announced her retirement from the stage, preferring, perhaps not unnaturally, to be one of the wealthiest women in America. Miss Templeton returned, however, in 1911, to play vaudeville but refused to appear in her home town of Pittsburgh or in any other town on the Eastern seaboard. By 1913 she had changed her mind and was headlining at Hammerstein's with an act which included songs from her Weber and Fields days, "Fishing" and "Rosey Posey." She also did a song from *Forty-Five Minutes from Broadway,* "So Long Mary," together with "Poor Little Buttercup" from Gilbert and Sullivan's *H.M.S. Pinafore* (in a 1911 revival of which she had starred) and a number which indicated her weight problem, "Though I'm Stouter Than I Have Been, Still I'm Thinner Than I Was." *Variety* (February 28, 1913) hailed her as a "great old-time favorite—and artist."

In 1912 Fay Templeton had reunited with Weber and Fields to Play Peachie Mullen in *Hokey-Pokey* and Bunty Biggar in *Bunty Bulls and Strings.* She came out of retirement again for Weber and Fields in June of 1925 to headline with them in an old-timers bill at the Palace. She sang Lillian Russell's famous song, "Come Down, My Evenin' Star," after being wheeled out in a wheel chair by Weber and Fields—a gag about Fay Templeton's massive weight. After performing some of her own hits of two decades earlier, "Ma Blushin' Rose," "Dinah," and "Lou," Fay Templeton broke down and wept. "There was many a dim eye in the audience that lighted with a new fire at the thoughts that came crowding back again," commented *Variety* (June 10, 1925).

Fay Templeton had one final, glorious moment in the theatre before her death in San Francisco on October 3, 1939. She played Aunt Minnie in the original 1933 production of *Roberta* and introduced Jerome Kern's haunting melody, "Yesterdays." And what yesterdays they had been for Fay Templeton, one of the great comic ladies of the American stage.

EVELYN NESBIT THAW

Had it not been for the sensational murder of architect Stanford White by Evelyn Nesbit's husband, millionaire Harry K. Thaw, there would have been no entry in this book on Evelyn Nesbit Thaw, whose stage career prior to her marriage was exclusively that of a chorus girl. But Evelyn Nesbit became more than a mere vaudevillian, she was the freak act of all time, who proved Willie Hammerstein's claim that vaudeville audiences would pay good money to see newspaper headliners, particularly when

Evelyn Nesbit Thaw

those headliners had been involved in sexual escapades that led to murder.

Evelyn Nesbit was born on December 25, 1884, in Tarentum, Pennsylvania and came to New York with her mother around 1900. In New York, Evelyn was an artist's model—in particular for Charles Dana Gibson's "The Eternal Question"—and eventually a chorus girl in *Florodora,* from which came the popular song, "Tell Me Pretty Maiden, Are There Any More at Home Like You?" Like many other chorus girls, apparently, Evelyn Nesbit met Stanford White, who seduced her, and one of whose favorite relaxations was to place Evelyn, often naked, on a red velvet swing in his studio apartment. Evelyn Nesbit was quite a girl from all accounts, for aside from swinging on the red velvet swing, she found time to have a tempestuous affair with the young John Barrymore. In addition, she met Harry K. Thaw, a Philadelphia millionaire who was obviously mentally unstable and who became infatuated with the young girl. On April 5, 1905, Evelyn and Thaw were married. Thaw had learned of Stanford White's part in his wife's losing her virginity and brooded about the matter constantly until, on June 25, 1906, during a performance of *Mamzelle Champagne* at the Roof Garden of Madison Square Garden, he shot White to death. Naturally, the murder and the trial, or to be more precise the two trials that followed, caused a sensation. "Stanny White was killed," Evelyn Nesbit reportedly said once, "but my fate was worse. I lived."

As early as October of 1908, Evelyn Nesbit Thaw was offered $3,000 a week to appear in vaudeville. All that was required of her was that she be seated in a box during an

audience song, but Mrs. Thaw declined, stating, "I will not consider the vaudeville stage under any circumstance." However by 1913 her circumstances had changed. Harry Thaw's mother was determined that her daughter-in-law should return to the gutter from which she was sure she had come, and Evelyn was having financial problems.

H. B. Marinelli, the highly successful international agent responsible for the fame of Gaby Deslys, among others, arranged for her to appear in the 1913 revue *Hello Ragtime* at the London Hippodrome. Marinelli found her a partner in the person of Jack Clifford (whose real name was Virgil Montani) who had been teaching English society how to dance the foxtrot and one-step. After her success in *Hello Ragtime,* Evelyn was booked by Willie Hammerstein into his Victoria Theatre at $1,750 a week. He did not believe the publicity would sustain Evelyn Nesbit Thaw's appearances at the theatre for more than two weeks, but she insisted on a four-week guarantee and, in fact, had no problem in filling the theatre for that length of time. The management netted a profit of $100,000, which established Evelyn as the biggest single drawing card in any vaudeville theatre.

As for the act itself, which, incidentally, marked Mrs. Thaw's first Broadway appearance in ten years, it consisted of three dances, which Evelyn performed in a transparent, yellow, ankle-length dress with her hair hanging down her back. In the final dance Evelyn clung around Clifford's neck while he swung her—shades of that red velvet swing! "It's a nice act if you don't stop to analyze too closely," reported *Variety* (August 8, 1913).

Later in 1913 Evelyn Nesbit Thaw toured for Comstock and Gest at a salary of $3,250 a week. In April of 1914 she announced she would drop the name of Thaw. The Thaw family was giving her problems, for aside from Harry's penchant for escaping from the various mental institutions in which he had been confined, his mother financed an organization of civic-minded religious leaders who would demand that Evelyn be arrested for immoral dancing.

In September of 1917 Evelyn Nesbit dropped Jack Clifford, whom she had married when her divorce from Thaw became final, from her act, and took a new dancing partner, Bobby O'Neill. Evelyn also made occasional film appearances. They included *Threads of Destiny* (1914), *Redemption* (1917), and *The Hidden Woman* (1922). "I just have to succeed. I must make money for myself and my little boy. There's his education and all the years to come. I *must* be successful," she pitifully told a 1919 fan magazine reporter.

Evelyn Nesbit's vaudeville career ended in the twenties, although she occasionally appeared at such night spots as Chicago's Moulin Rouge, where, in 1925, she sang "I'm a Broad-Minded Broad from Broadway." During the prohibition era she was involved in various roadhouses as a hostess and entertainer. In 1955 Hollywood produced a feature about her life, *The Girl in the Red Velvet Swing,* starring Joan Collins in the title role. It was not successful.

The last years of Evelyn Nesbit Thaw's life were spent in a downtown Los Angeles hotel room. She told a reporter in 1962, "I'm registered here under my maiden name, Evelyn Nesbit. I'm still reading and trying to understand, just as I did when I was a girl. I'm still interested in that world of art and music and beauty which Stanford White first showed me, so long ago." Thaw died in Miami, Florida, in 1947. Evelyn Nesbit died in a Santa Monica, California, nursing home on January 18, 1967. "The Tired Butterfly," the title of a famous photograph for which Evelyn posed on Stanford White's bearskin rug, died in an age which had forgotten her, and only a handful attended her funeral.

References: "Evelyn Nesbit, the Ambitious" by Harrison Haskins in *Motion Picture Magazine,* Vol. 16, No. 12 (January, 1919), pages 38–39 and 108. *Evelyn Nesbit and Stanford White: Love and Death in the Gilded Cage* by Michael Macdonald Mooney (William Morrow and Company, 1976).

VESTA TILLEY

Vesta Tilley was perhaps the greatest male impersonator of all time; she was certainly the best known. She was a slightly built, flat-chested woman, and her male characters, played in evening dress or military attire, were more reminiscent of boys than of men. Vesta Tilley played a dapper little man—as one critic wrote, "the dandiest fellah turned sixteen." There was little spontaneity to her characterization, for every movement and inflection had been carefully rehearsed. There are probably few people alive today who saw Vesta Tilley on the stage, and thus it is hard to explain her fame, which is probably based chiefly on the fact that she was the first woman to adopt a totally masculine attire in her act. Prior to Vesta Tilley, women had usually portrayed male characters in tights and strictly feminine versions of male clothing. But once she appeared on the scene there was no one who would argue with the statement in *Variety* (December 18, 1909), "For male impersonations Vesta Tilley is the standard."

She was born Matilda Alice Powles, in Worcester, England, on May 13, 1864. Her father, Harry Ball, was the chairman (a sort of master of ceremonies) at the St. George's Hall Music Hall in Nottingham. And it was on the stage of her father's theatre in 1868 that Vesta Tilley made her debut. She first appeared in male attire at the age of five, and she continued to adopt that guise for the rest of her career. In her 1934 autobiography, *Recollections of Vesta Tilley,* she wrote, "I concluded that female costume was rather a drag. I felt I could express myself better if I were dressed as a boy." By 1876 she was fairly popular in provincial British music halls; appearing with her father, she was billed as "The Great Little Tilley." Her London debut came on March 25, 1878, at the Royal Theatre in Holborn. Thereafter, Vesta Tilley became known as "The London Idol." At that first London engagement she sang "The Pet of Rotten Row" and "Near the Workhouse Door."

Vesta Tilley made her first American appearance at Tony Pastor's on April 16, 1894, and was hailed by critic Alan Dale as "The Irving of the Halls." At the Colonial in May of 1906, *Variety's* Chicot (Epes W. Sargent) saw

Vesta Tilley

her act and wrote, "She is the one male impersonator on the stage today who really looks like a boy; her costumes are exact and she wears a wig that might well be her own hair. . . . But Miss Tilley is something more than a clotheshorse. She is a leader of style and every detail of dress is merely the complement to her detail of rendition. She is an artist."

The songs for which Vesta Tilley is best remembered are "After the Ball" (the title of a 1957 British film loosely based on her life), "Following in Father's Footsteps," and "Algy" ("the Piccadilly Johnny with the Little Glass Eye"). During the First World War she sang "Jolly Good Luck to the Girl That Loves a Sailor," which became a recruiting song, as did her "I Joined the Army Yesterday, So the Army of Today's All Right." She was the first male impersonator to appear at a royal command performance, in 1912, and legend has it that Queen Mary was so offended by the idea of a woman dressed in man's clothing that she turned her back on the star.

On June 5, 1920, Vesta Tilley gave her farewell performance at the London Coliseum. She sang "Jolly Good Luck to the Girl That Loves a Sailor" and took seventeen curtain calls. Ellen Terry presented her with "The People's Tribute to Vesta Tilley," a number of volumes containing two million signatures of her admirers. Vesta Tilley had married Walter de Frece, who managed many British music halls, on August 6, 1890. Between 1920 and 1931 he was a member of the British Parliament, and his wife actively helped to promote his career. He died in Monaco in January of 1935. Vesta Tilley never returned to the stage after her 1920 farewell, preferring life as Lady de Frece, and she died in London on September 16, 1952.

At her farewell to the stage, Vesta Tilley sang "Girls, If You'd Like to Love a Soldier, You Can All Love Me." From the gallery came the shout, "We do."

FRANK TINNEY

Frank Tinney

Frank Tinney was perhaps the best of vaudeville's black-face comics, following in the footsteps of George "Honey Boy" Evans. Joe Cook called Tinney "the greatest natural comic ever developed in America," although his humor, considered today, and perhaps even in Tinney's day, is pretty dreadful, as the following indicates:

Lend me a dollar for a week, old man.
Who is the weak old man?
Why is an old maid like a green tomater?
Because it's hard to mate her.

Possibly the humor was as much in Tinney's delivery as in itself, for Wynn in *Variety* (June 4, 1910), reviewing one of Tinney's first vaudeville appearances, at the Fifth Avenue Theatre, wrote, "His material consists of a bunch of nothingness moulded together into seventeen minutes of original and rare humor. . . . Tinney's is the most original offering brought to Broadway this season." Usually, as he did in 1910, Tinney would chat with the orchestra conductor, but sometimes he would confide in the audience, perhaps telling them that the leading lady was so crazy about him she couldn't answer when he spoke to her, but simply looked at him without a word.

Frank Tinney was born in Philadelphia on March 29, 1878, and claimed to have made his first stage appearance in blackface at the age of four at Philadelphia's Bijou Theatre. From Philadelphia, his mother took him to Texas where he perfected his blackface comedy routine and where he was spotted by a vaudeville agent named Max Hart, whose clients included Eddie Cantor, Fred Stone, The Avon Comedy Four, and Blossom Seeley. Hart brought Tinney to New York and introduced him to big-time vaudeville, until by January of 1913 the comic was earning $1,000 a week at Hammerstein's. In 1913 Frank Tinney also made his London debut, at the Palace, and was an immediate success, described as "the most irresistible entertainer that America has sent us." Tinney returned to London in 1914, 1919, 1924, and 1925.

1913 was a big year for Tinney, for it also saw his performance in the *Ziegfeld Follies*, in which his ad-libbing assured him as much success as the *Follies'* other comedian, Leon Errol. (In 1924 Frank Tinney was to make headlines when he consistently beat up a Follies showgirl by the name of Imogene Wilson, with whom he was romantically involved. One sordid story had it that Tinney, in a fit of drunken rage, took a pair of scissors and cut off one of the girl's nipples. Imogene Wilson fled the country, obtained film work in Germany, and subsequently became a fairly popular American film star under the name of Mary Nolan.) Throughout his early career, Frank Tinney alternated vaudeville with appearances in such Broadway shows as *Watch Your Step* (1914), *The Century Girl* (1916), and *Doing Our Bit* (1917).

In the twenties Frank Tinney stopped appearing in blackface, but as he had never used a Negro dialect, it made no change in his act. He did reintroduce a novelty from the early years of vaudeville, that of making his navel whistle, reminiscent of a French act from the turn of the century in which the performer would play tunes and perform various feats with his anus. In 1926 Frank Tinney suffered a complete breakdown, probably brought on by the Imogene Wilson scandal, and retired from the stage. "The Revelation in Burnt Cork," as he was once billed, died in the Veterans Hospital at Northport, Long Island, on November 27, 1940; his service as a captain in the Quartermasters Corps during the First World War had made him eligible to enter the hospital.

ARTHUR TRACY

"Radio's Voice of Romance," Arthur Tracy, had a fine baritone voice with a hint of a rich Irish brogue. He was at his best singing sentimental ballads such as "Trees," "It's My Mother's Birthday Today," "In a Little Gypsy Tea Room," "Danny Boy," and, of course, Tracy's theme song, "Marta" (the "rambling rose of the wildwood" who rambled through radio, vaudeville, and films with considerable success during the thirties). Arthur Tracy took himself very seriously, which helped in view of the type of material he was expected to sing. Margaret Lockwood, who was Arthur Tracy's leading lady in the 1937 British film *The Street Singer,* once told me that he would sit for hours in his dressing room listening to his own recordings with tears in his eyes.

Arthur Tracy

Tracy was born in Philadelphia on June 25, 1903. "I started singing when I was about six years old," he recalls. "I sang in churches, synagogues, at weddings and parties, wherever I could get a dollar in those days." Initially he took lessons at four dollars a week, and he also learned a lot from his father. In addition, he would listen to Caruso's recordings, buy sheet music of the arias, and mark Caruso's nuances. As far as Tracy is concerned, Caruso was his teacher, although he also acknowledges a great debt to Horatio Connell, "a fine baritone," one of his instructors at Philadelphia's Curtis Institute. In Philadelphia in 1927, he was booked into the Logan Theatre on North Broad Street and played there for eleven months. There he sang the type of songs always associated with him and notes, "The audience itself teaches you how to behave on stage." At this time, Tracy was approached by the Philadelphia Opera Society to perform with them at $200 an appearance, but, as he admits now with regret, he turned down the offer because he was making $300 a week in vaudeville at the Logan.

On July 13, 1931, he was heard on 187 CBS stations with his own program, in which he was billed simply as "The Street Singer." "Overnight, I'm happy to report, it was sensational," he comments with pride, and soon Tracy had four fifteen-minute shows a week on CBS and was earning a salary of $3,000 a week. "I liked to be known only as the Street Singer," he recalls.

I loved the air of mystery on the program, with its closing announcement of "There he goes, your Street Singer, to pick new melodies for your entertainment." I was only known to the trade, the music men. By the third week of my appearances on the air I was getting two thousand letters a week, the majority asking who the Street Singer was. When Mr. Bill Paley gave me six weeks to do or die, as he said, I had six weeks in which to prepare my program. I worked to conceal my identity. I finally decided because of the international scope of my work—ten languages—and the types of songs that I would call myself the International Balladeer. Three days prior to my first program, I picked up the *New York Times,* turned to the theatre page, and found an item which said Freddie Lonsdale had just arrived with a new play titled *The Street Singer.* I thought, "My God, why didn't I think of that?" For fear of being accused of plagiarism I appended the phrase, "of the air"—calling myself the Street Singer of the Air—but then a lawyer told me I didn't need that because you can't copyright the English language.

After five months on radio, the identity of the Street Singer was revealed.

"Marta" became Arthur Tracy's theme song in August of 1931. He recalls, "Having adopted the title of Street Singer, I temporarily adopted 'East Side, West Side' as my theme song, but as I went on for some three or four weeks doing it, I realized it did not fit into my type of singing, my type of program. I went around in search of some beautiful melody to adopt, something new. I walked into Marks Music one day when I heard this beautiful strain coming from behind a closed door. I walked in, and there was a little Cuban—he was so tiny his feet didn't even touch the floor—and he was playing this beautiful strain. I wanted to buy the song, but Mr. Marks said, 'No, songs that are demonstrated in my office, I buy them.' So he bought it. Millions have been made off that song. The Cuban had peddled the song for eight years and no one would buy it." Arthur Tracy has recorded "Marta" many, many times in a recording career that began in 1931 with "I'm All Dressed Up with a Broken Heart" for RCA, and to date includes 750 recordings.

One of Tracy's earliest major vaudeville bookings was as "The Mystery Man of the Air" at the Hippodrome in December of 1931. *Variety* was not impressed by his act, describing Tracy as a neutral performer who used no showmanship. "What suggests a splendid voice is spoiled by a cold style of presentation," commented Rush at the end of his review. As Arthur Tracy's radio fame grew— in 1932 he was featured along with Ruth Etting and the Boswell Sisters on Chesterfield's "Music That Satisfies"— his vaudeville career expanded. Vaudeville offered radio listeners an opportunity to meet their favorite singer in person, and it also provided Tracy with the means to polish and perfect his act.

In 1935 Arthur Tracy went to England for a seven-week vaudeville tour and remained there for the next six years, starring in five films: *Flirtation* (1935), *Limelight* (1935), *The Street Singer* (1937), *Command Performance* (1937), and *Follow Your Star* (1938). (Tracy had also appeared in the 1932 Paramount film tribute to radio, *The Big Broadcast*.) His style seemed to suit the English mood; he still has a fan club in England and Tracy's recordings continue to be available there. Interestingly, Arthur Tracy's singing style is very similar to that of the English Cavan O'Connor, who began his career as a mystery singer on British radio in the early thirties, billed as "The Vagabond Lover."

Arthur Tracy returned to the United States in 1941 and has continued his career up to the present. The accordion he once used has been dropped, because, as Tracy is quick to admit, he is not a good accordionist and without the accordion he is able to use his hands eloquently. With his unsophisticated songs, Arthur Tracy is a pleasant throwback to an earlier, simpler, unamplified time in show business, when, as Tracy points out, an audience recognized that what came from the heart goes to the heart.

Reference: "Arthur Tracy" in *The Vaudevillians* by Bill Smith (Macmillan, 1976), pages 219–228.

SOPHIE TUCKER

Sophie Tucker was the "red-hot mama" who became the "big fat mama"—she changed the lyrics—as exemplified by her theme song, "Some of These Days"; along the way, she became an American institution. The plump Sophie Tucker of later years was described by one critic as "a glistening iceberg cut loose from its foundation"; to an earlier generation, to her vaudeville and burlesque audiences, she was slim, not exactly beautiful but certainly not unattractive, and she had a sexy, vibrant way with a song. She claimed to have originated jazz on the stage, and, who knows, perhaps she did, for she had a flair for songs like "We Are Simply Full of Jazz" and "When Fan Tan Takes Her Jazz Band to Tokyo." *Life* magazine captured the essence of her style when it noted, "Her exuberance and racy songs made people feel wicked without the wear and tear of being so." But there was a gentler side to her singing, a side which was exhibited less as she grew older, and Mrs. Gus Kahn remembers, "She could sing a ballad beautifully. She could sing anything—anything at all." Who else could have put such feeling into "My Yiddishe Mama"? The style of singing was brassy and loud, and Sophie Tucker talked a song as much as she sang it; there was worldliness in her voice, but there was also kindness and compassion.

As she grew older—and fatter—Sophie Tucker realized the need for glamorous clothes and for songs which poked gentle fun at her girth and her age, songs like "Life Begins at Forty." She would still sing the old standards, such as "Some of These Days," written in 1910 by Shelton Brooks, and "After You're Gone," written in 1918 by Henry Creamer and Turner Layton, but she added new, saucy numbers to her repertoire. With advancing years came "I'm the 3-D Momma with the Big Wide Screen," "I May Be Getting Older Every Day (But Getting Younger Every Night)," "There's No Business Like That Certain Business—That Certain Business Called Love," and, of course, "I'm the Last of the Red Hot Mamas." The

Sophie Tucker

title was self-given, but it was certainly deserved, summing up her vitality and zest for living.

As she writes in her autobiography, Sophie Tucker was born on the road, not on a vaudeville circuit but the road between Russia and the United States while the family was emigrating. Her parents' name was Kalish, but her father changed the name to Abuza, for fear of the Russians discovering he was a deserter from the military. Sophie Abuza was born, probably in Poland, on January 13, 1888, although in later years she claimed the year of her birth was 1884. Anyway, whatever the year, Sophie Tucker was three months old when her family arrived in the United States.

Sophie's parents opened a restaurant in Hartford, Connecticut, and there she began to sing for the customers. At the age of thirteen Sophie was singing in amateur concerts. While still in her teens, she was married, albeit briefly, to Louis Tuck, from whose last name her stage name originated. In 1906 she told Willie Howard—who was playing Poli's Theatre in New Haven with his brother Eugene—that she was determined to enter show business, and he gave her a letter of introduction to composer Harry Von Tilzer. ("Wait till the Sun Shines Nellie," "A Bird in a Gilded Cage," "I Want a Girl Just Like the Girl That Married Dear Old Dad," etc.). He was unable to help her, but at least Sophie was in New York, and eventually she got a job singing at the Cafe Monopol. "I worked on Second Avenue in one place where I not only sang but had to wash dishes and make knishes," she recalled. "Not many young performers of today would be willing to sacrifice their lives for their profession as we did in those days."

More amateur nights followed at the 125th Street Theatre, where Sophie Tucker performed her act in blackface for the first time. Blackface became an established part of her early act, and she was soon billed as "The World-Renowned Coon Shouter." Following her first professional New York vaudeville appearance at the 116th Street Music Hall, Sophie Tucker became a regular in small-town houses. She appeared at Tony Pastor's 14th Street Theatre, and was booked on the Manchester and Hills burlesque circuit. While playing a theatre in Holyoke, Massachusetts, Sophie Tucker was seen by Marc Klaw (of Klaw and Erlanger), and he offered her a part in the second edition of *The Ziegfeld Follies*.

There is some confusion as to what happened when Sophie Tucker went into the 1909 *Ziegfeld Follies*. During the show's tryout in Atlantic City, Miss Tucker claims in her autobiography that her songs went over too well for the comfort of the star, Nora Bayes, and she ordered the newcomer's numbers cut to one. This claim is not substantiated by *Variety*, which, in its issue of June 12, 1909, reported that the *Follies* had opened at the Apollo Theatre in Atlantic City the previous Monday and that "Sophie Tucker received little chance." Certainly, when the *Follies* opened in New York at the Jardin De Paris on June 14, 1909, Sophie Tucker was performing only one number in a "Kermit Roosevelt" jungle sketch. *Variety* made no specific comment on Miss Tucker's song, but in mentioning her and another burlesque star new to the *Follies,* a Miss MacMahon, it noted that "both the burlesquers made good." If Nora Bayes did best Sophie Tucker in 1909, then Tucker certainly got the best of Bayes in 1927, when both were on the bill at a National Vaudeville Association benefit at the Palace. An argument erupted between the two as to who would appear first; Bayes announced she was the head-liner and would not permit Sophie to go on before her, but Tucker won the fight, largely because Eddie Darling, the Palace booker, was tired of Bayes's temperament and inconsiderateness. Nora Bayes was publicly humiliated, and Sophie Tucker was, as usual, the hit of the show.

After the brief unproductive spell in the *Follies,* it was back to vaudeville and the slow climb to headliner status. *Variety* first reviewed Sophie Tucker on September 4, 1909, reporting, "The young woman has a way of ingratiating herself at once, and possesses not alone good looks but magnetism to back it." Under William Morris's guidance, Sophie Tucker's fame and popularity grew; when she appeared at the American Music Hall in Chicago, Ashton Stevens wrote of her, "If Julian Eltinge's singing voice was as virile as Miss Tucker's, he would be executing a long overdue male impersonation.... Miss Tucker can move an audience or a piano with equal address." On July 24, 1914, Sophie Tucker made her debut at the Palace, on a bill which also included Joseph Santley, Chic Sale, and Sam Barton, "the cycling pantominist." *Variety* (July 31, 1914) reported, "Sophie let loose her 40-h.p. voice and sang six songs," which included "There's a Girl in the Heart of Maryland," "The International Rag," and "Who Paid the Rent for Mrs. Rip Van Winkle (When Rip Van Winkle Went Away)?" In her

book on the Palace, Marian Spitzer wrote that "if any one person could be said to have symbolized the Palace in its greatest days, that person was Sophie Tucker." But Miss Tucker did more than merely symbolize the best of a Palace bill, she symbolized—she was—vaudeville.

In the summer of 1916 Miss Tucker added five young men to her act and billed them as the kings of syncopation. They added to the performance of such songs as "I've Got a Bungalow," with its lyric:

My bills are shocking,
But I've got a Santa Claus,
Who fills my stocking

As the *New York Dramatic Mirror* (July 15, 1916) reported of the new act at the Colonial, "Miss Tucker is entertaining in her vociferous offering. In fact, she is in better form than during the past two seasons." Around this time Sophie Tucker was taking credit for the introduction of the Shimmie, and she explained to the *New York Dramatic Mirror* (February 1, 1919), "When I was known as a coon shouter, I executed a Jazz and Shimmie rhythm with every song. As inventors of Jazz and Shimmie, these other birds are wonderful aviators—their imagination takes such long flights. But don't wake them up. Just let them dream, for I'm getting the stuff that buys Liberty Bonds."

Sophie Tucker deserted vaudeville late in 1918 for an extended engagement at Reisenweber's, a popular restaurant and cabaret at Eighth Avenue and Fifty-eighth Street. There she introduced one of her most famous blues numbers, "A Good Man Is Hard to Find," singing it nightly for ten consecutive weeks. From Reisenweber's,

Sophie Tucker went into the McIntyre and Heath show, *Hello Alexander,* and from that she returned to vaudeville, at the Colonial, singing "Vamp a Little Lady," "The Wonderful Kid from Madrid," and "Won't You Bless Everybody That's Worth Blessing in My Suwanee Home?," among others. "It's a great act," reported the *New York Dramatic Mirror* (December 25, 1919). "Here's hoping vaudeville doesn't let her get away again."

There have been many jokes about Sophie Tucker's endless farewell performances, but there might have been just as many jokes concerning her returns to vaudeville in the 1910s and 1920s with new acts and new songs. There were many personifications, but when all was said and done it was still the same beloved Sophie Tucker. In 1922 she was appearing on stage with two male piano players and discussing her private life with the audience. One of those piano players was Ted Shapiro, who remained with Sophie Tucker as her accompanist until she died; the other was Jack Carrol. In 1925 she was billing herself as Dame Sophie Tucker and singing "It's How Young You Feel" and "Polly, the Pest of Hollywood." (Before billing herself as Dame Sophie Tucker, she had adopted the title of Madame, causing *Variety*'s Sime Silverman to note, "There's a $2 Madame at the Palace this week.") In 1928 Sophie Tucker's son, Bert, was part of the act, together with six Tivoli Girls; it featured Sophie's rendition of "I'm Not Taking Orders from No-One," "Nobody Loves a Fat Girl," and a Yiddish rendition of "Bye, Bye Blackbird," titled "Bye, Bye Greenburg."

In addition to vaudeville, Sophie Tucker found time to play night clubs and to become popular in England through frequent appearances at the London Palladium. She was seen on Broadway in *Leave It to Me* (1938) and *High Kickers* (1941). She appeared in seven feature films: *Honky Tonk* (1929), *Gay Love* (1934), *Broadway Melody of 1938,* (1937), *Thoroughbreds Don't Cry* (1937), *Follow the Boys* (1944) *Sensations of 1945* (1944), and *Atlantic City* (1944). She never really retired, and only months before her death in New York City on February 9, 1966, she had been working in an act with George Jessel and Ted Lewis.

Her funeral was as popular as her act had been, attended by more than 3,000 mourners. Even the Teamsters Union, whose hearse drivers were on strike, called off their picketing in deference to her memory. She herself explained one of the reasons for her lasting popularity: "It may sound corny to some, but I also have a deep love and respect for my audiences. I have a file of 7,000 names, persons I've met on my travels, and never fail to send each of them a handwritten note telling them I'll be appearing in their communities. They also receive Christmas cards from me——handwritten, because I do not employ a secretary." Only Joan Crawford was as attentive to her fans as Sophie Tucker. On August 31, 1953, the *New York Times*, on the occasion of a Golden Jubilee testimonial dinner sponsored by the Jewish Theatrical Guild of America, published an editorial which also serves as Sophie Tucker's epitaph: "To a versatile and generous trouper, we say thanks for the half-century of songs, some sad, some comic, but always entertaining."

Reference: *Some of These Days* by Sophie Tucker (Doubleday and Company, 1945).

RUDY VALEE

Rudy Vallee

In the entertainment world, Rudy Vallee is a phenomenon. He has been a major figure in the field of popular music, one of the top stars of radio in the thirties, a delightful character comedian in films in the forties and fifties, and he is still entertaining audiences today with his one-man show. And despite his status as a living legend, Rudy Vallee remains amiable and retains a sense of humor that is often directed at himself.

Rudy Vallee was born Hubert Prior Vallee in Island Pond, Vermont, on July 28, 1901, the son of the town druggist. But it was in Westbrook, Maine, that he developed his charming New England style of delivering a song or a line of dialogue. At the age of fifteen, he decided that he wanted to be a musician, joined a local band as a drummer, and adopted the first name of his idol, saxophonist Rudy Weidoeft. After graduation from Yale in June of 1927, he toured for a while with the Yale Collegians. Then, in January of 1928, he got together his own group of musicians, the Connecticut Yankees, and with them he obtained an engagement at the Heigh-Ho Club in New York. As saxophonist and director of the group, Vallee's success was almost instantaneous, and his familiar greeting, "Heigh-Ho, everybody!" first used at the Club, soon became known to a new audience on radio and in vaudeville.

Vallee was first heard on radio over New York's

WABC, broadcasting from the Heigh-Ho Club in February of 1928. After a year on local radio Vallee was picked up by NBC, and "The Rudy Vallee Show," also known as "The Fleischmann Hour," was first heard nationally on October 24, 1929. It was the first major network variety show, and with its announcer Graham McNamee, and Vallee's theme song of "My Time Is Your Time," it was to be one of the most enduring programs on radio. Vallee was noted for introducing such new talent as Alice Faye, Frances Langford, Phil Baker, Joe Penner, and Bob Burns, and in the early forties his radio program was noted for the outrageous appearances of John Barrymore. Vallee left his radio program in July of 1943, when he joined the Coast Guard to become conductor of its band. He did return to radio after the war, but without the success that he had enjoyed in the thirties.

Thanks to his New York radio broadcasts, Vallee was able to embark on a short vaudeville tour in the spring of 1929. He opened at Keith's Eighty-first Street Theatre, broke all the house records and, as Vallee himself notes, quoting publicity at the time, created "an explosion in the theatrical world." From there he moved to the Coliseum, then to the Palace, ending his initial vaudeville tour at Proctor's Eighty-sixth Street Theatre. Vallee and his Connecticut Yankees performed such numbers as "Deep Night," "Sweetheart of My Dreams," and "Sweet Lorraine." Reviewing them at the Eighty-first Street Theatre, *Variety* (February 13, 1929) commented, "With silly little props such as an assortment of carnival hats and simple hokum pantomimic business to further stress the lyric significance of their ditties, theirs proved a pleasantly unique style of popular entertainment. The chief appeal is the quiet simplicity of their music. There is no fanfare, no heavy arrangements, no hullaballoo. They rely strongly on their vocal interludes, with some comedy derived from a couple of saucy lyrics. The keynote of their instrumentation is charming softness, with plenty of rhythm from piano and traps." At the Palace Rudy Vallee and His Connecticut Yankees appeared on the same bill with the Duncan Sisters, Van and Schenck, and Joe Laurie, Jr., but they easily stole the show and were held over for a second week (which also happened at the Eighty-first Street Theatre). It was, as *Variety* (March 6, 1929) noted, an amazing achievement "for an act that hadn't seen the back of a vaude stage a month ago."

From today's viewpoint, the most delightful, and still entertaining, of the Vallee songs from this period are what he described as "nut" songs, such as the somewhat risqué "You'll Do It Someday, So Why Not Now?" Vallee and his men would perform the song complete with appropriate gestures; when they sang "You may be kissing," they blew kisses in the air, and when they sang of the land "where men are men" they would bend their elbows to show their muscles. The eight members of the Connecticut Yankees had considerable personality, as evidenced by their work on songs such as "You'll Do It Someday, So Why Not Now?" but this personality completely fails to come across in the group's first feature film, *The Vagabond Lover,* produced by RKO in 1929, which Vallee is quick to brand as the worst film ever made.

"Vaudeville was not important to my career, but it was a delightful experience," Vallee told me. "I had always enjoyed vaudeville as a child, and to be appearing on the stage with these people was really something. . . . I learned more than anything, from watching the other acts perform, about what an audience would accept and how to gain audience approval."

Vallee feels this was particularly true of his second vaudeville engagement, a long-term stint at the Brooklyn Paramount presentation house in 1930. Here Vallee conducted a twenty-four-piece orchestra on stage and also acted as master of ceremonies. The Brooklyn Paramount was built over a two-year period at a cost of five million dollars, and when it opened on November 24, 1928, its 4,500 seats made it one of the largest theatres in the country. Vallee's act there was basically a revue, titled "A Night at Villa Vallee," and although, as *Variety* (March 12, 1930) noted, "Vallee's voice has a tough time with it even by the aid of a big megaphone," his thousands of devoted fans greeted the crooner's appearance enthusiastically. Had he wished, there is little question that Rudy Vallee could have continued for many more years in vaudeville.

References: *Vagabond Dreams Come True* by Rudy Vallee (Grosset and Dunlap, 1930). *My Time Is Your Time* by Rudy Vallee (Ivan Obolensky, 1962). *Let the Chips Fall* by Rudy Vallee (Stackpole Books, 1975). "Rudy Vallee" in *The Vaudevillians* by Bill Smith (Macmillan, 1976), pages 229–238.

VAN AND SCHENCK

Van and Schenck

"The Pennant Winning Battery of Songland"—a phrase invented by publicist Jack Lait—was the billing of Van and Schenck, one of vaudeville's favorite singing teams from the late 1910s on. Gus Van was the slightly overweight member of the team who specialized in dialect songs, while Joe Schenck played the piano, often using only one hand. The two sang in close harmony and also performed comedy dialect songs in Italian or Yiddish, numbers like "Pasta Vazoola" or "Hungry Women" (which is usually associated with Eddied Cantor, but which Gus Van sang with a pronounced Yiddish accent). The act was, as *The Billboard* commented on March 3, 1928, "The best of its kind in the business."

August van Glone, to give Gus Van his correct name, and Joseph T. Schenck were both born in Brooklyn, New York, and first met when both attended the same public school. As children they appeared at Brooklyn's Myrtle Avenue Picture House and also performed at the Lenore Club, which was later to become the Van and Schenck Club, and was located at twelve Cypress Hill Street, Glendale, Queens. While planning a professional stage act, Van and Schenck landed a job as trolley car operators, Schenck as the conductor, and Van as the pilot. Eventually they entered vaudeville, but not as a team, for Gus Van initially appeared as part of the Edwards, Ryan, and Keeney act. Around 1910 Van finally teamed up in vaudeville with Joe Schenck, who only played the piano until his voice changed to a pleasant tenor which blended well with Van's rich baritone. As early as August 30, 1912, *Variety* wrote of them, "Van and Schenck need never worry about anything as long as they stick together and their voices stick with them.... Van and Schenck form one of the best teams of its kind in vaudeville." By 1916 the two were fairly well known in vaudeville, and when, in May of that year, the couple headlined at the Royal Theatre, *Variety* (May 5, 1916) noted, "They set a pace rather difficult for others to follow. The pianist makes a strong bid for popular favor with a well trained tenor voice of commercial proportions, while the dialect singer stands out conspicuously as one of the best in his line. The boys have chosen a sensible repertoire, closing with 'Good Old Days Back Home,' although the pianist might have picked a better ballad for his solo.... They scored a decisive hit."

In 1916 Florenz Ziegfeld hired Van and Schenck to appear in his and Charles Dillingham's production of *The Century Girl,* which opened at the Century Theatre on November 16, 1916, with music by Victor Herbert and Irving Berlin. The stars of the show were Hazel Dawn, Elsie Janis, Leon Errol, and Frank Tinney. The following year, Van and Schenck went into Florenz Ziegfeld's *Midnight Frolic* on the Amsterdam Theatre Roof but quit in April of 1918 apparently after overhearing Ziegfeld make a disparaging remark about their being "cabaret hams." That comment notwithstanding, Van and Schenck were back with Ziegfeld in 1919 as two of the stars of that year's edition of the *Follies,* which opened at the Amsterdam Theatre on June 16. They were featured in the Minstrel Show sequence in the second half of the program, which included an impersonation of famed minstrel George Primrose by Marilyn Miller. Van and Schenck sang perhaps their most famous song, Irving Berlin's "Mandy, " and also performed a song routine with Eddie Dowling and John Steel. Through the 1921 edition of the *Follies,* Van and Schenck were regulars in the Ziegfeld company.

Radio's "The Eveready Hour" made its debut on New York station WEAF on December 4, 1923, and Van and Schenck were regulars on this pioneering major radio variety show. After Schenck's death, Gus Van was to be heard on radio for a while as the interlocuter on "The Sinclair Minstrel Show."

Aside from vaudeville, the team appeared in night clubs and also went to Hollywood, to appear in film shorts and one feature, for M-G-M, *They Learned about Women.* In this 1930 film they played major league baseball stars, supported by Bessie Love and Benny Rubin. Billed as "The Shahs of Songland," Van and Schenck made their last Palace Theatre appearance together the week of June 7, 1930. While appearing at the Fischer Theatre, Detroit, Joe Schenck suffered a heart attack. He died in Gus Van's arms at the Book Cadillac Hotel on June 28, 1930; he was thirty-nine years old. As a partnership, Gus and Van were almost unique in that they had remained friends since childhood and even owned homes within a block of each other.

After Schenck's death, Gus Van went solo, making his New York debut at the Albee Theatre in his home town of Brooklyn early in September of 1930. He opened with "Why Kentucky Bids the World Good Morning" and then spoke about the trolley route that he and Schenck had before entering vaudeville. Afterward he performed a number of dialect songs: an Irish, an Italian, and a Yiddish number, "Is dat Religion?" Two straight numbers completed the program: "That's the Kind of Baby I Am" and "I Like to Stay after School." As *Variety* (September 3, 1930) reported, Gus Van closed the show and stopped it. Gus Van explained that he always sang his numbers to the spirit of his dead partner: "I am as uncertain as every mortal about what happens to the soul after death, but if I didn't know absolutely that Joe Schenck's spirit was listening to my every note—that he is keeping me in pitch, so to speak—as he always did when we were partners, I would never make another public appearance."

Later in September of 1930 Gus Van returned as a solo act to the Palace. *Variety* (September 17, 1930) reported,

Palace audience Saturday afternoon had its first chance in a long while to go sentimental, and it did even more so than Gus Van, the subject of the demonstration, who appeared to have difficulty with his own emotions. Gus kept as straight-faced as possible while the reception lasted but was said to have broken down sobbing in his dressing room. No wonder.... It was a great tribute to this remaining member of vaudeville's greatest singing team. He did not mention the name of Joe Schenck at any time, an immediate sign of good taste, with the lamented Joe suggested only faintly by lyric. Announcing he had learned it the day before, thinking it particularly suited to this house, Gus sang that he's not so much alone. Gus was right when, while thanking the audience, he said that from the Palace response he sees a bright future for himself as a single entertainer. There is no doubt he will. This singer as a single is a jewel character man, a neat, smart-acting showman. No one in vaude so well versed in the various dialects. In the course of one number, wherein reference was made to the old car barn days by a nicely written introduction, Van does Hebe, Irish, Cockney, Wop, Dutch and Coon, the latter as a colored preacher delivering a sermon and the rest mainly snatches from the old repertoire. He impressed as a singer and single act despite the audience's sob. Van will not have any trouble with his single.

Gus Van continued to entertain through the forties, serving as president of the American Guild of Variety Artists, of which he was made a life member in 1949. Eventually he retired to Miami Beach, Florida, where he died after being struck by a car on March 13, 1968.

VASCO

A vaudeville performer with an act similar in style to that of Buddy Rogers in that he played all the various instruments of the orchestra, Vasco was known as "The Mad Musician." He could play twenty-eight instruments, and *Variety* (April 13, 1907) noted, "Not only does Vasco play each in a manner to indicate his ability, but finds time to inject comedy and acrobatics." He learned his trade at the British Army Musical Academy, Kneller Hall, and toured the world with Frank Fillis's Circus. Vasco made his American debut at the Alhambra in 1897 and continued to perform until the spring of 1923, when he made his last appearance with a circus in Madrid. He died in London on May 9, 1925, at the reported age of fifty-six.

VESTA VICTORIA

Vesta Victoria was a plump character songstress, noted for her low-pitched voice, clear diction, and energy, who became as popular in America as she was in her native England. Her songs were usually concerned with some misfortune of which she was the victim. "Waiting at the Church" told of her as a stranded bride at the altar. "Poor John," its successor, which became an instant hit when she first sang it at the Colonial Theatre in 1907, was the sad lament of a girl's first meeting with her prospective mother-in-law:

John took me round to see his mother!
His mother! His mother!
And while he introduced us to each other,
She weighed up everything that I had on.
She put me through a cross-examination,
I fairly boiled with aggravation,
Then she shook her head, looked at me and said,
Poor John! Poor John!

Other songs associated with Vesta Victoria include "I've Told His Missus about Him," "Just Because they Put Him

Vesta Victoria

into Trousers," "He Calls Me His Own Grace Darling," "You Can Do a Lot of Things at the Seaside (That You Can't Do in Town)," "Now I Have to Call Him Father," "Our Lodger's Such a Nice Young Man," "See What Percy's Picked Up in the Park," "Some Would Marry Anything with Trousers On," "The Next Horse I Ride On," and one song which will last forever, "Daddy Wouldn't Buy Me a Bow-wow." "It's All Right in the Summertime" had her as a sign-painter's wife; he longed to paint portraits in "the altogether," for which she was required to pose:

It's all right in the summertime,
In the summertime its lovely.
While my old man's a'paintin' 'ard,
Standin' 'ere a' posin' in the old back-yard.
But, oh my, in the wintertime;
It's a different thing, you know,
With a red, red nose, and very few clothes
And the stormy winds do blow.

Vesta Victoria was born in Leeds, England, on November 26, 1873, the daughter of Joe Lawrence, a music hall performer who appeared in blackface and was billed as "The Upside Down Comedian" because he sang songs standing on his head. She made her first stage appearance at the age of four as "Baby Victoria." She was subsequently billed as "Little Victoria," and under that name made her first London appearance at the Cambridge Music Hall on October 22, 1883. Vesta Victoria soon became a favorite of the London music halls with her first hit song, "Good for Nothing Nan." In 1893 she introduced "Daddy Wouldn't Buy Me a Bow-wow," which she sang that same year on her first American vaudeville tour.

In 1906 Vesta Victoria returned to America after an eight-year absence, and Sime Silverman hailed her as "the truly blown-in-the-bottle music hall artist of the first grade." Within a year, she was back in the States for a ten-week tour at $3,000 a week. At that time Sime Silverman, in *Variety* (January 19, 1907), called her "the magnetic, pretty, buxom character songstress, the idol of the New York public, unexcelled and impossible of imitation."

Vesta Victoria retired from the stage at the end of the First World War but made several highly successful returns to vaudeville. At London's Victoria Palace in 1926, she revived the songs she had made famous. In April of 1927 she headlined at New York's Palace, and Sime Silverman was in the audience again, noting, "There's something magic in the Vesta Victoria name in America." In the early thirties the singer toured in a British revue titled *Star Who Never Failed to Shine,* and in 1932 she appeared in the Royal Variety Show at the London Palladium. She died in London on April 3, 1956.

TED WALDMAN

Ted Waldman

Ted Waldman is typical of many vaudevillians who were the backbone of the medium but who, despite their lasting entertainment value, never became household names in vaudeville. Borrah Minevitch is the best-known harmonica player in vaudeville, but there is little doubt that Ted Waldman was more symbolic of what vaudeville was all about, and certainly his career playing the harmonica or mouth organ lasted far longer than that of Minevitch.

Born in Birmingham, Alabama, Waldman taught himself to play the mouth organ and at the age of sixteen was performing and working as a waiter at Brown's Cafe in Charlotte, North Carolina. The restaurant was next to the Piedmont Theatre, and many of the entertainers there heard Ted and urged him to join their shows, but he was too familiar with stranded companies and the other blights that affected entertainers to leave the security of Brown's cafe. Around 1911, tab—or tabloid—shows, which presented tabloid versions of musical comedies and were to remain popular through the late 1920s (when many of them had become little more than burlesque shows) were introduced. One such tab show was Harry Feldman's *Yankee Doodle Doos.* Ted Waldman was impressed by the show, liked Feldman and his soubrette wife, Agnes Gary, and agreed to join the company.

"We played all the oil fields, and a gusher would come in and fill the theatres with oil; sometimes we'd have to sleep in the dressing rooms," recalls Ted. When the tab shows played major two-a-day vaudeville houses like the Majestic Theatre in Dallas, Ted Waldman's harmonica playing received such attention that he quickly had offers to join mainstream vaudeville. Finally, he teamed up with Ned Norworth and the two played together for three years. Before the twenties; he had reached New York and, while playing one evening for fun at Lindy's restaurant, Waldman was seen and heard by Eva Tanguay. She invited him to join her act, playing the mouth organ while she changed costumes and engaging in repartee with her from the stage box. Ted remained with Tanguay for four years, earning as much as $25,000 a year.

In the twenties Waldman created an act called Blu-O-Logy with his brother, Al. Both appeared in blackface and Ted played the mouth organ (or to be more precise, various mouth organs of different sizes, eleven in all), becoming the first person to play blues on the harmonica. After fourteen years together, Al retired from show business in 1938 and Ted's wife, Priscilla, joined the act. Priscilla and Ted Waldman were kept busy with the U.S.O. during the Second World War and also toured Australia. Today, both are long-time and much-liked volunteers at the Motion Picture and Television Fund Country House and Hospital in Los Angeles, proud reminders of the folks who made vaudeville what it was.

FANNIE WARD

It may sound trite, but the best description available for Fannie Ward is that of the Marlene Dietrich of her era. Like Dietrich, Fannie Ward was ageless, as beautiful at sixty as she had been at twenty, and without the aid of a face lift. She once commented, "I posted a standing offer of $50,000 for anyone who could prove I ever had my face lifted." She was known as the Eternal Flapper, but her career began long before the age of the flapper, in fact, back in the last century in the era of the soubrette.

Fannie Ward was born Fannie Buchanan in St. Louis, Missouri, on February 22, 1872 (or possibly a few years earlier), and made her first stage appearance at New York's Broadway Theatre on November 26, 1890. It was theatrical impresario Daniel Frohman who changed her name to Ward, and she quickly became a popular favorite on the New York and London stages. It was in London in 1898 that she married her first husband, "Diamond" Joe Lewis, a South African millionaire. She divorced Lewis in 1913 and married Jack Dean, who had been named corespondent in the divorce action and who became her leading man on stage and in films. (Dean died in June of 1950).

Fannie Ward probably made her vaudeville debut in the 1890s. She certainly toured the vaudeville circuits as early as 1910, first in a thirty-minute playlet titled *Van Allen's Wife,* a somewhat sordid tale along the lines of her 1915 film success, *The Cheat,* but without the racial angle. *Variety* (January 15, 1910) was not impressed: "Miss Ward . . . will leave behind no yearning devotees of light entertainment to long for her return." Her second vaudeville playlet, *An Unlucky Star,* which she introduced in April of 1910, proved more popular. It concluded with its author appearing on stage to reveal that the audience was supposedly watching only a dress rehearsal; then followed a vigorous argument with the star, Miss Ward. Rush in *Variety* (April 2, 1910) found *An Unlucky Star* "an immensely refreshing sketch for the jaded vaudeville habitué."

It is because of her films rather than her stage roles that Fannie Ward is remembered today. She entered films in

Fannie Ward

1915 and starred in a number of silent features, including *The Cheat* (1915), in which she was an American businessman's wife who is branded by the Japanese from whom she borrows money, *The Yellow Ticket* (1918), and *Our Better Selves* (1919).

Fannie Ward returned to vaudeville in December of 1926 with a twenty-four-minute playlet titled *The Miracle Woman* at the Palace. The plot had her as a seemingly young woman with a daughter who looked as old as she. She showed her legs, appeared in a negligeé, and apparently received more floral tributes than the Palace stage generally saw in an entire season. One reason for this particular engagement was to promote Miss Ward's beauty shop. Fannie Ward was back at the Palace in February of 1928, billed as "the most remarkable looking woman for her age of our age," and singing "Grandma Blues," "Flapper Fannie," and "My Marine" (dressed as a French war bride).

The actress never officially retired, although from the thirties on she was more concerned with her social life as the mother of Lady Plunket than with her stage career. However, at the age of forty-five she could still pass for a fourteen-year-old on stage, and at the age of sixty she was proud to report that her legs were still slim and handsome. Reporters noted that a year before she died her face retained an unbelievable babylike softness. Fannie Ward died in New York City on January 27, 1952, her fountain of youth run dry. There were many explanations as to how she kept her youthful appearance. One had it that she had learned of a secret facial treatment from the French actress Gaby Deslys. Other secrets were supposedly a "Siberian show face mask," a young husband, and a diet of green vegetables.

Fannie Ward

ETHEL WATERS

Ethel Waters

Ethel Waters was born in Chester, Pennsylvania, on October 31, 1900, and her early life as a poor black child was one of squalor and degradation. She was married at the age of thirteen (her mother had been raped at the same age). Yet from these sordid beginnings, Ethel Waters emerged as perhaps the greatest popular black singer of this century, a performer who was equally at home with songs of pathos and songs of wit. "I'm Coming Virginia," "Am I Blue?," "You're Lucky to Me," "Harlem on My Mind," "Taking a Chance on Love," "Cabin in the Sky," and "Honey in the Honeycomb" are just a few of the songs that only she could sing to perfection. She would break your heart with a sentimental ballad such as "Cabin in the Sky" and the next minute have you sniggering at the out-and-out bawdy lyrics of "My Handy Man." No wonder that *Variety* hailed her in 1938 as "the prima donna of all colored warblers."

She entered vaudeville at the age of seventeen, making her debut at the Lincoln Theatre in Baltimore, teamed with the two Hill Sisters and billed as "Sweet Mama Stringbean." She recorded her first song in 1921, and by the mid-twenties she was a popular entertainer on the T.O.B.A. (Theatre Owners Booking Association) Negro vaudeville circuit. In 1925 Ethel Waters replaced Florence Mills at the Plantation Club and then signed a contract with Columbia Records. She made her Broadway debut in *Africana,* a musical revue by Donald Heyward which opened at the Daly Theatre on July 11, 1927, and ran for seventy-two performances.

Ethel Waters's "white" vaudeville debut came at the Palace Theatre in September of 1927. *Variety* (September 21, 1927) liked her act, and noted, " 'Shake That Thing' is to Miss Waters what 'I don't Care' is to Eva Tanguay. It's her trademark." In May of 1928 she was headlining at the Chicago Palace after taking *Africana* on the road. *Variety* (May 23, 1928) reported, "Miss Waters's first appearance was in a tattered plantation outfit, singing 'I'm Coming Virginia.' She had a friendly house and her handling of this number brought considerable extra recognition. Later she shocked the family customers by wearing almost nothing and going through a series of gyrations and grinds identified as B.B. It seemed a little too Harlem for the local momma and the kiddies down front.... There's no doubt as to this gal's ability with blues. Her husky voice and understanding delivery can make an ordinary number full of torrid implications or profound melancholy."

The singer returned to Broadway for *Lew Leslie's Blackbirds,* which opened at the Royale Theatre on October 22, 1930, and ran for a disappointing fifty-seven performances. The cast included Mantan Moreland, Buck and Bubbles, and Flourney Miller. In that show she introduced "You're Lucky to Me." Three years later at the Cotton Club she introduced "Stormy Weather," and that same year, 1937, she sang "Heat Wave" in *As Thousands Cheer.*

Ethel Waters with Eubie Blake

Ethel Waters was by now an established star; Brooks Atkinson described her as "the gleaming tower of dusky regality, who knows how to make a song stand on tiptoe." She had appeared in the 1929 Warner Bros. feature *On with the Show* and thus captured on film a rendering of two of her great songs, "Am I Blue?" and "Birmingham Bertha." Even in an unpretentious 1933 film short like *Bubbling Over,* she transforms the screen with her rendition of "That's Why Darkies Never Dream." Waters's other films include *Cabin in the Sky* (1943), based on the hit Broadway show of 1940 in which she starred, *Pinky* (1949), and, of course, *The Member of the Wedding* (1952), again based on a Broadway play in which she had appeared. Who will forget that heart-rending scene as Julie Harris and Brandon De Wilde lie cradled in her arms, and Ethel Waters sings "His Eye Is on the Sparrow":

Why should I feel discouraged?
Why should the shadows come?
Why should my heart be lonely?
And long for heaven and home?
When Jesus is my portion,
My constant friend is he.
His eye is on the sparrow
And I know he watches Me.

Yet for all her success, Ethel Waters suffered racial discrimination. In March of 1937, when she played Kansas City with her own vaudeville show, *Swing, Harlem, Swing,* the audience was segregated and Negroes were required to pay an extra admission fee to attend a midnight, all-black audience show. Angry blacks picketed the theatre, and it was reported that Miss Waters "was visibly shaken by the affair."

In the last years of her life, Ethel Waters devoted herself to religion. She would sing only religious numbers, a tragic loss for young people who had never had the opportunity to witness an Ethel Waters performance. "The Yvette Guilbert of her race," as critic Ashton Stevens described her, died in Chatsworth, California, on September 1, 1977.

Reference: *His Eye Is on the Sparrow* by Ethel Waters, with Charles Samuels (Doubleday and Company, 1951).

WEBER AND FIELDS

Weber and Fields not only represent old-fashioned knockabout comedy, they were its creators. It seems as if every joke and gag that is considered corny today was created by Weber and Fields. The trick of apparently poking your finger in your partner's eye, used by everyone from Laurel and Hardy to Dean Martin and Jerry Lewis, had its origins with Weber and Fields. Around 1887 Weber asked Fields, "Who is that lady I saw you with last night?," to which came the hoary answer, "She ain't no lady; she's my wife." Another favorite gag was to inveigle a valuable violin away from its owner, handle it roughly, get into an argument about it, and eventually smash it over the partner's head.

They were both born in New York City in 1867, Joseph Weber on August 11, and Lew Fields on January 1. They made their stage debuts together at New York's Chatham Square Museum in 1877, opening with a chorus of "Here

Weber and Fields as themselves

we are, a jolly pair" before embarking on their comedy act. For three dollars a week, they gave eight or nine shows a day. From the Chatham Square Museum, they took to appearing at other dime museums, vaudeville theatres, and beer gardens. Their entrance changed with the ethnic nature of their act. For blackface they sang, "Here we are, a colored pair"; for an Irish act, "Here we are, an Irish pair"; and so on. As Weber and Fields's biographer, Felix Isman, wrote, "They fit any figure, as did the second-hand suits in the Bowery schlockshops."

It was not until the 1880s that Weber and Fields became firmly established with a Dutch knockabout act titled Mike and Myer. Tall and bullying Fields was Myer, while the "knockee" was small and plump, trustful and innocent Weber as Mike. Sporting goatees and destroying the English language in a parody of German immigrants new to this country, their routine would include the following dialogue:

MIKE: I am delightfulness to meet you.
MYER: Der disgust is all mine.
MIKE: I receividid a letter from mein goil, but I don't know how to writteninin her back.
MYER: Writteninin her back! Such an edumucation you got it? Writteninin her back! You mean rotteninin her back. How can you answer her ven you don't know how to write?
MIKE: Dot makes no nefer mind. She don't know how to read.

MYER: If I'm cruel to you, Mike, it's because I luff you. (As he gouges Mike's eyes.)

MIKE: If you luffed me any more, I couldn't stand it.

The classic Mike and Myer sketch involved a pool table, which Weber and Fields introduced in 1889. Myer, the pool shark, is showing Mike how to play pool, and occasionally hitting him over the head with a cue, while telling him, "Ven I'm away from you, I cannot keep mein mind off you. Ven I'm mit you, I cannot keep mein hands from off you. Oh, how I luff you, Mike!" The game ended with the innocent Mike winning the betting money. The pool table sketch was new to vaudeville—W. C. Fields was a decade or two away—and with their act Weber and Fields offered a burlesque of reality. Felix Isman wrote, "The pool table skit told a story and held a mirror up to life; a farcical story and a distorted mirror, it is true, but a long step beyond the belled cap, the bladder, the stuffed club, and the topical joke."

It is interesting to note the sado-masochism in the Weber and Fields routines, which was carried through into the twentieth century, not so much on the vaudeville stage as in circuses, with their aggressive and passive clowns. Laurel and Hardy, in more recent times, have come closest to the violent nature of the Weber and Fields routines, but had their sketches been written by the latter, it would have been portly Hardy who bore the brunt of the violence. Certainly audiences have a need for violence, as evidenced by boxing matches and ice hockey in the area of sports, and Weber once commented that "all the public wanted to see was Fields knock the hell out of me." Fields explained, "I don't know why it was, but the audiences always seemed to have a grudge against him."

On September 5, 1896, the two opened their own theatre, the Weber and Fields Music Hall, which had formerly been the Imperial Theatre at Twenty-ninth Street and Broadway. It was the first burlesque theatre in the world, when burlesque did not mean the "girlie" shows with which the name has come to be associated today, but rather burlesques of popular theatrical productions such as *The Heart of Maryland* (in which Mrs. Leslie Carter was then starring), with which the theatre opened. *The Art of Maryland,* as the Weber and Fields burlesque was called, ran for six weeks and was followed by *The Geezer,* a burlesque on a recent musical comedy import from England, *The Geisha.* Among the shows that followed were *Under the Red Globe, Barbara Fidgety, Quo Vass Iss?, Fiddle-dee-dee, Pousse-Cafe, Hurly-Burly, Hoity-Toity,* and *Higgledy-Piggledy.* Aside from the introduction of burlesque, the Weber and Fields Music Hall also introduced, or made popular, some of that era's most famous vaudeville and light opera stars, including Lillian Russell, DeWolf Hopper, Fay Templeton, Bessie Clayton, David Warfield, and Sam Bernard. The *New York Clipper* (December 27, 1900) described Weber and Fields as "among the most popular actor-managers in this country," adding "They have placed their cozy little house not only in the front rank of amusement resorts in the metropolis but in the world."

Weber and Fields as Mike and Myer

For seven years the Weber and Fields Music Hall prospered, until the Iroquois Theatre fire in Chicago caused New York City to revise its theatre building codes. The Weber and Fields Music Hall would have to be rebuilt or close down; Weber and Fields chose the latter course, and on January 30, 1904, the Weber and Fields Music Hall gave its last performance. A few months later, on April 25, Weber and Fields dissolved their partnership, with Joe Weber paying Lew Fields $40,000 for the rights to the name of Weber and Fields Music Hall. May 29, 1904, was their final performance in *Whoop-dee-doo* at the New Amsterdam Theatre and the final appearance of Weber and Fields on stage together for a number of years. "We can only say that we are sorry," said Weber, to which Fields added, "I can only echo Mr. Weber's sentiment."

Lew Fields leased a theatre on West Forty-second Street and renamed it Fields Theatre, moving in 1906 to the Herald Square Theatre where he continued to produce burlesques, beginning with *It Happened in Nordland.* Other productions included *The Music Master* (1905), *About Town* (1906), *The Girl behind the Counter* (1907), *Old Dutch* (1909), *The Henpecks* (1911), and *The Neverhomes* (1911). Joe Weber also continued with burlesques at Weber's Music Hall, which reopened in the fall of 1904.

In January of 1912 Lew Fields's father died, and Weber and Fields attended the funeral together. Weber confirmed that he was giving up the Music Hall, and Fields suggested that they get together again. Lillian Russell, Fay Templeton, George Beban, Bessie Clayton, and others joined Weber and Fields for the reunion which took place at the Broadway Theatre on February 8, 1912. The Weber and Fields Music Hall reopened at the Forty-fourth Street Theatre on November 21, 1912, but survived only one season, because, Weber and Fields's biographer claims, it was too large for burlesque.

Weber and Fields continued to appear separately and together in musical comedy and revue. In February of 1914 they appeared in a thirty-minute sketch, "Mike and Myer's Trip Abroad," at the Auditorium in Chicago, assisted by Nora Bayes, George Beban, and Harry Clark. In the sketch, Weber and Fields were required to pose as statues and be subjected to all types of annoyances. *Variety* (February 27, 1914) reported, "The comedy is fast and furious. Some of it is new and some old. . . . It is an act such as suits the people in it, but demands just such people to put it over." On August 9, 1915, Weber and Fields made their debut at the Palace, receiving $3,800 a week. (In 1883 Weber and Fields had been earning forty dollars a week.)

The team appeared together in a number of films from 1915 on, including *Two of the Finest* (1915), *The Worst of Enemies* (1916), *Friendly Enemies* (1925), and *Blossoms on Broadway* (1937), and, in addition, Lew Fields played himself in *The Story of Vernon and Irene Castle* (1939). In 1912 they were paid $10,000 to make a phonograph recording of their "Dutch Sidewalk Conversation," which contains this classic exchange:

MIKE: Do you have any money?
MYER: No.
MIKE: Well, all I have is a nickel—just enough for one beer.
MYER: Why don't you have one. I don't want a drink just now.
MIKE: Oh good. But it wouldn't look good if we both went in and I ordered a beer without offering one to you. Tell you what we'll do. We'll go into this bar. I'll ask you if you want beer, and you say, "I don't care for any."
MYER: Okay, I'll do that. (There is the sound of a door opening. A pause. Then the sound of the door opening as they come out.)
MIKE: Oh, you idiot! Now see what you've done.
MYER: Why, I just done what you told me. When you asked me if I wanted a beer. . . .
MIKE: You said, "I don't care if I do." And the bartender gave you the beer, and I had to pay my last nickel.

In 1925 Weber and Fields headlined on the Palace Theatre's old-timer bill. Their popularity never really waned. The opening night program at the Radio City Music Hall on December 27, 1932, included Ray Bolger, Jan Peerce, Dr. Rockwell, DeWolf Hopper, and Weber and Fields. The couple closed the show but unfortunately, it was by then so late in the evening that the *New York Times's* Brooks Atkinson decided not to wait for the act to report on it in his column. In 1930 both comedians had taken up residence in Los Angeles; Lew Fields died there on July 20, 1941, and Joe Weber a year later, on May 10, 1942.

Their catchphrase, heard plaintively from the wings, "Don't poosh me, Myer," was one of the most famous in the early years of vaudeville. As Douglas Gilbert wrote, "Theirs was an inherent aptness for the ridiculousness of pseudo pomp and they laid bare many a fool in their latter day clowning."

Reference: *Weber and Fields* by Felix Isman (Boni and Liveright, 1924).

SEÑOR WENCES

Vaudeville may have been dying in the thirties, but one act that carried on the vaudeville tradition to the present, and which proves that artistry and talent are not completely dead in the field of live entertainment, is Señor Wences. To call Señor Wences a ventriloquist is comparable to stating that Eddie Cantor was just a comedian or that Belle Baker was just another popular songstress, for his ventriloquism act was totally unique and incomparable to any other performer's routines in that field before or since. The act usually featured two characters. The first was a doll, created by painting a mouth with lipstick and adding two onyx rings for eyes and a tiny red wig to Señor Wences's left hand. The result was a character both impudent and funny. The other "dummy" was nothing more than the head of a Moorish-type character in a wooden box. The head was always arguing and threatening, and so good was—and is—Señor Wences that as he began to shut the box, the voice of the head would become gradually muffled. Often there would be a three-way argument in the act between Señor Wences, the doll, and the disembodied head.

Señor Wences was born Wenceslao Moreno Cetena in Spain, and at the age of twelve he had become a bullfighter. After an unpleasant accident with a bull, he turned to conjuring and from that to ventriloquism. He learned the art of turning his hand into a dummy from his father. After a successful career in Europe, he came to New York in 1936 and made his first appearance there at the El Chico Club in Greenwich Village. The *London Times* (November 10, 1937) had seen Señor Wences at the Holborn Empire and reported, "Wences is a ventriloquist who had a dummy of individuality, a dummy who not so much departs as strides away vigorously from the methods of his master." Señor Wences made his vaudeville debut in an eleven-minute act at the Paramount Theatre in November of 1938, billed incorrectly as "The Wences," which, as *Variety* noted, made him sound like a dance team. He was an instant success with the audience. The high spot of his routine was the doll singing a high soprano while Señor Wences drank a glass of water and smoked a cigarette. Abel Green in *Variety* (November 2, 1938) reported, "He walks off the Par. stage with a resounding personal score, working hard, fast, and effectively. . . . Act is a happy blend of comedy and generally good pacing." (On the same bill was a young tap dancer named Ann Miller, but she did not have the same audience impact as Señor Wences.)

Prior to his Paramount Theatre appearance, Señor Wences had appeared outside of New York, chiefly in *Ice Carnival* with Chester Morris and the Frazee Sisters at the Hippodrome, Baltimore, in September of 1938. After his New York success, he was booked for a lengthy vaudeville tour with Martha Raye which opened at the Earle Theatre in Philadelphia on October 14, 1939. The act went over well, although there were complaints from the Midwest that Señor Wences's foreign accent was confusing to corn-belt audiences. On August 26, 1942, *Variety* hailed him as "one of the best ventriloquists around."

As the years went by, Señor Wences tended to appear more in Europe than in this country, although, fortunately, he did film his act for posterity in the 1947 Betty Grable vehicle *Mother Wore Tights.* One of his last major American appearances was in "One-Man Show," which was televised on February 14, 1970. Much of the material was that which he had used since the thirties, although he did introduce a chicken named Cecelia, and for his finale he juggled four plates on sticks while speaking in four separate voices. It was, as *Variety* (February 18, 1970) reported, "a reminder that great vaude turns are getting scarce."

References: "Señor Wences Has Seven Voices but Audiences Believe Only Five" by Helen Ormsbee in the *New York Herald Tribune* (September 26, 1943), page 2. "Look Who's Talking!" by Ed Wallace in the *New York World-Telegram and Sun* (May 26, 1953), page 21.

MAE WEST

Mae West

Reviewing Mae West's vaudeville act in 1912, *Variety* (January 20, 1912) noted that "Miss West is a lively piece of femininity," and went on to say, "The girl is of the eccentric type." As a criticism of Miss West, it could have been applied to any period of her career, from vaudeville through musical comedy and her sex-related dramas to her classic feature films of the thirties.

Born in Brooklyn, New York, on August 17, 1893, Mae West began appearing in amateur productions as a child, and by the time she was eleven she had toured in stock companies in New York and on the road. In September of 1911 she appeared in *A la Broadway* at the Henry B. Harris and Jesse L. Lasky cabaret restaurant, the Folies Bergere. It was followed a few months later by an appearance in the revue *Vera Violetta,* which starred Al Jolson and Gaby Deslys, at the Winter Garden. Mae West made her big-time vaudeville debut as a single—she had certainly been on the vaudeville stage earlier and in January of 1912 had appeared in a vaudeville act with the Girard Brothers—in May of 1912. Sime Silverman, writing in *Variety* (May 25, 1912) noted, "She sings rag melodies and dresses oddly, but still lacks that touch of class that is becoming requisite now in the first-class houses."

In 1916 Mae West was teamed with her sister, Beverly, in vaudeville. She sang "I Want To Be Loved in the Old Fashioned Way" and "They Called It Dixieland," then appeared in male attire, complete with silk hat, to sing "Walkin' th' Dog." *Variety* (July 7, 1916) was not particularly impressed: "Mae West in big-time vaudeville may only be admired for her persistency in believing she is a big-time act and trying to make vaudeville accept her as such." Miss West had made a curtain speech in which she said, "I am very pleased, ladies and gentlemen, you like my new act. It's the first time I have appeared with my sister. They all like her, especially the boys, who always fall for her, but that's where I come in—I always take them away from her." *Variety* suggested that Mae West would do better in vaudeville if she were to wear men's dress all the while on stage, and that "With 'Sister' they could do a boy-and-girl 'sister' act."

Miss West came to prominence on the musical comedy stage when she opened as the star of the Rudolf Friml musical romance *Sometime* on October 4, 1918, at the Shubert Theatre. She was a big hit with a dance that was a combination of the cooch and the shimmy, and was called "The Shimmy Shawabble." *Variety* (October 11, 1918) commented, "Miss West has improved somewhat in looks but is still the rough hand-on-the-hip character that she first conceived as the ideal type of a woman single in vaudeville." Two of Mae West's songs from this show, "Any Kind of Man" and "All I Want Is Just a Little Lovin'," typified the kind of material which was to be associated with the star in the years to come.

In September of 1919 Mae West returned to vaudeville after an absence of two years, and *Variety* (September 19, 1919) was a little kinder to her, commenting that "Miss West shows a marked improvement in method and delivery since last appearing in vaudeville." She was on the bill of the opening program at the Capitol Theatre on October 24, 1919, with a burlesque shimmy dance and the song,

"Oh, What a Moanin' Man." Also on the program was the Douglas Fairbanks film *His Majesty the American* and Muriel De Forrest singing George Gershwin's "Swanee," its first performance. In August of 1920 Mae West opened at the Colonial with a new, eighteen-minute vaudeville act titled "Songalog," in which she performed "I Want a Cave Man," "I'm a Night School Teacher," and "The Manni-kin," wearing a black, silver-jetted, one-piece gown. "Miss West has acquired ease and a legitimate repose in charac-ter comedy since last seen around, getting every point over without the slightest effort and for full value. . . . Miss West looks set as a big-time feature," reported *Variety* (August 13, 1920). In fact, by now Mae West was an established star in both vaudeville and musical comedy; she was featured on the cover of the December 25, 1919, issue of the *New York Dramatic Mirror,* described as a "Popular Broadway Comedienne."

During the twenties Mae West had little time for the vaudeville stage. On August 15, 1921, she opened at the Century Theatre in *The Mimic World of 1921,* the high spot—or low spot, depending on your point of view—of which was Miss West's dancing a shimmy dressed as Our Lady of Fatima. She did return to vaudeville in 1922 with Harry Richman as her pianist, and when the two appeared at the Riverside Theatre, *Variety* (June 23, 1922) re-ported, "She rises to heights undreamed of for her and reveals unsuspected depths as a delineator of character songs, a dramatic reader of ability, and a girl with a flare for farce that will some day land her on the legitimate Olympus." Richman departed in the fall of 1922, and Mae West apparently turned her attention to sex and its possi-bilities as a dramatic subject. The result was her play *Sex,* which opened at the Daly Theatre on April 26, 1926, and which, according to the *New York Herald Tribune,* "wins high mark for depravity (and) dullness." Miss West also starred in *Sex,* but she did not appear in her 1927 play, *The Drag,* which dealt very explicitly with homosexuality, or in her next production, a satirical comedy titled *The Wicked Age.*

Mae West's most successful play was *Diamond Lil,* "a drama of the underworld," which opened at the Royale Theatre on April 9, 1928, and ran for 323 performances. It was to be followed by two other lurid plays, *Pleasure Man* (1928) and *The Constant Sinner* (1931). Prior to starring in *The Constant Sinner,* Mae West had returned to the vaudeville stage with a fourteen-minute act which made its debut at the Fox Audubon—where the cooch dance was ordered removed—in May of 1930. Reviewing the act at The Academy, a presentation house, *Variety* (May 21, 1930) reported, "Miss West has been out of vaude since about 1925 or thereabouts and in the interim has become an accomplished and at the same time notori-ous legitimate authoress, producer, and actress. In her new vaude act she mentions all of that legit career, includ-ing the shows and the trouble. In talking, she's the nearest to a female Jimmy Durante as, when talk-singing about the 'Pleasure Man' bunch, she pipes 'They (the police) said these guys is fairies.' "

At that time Mae West announced, somewhat prema-turely, that she was departing for Hollywood. In fact, she

did not enter films until 1932; her appearances in *Night after Night* (1932), *She Done Him Wrong* (1933), *I'm No Angel* (1933), *Goin' to Town* (1935), *Go West, Young Man* (1936), *My Little Chickadee* (1940), and *Myra Breckin-ridge* (1970), among others, precluded any further appear-ances on the vaudeville stage. She died in Los Angeles on November 22, 1980.

(In 1911 Mae West was briefly married to a song-and-dance man named Frank Wallace and toured with him. Billed as "Mister Mae West," Wallace opened in bur-lesque at the Eltinge Theatre on September 27, 1935, in an act with Trixie LeMae that he claimed he had performed with Mae West.)

References: *Goodness Had Nothing To Do with It* by Mae West (Prentice-Hall, 1959). *The Films of Mae West* by Jon Tuska (The Citadel Press, 1973).

WHEELER AND WOOLSEY

To most people familiar with the films of Wheeler and Woolsey—*The Cuckoos* (1930), *Hook, Line and Sinker* (1930), *Cracked Nuts* (1931), *Diplomaniacs* (1933), *Hips, Hips, Hooray!* (1934), *Cockeyed Cavaliers* (1934), *The Nitwits* (1935), and the like—the funny man was the one with the lean face and glasses, Robert Woolsey. The baby-faced, better-looking one, Bert Wheeler, is often mistaken for the straight man of the team, and few realize that Wheeler's career prospered both before and after the teaming with Woolsey; if anything, this essay should be devoted entirely to Bert Wheeler.

Vaudevillian Ted Waldman recalls that Bert Wheeler would walk out on stage carrying a joke book and an-nounce to the audience that he would read to them from the book. So funny was Wheeler that when he proceeded to do this, the audience was convulsed. The jokes might be corny (for example, "The headwaiter kept asking me if I had a reservation. What does he think I am? An In-dian?"), but they never failed to amuse a vaudeville crowd. Many times Bert Wheeler would simply sit on the edge of the stage, perhaps eating a sandwich, and just talk with the audience; sometimes he would cry and accidentally wipe his eyes on the sandwich and eat his handkerchief.

Albert Jerome Wheeler was born in Paterson, New Jer-sey, on April 17, 1895, and his early career included a spell with Gus Edwards's company and a vaudeville act with his first wife, Betty, whom he married while still a teen-ager. (She later married Clarence Stroud of the Stroud Twins, and Wheeler was to marry three more times, all of which unions ended in divorce.) In 1923 Bert Wheeler was featured in *The Ziegfeld Follies,* and as a result of his success in that show Florenz Ziegfeld offered him a five-year contract. It was Ziegfeld who teamed Bert Wheeler with Robert Woolsey for *Rio Rita,* which opened at the Ziegfeld Theatre on February 2, 1926. Wheeler played Chick Bean, while Woolsey was Ed Lovett; J. Harold Murray was Jim and Ethelind Terry played Rio Rita.

Robert Woolsey was born in Oakland, California, on August 14, 1889, and had been an exercise boy and a jockey before a riding accident forced him to change ca-

Wheeler and Woolsey

reers. He entered show business playing in stock companies and performing in Gilbert and Sullivan operettas. He made his New York debut, as Drake in *Nothing But Love,* at the Lyric Theatre on October 14, 1919, and was later featured in *The Right Girl* (1921), *The Blue Kitten* (1922), *Poppy* (1923), *The Dream Girl* (1924), *Mayflowers* (1925), and *Honest Liars* (1926).

Rio Rita made the continuation of the Wheeler and Woolsey partnership inevitable, for as the 1929 film version indicates, the two reacted to one another with perfect, split-second timing. In addition, the film illustrates what a delightful singing voice Bert Wheeler had, particularly in the charming duet "Sweetheart, We Need Each Other" with Dorothy Lee. A film career for Wheeler and Woolsey followed, and the two starred in twenty-one features. "They were pretty bad, but they all made money," Wheeler once commented. They split up in May of 1932, with Woolsey explaining, "I wish it understood that Wheeler and I never really formed a team at any time. He had his manager and attorney and I had mine." However, a reconciliation was worked out in July of the same year, and the two were immediately starred in their only film for Columbia, *So This Is Africa*—all the other Wheeler and Woolsey features were produced by RKO.

Robert Woolsey died at his Malibu, California, home on October 31, 1938, at the age of forty-nine, and after his death Bert Wheeler never appeared in another film. Wheeler returned to vaudeville and was also to be heard on radio and seen on early television. He took on several partners, including Betty Grable, Harry Jans, Sid Slate, and Jack Pepper, and for a number of years he appeared

in drag, as an elderly lady, with Tom Dillon playing his abusive son. On October 26, 1966, the small theatre inside New York's Dixie Hotel was named in his honor.

Wheeler's last years were spent on the borderline of poverty, but he enjoyed participating in various entertainments at the Lambs Club, explaining, "I make all I need." Bert Wheeler made his last public appearance at the Garden City Hotel, Long Island, in December of 1966. He died in New York City on January 18, 1968, at which time the then-president of the Lambs Club, Harry Hershfield, said of him, "Bert had a pixie face and remained a pixie to the end."

Reference: "Bert Wheeler, 73, Always a Pixie" by Joe Cohen in *Variety,* Vol. 249, No. 10 (January 24, 1968), pages 2 and 70.

FRANCES WHITE see William Rock and Frances White

BERT WILLIAMS

Bert Williams

Without a doubt, Bert Williams was one of the finest pantomimists and comedians vaudeville has ever known. The *New York Dramatic Mirror* (December 7, 1918) called him "one of the great comedians of the world." W. C. Fields described him as "the funniest man I ever saw." Eddie Cantor regarded Williams as both his teacher and his friend; "the man to whom I owe so much," and wrote of him: "In my seventy years, I've known many outstanding people in and out of the theater. A Will Rogers, an Al

Bert Williams

Jolson, comes once in a generation. Bert Williams . . . once in a lifetime."

Bert Williams was also black, and in an age when black performers were not welcome on the "white" vaudeville stage he was very much a pioneer. He was the only black the Keith circuit could book on a white bill in Washington, D.C. In 1904 he played a command performance in England before King Edward VII. He was a Mason, and had the distinction, if such it be, of being the first black to be buried by a white Masonic lodge. His humor did not poke fun at his race as did, say, the comedy of blackface comedians like Moran and Mack; rather he found mirth in situations which might apply equally well to any poor folk. Yet he always performed—as was the style of the day —in blackface make-up, overemphasizing his racial background.

There is no question that his color did hurt him both commercially and emotionally. Some white vaudevillians would not appear on the same bill with Williams, while others objected when his material seemed superior to theirs. He once told Eddie Cantor how much it hurt that he should be allowed to stay at the same hotels as his fellow white performers but be required to take the back elevators: "It wouldn't be so bad, Eddie, if I didn't still hear the applause ringing in my ears."

Williams was born in New Providence, Nassau, in the British West Indies. His entry into show business came in 1893 when he joined Martin and Seig's Mastodon Minstrels, along with a black song-and-dance man named George Walker. The two teamed up as Williams and Walker and were to become a highly popular act until

Walker's death in 1911. Their New York debut came in 1898 in a short-lived show, *The Gold Bug,* at the Casino Theatre. Williams and Walker entertained with songs and with a quick-paced patter act in which Walker was always trying to persuade the slower and more cautious Williams to participate in one of his get-rich-quick schemes.

When Walker became sick in 1909, Bert Williams embarked on a single act which led to his being signed by Florenz Ziegfeld as one of the stars of *The Ziegfeld Follies* in 1910. Williams played in the *Follies* almost continuously from 1910 through 1919, taking breaks only in 1913 and 1918. Eddie Cantor and Williams first played together in the 1917 *Ziegfeld Follies,* in which Cantor portrayed the black comedian's son in a sketch set at Grand Central Station. Cantor recalled, "As a performer, he was close to genius. As a man, he was everything the rest of us would like to have been. As a friend, he was without envy or jealousy. . . . A master of pantomime, he was a miser with gestures, never raising his hand six inches if three would suffice. Whatever sense of timing I have, I learned from him. Years later when I was in pictures that called for pantomime—*The Kid from Spain* and *Roman Scandals*— I'd ask myself, 'How would Bert Williams handle this scene?' "

Bert Williams's most famous pantomime was that of a player in a poker game. His head and shoulders would be lit by a single spotlight as he mimicked all the gestures of the player, from the draw to losing the game. When he returned to vaudeville in 1918 to top the bill at the Palace, he climaxed his act with this sketch, and the *New York Dramatic Mirror* (December 14, 1918) noted that despite its familiarity, the pantomime "holds fresh interest with every resurrection."

In addition to the poker game, Bert Williams introduced many popular songs of the day, including "You Ain't So Warm," "That's Harmony," "You Got the Right Church but the Wrong Pew," "He's a Cousin of Mine," "My Castle on the Nile," and, of course, "Nobody." This writer's own particular favorite is "Bring Back Those Wonderful Days," which Williams recorded for Columbia around 1920 and in which he pleads at the dawn of prohibition for the saloon and "the ale that was always musty," and asks that we take back the income tax collector and the Red Flag agitator. Aside from the songs, Bert Williams was a natural storyteller, with a calm deliberation to his delivery. A typical yarn, as recalled by Douglas Gilbert, concerned his home:

Where I'm living now is a nice place, but you have to go along a road between two graveyards to get to it. One night last week I was coming home kind of late, and I got about halfway home when I happened to look over my shoulder and saw a ghost following me. I started to run. I run till I was 'most ready to drop. And then I looked around. But I didn't see no ghost, so I sat down on the curbstone to rest. Then out of the corner of my eye I could see something white, and when I turned square around, there was that ghost sitting alongside of me. The ghost says, "That was a fine run we had. It was the best running

I ever saw." I says: "Yes. And soon as I get my breath you're going to see some more."

Even without Williams's delivery, a simple reading of this tale confirms the comment by Rush in *Variety* (December 26, 1913) that "Williams has the story telling gift in a degree possessed by few."

Bert Williams even found time for a brief film career with the American Biograph Company in the summer of 1916. One of the films in which he appeared, *A Natural Born Gambler,* released by the General Film Company on July 24, 1916, was inspired by his celebrated poker game. The critic for *The Moving Picture World* (August 12, 1916) reported, "The actors are all colored persons of the male sex and they are all addicted to gambling. Williams attempts to annex the roll of a swell sport from the city, but the game is raided and when last seen the natural born gambler is sadly dealing out imaginary hands behind the bars of a prison. The business of some of the scenes could be improved, but Bert Williams's skill at pantomime shows up well on the screen."

In 1920 Bert Williams left Ziegfeld and signed with the Shuberts. On February 21, 1922, while touring in their production of *Under the Bamboo Tree,* he collapsed on stage at the Shubert-Garrick Theatre in Detroit. Williams returned to New York and died in his home at 2309 Seventh Avenue on March 4, at the reported age of forty-nine.

Many black performers have come along since Bert Williams's death, from Sammy Davis, Jr. to Ben Vereen, but none will ever have the appeal or the personality of the man who made vaudeville audiences accept black performers, and coincidentally proved they could be better than many white entertainers of that era.

Reference: "Bert Williams" by Eddie Cantor in *As I Remember Them* (Duell, Sloan and Pearce, 1963), pages 48–51.

WILLIE, WEST, AND McGINTY

Willie, West, and McGinty were a popular trio in vaudeville from the late twenties through the late thirties, and their act lingered on into television in the fifties. Their slapstick routine was billed as "A Billion Builders Blunders" or "A Comedy of Errors" and they appeared as three workmen attempting to build a house; everything went wrong as they were hit by buckets, planks of wood, and the like. With perfect timing, the trio would awkwardly manipulate the assorted paraphernalia with disastrous results. When they played their first major New York engagement at the Hippodrome in August of 1924, *Variety* (August 27, 1924) commented, "This manner of clowning made several Billy Reeves and Charlie Chaplin stars, and is sound, wholesome, and entirely welcome whenever it is efficiently done." It was slapstick pure and simple, but it was, as *Variety* (February 19, 1930) noted, "a good act with plenty of laughs," and it proved hugely successful on variety stages in the United States and England. The act is still copied today by circus clowns. Willie, West, and McGinty reached their zenith in 1939 when

they were the star attraction of *Billy Rose's Aquacade* at the New York World's Fair.

NAT WILLS

Nat Wills

Billed as "The Happy Tramp" in vaudeville, Wills's life was apparently far from happy, and he died under mysterious circumstances, possibly a suicide victim. Wills would appear on stage as a genial bum with his front teeth blacked out, several days growth of beard on his chin, and his hair awry. He was a monologist and was notorious for the large sums of money that he paid out to writers to provide him with fresh materal. *Variety* claimed that Wills would pay any amount for new material.

Nat Wills was born in Fredericksburg, Virginia, in 1873. Originally he worked with a partner, Dave Halpin, in an act which was called "The Tramp and the Policeman." Next he introduced an act with his wife, Loretta, known, not surprisingly, as Wills and Loretta. When Loretta died, Wills married May Montrief and worked with her. When she died, he married "La Belle Titcomb," who had a vaudeville act that Douglas Gilbert recalls as consisting of her riding a white horse and singing operatic arias. When the couple divorced in 1914, Wills was married for the fourth and last time, to May Day, who had been with *The Ziegfeld Follies* and was known professionally as May Harrison.

Wills was earning a salary of $800 a week in vaudeville and was a favorite at the New York Hippodrome, but he was forced to pay out a considerable weekly sum in alimony to "La Belle Titcomb." His financial obligations weighed heavily on him and Wills constantly worried that his material might become stale. On December 9, 1917, Nat Wills went into the garage of his home in Woodcliff, New Jersey, turned on the motor of his car, and was later found dead of carbon monoxide poisoning by his wife. He left an estate valued at twenty-three dollars.

ED WYNN

Ed Wynn in 1923

"A comic is a monologist who tells jokes but he isn't necessarily funny," Ed Wynn once explained. "He's a man who doesn't do funny things but does things funny. He doesn't open a funny door, he opens a door funny." He was known as "The Perfect Fool," after a 1921 musical of that name in which he starred, and also noted as "The Fire Chief," from the Texaco-sponsored radio show which began in 1932. Ed Wynn had a bespectacled baby face, a silly giggle, an effeminate walk, and expressive hands which always seemed to be on the move. (In many respects, silent film comedian Harry Langdon was a mute version of Ed Wynn.) As an act on the vaudeville stage for ten minutes or so, Ed Wynn could obviously be very entertaining, but based on surviving film footage of Wynn and his act, after half an hour he could become extremely tiresome.

Ed Wynn was famous for his silly inventions, such as an eleven-foot, four-and-a-half-inch pole for people you wouldn't touch with a ten-foot pole. He invented a windshield wiper for people to use when they ate grapefruit, and there was also a device for eating corn on the cob which was somewhat similar to a modified typewriter carriage. It was these inventions which led Fred Allen to describe Wynn as the greatest visual comedian of his time. Wynn's jokes were corny in the extreme. In a 1930 film titled *Follow the Leader,* in which Wynn was co-starred with Lou Holtz, the latter announces, "A man was shot under my nose." Ed Wynn looks closely at Holtz's nose and comments, "That could happen." The film was based on Wynn's 1927 Broadway musical success *Manhattan Mary,* and captures for posterity the classic, corny

gag which has a gangster announcing to waiter Wynn, "I'm so hungry, I could eat a horse!" Wynn runs out of the restaurant and returns leading a horse. The comedian's next line was, "Will you have mustard or ketchup?" According to old-timers, that joke was the biggest clean laugh in the history of show business.

Ed Wynn was a comedian who was idolized by his peers. George Burns said of him, "Ed Wynn is the greatest of us all. Every comedian alive today has borrowed or learned something from him." Jack Benny noted, "In more than fifty years he never used a naughty word or a suggestive line, yet he could keep you screaming for two hours and a half." To Red Skelton, Wynn was simply "A funny, funny man."

Isaiah Edwin Leopold was born in Philadelphia on November 9, 1886, the son of a well-to-do millinery manufacturer who would have preferred that he become a businessman rather than an entertainer. "I was twelve when, at the People's Theatre in Philadelphia, I got on a stage for the first time," recalled Ed Wynn.

> Howard Thurston, the magician, called for volunteers to help him do a mind-reading act. Blindfolded, he would identify objects handed to his girl assistant down in the aisles. "I know this trick. I can do this!" I exclaimed, as I tied the scarf around Thurston's eyes. Thurston lifted the blindfold. "You can?" he cried, as though delighted to meet someone who shared his occult powers. "Then you do it, by all means!" Of course, I couldn't. It was done with a code of signals in the apparently innocuous patter of his girl assistant; the spacing of the words, their very tone—all had meaning. If she kept talking, Thurston could read the serial numbers on a dollar bill handed to her by anyone in the audience. It sounds naive today, but it was high drama then. Thurston gasped out the numbers, tortured by the intensity of his concentration. The applause was deafening when the owner of the money cried, "By gosh, that's right!" I think Thurston actually welcomed interruptions like mine, which challenged his power over an audience. For years he was, to me, the ideal showman.

Ed Wynn—taken from his middle name—made his first professional stage appearance in 1901. A year later he teamed up with Jack Lewis, ten years his senior, to form an act titled the Rah, Rah Boys. "I wrote an act around two college boys that required a fairly high level of intelligence. From the audience, I had squirmed through too many low comedy acts. I knew I wasn't that dumb, and I didn't think other people were, either. We also agreed that we would use no 'blue' lines, no dirt," Wynn recalled years later. The two men persuaded "Gentleman Jim" Corbett to introduce their act; he did, pretending that Wynn and Lewis were an act from the West new to New York, and they were an instantaneous success. A typical Wynn and Lewis routine went something like this:

LEWIS: Has your brother read the novels of Dickens and Thackeray?
WYNN: No, he hasn't.

LEWIS: What has your brother read?
WYNN: He has red hair.

Wynn maintained, "We revolutionized the two-man comedy act. Up to then the straight man used to swat his partner with a bladder or rolled-up newspaper after every joke and chase him around the stage. We stood still and cut out swatting."

In 1904 Wynn split with Jack Lewis and would sometimes work as a solo in vaudeville and sometimes with a partner. In 1909 he teamed with Al Lee for an act titled *The Billiken Freshman*, which Sime Silverman, writing in *Variety* (July 12, 1909), thought "a good comedy number, Lee playing the 'straight.'" In 1910 P. O'Malley Jennings from the legitimate stage was Wynn's partner, playing an asinine Englishman. "It is a clever comedy turn worked out along familiar lines," reported *Variety* (December 17, 1910).

"Mr. Busybody" was a twenty-nine-minute vaudeville musical comedy sketch that Ed Wynn introduced to New York audiences at Brooklyn's Greenpoint Theatre in October of 1908. Wynn's leading lady in the sketch was Minerva Courtney, who in later years entertained on the vaudeville stage with her impersonations of Charlie Chaplin. Wynn was a department store customer named Appiuscanbee, while Miss Courtney portrayed "a superior shopgirl" named Navva Fitzhugh. Even *Variety* (October 31, 1908) had to admit that most of the jokes in the sketch, which like all of Ed Wynn's material was written by the star, were corny; "There is no novelty in the piece," *Variety* complained.

Ed Wynn has the distinction of being, from today's standpoint, the best-known name on the March 24, 1913, opening bill of the Palace Theatre. His fourteen-minute comedy routine, titled "The King's Jester," had Wynn as the jester trying to make the King (Frank Wunderlee) laugh. The premise was that if Wynn failed, he would die, a premise which led *Variety* (March 28, 1913) to note that the audience was not the King. Ed Wynn played ragtime —badly—on the piano, and at the close of the act whispered in the King's ear. The King, who had remained silent throughout the act, roared with laughter and Wynn asked, "Why didn't you tell me you wanted to hear that kind of a story?" While at the Palace, Wynn claimed to have been vaudeville's first master of ceremonies, announcing the acts when the electric sign on the proscenium arch, used for that purpose, failed to operate.

From 1914 on, Ed Wynn turned his back on vaudeville and devoted his energies to the musical comedy and revue stage. He was featured in the 1914 and 1915 editions of *The Ziegfeld Follies* and in the 1916 edition of *The Passing Show*. Wynn starred in *Doing Our Bit* (1917), *Over the Top* (1917), *Sometime* (1918), *The Shubert Gaieties of 1919*, *The Ed Wynn Carnival* (1920), *The Perfect Fool* (1921), *The Grab Bag* (1924), *Manhattan Mary* (1927), *Simple Simon* (1930), *The Laugh Parade* (1931), and many others. In the 1915 *Follies* was the famous incident in which he hid under W. C. Fields's pool table, making faces at the audience, until Fields discovered him and hit him with a billiard cue. From *The Grab Bag* came the gag

with an inch-long harmonica, which Wynn swallowed and which caused him to wheeze throughout the show. In a 1942 revue, *Boys and Girls Together,* Wynn entered in the middle of an Indian Club throwing routine, climbed a ladder to catch one of the Clubs, and then walked off the stage without even acknowledging the audience.

In 1919 Wynn was one of the leaders of the Actors' Equity strike. Although not a member of Equity, he was sympathetic toward the plight of his fellow performers, and it was he who suggested that Equity join the American Federation of Labor. Wynn personally approached A. F. of L. founder Samuel Gompers for support. For his efforts, Ed Wynn was blacklisted, but in some respects the blacklist paid off for him as it led to his writing, producing, directing, and starring in his own show, *The Ed Wynn Carnival,* which opened at the New Amsterdam Theatre in April of 1920.

Ed Wynn's radio show, "The Fire Chief," had its premiere on April 26, 1932, and the comedian and his catchphrase, "S-o-o-o-o," immediately caught on with listeners. He remained on radio through 1937, then retired from the air until 1944 when his fantasy show, "Happy Island," had its debut. It was not a success and was cancelled in 1945. When told that the show was sponsored by Borden, makers of homogenized milk, Wynn quipped, "Why I have an uncle who used to go out every Saturday night to get homogenized." Television in the late forties offered Ed Wynn a new career, and when television no longer wanted him the comedian turned to films, in which he had made his debut in 1927 with *Rubber Tires*. In his early films Wynn had been strictly a comic but in the fifties he became a character actor in motion pictures such as *The Great Man* (1956), *Marjorie Morningstar* (1959), *The Absent-Minded Professor* (1960), *Mary Poppins* (1964), *The Greatest Story Ever Told* (1965), *The Warning Shot* (1967), and his last film, *The Gnomemobile* (1967). Wynn was nominated for an Academy Award for best supporting actor for his role in *The Diary of Anne Frank* (1959); as early as 1956 he had appeared in a serious role on television, in *Requiem for a Heavyweight,* which also featured his son, Keenan.

Ed Wynn died in Los Angeles on June 19, 1966, after seeing his career evolve from the perfect fool to the perfect character actor. Jack Benny, on being told of Wynn's death, said, "The reason he was also such a great dramatic actor was because he was what I call an 'honest comedian.' When he said anything funny, you believed everything he said. It made no difference how ridiculous the joke was. If he said he had an uncle who was walking around without his head, you absolutely believed it because of his delivery. . . . Just like Al Jolson was the world's greatest entertainer, Ed Wynn was definitely, in my opinion, the world's greatest comedian."

References: "August Clown" by Joel Sayre in *Life* (July 26, 1948), pages 65–6, 69, 70, 73–4, 76. "Grand Old Man's New Career" by John Reese in *Saturday Evening Post* (April 4, 1959), pages 24–5, 112, 114, 117. "The People I Have Laughed With" by Ed Wynn in *Good Housekeeping* (February 1959), pages 47, 197–200.

SELECT BIBLIOGRAPHY

(Books and magazine articles on individual performers are listed after the entries on those performers.)

The ASCAP Biographical Dictionary of Composers, Authors and Publishers. The American Society of Composers, Authors and Publishers, 1966.

Albee, E. F. "E. F. Albee on Vaudeville," *Variety, Vol. 72, No. 3 (September 6, 1923),* pages 1 and 18.

Baral, Robert. *Revue.* Fleet Publishing Corporation, 1962.

Barnard, Eunice Fuller. "Nimble Vaudeville Is a Centenarian, "The *New York Times* Magazine (April 24, 1927), pages 6, 7, and 16.

Blum, Daniel. *A Pictorial History of the American Theatre, 1860-1970.* Crown, 1969.

Browne, Walter, and Koch, E. De Roy. *Who's Who on the Stage, 1908.* B. W. Dodge Company, 1909.

Busby, Roy. *British Music Hall: An Illustrated Who's Who from 1850 to the Present.* Paul Elek, 1976.

Carter, Randolph. *The World of Flo Ziegfeld.* Praeger, 1974.

"Critics Analyze Vaudeville's Chances," *The Billboard,* Vol. 51, No. 14 (April 8, 1939), page 32.

Clarke, Norman. *The Mighty Hippodrome.* A. S. Barnes, 1968.

Csida, Joseph, and Csida, June Bundy. *American Entertainment.* A Billboard Book/Watson-Guptill Publications, 1978.

Davies, Acton. "What Do I Know about Vaudeville?" *Variety,* Vol. 1, No. 1 (December 16, 1905), page 2.

DiMeglio, John E. *Vaudeville U.S.A.* Bowling Green University Popular Press, 1973.

Dunning, John. *Tune in Yesterday.* Prentice-Hall, 1976.

Fisher, John. *Funny Way To Be a Hero.* Frederick Muller, 1973.

Gilbert, Douglas. *American Vaudeville: Its Life and Times.* Whittlesey House, 1940.

Gould, William. "Vaudeville versus Musical Comedy," *Variety,* Vol. 9, No. 1 (December 14, 1907), pages 19 and 65.

Granlund, Nils Thor, with Feder, Sid and Hancock, Ralph, *Blondes, Brunettes, and Bullets.* David McKay Company, 1957.

Grau, Robert. *The Business Man in the Amusement World.* Broadway Publishing Company, 1910.

Green, Abel, editor. *The Spice of Variety.* Henry Holt and Company, 1952.

Green, Abel, and Laurie, Joe, Jr. *Show Biz: From Vaude to Video.* Henry Holt and Company, 1951.

Grinde, Nick. "Where's Vaudeville At?" The *Saturday Evening Post* (January 11, 1930), pages 44, 46, 158, and 161.

Hoyt, Harlowe R. *Town Hall Tonight.* Prentice-Hall, 1955.

Hughes, Langston, and Meltzer, Milton. *Black Magic: A Pictorial History of the Negro in American Entertainment.* Prentice-Hall, 1967.

Laurie, Joe, Jr. *Vaudeville: From the Honky-Tonks to the Palace.* Henry Holt and Company, 1953.

Leslie, Peter. *A Hand Act To Follow.* Paddington Press, 1978.

Mander, Raymond, and Michenson, Joe. *British Music Hall.* Studio Vista, 1974.

Mantle, Burns, and Sherwood, Garrison P. editors *The Best Plays of 1899-1909.* Dodd, Mead and Company, 1944.
    The Best Plays of 1909-1919. Dodd, Mead and Company, 1943.

Marston, William Moulton, and Feller, John Henry. *F. F. Proctor: Vaudeville Pioneer.* Richard R. Smith, 1943.

Mattfeld, Julius. *Variety Music Cavalcade, 1620-1969.* Prentice-Hall, 1971.

Page, Will A. *Behind the Curtains of Broadway's Beauty Trust.* The Edward A. Miller Publishing Company, 1927.

Rust, Brian, with Debus, Allen G. *The Complete Entertainment Discography.* Arlington House, 1973.

Short, Ernest. *Fifty Years of Vaudeville.* Eyre and Spottiswoode, 1946.

Sobel, Bernard. *A Pictorial History of Vaudeville.* The Citadel Press, 1961.

Spitzer, Marion. *The Palace.* Athenaeum, 1969.

Toll, Robert C. *Blacking Up.* Oxford University Press, 1974.
    On with the Show. Oxford University Press, 1976.

Vance, Mark. "Musical Comedy Invades Vaudeville," the *New York Dramatic Mirror* (January 1, 1920), pages 2058-2059.

Who Was Who in the Theatre, 1912-1976. Gale Research Company, 1978.

Wilde, Larry. *The Great Comedians Talk about Comedy.* The Citadel Press, 1968.